Invent Your Own
Computer Games with Python

2nd Edition

Al Sweigart

*For Caro, with more love
than I ever knew I had.*

A Note to Parents and Fellow Programmers

Thank your for reading this book. My motivation for writing this book comes from a gap I saw in today's literature for kids interested in learning to program. I started programming when I was 9 years old in the BASIC language with a book similar to this one. During the course of writing this, I've realized how a modern language like Python has made programming far easier and versatile for a new generation of programmers. Python has a gentle learning curve while still being a serious language that is used by programmers professionally.

The current crop of programming books for kids that I've seen fell into two categories. First, books that did not teach programming so much as "game creation software" or a dumbed-down languages to make programming "easy" (to the point that it is no longer programming). Or second, they taught programming like a mathematics textbook: all principles and concepts with little application given to the reader. This book takes a different approach: show the source code for games right up front and explain programming principles from the examples.

I have also made this book available under the Creative Commons license, which allows you to make copies and distribute this book (or excerpts) with my full permission, as long as attribution to me is left intact and it is used for noncommercial purposes. (See the copyright page.) I want to make this book a gift to a world that has given me so much. Thank you again for reading this book, and feel free to email me any questions or comments.

Al Sweigart
al@inventwithpython.com

The full text of this book is available in HTML or PDF format at:
http://inventwithpython.com

Who is this book for?

Programming isn't hard. But it is hard to find learning materials that teach you to do interesting things with programming. Other computer books go over many topics that most newbie coders don't need. This book will teach you how to program your own computer games. You will learn a useful skill and have fun games to show for it!

This book is for:

- Complete beginners who wants to teach themselves computer programming, even if they have no previous experience programming.
- Kids and teenagers who want to learn computer programming by creating games. Kids as young as 9 or 10 years old should be able to follow along.
- Adults and teachers who wish to teach others programming.
- Anyone, young or old, who wants to learn how to program by learning a professional programming language.

Table of Contents

Chapter 1
Installing Python

Topics Covered In This Chapter:

- Downloading and installing the Python interpreter.
- Using IDLE's interactive shell to run instructions.
- How to use this book.
- The book's website at *http://inventwithpython.com*

Hello! This is a book that will teach you how to program by showing you how to create computer games. Once you learn how the games in this book work, you'll be able to create your own games. All you'll need is a computer, some software called the Python Interpreter, and this book. The software you'll need is free and you can download it from the Internet.

When I was a kid, I found a book like this that taught me how to write my first programs and games. It was fun and easy. Now as an adult, I still have fun programming computers, and I get paid for it. But even if you don't become a computer programmer when you grow up, programming is a useful and fun skill to have.

Computers are very useful machines. The good news is that learning to program a computer is easy. If you can read this book, you can program a computer. A computer **program** is just a bunch of instructions run by a computer, just like a storybook is just a whole bunch of sentences read by the reader.

These instructions are like the turn-by-turn instructions you might get for walking to a friend's house. (Turn left at the light, walk two blocks, keep walking until you find the first blue house on the right.) The computer follows each instruction that you give it in the order that you give it. Video games are themselves nothing but computer programs. (And very fun computer programs!)

In this book, any words you need to know will look like **this**. For example, the word "program" is defined in the previous paragraph.

In order to tell a computer what you want it to do, you write a program in a language that the computer understands. The programming language this book teaches is named Python. There are many different programming languages including BASIC, Java, Pascal, Haskell, and C++ (pronounced, "c plus plus").

When I was a kid most people learned to program in BASIC as their first language. But new programming languages have been invented since then, including Python. Python is even easier to learn than BASIC and it's a serious programming language used by professional computer programmers. Many adults use Python in their work (and when programming just for fun).

The first few games we'll create together in this book will probably seem simple compared to the games you've played on the Xbox, Playstation, or Wii. They don't have fancy graphics or music but that's because they're meant to teach you the basics. They're purposely simple so that we can focus on learning to program. Games don't have to be complicated to be fun. Hangman, Tic Tac Toe, and making secret codes are simple to program but are also fun.

We'll also learn how to make the computer solve some math problems in the Python shell. (Don't worry if you don't know a lot of mathematics. If you know how to add and multiply, you know enough math to do programming. Programming is more about problem solving and making plans than it is about solving math problems.)

Downloading and Installing Python

Before we can begin programming you'll need to install software called the Python interpreter. (You may need to ask an adult for help here.) The **interpreter** is a program that understands the instructions that you'll write in the Python language. Without the interpreter, your computer won't understand these instructions and your programs won't work. (We'll just refer to "the Python interpreter" as "Python" from now on.)

Because we'll be writing our games in the Python language we need to download Python first, from the official website of the Python programming language, *http://www.python.org*

I'm going to give you instructions for installing Python on Microsoft Windows, not because that's my favorite operating system but because chances are that's the operating system that your computer is running. You might want the help of someone else to download and install the Python software.

When you get to python.org, you should see a list of links on the left (About, News, Documentation, Download, and so on.) Click on the **Download** link to go to the download page, then look for the file called **Python 3.1 Windows Installer** (Windows binary -- does not include source) and click on its link to download Python for Windows.

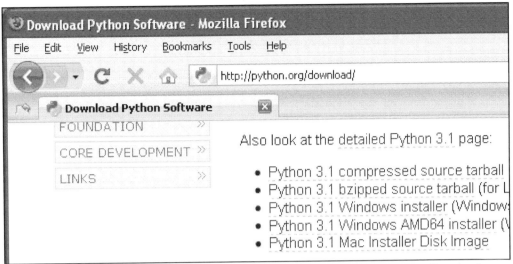

Figure 1-1: Click the Windows installer link to download Python for Windows from *http://www.python.org*

Double-click on the *python-3.1.msi* file that you've just downloaded to start the Python installer. (If it doesn't start, try right-clicking the file and choosing Install.) Once the installer starts up, click the **Next** button and just accept the choices in the installer as you go (no need to make any changes). When the install is finished, click **Finish**.

Important Note! Be sure to install Python 3, and not Python 2. The programs in this book use Python 3, and you'll get errors if you try to run them with Python 2.

The installation for Mac OS is similar. Instead of downloading the .msi file from the Python website, download the .dmg Mac Installer Disk Image file instead. The link to this file will look something like "Mac Installer disk image (3.1.1)" on the "Download Python Software" web page.

If your operating system is Ubuntu, you can install Python by opening a terminal window (click on Applications > Accessories > Terminal) and entering sudo apt-get install python3 then pressing Enter. You will need to enter the root password to install Python, so ask the person who owns the computer to type in this password.

There may be a newer version of Python available than 3.1. If so, then just download the latest version. The game programs in this book will work just the same. If you have any problems, you can always Google for "installing Python on <your operating system's name>". Python is a very popular language, so you should have no difficulty finding help.

A video tutorial of how to install Python is available from this book's website at *http://inventwithpython.com/videos/*.

Starting Python

If your operating system is Windows XP, you should be able to run Python by choosing **Start, Programs, Python 3.1, IDLE (Python GUI)**. When it's running it should looking something like Figure 1-2. (But different operating systems will look slightly different.)

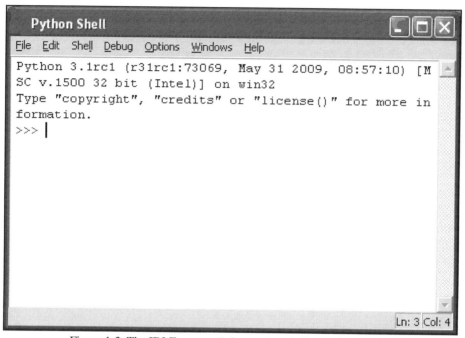

Figure 1-2: The IDLE program's interactive shell on Windows.

IDLE stands for **I**nteractive **D**eve**L**opment **E**nvironment. The development environment is software that makes it easy to write Python programs. We will be using IDLE to type in our programs and run them.

The window that appears when you first run IDLE is called the interactive shell. A shell is a program that lets you type instructions into the computer. The Python shell lets you type Python instructions, and the shell sends these instructions to software called the Python interpreter to perform. We can type Python instructions into the shell and, because the shell is interactive, the computer will read our instructions and respond in some way. (Ideally in a way that we expect but that will depend on whether we write the correct instructions.)

How to Use This Book

There are a few things you should understand about this book before you get started. "Invent with Python" is different from other programming books because it focuses on the complete source code for different games. Instead of teaching you programming concepts and leaving it up to you to figure out how to make fun games with those concepts, this book shows you fun games and then explains how they are put together.

The Featured Programs

Most chapters begin with a sample run of the featured program. This sample run shows you what the program's output looks like, with what the user types in shown as **bold** print. This will give you an idea of what the complete game will look like when you have entered the code and run it.

Some chapters also show the complete source code of the game, but remember: you don't have to enter every line of code right now. Instead, you can read the chapter first to understand what each line of code does and then try entering it later.

You can also download the source code file from this book's website. Go to the URL *http://inventwithpython.com/source* and follow the instructions to download the source code file.

Line Numbers and Spaces

When entering the source code yourself, do **not** type the line numbers that appear at the beginning of each line. For example, if you see this in the book:

```
9. number = random.randint(1, 20)
```

You do not need to type the "9." on the left side, or the space that immediately follows it. Just type it like this:

```
number = random.randint(1, 20)
```

Those numbers are only used so that this book can refer to specific lines in the code. They are not a part of the actual program.

Aside from the line numbers, be sure to enter the code exactly as it appears. Notice that some of the lines don't begin at the leftmost edge of the page, but are indented by four or eight spaces. Be sure to put in the correct number of spaces at the start of each line. (Since each character in IDLE is the same width, you can count the number of spaces by counting the number of characters above or below the line you're looking at.)

For example, you can see that the second line is indented by four spaces because the four characters ("whil") on the line above are over the indented space. The third line is indented by another four spaces (the four characters, "if n" are above the third line's indented space):

```
while guesses < 10:
    if number == 42:
        print('Hello')
```

Text Wrapping in This Book

Some lines of code are too long to fit on one line on the page, and the text of the code will wrap around to the next line. When you type these lines into the file editor, enter the code all on one line without pressing Enter.

You can tell when a new line starts by looking at the line numbers on the left side of the code. For example, the code below has only two lines of code, even though the first line wraps around:

```
1. print('This is the first line! xxxxxxxxxxxxxx
   xxxxxxxxxxx')
2. print('This is the second line! ')
```

Tracing the Program Online

You can visit *http://inventwithpython.com/traces* to see a trace through each of the programs in this book. Tracing a program means to step through the code one line at a time, in the same way that a computer would execute it. The traces web page has notes and helpful reminders at each step of the trace to explain what the program is doing, so it can help you better understand why these programs work the way they do.

Checking Your Code Online

Some of the games in this book are a little long. Although it is very helpful to learn Python by typing out the source code for these games, you may accidentally make typos that cause your game programs to crash. It may not be obvious where the typo is.

You can copy and paste the text of your source code to the online diff tool on the book's website. The diff tool will show any differences between the source code in the book and the source code you've typed. This is an easy way of finding any typos in your program.

Copying and pasting text is a very useful computer skill, especially for computer programming. There is a video tutorial on copying and pasting at this book's website at *http://inventwithpython.com/videos/*.

The online diff tool is at this web page: *http://inventwithpython.com/diff*. A video tutorial of how to use the diff tool is available from this book's website at *http://inventwithpython.com/videos/*.

Summary

This chapter has helped you get started with the Python software by showing you the python.org website where you can download it for free. After installing and starting the Python IDLE software, we will be ready to learn programming starting in the next chapter.

This book's website at *http://inventwithpython.com* has more information on each of the chapters, including an online tracing website that can help you understand what exactly each line of the programs do.

Chapter 2
The Interactive Shell

Topics Covered In This Chapter:

- Integers and Floating Point Numbers
- Expressions
- Values
- Operators
- Evaluating Expressions
- Storing Values in Variables
- Overwriting variables

Before we start writing computer games, we should learn some basic programming concepts first. These concepts are values, operators, expressions, and variables. We won't start programming in this chapter, but knowing these concepts and the names of things will make learning to program much easier. This is because most programming is built on only a few simple concepts combined together to make advanced programs.

Let's start by learning how to use Python's interactive shell.

Some Simple Math Stuff

To open IDLE on Windows, click on **Start**, then **Programs**, then **Python 3.1**, then **IDLE (Python GUI)**. With IDLE open, let's do some simple math with Python. The interactive shell can work just like a calculator. Type 2+2 into the shell and press the Enter key on your keyboard. (On some keyboards, this is the Return key.) As you can see in Figure 2-1, the computer should respond with the number 4; the sum of 2+2.

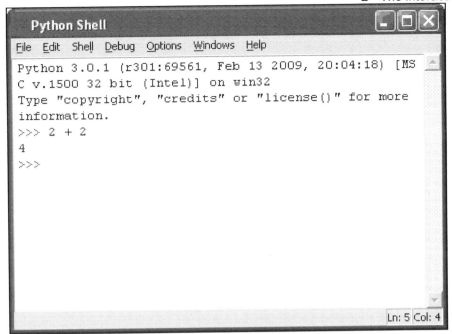

Figure 2-1: Type 2+2 into the shell.

As you can see, we can use the Python shell just like a calculator. This isn't a program by itself because we are just learning the basics right now. The + sign tells the computer to add the numbers 2 and 2. To subtract numbers use the – sign, and to multiply numbers use an asterisk (*), like so:

Table 2-1: The various math operators in Python.

2+2	addition
2–2	subtraction
2*2	multiplication
2/2	division

When used in this way, +, -, *, and / are called **operators** because they tell the computer to perform the specified operation on the numbers surrounding them.

Integers and Floating Point Numbers

In programming (and also in mathematics), whole numbers like 4, 0, and 99 are called **integers**. Numbers with fractions or decimal points (like 3.5 and 42.1 and 5.0) are not integers. In Python, the number 5 is an integer, but if we wrote it as 5.0 it would not be an integer. Numbers with a decimal point are called **floating point numbers**. In mathematics, 5.0 is still considered an integer and the same as the number 5, but in computer programming the computer considers any number with a decimal point as not an integer.

Expressions

Try typing some of these math problems into the shell, pressing Enter key after each one.

```
2+2+2+2+2
8*6
10-5+6
2   +       2
```

Figure 2-2 is what the interactive shell in IDLE will look like after you type in the instructions above.

```
interface and no data is sen
**************************
IDLE 1.2.1
>>> 2+2
4
>>> 2+2+2+2+2
10
>>> 8*6
48
>>> 10-5+6
11
>>> 2   +       2
4
>>> |
```

Figure 2-2: What the IDLE window looks like after entering instructions.

These math problems are called expressions. Computers can solve millions of these problems in seconds. Expressions are made up of **values** (the numbers) connected by **operators** (the math signs). Let's learn exactly what values and operators are.

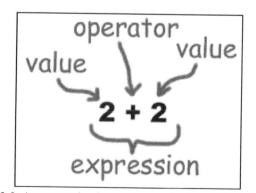

Figure 2-3: An expression is a made up of values and operators.

As you can see with the last expression in the above example, you can put any amount of spaces in between the integers and these operators. (But be sure to always start at the very beginning of the line, with no spaces in front.)

Numbers are a type of value. Integers are a type of number. But, even though integers are numbers, not all numbers are integers. (For example, fractions and numbers with decimal points like 2.5 are numbers that are not integers.)

This is like how a cat is a type of pet, but not all pets are cats. Someone could have a pet dog or a pet hermit crab. An **expression** is made up of values (such as integers like 8 and 6) connected by an operator (such as the * multiplication sign). A single value by itself is also considered an expression.

In the next chapter, we will learn about working with text in expressions. Python isn't limited to just numbers. It's more than just a fancy calculator!

Evaluating Expressions

When a computer solves the expression 10 + 5 and gets the value 15, we say it has **evaluated** the expression. Evaluating an expression reduces the expression to a single value, just like solving a math problem reduces the problem to a single number: the answer.

The expressions 10 + 5 and 10 + 3 + 2 have the same value, because they both evaluate to 15. Even single values are considered expressions: The expression 15 evaluates to the value 15.

However, if you just type 5 + into the interactive shell, you will get an error message.

```
>>> 5 +
SyntaxError: invalid syntax
```

This error happened because 5 + is not an expression. Expressions have values connected by operators, but the + operator always expects to connect two things in Python. We have only given it one. This is why the error message appeared. A syntax error means that the computer does not understand the instruction you gave it because you typed it incorrectly. Python will always display an error message if you enter an instruction that it cannot understand.

This may not seem important, but a lot of computer programming is not just telling the computer what to do, but also knowing exactly how to tell the computer to do it.

Expressions Inside Other Expressions

Expressions can also contain other expressions. For example, in the expression 2 + 5 + 8, the 2 + 5 part is its own expression. Python evaluates 2 + 5 to 7, so the original expression becomes 7 + 8. Python then evaluates this expression to 15.

Think of an expression as being a stack of pancakes. If you put two stacks of pancakes together, you still have a stack of pancakes. And a large stack of pancakes can be made up of smaller stacks of pancakes that were put together. Expressions can be combined together to form larger expressions in the same way. But no matter how big an expression is it also evaluates to a single answer, just like 2 + 5 + 8 evaluates to 15.

Storing Values in Variables

When we program, we will often want to save the values that our expressions evaluate to so we can use them later in the program. We can store values in **variables**.

Think of variables like a box that can hold values. You can store values inside variables with the = sign (called the **assignment operator**). For example, to store the value 15 in a variable named "spam", enter `spam = 15` into the shell:

```
>>> spam = 15
>>>
```

You can think of the variable like a box with the value 15 inside of it (as shown in Figure 2-4). The variable name "spam" is the label on the box (so we can tell one variable from another) and the value stored in it is like a small note inside the box.

When you press Enter you won't see anything in response, other than a blank line. Unless you see an error message, you can assume that the instruction has been executed successfully. The next >>> prompt will appear so that you can type in the next instruction.

Figure 2-4: Variables are like boxes that can hold values in them.

This instruction (called an **assignment statement**) creates the variable spam and stores the value 15 in it. Unlike expressions, **statements** are instructions that do not evaluate to any value, which is why there is no value displayed on the next line in the shell.

It might be confusing to know which instructions are expressions and which are statements. Just remember that if the instruction evaluates to a single value, it's an expression. If the instruction does not, then it's a statement.

An assignment statement is written as a variable, followed by the = equal sign, followed by an expression. The value that the expression evaluates to is stored inside the variable. The value 15 by itself is an expression. Expressions made up of a single value by itself are easy to evaluate. These expressions just evaluate to the value itself. For example, the expression 15 evaluates to 15!

Remember, variables store values, not expressions. For example, if we had the statement, spam = 10 + 5, then the expression 10 + 5 would first be evaluated to 15 and then the value 15 would be stored in the variable, spam.

The first time you store a value inside a variable by using an assignment statement, Python will create that variable. Each time after that, an assignment statement will only replace the value stored in the variable.

Now let's see if we've created our variable properly. If we type spam into the shell by itself, we should see what value is stored inside the variable spam.

```
>>> spam = 15
>>> spam
15
>>>
```

Now, spam evaluates to the value inside the variable, 15.

And here's an interesting twist. If we now enter spam + 5 into the shell, we get the integer 20, like so.

```
>>> spam = 15
>>> spam + 5
20
>>>
```

That may seem odd but it makes sense when we remember that we set the value of spam to 15. Because we've set the value of the variable spam to 15, writing spam + 5 is like writing the expression 15 + 5.

If you try to use a variable before it has been created, Python will give you an error because no such variable would exist yet. This also happens if you mistype the name of the variable.

We can change the value stored in a variable by entering another assignment statement. For example, try the following:

```
>>> spam = 15
>>> spam + 5
20
>>> spam = 3
>>> spam + 5
8
>>>
```

The first time we enter spam + 5, the expression evaluates to 20, because we stored the value 15 inside the variable spam. But when we enter spam = 3, the value 15 is replaced, or overwritten, with the value 3. Now, when we enter spam + 5, the expression evaluates to 8 because the value of spam is now 3.

To find out what the current value is inside a variable, just enter the variable name into the shell.

Now here's something interesting. Because a variable is only a name for a value, we can write expressions with variables like this:

```
>>> spam = 15
>>> spam + spam
30
>>> spam - spam
0
>>>
```

When the variable spam has the integer value 15 stored in it, entering spam + spam is the same as entering 15 + 15, which evaluates to 30. And spam - spam is the same as 15 - 15, which evaluates to 0. The expressions above use the variable spam twice. You can use variables as many times as you want in expressions. Remember that Python will evaluate a variable name to the value that is stored inside that variable, each time the variable is used.

We can even use the value in the spam variable to assign spam a new value:

```
>>> spam = 15
>>> spam = spam + 5
20
>>>
```

The assignment statement spam = spam + 5 is like saying, "the new value of the spam variable will be the current value of spam plus five." Remember that the variable on the left side of the = sign will be assigned the value that the expression on the right side evaluates to. We can also keep increasing the value in spam by 5 several times:

```
>>> spam = 15
>>> spam = spam + 5
>>> spam = spam + 5
>>> spam = spam + 5
>>> spam
30
>>>
```

Using More Than One Variable

When we program we won't always want to be limited to only one variable. Often we'll need to use multiple variables.

For example, let's assign different values to two variables named eggs and fizz, like so:

```
>>> fizz = 10
>>> eggs = 15
```

Now the fizz variable has 10 inside it, and eggs has 15 inside it.

Figure 2-5: The "fizz" and "eggs" variables have values stored in them.

Without changing the value in our spam variable, let's try assigning a new value to the spam variable. Enter spam = fizz + eggs into the shell then enter spam into the shell to see the new value of spam. Can you guess what it will be?

```
>>> fizz = 10
>>> eggs = 15
>>> spam = fizz + eggs
>>> spam
25
>>>
```

The value in spam is now 25 because when we add fizz and eggs we are adding the values stored inside fizz and eggs.

Overwriting Variables

Changing the value stored inside a variable is easy. Just perform another assignment statement with the same variable. Look what happens when you enter the following code into the interactive shell:

```
>>> spam = 42
>>> print(spam)
42
>>> spam = 'Hello'
>>> print(spam)
Hello
```

Initially, the spam variable had the integer 42 placed inside of it. This is why the first print(spam) prints out 42. But when we execute spam = 'Hello', the 42 value is tossed out of the variable and forgotten as the new 'Hello' string value is placed inside the spam variable.

Replacing the value in a variable with a new value is called **overwriting** the value. It is important to know that the old value is permanently forgotten. If you want to remember this value so you can use it later in your program, store it in a different variable before overwriting the value:

```
>>> spam = 42
>>> print(spam)
42
>>> oldSpam = spam
>>> spam = 'Hello'
>>> print(spam)
Hello
>>> print(oldSpam)
42
```

In the above example, before overwriting the value in spam, we copy that value to a variable named oldSpam. At that point, both spam and oldSpam store the value 42. On the next line, the string 'Hello' is stored in spam but oldSpam is left untouched.

Summary

In this chapter you learned the basics about writing Python instructions. Python needs you to tell it exactly what to do in a strict way, because computers don't have common sense and only understand very simple instructions. You have learned that Python can evaluate expressions (that is, reduce the expression to a single value), and that expressions are values (such as 2 or 5) combined with operators (such as + or –). You have also learned that you can store values inside of variables so that your program can remember them in order to use them later on.

In the next chapter, we will go over some more basic concepts, and you will write your first program!

Chapter 3

Strings

Topics Covered In This Chapter:

- Flow of execution
- Strings
- String concatenation
- Data types (such as strings or integers)
- Using IDLE to write source code.
- Saving and running programs in IDLE.
- The `print()` function.
- The `input()` function.
- Comments
- Capitalizing variables
- Case-sensitivity

That's enough of integers and math for now. Python is more than just a calculator. Now let's see what Python can do with text. In this chapter, we will learn how to store text in variables, combine text together, and display them on the screen. Many of our programs will use text to display our games to the player, and the player will enter text into our programs through the keyboard. We will also make our first program, which greets the user with the text, "Hello World!" and asks for the user's name.

Strings

In Python, we work with little chunks of text called **strings**. We can store string values inside variables just like we can store number values inside variables. When we type strings, we put them in between two single quotes ('), like this:

```
>>> spam = 'hello'
>>>
```

The single quotes are there only to tell the computer where the string begins and ends (and are not part of the string value).

Now, if you type spam into the shell, you should see the contents of the spam variable (the 'hello' string.) This is because Python will evaluate a variable to the value stored inside the variable (in this case, the string 'Hello').

```
>>> spam = 'hello'
>>> spam
'hello'
>>>
```

Strings can have almost any keyboard character in them. (Strings can't have single quotes inside of them without using escape characters. Escape characters are described later.) These are all examples of strings:

```
'hello'
'Hi there!'
'KITTENS'
'7 apples, 14 oranges, 3 lemons'
'Anything not pertaining to elephants is
irrelephant.'
'A long time ago in a galaxy far, far away...'
'O*&#wY%*&OCfsdYO*&gfC%YO*&%3yc8r2'
```

As we did with numerical values in the previous chapter, we can also combine string values together with operators to make expressions.

String Concatenation

You can add one string to the end of another by using the + operator, which is called string concatenation. Try entering 'Hello' + 'World!' into the shell:

```
>>> 'Hello' + 'World!'
'HelloWorld!'
>>>
```

To keep the strings separate, put a space at the end of the 'Hello' string, before the single quote, like this:

```
>>> 'Hello ' + 'World!'
'Hello World!'
>>>
```

The + operator works differently on strings and integers because they are different **data types**. All values have a data type. The data type of the value 'Hello' is a string. The data type of the value 5 is an integer. The data type of the data that tells us (and the computer) what kind of data the value is.

Writing Programs in IDLE's File Editor

Until now we have been typing instructions one at a time into the interactive shell. When we write programs though, we type in several instructions and have them run all at once. Let's write our first program!

The name of the program that provides the interactive shell is called IDLE, the Interactive DeveLopement Environment. IDLE also has another part called the file editor.

Click on the **File** menu at the top of the Python Shell window, and select **New Window**. A new blank window will appear for us to type our program in. This window is the **file editor**.

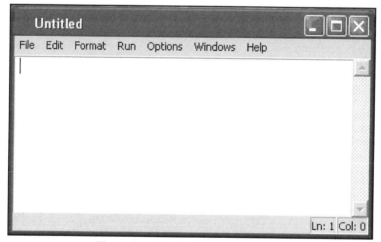

Figure 3-1: The file editor window.

Hello World!

A tradition for programmers learning a new language is to make their first program display the text "Hello world!" on the screen. We'll create our own Hello World program now.

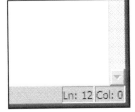

Figure 3-2: The bottom right of the file editor window tells you where the cursor is. The cursor is currently on line 12.

When you enter your program, don't enter the numbers at the left side of the code. They're there so we can refer to each line by number in our explanation. If you look at the bottom-right corner of the file editor window, it will tell you which line the cursor is currently on.

Enter the following text into the new file editor window. We call this text the program's source code because it contains the instructions that Python will follow to determine exactly how the program should behave. (Remember, don't type in the line numbers!)

IMPORTANT NOTE! The following program should be run by the Python 3 interpreter, not the Python 2.6 (or any other 2.x version). Be sure that you have the correct version of Python installed. (If you already have Python 2 installed, you can have Python 3 installed at the same time.) To download Python 3, go to *http://python.org/download/releases/3.1.1/* and install this version.

---

hello.py

This code can be downloaded from *http://inventwithpython.com/hello.py*
If you get errors after typing this code in, compare it to the book's code with the online diff tool at *http://inventwithpython.com/diff* or email the author at al@inventwithpython.com

```
1. # This program says hello and asks for my name.
2. print('Hello world!')
3. print('What is your name?')
4. myName = input()
5. print('It is good to meet you, ' + myName)
```

The IDLE program will give different types of instructions different colors. After you are done typing this code in, the window should look like this:

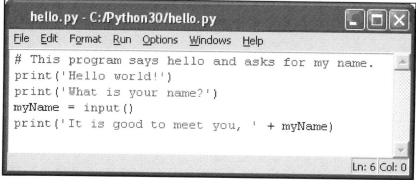

Figure 3-3: The file editor window will look like this after you type in the code.

Saving Your Program

Once you've entered your source code, save it so that you won't have to retype it each time we start IDLE. To do so, choose the File menu at the top of the File Editor window, and then click on **Save As**. The Save As window should open. Enter *hello.py* in the File Name box then press **Save**. (See Figure 3-4.)

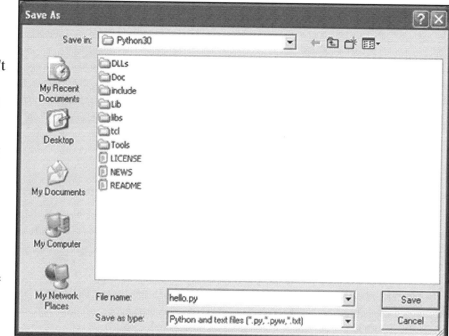

Figure 3-4: Saving the program.

You should save your programs every once in a while as you type them. That way, if the computer crashes or you accidentally exit from IDLE, only the typing you've done since your last save will be lost. Press Ctrl-S to save your file quickly, without using the mouse at all.

A video tutorial of how to use the file editor is available from this book's website at *http://inventwithpython.com/videos/*.

If you get an error that looks like this:

```
Hello world!
What is your name?
```

```
Albert

Traceback (most recent call last):
  File "C:/Python26/test1.py", line 4, in <module>
    myName = input()
  File "<string>", line 1, in <module>
NameError: name 'Albert' is not defined
```

...then this means you are running the program with Python 2, instead of Python 3. You can either install Python 3, or convert the source code in this book to Python 2. Appendix A lists the differences between Python 2 and 3 that you will need for this book.

Opening The Programs You've Saved

To load a saved program, choose **File > Open**. Do that now, and in the window that appears choose *hello.py* and press the **Open** button. Your saved *hello.py* program should open in the File Editor window.

Now it's time to run our program. From the File menu, choose **Run > Run Module** or just press the F5 key on your keyboard. Your program should run in the shell window that appeared when you first started IDLE. Remember, you have to press F5 from the file editor's window, not the interactive shell's window.

When your program asks for your name, go ahead and enter it as shown in Figure 3-5:

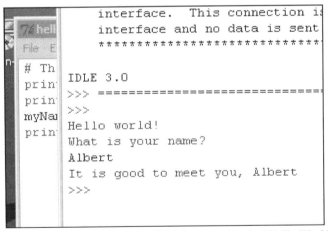

Figure 3-5: What the interactive shell looks like when running the "Hello World" program.

Now, when you push Enter, the program should greet you (the **user**) by name. Congratulations! You've written your first program. You are now a beginning computer programmer. (You can run this program again if you like by pressing F5 again.)

How the "Hello World" Program Works

How does this program work? Well, each line that we entered is an instruction to the computer that is interpreted by Python in a way that the computer will understand. A computer program is a lot like a recipe. Do the first step first, then the second, and so on until you reach the end. Each instruction is followed in sequence, beginning from the very top of the program and working down the list of instructions. After the program executes the first line of instructions, it moves on and executes the second line, then the third, and so on.

We call the program's following of instructions step-by-step the **flow of execution**, or just the **execution** for short.

Now let's look at our program one line at a time to see what it's doing, beginning with line number 1.

Comments

```
1. # This program says hello and asks for my name.
```

This line is called a **comment**. Any text following a # sign (called the **pound sign**) is a comment. Comments are not for the computer, but for you, the programmer. The computer ignores them. They're used to remind you of what the program does or to tell others who might look at your code what it is that your code is trying to do.

Programmers usually put a comment at the top of their code to give their program a title. The IDLE program displays comments in red to help them stand out.

Functions

A **function** is kind of like a mini-program inside your program. It contains lines of code that are executed from top to bottom. Python provides some built-in functions that we can use. The great thing about functions is that we only need to know what the function does, but not how it does it. (You need to know that the print() function displays text on the screen, but you don't need to know how it does this.)

A **function call** is a piece of code that tells our program to run the code inside a function. For example, your program can call the print() function whenever you want to display a string on the screen. The print() function takes the string you type in between the parentheses as input and displays the text on the screen. Because we want to display Hello world! on the screen, we type the print function name, followed by an opening parenthesis, followed by the 'Hello world!' string and a closing parenthesis.

The `print()` Function

```
2. print('Hello world!')
3. print('What is your name?')
```

This line is a call to the **print** function, usually written as `print()` (with the string to be printed going inside the parentheses).

We add parentheses to the end of function names to make it clear that we're referring to a function named `print()`, not a variable named `print`. The parentheses at the end of the function let us know we are talking about a function, much like the quotes around the number `'42'` tell us that we are talking about the string `'42'` and not the integer `42`.

Line 3 is another `print()` function call. This time, the program displays "What is your name?"

The `input()` Function

```
4. myName = input()
```

This line has an assignment statement with a variable (`myName`) and a function call (`input()`). When `input()` is called, the program waits for input; for the user to enter text. The text string that the user enters (your name) becomes the function's output value.

Like expressions, function calls evaluate to a single value. The value that the function call evaluates to is called the **return value**. (In fact, we can also use the word "returns" to mean the same thing as "evaluates".) In this case, the return value of the `input()` function is the string that the user typed in-their name. If the user typed in Albert, the `input()` function call evaluates to the string `'Albert'`.

The function named `input()` does not need any input (unlike the `print()` function), which is why there is nothing in between the parentheses.

```
5. print('It is good to meet you, ' + myName)
```

On the last line we have a `print()` function again. This time, we use the plus operator (+) to concatenate the string `'It is good to meet you, '` and the string stored in the `myName` variable, which is the name that our user input into the program. This is how we get the program to greet us by name.

Ending the Program

Once the program executes the last line, it stops. At this point it has **terminated** or **exited** and all of the variables are forgotten by the computer, including the string we stored in `myName`. If you try running the program again with a different name, like Carolyn, it will think that's your name.

```
Hello world!
What is your name?
Carolyn
It is good to meet you, Carolyn
```

Remember, the computer only does exactly what you program it to do. In this, our first program, it is programmed to ask you for your name, let you type in a string, and then say hello and display the string you typed.

But computers are dumb. The program doesn't care if you type in your name, someone else's name, or just something dumb. You can type in anything you want and the computer will treat it the same way:

```
Hello world!
What is your name?
poop
It is good to meet you, poop
```

Variable Names

The computer doesn't care what you name your variables, but you should. Giving variables names that reflect what type of data they contain makes it easier to understand what a program does. Instead of `name`, we could have called this variable `abrahamLincoln` or `nAmE`. The computer will run the program the same (as long as you consistently use `abrahamLincoln` or `nAmE`).

Variable names (as well as everything else in Python) are case-sensitive. **Case-sensitive** means the same variable name in a different case is considered to be an entirely separate variable name. So `spam`, `SPAM`, `Spam`, and `sPAM` are considered to be four different variables in Python. They each can contain their own separate values.

It's a bad idea to have differently-cased variables in your program. If you stored your first name in the variable `name` and your last name in the variable `NAME`, it would be very confusing when you read your code weeks after you first wrote it. Did `name` mean first and `NAME` mean last, or the other way around?

If you accidentally switch the name and NAME variables, then your program will still run (that is, it won't have any syntax errors) but it will run incorrectly. This type of flaw in your code is called a **bug**. It is very common to accidentally make bugs in your programs while you write them. This is why it is important that the variable names you choose make sense.

It also helps to capitalize variable names if they include more than one word. If you store a string of what you had for breakfast in a variable, the variable name `whatIHadForBreakfastThisMorning` is much easier to read than `whatihadforbreakfastthismorning`. This is a **convention** (that is, an optional but standard way of doing things) in Python programming. (Although even better would be something simple, like `todaysBreakfast`. Capitalizing the first letter of each word in variable names makes the program more readable.

Summary

Now that we have learned how to deal with text, we can start making programs that the user can run and interact with. This is important because text is the main way the user and the computer will communicate with each other. The player will enter text to the program through the keyboard with the `input()` function. And the computer will display text on the screen when the `print()` function is executed.

Strings are just a different data type that we can use in our programs. We can use the + operator to concatenate strings together. Using the + operator to concatenate two strings together to form a new string is just like using the + operator to add two integers to form a new integer (the sum).

In the next chapter, we will learn more about variables so that our program will remember the text and numbers that the player enters into the program. Once we have learned how to use text, numbers, and variables, we will be ready to start creating games.

Chapter 4
Guess the Number

Topics Covered In This Chapter:

- `import` statements
- Modules
- Arguments
- `while` statements
- Conditions
- Blocks
- Booleans
- Comparison operators
- The difference between = and ==.
- `if` statements
- The `break` keyword.
- The `str()` and `int()` functions.
- The `random.randint()` function.

The "Guess the Number" Game

We are going to make a "Guess the Number" game. In this game, the computer will think of a random number from 1 to 20, and ask you to guess the number. You only get six guesses, but the computer will tell you if your guess is too high or too low. If you guess the number within six tries, you win.

This is a good game for you to start with because it uses random numbers, loops, and input from the user in a fairly short program. As you write this game, you will learn how to convert values to different data types (and why you would need to do this).

Because this program is a game, we'll call the user the **player**, but the word "user" would be correct too.

Sample Run of "Guess the Number"

Here is what our game will look like to the player when the program is run. The text that the player types in is in **bold**.

```
Hello! What is your name?
Albert
Well, Albert, I am thinking of a number between 1
and 20.
Take a guess.
10
Your guess is too high.
Take a guess.
2
Your guess is too low.
Take a guess.
4
Good job, Albert! You guessed my number in 3
guesses!
```

Enter this code exactly as it appears here, and then save it by clicking on the **File** menu and then **Save As**. Give it a file name like *guess.py* then run it by pressing the F5 key. Don't worry if you don't understand the code now, I'll explain it step by step.

Guess the Number's Source Code

Here is the source code for our Guess the Number game. When you enter this code into the file editor, be sure to pay attention to the spacing at the front of some of the lines. Some lines have four or eight spaces in front of them. After you have typed in the code, save the file as *guess.py*. You can run the program from the file editor by pressing F5. If you see an error message, check that you have typed the program in exactly as written.

If you don't want to type all this code, you can download it from this book's website at the URL *http://inventwithpython.com/chapter4*.

Important Note! Be sure to run this program with Python 3, and not Python 2. The programs in this book use Python 3, and you'll get errors if you try to run them with Python 2. You can click on **Help** and then **About IDLE** to find out what version of Python you have.

guess.py

This code can be downloaded from *http://inventwithpython.com/guess.py*

If you get errors after typing this code in, compare it to the book's code with the online diff tool at *http://inventwithpython.com/diff* or email the author at al@inventwithpython.com

```
1. # This is a guess the number game.
2. import random
3.
4. guessesTaken = 0
5.
6. print('Hello! What is your name?')
7. myName = input()
8.
9. number = random.randint(1, 20)
10. print('Well, ' + myName + ', I am thinking of a number
    between 1 and 20.')
11.
12. while guessesTaken < 6:
13.     print('Take a guess.') # There are four spaces in
    front of print.
14.     guess = input()
15.     guess = int(guess)
16.
17.     guessesTaken = guessesTaken + 1
18.
19.     if guess < number:
20.         print('Your guess is too low.') # There are eight
    spaces in front of print.
21.
22.     if guess > number:
23.         print('Your guess is too high.')
24.
25.     if guess == number:
26.         break
27.
28. if guess == number:
29.     guessesTaken = str(guessesTaken)
30.     print('Good job, ' + myName + '! You guessed my
    number in ' + guessesTaken + ' guesses!')
31.
32. if guess != number:
33.     number = str(number)
34.     print('Nope. The number I was thinking of was ' +
    number)
```

Even though we are entering our source code into a new file editor window, we can return to the shell to enter individual instructions in order to see what they do. The interactive shell is very good for experimenting with different instructions when we are not running a program. You can return to the interactive shell by clicking on its window or on its taskbar button. In Windows or Mac OS X, the taskbar or dock is on the bottom of the screen. On Linux the taskbar may be located along the top of the screen.

If the program doesn't seem to work after you've typed it, check to see if you have typed the code exactly as it appears in this book. You can also copy and paste your code to the online "diff" tool at *http://inventwithpython.com/diff*. The diff tool will show you how your code is different from the source code in this book. In the file editor, press Ctrl-A to "Select All" the text you've typed, then press Ctrl-C to copy the text to the clipboard. Then, paste this text by clicking in the diff tool's text field on the website and click the "Compare" button. The website will show you any differences between your code and the code in this book.

There is a diff tool for each program in this book on the *http://inventwithpython.com* website. A video tutorial of how to use the diff tool is available from this book's website at *http://inventwithpython.com/videos/*.

The `import` Statement

Let's look at each line of code in turn to see how this program works.

```
1. # This is a guess the number game.
```

This line is a comment. Comments were introduced in our Hello World program in Chapter 3. Remember that Python will ignore everything after the # sign. This just reminds us what this program does.

```
2. import random
```

This is an **import statement**. Statements are not functions (notice that neither `import` nor `random` has parentheses after its name). Remember, statements are instructions that perform some action but do not evaluate to a value. You have already seen statements: assignment statements store a value into a variable (but the statement does not evaluate to anything).

While Python includes many built-in functions, some functions exist in separate programs called modules. **Modules** are Python programs that contain additional functions. We use the functions of these modules by bringing them into our programs with the `import` statement. In this case, we're importing the module `random`.

The `import` statement is made up of the `import` keyword followed by the module name. Together, the keyword and module name make up the statement. Line 2 then is an `import` statement that imports the module named `random` which contains several functions related to random numbers. (We'll use one of these functions later to have the computer come up with a random number for us to guess.)

```
4. guessesTaken = 0
```

This line creates a new variable named guessesTaken. We'll store the number of guesses the player makes in this variable. Since the player hasn't made any guesses so far, we store the integer 0 here.

```
6. print('Hello! What is your name?')
7. myName = input()
```

Lines 6 and 7 are the same as the lines in the Hello World program that we saw in Chapter 3. Programmers often reuse code from their other programs when they need the program to do something that they've already coded before.

Line 6 is a function call to the print() function. Remember that a function is like a mini-program that our program runs, and when our program calls a function it runs this mini-program. The code inside the print() function displays the string you passed it inside the parentheses on the screen.

When these two lines finish executing, the string that is the player's name will be stored in the myName variable. (Remember, the string might not really be the player's name. It's just whatever string the player typed in. Computers are dumb and just follow their programs no matter what.)

The `random.randint()` Function

```
9. number = random.randint(1, 20)
```

In Line 9 we call a new function named randint(), and then store the return value in a variable named number. Remember that function calls are expressions because they evaluate to a value. We call this value the function call's return value.

Because the randint() function is provided by the random module, we precede it with random. (don't forget the period!) to tell our program that the function randint() is in the random module.

The randint() function will return a random integer between (and including) the two integers we give it. Here, we give it the integers 1 and 20 between the parentheses that follow the function name (separated by a comma). The random integer that randint() returns is stored in a variable named number; this is the secret number the player is trying to guess.

Just for a moment, go back to the interactive shell and enter import random to import the random module. Then enter random.randint(1, 20) to see what the function call evaluates to. It should return an integer between 1 and 20. Now enter the same code again and the function call will probably return a different integer. This is because each time the randint() function is called, it returns some random number, just like when you roll dice you will get a random number each time.

```
>>> import random
>>> random.randint(1, 20)
12
>>> random.randint(1, 20)
18
>>> random.randint(1, 20)
3
>>> random.randint(1, 20)
18
>>> random.randint(1, 20)
7
>>>
```

Whenever we want to add randomness to our games, we can use the `randint()` function. And we use randomness in most games. (Think of how many board games use dice.)

You can also try out different ranges of numbers by changing the arguments. For example, enter `random.randint(1, 4)` to only get integers between 1 and 4 (including both 1 and 4). Or try `random.randint(1000, 2000)` to get integers between 1000 and 2000. Below is an example of calling the `random.randint()` function and seeing what values it returns. The results you get when you call the `random.randint()` function will probably be different (it is random, after all).

```
>>> random.randint(1, 4)
3
>>> random.randint(1, 4)
4
>>> random.randint(1000, 2000)
1294
>>> random.randint(1000, 2000)
1585
>>>
```

We can change the game's code slightly to make the game behave differently. Try changing line 9 and 10 from this:

```
 9. number = random.randint(1, 20)
10. print('Well, ' + name + ', I am thinking of a number
    between 1 and 20.')
```

into these lines:

```
 9. number = random.randint(1, 100)
10. print('Well, ' + name + ', I am thinking of a number
    between 1 and 100.')
```

And now the computer will think of an integer between 1 and 100. Changing line 9 will change the range of the random number, but remember to change line 10 so that the game also tells the player the new range instead of the old one.

Calling Functions that are Inside Modules

By the way, be sure to enter `random.randint(1, 20)` and not just `randint(1, 20)`, or the computer will not know to look in the `random` module for the `randint()` function and you'll get an error like this:

```
>>> randint(1, 20)
Traceback (most recent call last):
  File "<stdin>", line 1, in <module>
NameError: name 'randint' is not defined
>>>
```

Remember, your program needs to run `import random` before it can call the `random.randint()` function. This is why `import` statements usually go at the beginning of the program.

Passing Arguments to Functions

The integer values between the parentheses in the `random.randint(1, 20)` function call are called arguments. **Arguments** are the values that are passed to a function when the function is called. Arguments tell the function how to behave. Just like the player's input changes how our program behaves, arguments are inputs for functions.

Some functions require that you pass them values when you call them. For example, look at these function calls:

```
input()
print('Hello')
random.randint(1, 20)
```

The `input()` function has no arguments but the `print()` function call has one and the randint() function call has two. When we have more than one argument, we separate each with commas, as you can see in this example. Programmers say that the arguments are **delimited** (that is, separated) by commas. This is how the computer knows where one value ends and another begins.

If you pass too many or too few arguments in a function call, Python will display an error message, as you can see below. In this example, we first called `randint()` with only one argument (too few), and then we called `randint()` with three arguments (too many).

```
>>> random.randint(1)
Traceback (most recent call last):
  File "<pyshell#1>", line 1, in <module>
random.randint(1)
TypeError: randint() takes exactly 3 positional
arguments (2 given)
>>> random.randint(1, 2, 3)
Traceback (most recent call last):
  File "<pyshell#2>", line 1, in <module>
random.randint(1, 2, 3)
TypeError: randint() takes exactly 3 positional
arguments (4 given)
>>>
```

Notice that the error message says we passed 2 and 4 arguments instead of 1 and 3. This is because Python always passes an extra, invisible argument. This argument is beyond the scope of this book, and you don't have to worry about it.

Welcoming the Player

Lines 10 and 12 greets the player and tells them about the game, and then starts letting the player guess the secret number. Line 10 is fairly simple, but line 12 introduces a useful concept called a loop.

```
10. print('Well, ' + myName + ', I am thinking of a number
       between 1 and 20.')
```

In Line 10 the `print()` function welcomes the player by name, and tells them that the computer is thinking of a random number.

But wait - didn't I say that the `print()` function takes only one string? It may look like there's more than one string there. But look at the line carefully. The plus signs concatenate the three strings to evaluate down to one string, and that is the one string the `print()` function prints. It might look like the commas are separating the strings, but if you look closely you see that the commas are *inside* the quotes, and part of the strings themselves.

Loops

Line 12 has something called a `while` statement, which indicates the beginning of a while loop. **Loops** are parts of code that are executed over and over again. But before we can learn about `while` loops, we need to learn a few other concepts first. Those concepts are blocks, Booleans, comparison operators, conditions, and finally, the `while` statement.

Blocks

A **block** is one or more lines of code grouped together with the same minimum amount of indentation. You can tell where a block begins and ends by looking at the line's **indentation** (that is, the number of spaces in front of the line).

A block begins when a line is indented by four spaces. Any following line that is also indented by four spaces is part of the block. A block within a block begins when a line is indented with another four spaces (for a total of eight spaces in front of the line). The block ends when there is a line of code with the same indentation before the block started.

Below is a diagram of the code with the blocks outlined and numbered. The spaces have black squares filled in to make them easier to count.

```
12. while guessesTaken < 6:                          1
13. ••••print('Take a guess.')
14. ••••guess = input()
15. ••••guess = int(guess)
16.
17. ••••guessesTaken = guessesTaken + 1
18.                                                  2
19. ••••if guess < number:
20. ••••••••print('Your guess is too low.')
21.                                                  3
22. ••••if guess > number:
23. ••••••••print('Your guess is too high.')
```

Figure 4-1: Blocks and their indentation. The black dots represent spaces.

For example, look at the code in Figure 4-1. The spaces have been replaced with dark squares to make them easier to count. Line 12 has an indentation of zero spaces and is not inside any block. Line 13 has an indentation of four spaces. Since this indentation is larger than the previous line's indentation, we can tell that a new block has started. Lines 14, 15, 17 and 19 also have four spaces for indentation. Both of these lines have the same amount of indentation as the previous line, so we know they are in the same block. (We do not count blank lines when we look for indentation.)

Line 20 has an indentation of eight spaces. Eight spaces is more than four spaces, so we know a new block has started. This is a block that is inside of another block.

Line 22 only has four spaces. The line before line 22 had a larger number of spaces. Because the indentation has decreased, we know that block has ended. Line 22 is in the same block as the other lines with four spaces.

Line 23 increases the indentation to eight spaces, so again a new block has started.

To recap, line 12 is not in any block. Lines 13 to 23 all in one block (marked with the circled 1). Line 20 is in a block in a block (marked with a circled 2). And line 23 is the only line in another block in a block (marked with a circled 3).

When you type code into IDLE, each letter is the same width. You can count the number of letters above or below the line to see how many spaces you have put in front of that line of code.

In this figure, the lines of code inside box 1 are all in the same block, and blocks 2 and 3 are inside block 1. Block 1 is indented with at least four spaces from the left margin, and blocks 2 and 3 are indented eight spaces from the left margin. A block can contain just one line. Notice that blocks 2 and 3 are only one line each.

The Boolean Data Type

The Boolean data type has only two values: `True` or `False`. These values are case-sensitive and they are not string values; in other words, you do **not** put a ' quote character around them. We will use Boolean values (also called **bools**) with comparison operators to form conditions. (Explained next.)

Comparison Operators

In line 12 of our program, the line of code containing the `while` statement:

```
12. while guessesTaken < 6:
```

The expression that follows the `while` keyword (`guessesTaken < 6`) contains two values (the value in the variable `guessesTaken`, and the integer value 6) connected by an operator (the < sign, the "less than" sign). The < sign is called a **comparison operator**.

The comparison operator is used to compare two values and evaluate to a `True` or `False` Boolean value. A list of all the comparison operators is in Table 4-1.

Table 4-1: Comparison operators.

Operator Sign	Operator Name
<	Less than
>	Greater than
<=	Less than or equal to
>=	Greater than or equal to
==	Equal to
!=	Not equal to

Conditions

A **condition** is an expression that combines two values with a comparison operator (such as < or >) and evaluates to a Boolean value. A condition is just another name for an expression that evaluates to `True` or `False`. You'll find a list of other comparison operators in Table 4-1.

Conditions always evaluate to a Boolean value: either `True` or `False`. For example, the condition in our code, `guessesTaken < 6` asks "is the value stored in `guessesTaken` less than the number 6?" If so, then the condition evaluates to `True`. If not, the condition evaluates to `False`.

In the case of our Guess the Number program, in line 4 we stored the value 0 in `guessesTaken`. Because 0 is less than 6, this condition evaluates to the Boolean value of `True`. Remember, a condition is just a name for an expression that uses comparison operators such as < or !=.

Experiment with Booleans, Comparison Operators, and Conditions

Enter the following expressions in the interactive shell to see their Boolean results:

```
>>> 0 < 6
True
>>> 6 < 0
False
>>> 50 < 10
False
>>> 10 < 11
True
```

```
>>> 10 < 10
False
```

The condition $0 < 6$ returns the Boolean value True because the number 0 is less than the number 6. But because 6 is not less than 0, the condition $6 < 0$ evaluates to False. 50 is not less than 10, so $50 < 10$ is False. 10 is less than 11, so $10 < 11$ is True.

But what about $10 < 10$? Why does it evaluate to False? It is False because the number 10 is not smaller than the number 10. They are exactly the same size. If a girl named Alice was the same height as a boy named Bob, you wouldn't say that Alice is taller than Bob or that Alice is shorter than Bob. Both of those statements would be false.

Try entering some conditions into the shell to see how these comparison operators work:

```
>>> 10 == 10
True
>>> 10 == 11
False
>>> 11 == 10
False
>>> 10 != 10
False
>>> 10 != 11
True
>>> 'Hello' == 'Hello'
True
>>> 'Hello' == 'Good bye'
False
>>> 'Hello' == 'HELLO'
False
>>> 'Good bye' != 'Hello'
True
```

Notice the difference between the assignment operator (=) and the "equal to" comparison operator (==). The equal (=) sign is used to assign a value to a variable, and the equal to (==) sign is used in expressions to see whether two values are equal. It's easy to accidentally use one when you meant to use the other, so be careful of what you type in.

Two values that are different data types will **always** be not equal to each other. For example, try entering the following into the interactive shell:

```
>>> 42 == 'Hello'
False
```

```
>>> 42 != '42'
False
```

Looping with `while` Statements

The `while` statement marks the beginning of a loop. Sometimes in our programs, we want the program to do something over and over again. When the execution reaches a `while` statement, it evaluates the condition next to the `while` keyword. If the condition evaluates to `True`, the execution moves inside the while-block. (In our program, the while-block begins on line 13.) If the condition evaluates to `False`, the execution moves all the way past the while-block. (In our program, the first line after the while-block is line 28.)

A `while` statement always has a colon (the : sign) after the condition.

```
12. while guessesTaken < 6:
```

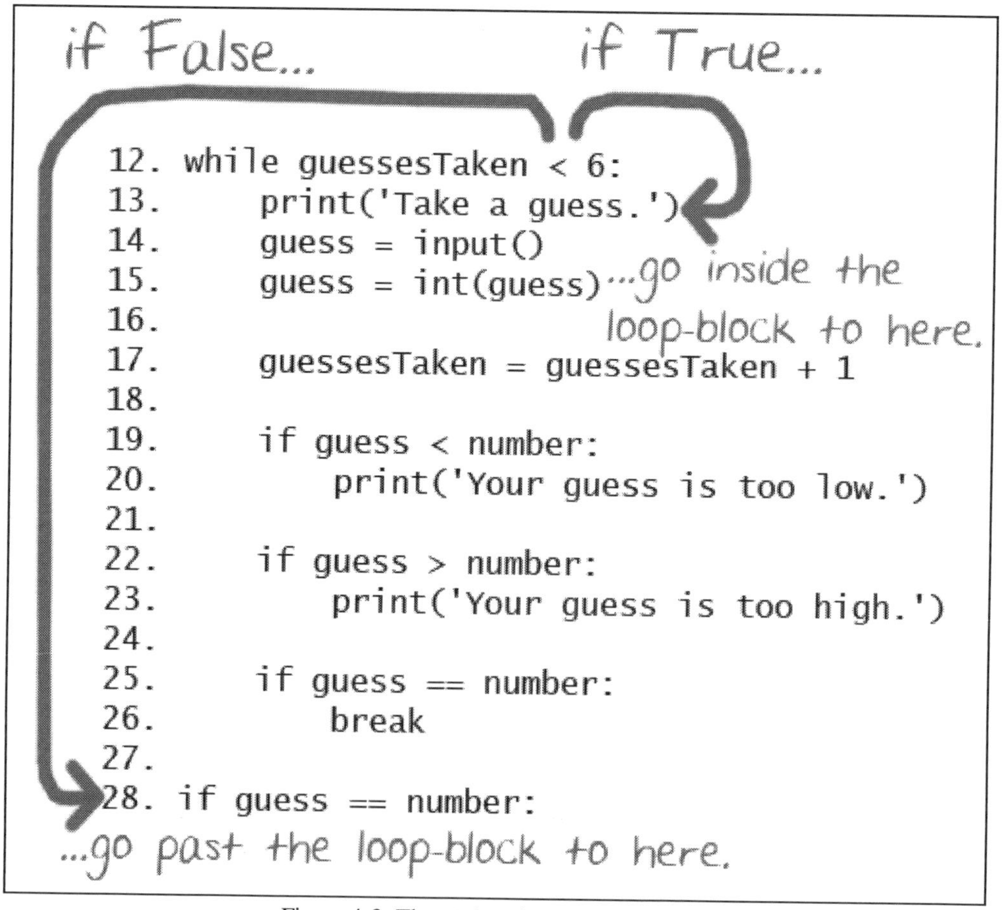

Figure 4-2: The `while` loop's condition.

Figure 4-2 shows how the execution flows depending on the condition. If the condition evaluates to `True` (which it does the first time, because the value of `guessesTaken` is

0), execution will enter the while-block at line 13 and keep going down. Once the program reaches the end of the while-block, instead of going down to the next line, it jumps back up to the `while` statement's line (line 12). It then re-evaluates the condition, and if it still evaluates to `True` we enter the while-block again.

This is how the loop works. As long as the condition is `True`, the program keeps executing the code inside the while-block repeatedly until we reach the end of the while-block and the condition is `False`. And, until `guessesTaken` is equal to or greater than 6, we will keep looping.

Think of the `while` statement as saying, "while this condition is true, keep looping through the code in this block".

You can make this game harder or easier by changing the number of guesses the player gets. All you have to do is change this line:

```
12. while guessesTaken < 6:
```

into this line:

```
12. while guessesTaken < 4:
```

...and now the player only gets four guesses instead of six guesses. By setting the condition to `guessesTaken < 4`, we ensure that the code inside the loop only runs four times instead of six. This makes the game much more difficult. To make the game easier, set the condition to `guessesTaken < 8` or `guessesTaken < 10`, which will cause the loop to run a few more times than before and accept more guesses from the player.

Of course, if we removed line 17 (`guessesTaken = guessesTaken + 1`) altogether then the `guessesTaken` would never increase and the condition would always be `True`. This would give the player an unlimited number of guesses.

The Player Guesses

Lines 13 to 17 ask the player to guess what the secret number is and lets them enter their guess. We store this guess in a variable, and then convert that string value into an integer value.

```
13.     print('Take a guess.') # There are four spaces in
     front of print.
14.     guess = input()
```

The program now asks us for a guess. We type in our guess and that number is stored in a variable named `guess`.

Converting Strings to Integers with the `int()` Function

```
15.        guess = int(guess)
```

In line 15, we call a new function called `int()`. The `int()` function takes one argument. The `input()` function returned a string of text that player typed. But in our program, we will want an integer, not a string. If the player enters 5 as their guess, the `input()` function will return the string value `'5'` and not the integer value 5. Remember that Python considers the string `'5'` and the integer 5 to be different values. So the `int()` function will take the string value we give it and return the integer value form of it.

Let's experiment with the `int()` function in the interactive shell. Try typing the following:

```
>>> int('42')
42
>>> int(42)
42
>>> int('hello')

Traceback (most recent call last):
  File "<pyshell#4>", line 1, in <module>
int('forty-two')
ValueError: invalid literal for int() with base
10: 'hello'
>>> int('forty-two')

Traceback (most recent call last):
  File "<pyshell#5>", line 1, in <module>
int('forty-two')
ValueError: invalid literal for int() with base
10: 'forty-two'
>>> int(' 42 ')
42
>>> 3 + int('2')
5
```

We can see that the `int('42')` call will return the integer value 42, and that `int(42)` will do the same (though it is kind of pointless to convert an integer to an integer). However, even though you can pass a string to the `int()` function, you cannot just pass any string. For example, passing `'hello'` to `int()` (like we do in the `int('hello')` call) will result in an error. The string we pass to `int()` must be made up of numbers.

The integer we pass to `int()` must also be numerical, rather than text, which is why `int('forty-two')` also produces an error. That said, the `int()` function is slightly forgiving; if our string has spaces on either side, it will still run without error. This is why the `int(' 42 ')` call works.

The `3 + int('2')` line shows an expression that adds an integer 3 to the return value of `int('2')` (which is the integer 2). The expression evaluates to `3 + 2`, which then evaluates to 5. So even though we cannot add an integer and a string (`3 + '2'` would show us an error), we can add an integer to a string that has been converted to an integer.

Remember, back in our program on line 15 the `guess` variable originally held the string value of what the player typed. We will overwrite the string value stored in `guess` with the integer value returned by the `int()` function. This is because we will later compare the player's guess with the random number the computer came up with. We can only compare two integer values to see if one is greater (that is, higher) or less (that is, lower) than the other. We cannot compare a string value with an integer value to see if one is greater or less than the other, even if that string value is numeric such as `'5'`.

In our Guess the Number game, if the player types in something that is not a number, then the function call `int()` will result in an error and the program will crash. In the other games in this book, we will add some more code to check for error conditions like this and give the player another chance to enter a correct response.

Notice that calling `int(guess)` does not change the value in the `guess` variable. The code `int(guess)` is an expression that evaluates to the integer value form of the string stored in the guess variable. We must assign this return value to guess in order to change the value in guess to an integer with this full line: `guess = int(guess)`

Incrementing Variables

```
17.        guessesTaken = guessesTaken + 1
```

Once the player has taken a guess, we want to increase the number of guesses that we remember the player taking.

The first time that we enter the loop block, `guessesTaken` has the value of 0. Python will take this value and add 1 to it. `0 + 1` is 1. Then Python will store the new value of 1 to `guessesTaken`.

Think of line 17 as meaning, "the `guessesTaken` variable should be one more than what it already is".

When we add one to an integer value, programmers say they are **incrementing** the value (because it is increasing by one). When we subtract one from a value, we are **decrementing** the value (because it is decreasing by one). The next time the loop block loops around, guessesTaken will have the value of 1 and will be incremented to the value 2.

if Statements

Is the Player's Guess Too Low?

Lines 19 and 20 check if the number that the player guessed is less than the secret random number that the computer came up with. If so, then we want to tell the player that their guess was too low by printing this message to the screen.

```
19.      if guess < number:
20.          print('Your guess is too low.') # There are
    eight spaces in front of print.
```

Line 19 begins an if statement with the keyword, if. Next to the if keyword is the condition. Line 20 starts a new block (you can tell because the indentation has increased from line 19 to line 20.) The block that follows the if keyword is called an if-block. An if statement is used if you only want a bit of code to execute if some condition is true. Line 19 has an if statement with the condition guess < number. If the condition evaluates to True, then the code in the if-block is executed. If the condition is False, then the code in the if-block is skipped.

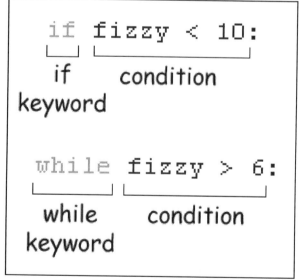

If the integer the player enters is less than the random integer the computer thought up, the program displays Your guess is too low. If the integer the player enters is equal to or larger than the random integer (in which case, the

Figure 4-3: if and while statements.

Like the while statement, the if statement also has a keyword, followed by a condition, a colon, and then a block of code. See Figure 4-3 for a comparison of the two statements.

The `if` statement works almost the same way as a `while` statement, too. But unlike the while-block, execution does not jump back to the `if` statement at the end of the if-block. It just continues on down to the next line. In other words, `if` statements won't loop.

If the condition is `True`, then all the lines inside the if-block are executed. The only line inside this if-block on line 19 is a `print()` function call.

condition next to the `if` keyword would have been `False`), then this block would have been skipped over.

Is the Player's Guess Too High?

Lines 22 to 26 in our program check if the player's guess is either too big or exactly equal to the secret number.

```
22.        if guess > number:
23.            print('Your guess is too high.')
```

If the player's guess is larger than the random integer, we enter the if-block that follows the `if` statement. The `print()` line tells the player that their guess is too big.

Leaving Loops Early with the `break` Statement

```
25.        if guess == number:
26.            break
```

This `if` statement's condition checks to see if the guess is equal to the random integer. If it is, we enter line 26, the if-block that follows it.

The line inside the if-block is a **break** statement that tells the program to immediately jump out of the while-block to the first line after the end of the while-block. (The `break` statement does not bother re-checking the `while` loop's condition, it just breaks out immediately.)

The `break` statement is just the `break` keyword by itself, with no condition or colon.

If the player's guess is not equal to the random integer, we do not break out of the while-block, we will reach the bottom of the while-block anyway. Once we reach the bottom of the while-block, the program will loop back to the top and recheck the condition (`guessesTaken < 6`). Remember after the `guessesTaken = guessesTaken + 1` line of code executed, the new value of `guessesTaken` is 1. Because 1 is less than 6, we enter the loop again.

If the player keeps guessing too low or too high, the value of `guessesTaken` will change to 2, then 3, then 4, then 5, then 6. If the player guessed the number correctly, the condition in the `if guess == number` statement would be `True`, and we would have executed the `break` statement. Otherwise, we keep looping. But when `guessesTaken` has the number 6 stored, the `while` statement's condition is `False`, since 6 is not less than 6. Because the `while` statement's condition is `False`, we will not enter the loop and instead jump to the end of the while-block.

The remaining lines of code run when the player has finished guessing (either because the player guessed the correct number, or because the player ran out of guesses). The reason the player exited the previous loop will determine if they win or lose the game, and the program will display the appropriate message on the screen for either case.

Check if the Player Won

```
28. if guess == number:
```

Unlike the code in line 25, this line has no indentation, which means the while-block has ended and this is the first line outside the while-block. When we left the `while` block, we did so either because the `while` statement's condition was `False` (when the player runs out of guesses) or if we executed the `break` statement (when the player guesses the number correctly). With line 28, check again to see if the player guessed correctly. If so, we enter the if-block that follows.

```
29.     guessesTaken = str(guessesTaken)
30.     print('Good job, ' + myName + '! You guessed my
    number in ' + guessesTaken + ' guesses!')
```

Lines 29 and 30 are inside the if-block. They only execute if the condition in the `if` statement on line 28 was `True` (that is, if the player correctly guessed the computer's number).

In line 29 we call the new function `str()`, which returns the string form of an argument. We use this function because we want to change the integer value in `guessesTaken` into its string version because we can only use strings in calls to `print()`.

Line 29 tells the player that they have won, and how many guesses it took them. Notice in this line that we change the `guessesTaken` value into a string because we can only add (that is, concatenate) strings to other strings. If we were to try to add a string to an integer, the Python interpreter would display an error.

Check if the Player Lost

```
32. if guess != number:
```

In Line 32, we use the comparison operator != with the if statement's condition to mean "is not equal to." If the value of the player's guess is lower or higher than (and therefore, not equal to) the number chosen by the computer, then this condition evaluates to True, and we enter the block that follows this if statement on line 33.

Lines 33 and 34 are inside the if-block, and only execute if the condition is True.

```
33.     number = str(number)
34.     print('Nope. The number I was thinking of was ' +
    number)
```

In this block, we tell the player what the number is because they failed to guess correctly. But first we have to store the string version of number as the new value of number.

This line is also inside the if-block, and only executes if the condition was True. At this point, we have reached the end of the code, and the program terminates.

Congratulations! We've just programmed our first real game!

Summary: What Exactly is Programming?

If someone asked you, "What exactly is programming anyway?" what could you say to them? Programming is just the action of writing code for programs, that is, creating programs that can be executed by a computer.

"But what exactly is a program?" When you see someone using a computer program (for example, playing our Guess The Number game), all you see is some text appearing on the screen. The program decides what exact text to show on the screen (which is called the **output**), based on its instructions (that is, the program) and on the text that the player typed on the keyboard (which is called the **input**). The program has very specific instructions on what text to show the user. A **program** is just a collection of instructions.

"What kind of instructions?" There are only a few different kinds of instructions, really.

1. Expressions, which are made up of values connected by operators. Expressions are all evaluated down to a single value, like 2 + 2 evaluates to 4 or 'Hello' + ' ' + 'World' evaluates to 'Hello World'. Function calls are also part of expressions because they evaluate to a single value themselves, and this value can be connected by operators to other values. When expressions are next to the if and while keywords, we also call them conditions.

2. Assignment statements, which simply store values in variables so we can remember the values later in our program.

3. `if`, `while` and `break` are **flow control statements** because they decide which instructions are executed. The normal flow of execution for a program is to start at the top and execute each instruction going down one by one. But these flow control statements can cause the flow to skip instructions, loop over instructions, or break out of loops. Function calls also change the flow of execution by jumping to the start of a function.

4. The `print()` function, which displays text on the screen. Also, the `input()` function can get text from the user through the keyboard. This is called **I/O** (pronounced like the letters, "eye-oh"), because it deals with the input and output of the program.

And that's it, just those four things. Of course, there are many details about those four types of instructions. In this book you will learn about new data types and operators, new flow control statements besides `if`, `while` and `break`, and several new functions. There are also different types of I/O (input from the mouse, and outputting sound and graphics and pictures instead of just text.)

For the person using your programs, they really only care about that last type, I/O. The user types on the keyboard and then sees things on the screen or hears things from the speakers. But for the computer to figure out what sights to show and what sounds to play, it needs a program, and programs are just a bunch of instructions that you, the programmer, have written.

A Web Page for Program Tracing

If you have access to the Internet and a web browser, you can go to this book's website at *http://inventwithpython.com/traces* you will find a page that traces through each of the programs in this book. By following along with the trace line by line, it might become more clear what the Guess the Number program does. This website just shows a simulation of what happens when the program is run. No actual code is really being executed.

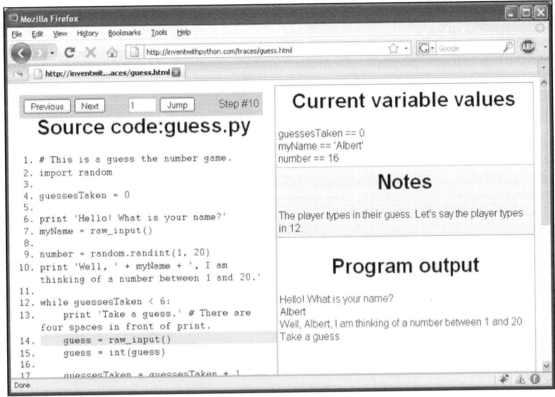

Figure 4-4: The tracing web page.

The left side of the web page shows the source code, and the highlighted line is the line of code that is about to be executed. You execute this line and move to the next line by clicking the "Next" button. You can also go back a step by clicking the "Previous" button, or jump directly to a step by typing it in the white box and clicking the "Jump" button.

On the right side of the web page, there are three sections. The "Current variable values" section shows you each variable that has been assigned a value, along with the value itself. The "Notes" section will give you a hint about what is happening on the highlighted line. The "Program output" section shows the output from the program, and the input that is sent to the program. (This web page automatically enters text to the program when the program asks.)

So go to each of these web pages and click the "Next" and "Previous" buttons to trace through the program like we did above.

A video tutorial of how to use the online tracing tool is available from this book's website at *http://inventwithpython.com/videos/*.

Chapter 5
Jokes

Topics Covered In This Chapter:

- Using `print()`'s `end` keyword argument to skip newlines.
- Escape characters.
- Using single quotes and double quotes for strings.

Make the Most of `print()`

Most of the games in this book will have simple text for input and output. The input is typed by the user on the keyboard and entered to the computer. The output is the text displayed on the screen. In Python, the `print()` function can be used for displaying textual output on the screen. We've learned how the basics of using the `print()` function, but there is more to learn about how strings and `print()` work in Python.

Sample Run of Jokes

```
What do you get when you cross a snowman with a vampire?

Frostbite!

What do dentists call an astronaut's cavity?

A black hole!

Knock knock.
```

```
Who's there?

Interrupting cow.

Interrupting cow wh-MOO!
```

Joke's Source Code

Here is the source code for our short jokes program. Type it into the file editor and save it as *jokes.py*. If you do not want to type this code in, you can also download the source code from this book's website at the URL *http://inventwithpython.com/chapter5*.

Important Note! Be sure to run this program with Python 3, and not Python 2. The programs in this book use Python 3, and you'll get errors if you try to run them with Python 2. You can click on **Help** and then **About IDLE** to find out what version of Python you have.

---

jokes.py

This code can be downloaded from *http://inventwithpython.com/jokes.py*
If you get errors after typing this code in, compare it to the book's code with the online diff tool at *http://inventwithpython.com/diff* or email the author at al@inventwithpython.com

```python
 1. print('What do you get when you cross a snowman with a
       vampire?')
 2. input()
 3. print('Frostbite!')
 4. print()
 5. print('What do dentists call a astronaut\'s cavity?')
 6. input()
 7. print('A black hole!')
 8. print()
 9. print('Knock knock.')
10. input()
11. print("Who's there?")
12. input()
13. print('Interrupting cow.')
14. input()
15. print('Interrupting cow wh', end='')
16. print('-MOO!')
```

Don't worry if you don't understand everything in the program. Just save and run the program. Remember, if your program has bugs in it, you can use the online diff tool at *http://inventwithpython.com/chapter5*.

How the Code Works

Let's look at the code more carefully.

```
1. print('What do you get when you cross a snowman with a
   vampire?')
2. input()
3. print('Frostbite!')
4. print()
```

Here we have three `print()` function calls. Because we don't want to tell the player what the joke's punch line is, we have a call to the `input()` function after the first `print()`. The player can read the first line, press Enter, and then read the punch line.

The user can still type in a string and hit Enter, but because we aren't storing this string in any variable, the program will just forget about it and move to the next line of code.

The last `print()` function call has no string argument. This tells the program to just print a blank line. Blank lines can be useful to keep our text from being bunched up together.

Escape Characters

```
5. print('What do dentists call a astronaut\'s cavity?')
6. input()
7. print('A black hole!')
8. print()
```

In the first `print()` above, you'll notice that we have a slash right before the single quote (that is, the apostrophe). This backslash (\ is a backslash, / is a forward slash) tells us that the letter right after it is an **escape character**. An escape character helps us print out letters that are hard to enter into the source code. There are several different escape characters, but in our call to `print()` the escape character is the single quote.

We have to have the single quote escape character because otherwise the Python interpreter would think that this quote meant the end of the string. But we want this quote to be a part of the string. When we print this string, the backslash will not show up.

Some Other Escape Characters

What if you really want to display a backslash? This line of code would not work:

```
>>> print('He flew away in a green\teal
helicopter.')
```

That `print()` function call would show up as:

```
He flew away in a green       eal helicopter.
```

This is because the "t" in "teal" was seen as an escape character since it came after a backslash. The escape character t simulates pushing the Tab key on your keyboard. Escape characters are there so that strings can have characters that cannot be typed in.

Instead, try this line:

```
>>> print('He flew away in a green\\teal
helicopter.')
```

Here is a list of escape characters in Python:

Table 5-1: Escape Characters

Escape Character	What Is Actually Printed
\\	Backslash (\)
\'	Single quote (')
\"	Double quote (")
\n	Newline
\t	Tab

Quotes and Double Quotes

Strings don't always have to be in between single quotes in Python. You can also put them in between double quotes. These two lines print the same thing:

```
>>> print('Hello world')
Hello world
>>> print("Hello world")
Hello world
```

But you cannot mix quotes. This line will give you an error if you try to use them:

```
>>> print('Hello world")
SyntaxError: EOL while scanning single-quoted
```

```
string
>>>
```

I like to use single quotes because I don't have to hold down the shift key on the keyboard to type them. It's easier to type, and the computer doesn't care either way.

But remember, just like you have to use the escape character \' to have a single quote in a string surrounded by single quotes, you need the escape character \" to have a double quote in a string surrounded by double quotes. For example, look at these two lines:

```
>>> print('I asked to borrow Abe\'s car for a
week. He said, "Sure."')
I asked to borrow Abe's car for a week. He said,
"Sure."
>>> print("He said, \"I can't believe you let him
borrow your car.\"")
He said, "I can't believe you let him borrow your
car."
```

Did you notice that in the single quote strings you do not need to escape double quotes, and in the double quote strings you do not need to escape single quotes? The Python interpreter is smart enough to know that if a string starts with one type of quote, the other type of quote doesn't mean the string is ending.

The end Keyword Argument

```
 9. print('Knock knock.')
10. input()
11. print("Who's there?")
12. input()
13. print('Interrupting cow.')
14. input()
15. print('Interrupting cow wh', end='')
16. print('-MOO!')
```

Did you notice the second parameter on line 15's print()? Normally, print() adds a newline character to the end of the string it prints. (This is why a blank print() function will just print a newline.) But the print() function can optionally have a second parameter (which has the name end.) The blank string we are passing is called a **keyword argument**. The end parameter has a specific name, and to pass an argument to this specific parameter we need to use the end= syntax.

Notice that when you type the keyword and the keyword argument, you use only one = sign. It is end=' ', and not end==' '.

By passing a blank string for the end we tell the print() function to not add a newline at the end of the string, but instead add a blank string. This is why '-MOO!' appears next to the previous line, instead of on its own line. There was no newline printed after the 'Interrupting cow wh' string.

Summary

This chapter explores the different ways you can use the print() function. Escape characters are used for characters that are difficult or impossible to type into the code with the keyboard. Escape characters are typed into strings beginning with a backslash \ followed by a single letter for the escape character. For example, \n would be a newline. To include a backslash in a string, you would use the escape character \\.

The print() function automatically appends a newline character to the end of the string we pass it to be displayed on the screen. Most of the time, this is a helpful shortcut. But sometimes we don't want a newline character at the end. To change this, we pass the end keyword argument with a blank string. For example, to print "spam" to the screen without a newline character, you would call print('spam', end='').

By adding this level of control to the text we display on the screen, we have much more flexible ways to display text on the screen the exact way we want to.

Chapter 6
Dragon Realm

Topics Covered In This Chapter:

- The `time` module.
- The `time.sleep()` function.
- The `return` keyword.
- Creating our own functions with the `def` keyword.
- The `and` and `or` and `not` Boolean operators.
- Truth tables
- Variable scope (Global and Local)
- Parameters and Arguments
- Flow charts

Introducing Functions

We've already used two functions in our previous programs: `input()` and `print()`. In our previous programs, we have called these functions to execute the code that is inside these functions. In this chapter, we will write our own functions for our programs to call. A function is like a mini-program that is inside of our program. Many times in a program we want to run the exact same code multiple times. Instead of typing out this code several times, we can put that code inside a function and call the function several times. This has the added benefit that if we make a mistake, we only have one place in the code to change it.

The game we will create to introduce functions is called "Dragon Realm", and lets the player make a guess between two caves which randomly hold treasure or certain doom.

How to Play "Dragon Realm"

In this game, the player is in a land full of dragons. The dragons all live in caves with their large piles of collected treasure. Some dragons are friendly, and will share their treasure with you. Other dragons are greedy and hungry, and will eat anyone who enters their cave. The player is in front of two caves, one with a friendly dragon and the other with a hungry dragon. The player is given a choice between the two.

Open a new file editor window by clicking on the **File** menu, then click on **New Window**. In the blank window that appears type in the source code and save the source code as *dragon.py*. Then run the program by pressing F5.

Sample Run of Dragon Realm

```
You are in a land full of dragons. In front of you,
you see two caves. In one cave, the dragon is friendly
and will share his treasure with you. The other dragon
is greedy and hungry, and will eat you on sight.

Which cave will you go into? (1 or 2)
1
You approach the cave...
It is dark and spooky...
A large dragon jumps out in front of you! He opens his jaws
and...

Gobbles you down in one bite!
Do you want to play again? (yes or no)
no
```

Dragon Realm's Source Code

Here is the source code for the Dragon Realm game. Typing in the source code is a great way to get used to the code. But if you don't want to do all this typing, you can download the source code from this book's website at the URL *http://inventwithpython.com/chapter6*. There are instructions on the website that will tell you how to download and open the source code file. If you type in the code yourself, you can use the online diff tool on the website to check for any mistakes in your code.

One thing to know as you read through the code below: The blocks that follow the `def` lines define a function, but the code in that block does not run until the function is called. The code does not execute each line in this program in top down order. This will be explained in more detail later in this chapter.

Important Note! Be sure to run this program with Python 3, and not Python 2. The programs in this book use Python 3, and you'll get errors if you try to run them with Python 2. You can click on **Help** and then **About IDLE** to find out what version of Python you have.

---

dragon.py

This code can be downloaded from *http://inventwithpython.com/dragon.py*

If you get errors after typing this code in, compare it to the book's code with the online diff tool at *http://inventwithpython.com/diff* or email the author at al@inventwithpython.com

```
 1. import random
 2. import time
 3.
 4. def displayIntro():
 5.     print('You are in a land full of dragons. In front of
    you,')
 6.     print('you see two caves. In one cave, the dragon is
    friendly')
 7.     print('and will share his treasure with you. The
    other dragon')
 8.     print('is greedy and hungry, and will eat you on
    sight.')
 9.     print()
10.
11. def chooseCave():
12.     cave = ''
13.     while cave != '1' and cave != '2':
14.         print('Which cave will you go into? (1 or 2)')
15.         cave = input()
16.
17.     return cave
18.
19. def checkCave(chosenCave):
20.     print('You approach the cave...')
21.     time.sleep(2)
22.     print('It is dark and spooky...')
23.     time.sleep(2)
24.     print('A large dragon jumps out in front of you! He
    opens his jaws and...')
25.     print()
26.     time.sleep(2)
27.
28.     friendlyCave = random.randint(1, 2)
29.
30.     if chosenCave == str(friendlyCave):
31.         print('Gives you his treasure!')
32.     else:
33.         print('Gobbles you down in one bite!')
34.
35. playAgain = 'yes'
36. while playAgain == 'yes' or playAgain == 'y':
```

```
37.
38.     displayIntro()
39.
40.     caveNumber = chooseCave()
41.
42.     checkCave(caveNumber)
43.
44.     print('Do you want to play again? (yes or no)')
45.     playAgain = input()
```

How the Code Works

Let's look at the source code in more detail.

```
1. import random
2. import time
```

Here we have two `import` statements. We import the `random` module like we did in the Guess the Number game. In Dragon Realm, we will also want some time-related functions that the `time` module includes, so we will import that as well.

Defining the `displayIntro()` Function

```
4. def displayIntro():
5.     print('You are in a land full of dragons. In front of
   you,')
6.     print('you see two caves. In one cave, the dragon is
   friendly')
7.     print('and will share his treasure with you. The
   other dragon')
8.     print('is greedy and hungry, and will eat you on
   sight.')
9.     print()
```

Figure 6-1 shows a new type of statement, the **def statement**. The `def` statement is made up of the `def` keyword, followed by a function name with parentheses, and then a colon (the : sign). There is a block after the statement called the def-block.

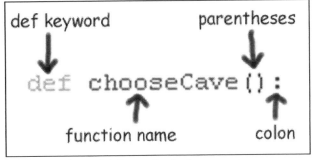

Figure 6-1: Parts of a `def` statement.

def Statements

The def statement isn't a call to a function named displayIntro(). Instead, the def statement means we are creating, or **defining**, a new function that we can call later in our program. After we *define* this function, we can call it the same way we call other functions. When we *call* this function, the code inside the def-block will be executed.

We also say we define variables when we create them with an assignment statement. The code spam = 42 defines the variable spam.

Remember, the def statement doesn't execute the code right now, it only defines what code is executed when we call the displayIntro() function later in the program. When the program's execution reaches a def statement, it skips down to the end of the def-block. We will jump back to the top of the def-block when the displayIntro() function is called. It will then execute all the print() statements inside the def-block. So we call this function when we want to display the "You are in a land full of dragons..." introduction to the user.

When we call the displayIntro() function, the program's execution jumps to the start of the function on line 5. When the function's block ends, the program's execution returns to the line that called the function.

We will explain all of the functions that this program will use before we explain the main part of the program. It may be a bit confusing to learn the program out of the order that it executes. But just keep in mind that when we define the functions they just silently sit around waiting to be called into action.

Defining the chooseCave() Function

```
11. def chooseCave():
```

Here we are defining another function called chooseCave. The code in this function will prompt the user to select which cave they should go into.

```
12.      cave = ''
13.      while cave != '1' and cave != '2':
```

Inside the chooseCave() function, we create a new variable called cave and store a blank string in it. Then we will start a while loop. This while statement's condition contains a new operator we haven't seen before called and. Just like the - or * are mathematical operators, and == or != are comparison operators, the and operator is a Boolean operator.

Boolean Operators

Boolean logic deals with things that are either true or false. This is why the Boolean data type only has two values, `True` and `False`. Boolean expressions are always either `True` or `False`. If the expression is not `True`, then it is `False`. And if the expression is not `False`, then it is `True`.

Boolean operators compare two Boolean values (also called bools) and evaluate to a single Boolean value. Do you remember how the `*` operator will combine two integer values and produce a new integer value (the product of the two original integers)? And do you also remember how the `+` operator can combine two strings and produce a new string value (the concatenation of the two original strings)? The `and` Boolean operator combines two Boolean values to produce a new Boolean value. Here's how the `and` operator works.

Think of the sentence, "Cats have whiskers and dogs have tails." This sentence is true, because "cats have whiskers" is true and "dogs have tails" is also true.

But the sentence, "Cats have whiskers and dogs have wings" would be false. Even though "cats have whiskers" is true, dogs do not have wings, so "dogs have wings" is false. The entire sentence is only true if both parts are true because the two parts are connected by the word "and." If one or both parts are false, then the entire sentence is false.

The `and` operator in Python works this way too. If the Boolean values on both sides of the `and` keyword are `True`, then the expression with the and operator evaluates to `True`. If either of the Boolean values are `False`, or both of the Boolean values are `False`, then the expression evaluates to `False`.

Evaluating an Expression That Contains Boolean Operators

So let's look at line 13 again:

```
13.       while cave != '1' and cave != '2':
```

This condition is has two expressions connected by the `and` Boolean operator. We first evaluate these expressions to get their Boolean (that is, `True` or `False`) values. Then we evaluate the Boolean values with the `and` operator.

The string value stored in cave when we first execute this `while` statement is the blank string, `''`. The blank string does not equal the string `'1'`, so the left side evaluates to `True`. The blank string also does not equal the string `'2'`, so the right side evaluates to `True`. So the condition then turns into `True and True`. Because both Boolean values are `True`, the condition finally evaluates to `True`. And because the `while` statement's condition is `True`, the program execution enters the while-block.

This is all done by the Python interpreter, but it is important to understand how the interpreter does this. This picture shows the steps of how the interpreter evaluates the condition (if the value of cave is the blank string):

```
while cave != '1' and cave != '2':
         ⬇
while '' != '1' and cave != '2':
         ⬇
while True and cave != '2':
         ⬇
while True and '' != '2':
         ⬇
while True and True:
         ⬇
while True:
```

Experimenting with the **and** and **or** Operators

Try typing the following into the interactive shell:

```
>>> True and True
True
>>> True and False
False
>>> False and True
False
>>> False and False
False
```

There are two other Boolean operators. The next one is the or operator. The or operator works similar to the and, except it will evaluate to True if *either* of the two Boolean values are True. The only time the or operator evaluates to False is if both of the Boolean values are False.

The sentence "Cats have whiskers or dogs have wings." is true. Even though dogs don't have wings, when we say "or" we mean that one of the two parts is true. The sentence "Cats have whiskers or dogs have tails." is also true. (Most of the time when we say "this or that", we mean one thing is true but the other thing is false. In programming, "or" means that either of the things are true, or maybe both of the things are true.)

Try typing the following into the interactive shell:

```
>>> True or True
True
>>> True or False
True
>>> False or True
True
>>> False or False
False
```

Experimenting with the not Operator

The third Boolean operator is not. The not operator is different from every other operator we've seen before, because it only works on one value, not two. There is only value on the right side of the not keyword, and none on the left. The not operator will evaluate to True as False and will evaluate False as True.

Try typing the following into the interactive shell:

```
>>> not True
False
>>> not False
True
>>> True not
SyntaxError: invalid syntax (<pyshell#0>, line 1)
```

Notice that if we put the Boolean value on the left side of the not operator results in a syntax error.

We can use both the and and not operators in a single expression. Try typing True and not False into the shell:

```
>>> True and not False
True
```

Normally the expression True and False would evaluate to False. But the True and not False expression evaluates to True. This is because not False evaluates to True, which turns the expression into True and True, which evaluates to True.

Truth Tables

If you ever forget how the Boolean operators work, you can look at these charts, which are called **truth tables**:

Table 6-1: The `and` operator's truth table.

A	and	B	is	Entire statement
True	and	True	is	True
True	and	False	is	False
False	and	True	is	False
False	and	False	is	False

Table 6-2: The `or` operator's truth table.

A	or	B	is	Entire statement
True	or	True	is	True
True	or	False	is	True
False	or	True	is	True
False	or	False	is	False

Table 6-3: The `not` operator's truth table.

not A	is	Entire statement
not True	is	False
not False	is	True

Getting the Player's Input

```
13.     while cave != '1' and cave != '2':
14.         print('Which cave will you go into? (1 or 2)')
15.         cave = input()
```

On line 14 the player is asked to enter which cave they chose to enter by typing in 1 or 2 and hitting Enter. Whatever string the player typed will be stored in `cave`. After this code is executed, we jump back to the top of the `while` statement and recheck the condition. Remember that the line was:

If this condition evaluates to `True`, we will enter the while-block again and ask the player for a cave number to enter. But if the player typed in 1 or 2, then the `cave` value will either be `'1'` or `'2'`. This causes the condition to evaluate to `False`, and the program execution will continue on past the `while` loop.

The reason we have a loop here is because the player may have typed in 3 or 4 or HELLO. Our program doesn't make sense of this, so if the player did not enter 1 or 2, then the program loops back and asks the player again. In fact, the computer will patiently ask the player for the cave number over and over again until the player types in 1 or 2. When the player does that, the while-block's condition will be `False`, and we will jump down past the while-block and continue with the program.

Return Values

```
17.       return cave
```

This is the **return** keyword, which only appears inside def-blocks. Remember how the `input()` function returns the string value that the player typed in? Or how the `randint()` function will return a random integer value? Our function will also return a value. It returns the string that is stored in `cave`.

This means that if we had a line of code like `spam = chooseCave()`, the code inside `chooseCave()` would be executed and the function call will evaluate to `chooseCave()`'s return value. The return value will either be the string `'1'` or the string `'2'`. (Our `while` loop guarantees that `chooseCave()` will *only* return either `'1'` or `'2'`.)

The `return` keyword is only found inside def-blocks. Once the `return` statement is executed, we immediately jump out of the def-block. (This is like how the `break` statement will make us jump out of a while-block.) The program execution moves back to the line that had called the function.

You can also use the `return` keyword by itself just to break out of the function, just like the `break` keyword will break out of a `while` loop.

Variable Scope

Just like the values in our program's variables are forgotten after the program ends, variables created inside the function are forgotten after the execution leaves the function. Not only that, but when execution is inside the function, we cannot change the variables outside of the function, or variables inside other functions. The variable's **scope** is this range that variables can be modified in. The only variables that we can use inside a function are the ones we create inside of the function (or the parameter variables, described later). That is, the scope of the variable is inside in the function's block. The scope of variables created outside of functions is outside of all functions in the program.

Not only that, but if we have a variable named `spam` created outside of a function, and we create a variable named `spam` inside of the function, the Python interpreter will consider them to be two separate variables. That means we can change the value of `spam` inside the function, and this will not change the `spam` variable that is outside of the function. This is because these variables have different scopes, the global scope and the local scope.

Global Scope and Local Scope

We have names for these scopes. The scope outside of all functions is called the **global scope**. The scope inside of a function is called the **local scope**. The entire program has only one global scope, and each function has a local scope of its own. Scopes are also called **namespaces**.

Variables defined in the global scope can be read outside and inside functions, but can only be modified outside of all functions. Variables defined in a function's local scope can only be read or modified inside that function.

Specifically, we can read the value of global variables from the local scope, but attempting to change the value in a global variable from the local scope will leave the global variable unchanged. What Python actually does is create a local variable with the **same name** as the global variable. But Python will consider these to be two different variables.

Also, global variables cannot be read from a local scope if you modify that variable inside the local scope. For example, if you had a variable named spam in the global scope but also modified a variable named spam in the local scope (say, with an assignment statement) then the name "spam" can **only** refer to the local scope variable.

Look at this example to see what happens when you try to change a global variable from inside a local scope. Remember that the code in the funky() function isn't run until the funky() function is called. The comments explain what is going on:

```
# This block doesn't run until funky() is called:
def funky():
    # We create a local variable named "spam"
    # instead of changing the value of the global
    # variable "spam":
    spam = 99

    # The name "spam" now refers to the local
    # variable only for the rest of this
    # function:
    print(spam)     # 99

# A global variable named "spam":
spam = 42
print(spam) # 42

# Call the funky() function:
funky()
```

```
# The global variable was not changed in funky():
print(spam)     # 42
```

When run, this code will output the following:

```
42
99
42
```

It is important to know when a variable is defined because that is how we know the variable's scope. A variable is defined the first time we use it in an assignment statement. When the program first executes the line:

```
12.     cave = ''
```

...the variable cave is defined.

If we call the chooseCave() function twice, the value stored in the variable the first time won't be remember the second time around. This is because when the execution left the chooseCave() function (that is, left chooseCave()'s local scope), the cave variable was forgotten and destroyed. But it will be defined again when we call the function a second time because line 12 will be executed again.

The important thing to remember is that the value of a variable in the local scope is not remembered in between function calls.

Defining the checkCave() Function

```
19. def checkCave(chosenCave):
```

Now we are defining yet another function named checkCave(). Notice that we put the text chosenCave in between the parentheses. The variable names in between the parentheses are called **parameters**.

Remember, for some functions like for the str() or randint(), we would pass an argument in between the parentheses:

```
>>> str(5)
'5'
>>> random.randint(1, 20)
14
```

When we call `checkCave()`, we will also pass one value to it as an argument. When execution moves inside the `checkCave()` function, a new variable named `chosenCave` will be assigned this value. This is how we pass variable values to functions since functions cannot read variables outside of the function (that is, outside of the function's local scope).

Parameters are local variables that get defined when a function is called. The value stored in the parameter is the argument that was passed in the function call.

Parameters

For example, here is a short program that demonstrates parameters. Imagine we had a short program that looked like this:

```
def sayHello(name):
    print('Hello, ' + name)

print('Say hello to Alice.')
fizzy = 'Alice'
sayHello(fizzy)
print('Do not forget to say hello to Bob.')
sayHello('Bob')
```

If we run this program, it would look like this:

```
Say hello to Alice.
Hello, Alice
Do not forget to say hello to Bob.
Hello, Bob
```

This program calls a function we have created, `sayHello()` and first passes the value in the `fizzy` variable as an argument to it. (We stored the string `'Alice'` in `fizzy`.) Later, the program calls the `sayHello()` function again, passing the string `'Bob'` as an argument.

The value in the `fizzy` variable and the string `'Bob'` are arguments. The `name` variable in `sayHello()` is a parameter. The difference between arguments and parameters is that arguments are the values passed in a function call, and parameters are the local variables that store the arguments. It might be easier to just remember that the thing in between the parentheses in the `def` statement is an parameter, and the thing in between the parentheses in the function call is an argument.

We could have just used the `fizzy` variable inside the `sayHello()` function instead of using a parameter. (This is because the local scope can still see variables in the global scope.) But then we would have to remember to assign the `fizzy` variable a string each time before we call the sayHello() function. Parameters make our programs simpler. Look at this code:

```
def sayHello():
    print('Hello, ' + fizzy)

print('Say hello to Alice.')
fizzy = 'Alice'
sayHello()
print('Do not forget to say hello to Bob.')
sayHello()
```

When we run this code, it looks like this:

```
Say hello to Alice.
Hello, Alice
Do not forget to say hello to Bob.
Hello, Alice
```

This program's sayHello() function does not have a parameter, but uses the global variable fizzy directly. Remember that you can read global variables inside of functions, you just can't modify the value stored in the variable.

Without parameters, we have to remember to set the fizzy variable before calling sayHello(). In this program, we forgot to do so, so the second time we called sayHello() the value of fizzy was still 'Alice'. Using parameters instead of global variables makes function calling simpler to do, especially when our programs are very big and have many functions.

Where to Put Function Definitions

A function's definition (where we put the def statement and the def-block) has to come before you call the function. This is like how you must assign a value to a variable before you can use the variable. If you put the function call before the function definition, you will get an error. Look at this code:

```
sayGoodBye()

def sayGoodBye():
    print('Good bye!')
```

If you try to run it, Python will give you an error message that looks like this:

```
Traceback (most recent call last):
  File "C:\Python31\foo.py", line 1, in <module>
sayGoodBye()
NameError: name 'sayGoodBye' is not defined
```

To fix this, put the function definition before the function call:

```
def sayGoodBye():
    print('Good bye!')

sayGoodBye()
```

Displaying the Game Results

Back to the game's source code:

```
20.     print('You approach the cave...')
21.     time.sleep(2)
```

We display some text to the player, and then call the `time.sleep()` function. Remember how in our call to `randint()`, the function `randint()` is inside the `random` module? In the Dragon Realm game, we also imported the `time` module. The `time` module has a function called `sleep()` that will pause the program for a few seconds. We pass the integer value 2 as an argument to the `time.sleep()` function to tell it to pause for exactly 2 seconds.

```
22.     print('It is dark and spooky...')
23.     time.sleep(2)
```

Here we print some more text and wait again for another 2 seconds. These short pauses add suspense to the game, instead of displaying all the text all at once. In our jokes program, we called the `input()` function to wait until the player pressed the Enter key. Here, the player doesn't have to do anything at all except wait.

```
24.     print('A large dragon jumps out in front of you! He
    opens his jaws and...')
25.     print()
26.     time.sleep(2)
```

What happens next? And how does the program decide what happens?

Deciding Which Cave has the Friendly Dragon

```
28.        friendlyCave = random.randint(1, 2)
```

Now we are going to have the program randomly chose which cave had the friendly dragon in it. Our call to the `random.randint()` function will return either the integer 1 or the integer 2, and store this value in a variable called `friendlyCave`.

```
30.        if chosenCave == str(friendlyCave):
31.            print('Gives you his treasure!')
```

Here we check if the integer of the cave we chose (`'1'` or `'2'`) is equal to the cave randomly selected to have the friendly dragon. But wait, the value in `chosenCave` was a string (because `input()` returns strings) and the value in `friendlyCave` is an integer (because `random.randint()` returns integers). We can't compare strings and integers with the `==` sign, because they will always be different (`'1'` does not equal 1).

Comparing values of different data types with the `==` operator will always evaluate to `False`.

So we are passing `friendlyCave` to the `str()` function, which returns the string value of `friendlyCave`.

What the condition in this `if` statement is really comparing is the string in `chosenCave` and the string returned by the `str()` function. We could have also had this line instead:

```
if int(chosenCave) == friendlyCave:
```

Then the `if` statement's condition would compare the integer value returned by the `int()` function to the integer value in `friendlyCave`. The return value of the `int()` function is the integer form of the string stored in `chosenCave`.

If the `if` statement's condition evaluates to `True`, we tell the player they have won the treasure.

```
32.        else:
33.            print('Gobbles you down in one bite!')
```

Line 32 has a new keyword. The `else` keyword always comes after the if-block. The else-block that follows the else keyword executes if the condition in the `if` statement was `False`. Think of it as the program's way of saying, "If this condition is true then execute the if-block or else execute the else-block."

Remember to put the colon (the : sign) after the else keyword.

The Colon :

You may have noticed that we always place a colon at the end of if, else, while, and def statements. The colon marks the end of the statement, and tells us that the next line should be the beginning of a new block.

Where the Program Really Begins

```
35. playAgain = 'yes'
```

This is the first line that is not a def statement or inside a def-block. This line is where our program really begins. The previous def statements merely defined the functions, it did not run the code inside of the functions. Programs must always define functions before the function can be called. This is exactly like how variables must be defined with an assignment statement before the variable can be used in the program.

```
36. while playAgain == 'yes' or playAgain == 'y':
```

Here is the beginning of a while loop. We enter the loop if playAgain is equal to either 'yes' or 'y'. The first time we come to this while statement, we have just assigned the string value 'yes' to the playAgain variable. That means this condition will be True.

Calling the Functions in Our Program

```
38.        displayIntro()
```

Here we call the displayIntro() function. This isn't a Python function, it is our function that we defined earlier in our program. When this function is called, the program execution jumps to the first line in the displayIntro() function on line 5. When all the lines in the function are done, the execution jumps back down to the line after this one.

```
40.        caveNumber = chooseCave()
```

This line also calls a function that we created. Remember that the chooseCave() function lets the player type in the cave they choose to go into. When the return cave line in this function executes, the program execution jumps back down here, and the parameter cave's value is the return value of this function. The return value is stored in a new variable named caveNumber. Then the execution moves to the next line.

```
42.        checkCave(caveNumber)
```

This line calls our `checkCave()` function with the argument of caveNumber's value. Not only does execution jump to line 20, but the value stored in `caveNumber` is copied to the parameter `chosenCave` inside the `checkCave()` function. This is the function that will display either `'Gives you his treasure!'` or `'Gobbles you down in one bite!'` depending on the cave the player chose to go in.

Asking the Player to Play Again

```
44.        print('Do you want to play again? (yes or no)')
45.        playAgain = input()
```

After the game has been played, the player is asked if they would like to play again. The variable `playAgain` stores the string that the user typed in. Then we reach the end of the while-block, so the program rechecks the `while` statement's condition: `playAgain == 'yes'` or `playAgain == 'y'`

The difference is, now the value of `playAgain` is equal to whatever string the player typed in. If the player typed in the string `'yes'` or `'y'`, then we would enter the loop again at line 38.

If the player typed in `'no'` or `'n'` or something silly like `'Abraham Lincoln'`, then the `while` statement's condition would be `False`, and we would go to the next line after the while-block. But since there are no more lines after the while-block, the program terminates.

But remember, the string `'YES'` is different from the string `'yes'`. If the player typed in the string `'YES'`, then the `while` statement's condition would evaluate to `False` and the program would still terminate.

We've just completed our second game! In our Dragon Realm game, we used a lot of what we learned in the "Guess the Number" game and picked up a few new tricks as well. If you didn't understand some of the concepts in this program, then read the summary at the end of this chapter, or go over each line of the source code again, or try changing the source code and see how the program changes. In the next chapter we won't create a game, but learn how to use a feature of IDLE called the debugger. The debugger will help us figure out what is going on in our program as it is running.

We went through the source code from top to bottom. If you would like to go through the source code in the order that the execution flows, then check out the online tracing web site for this program at the URL *http://inventwithpython.com/traces/dragon.html*.

Designing the Program

Dragon Realm was a pretty simple game. The other games in this book will be a bit more complicated. It sometimes helps to write down everything you want your game or program to do before you start writing code. This is called "designing the program."

For example, it may help to draw a **flow chart**. A flow chart is a picture that shows every possible action that can happen in our game, and in what order. Normally we would create a flow chart before writing our program, so that we remember to write code for each thing that happens in the game. Figure 6-2 is a flow chart for Dragon Realm.

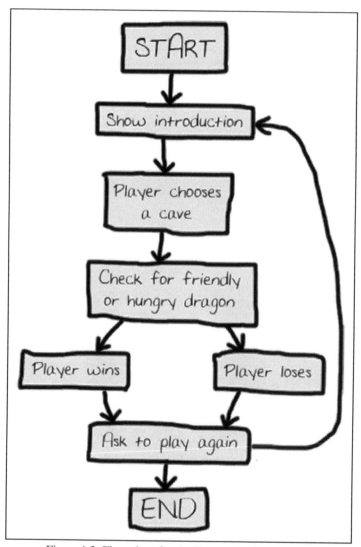

Figure 6-2: Flow chart for the Dragon Realm game.

To see what happens in the game, put your finger on the "Start" box and follow one arrow from the box to another box. Your finger is kind of like the program execution. Your finger will trace out a path from box to box, until finally your finger lands on the "End" box. As you can see, when you get to the "Check for friendly or hungry dragon" box, the program could either go to the "Player wins" box or the "Player loses" box. Either way, both paths will end up at the "Ask to play again" box, and from there the program will either end or show the introduction to the player again.

Summary

In the "Dragon Realm" game, we created our own functions that the main section of the program called. You can think of functions as mini-programs within our program. The code inside the function is run when our program calls that function. By breaking up our code into functions, we can organize our code into smaller and easier to understand sections. We can also run the same code by placing it inside of a function, instead of typing it out each time we want to run that code.

The inputs for functions are the arguments we pass when we make a function call. The function call itself evaluates to a value called the return value. The return value is the output of the function.

We also learned about variable scopes. Variables that are created inside of a function exist in the local scope, and variables created outside of all functions exist in the global scope. Code in the global scope can not make use of local variables. If a local variable has the same name as a variable in the global scope, Python considers it to be a separate variable and assigning new values to the local variable will not change the value in the global variable.

Variable scopes might seem complicated, but they are very useful for organizing functions as pieces of code that are separate from the rest of the function. Because each function has it's own local scope, we can be sure that the code in one function will not cause bugs in other functions.

All nontrivial programs use functions because they are so useful, including the rest of the games in this book. By understanding how functions work, we can save ourselves a lot of typing and make our programs easier to read later on.

Chapter 7
Using the Debugger

Topics Covered In This Chapter:

- 3 Different Types of Errors
- IDLE's Debugger
- Stepping Into, Over, and Out
- Go and Quit
- Break Points

Bugs!

"On two occasions I have been asked, 'Pray, Mr. Babbage, if you put into the machine wrong figures, will the right answers come out?' I am not able rightly to apprehend the kind of confusion of ideas that could provoke such a question."

-Charles Babbage, 19th century English mathematician, philosopher, inventor and mechanical engineer who originated the concept of a programmable computer.
http://en.wikipedia.org/wiki/Charles_Babbage

If you enter the wrong code, the computer will not give you the right program. A computer program will always do what you tell it to, but what you *tell* the program to do might not be the same as what you *wanted* the program to do. A **bug** is another name for an error or problem in a computer program. Bugs happen when the programmer has not carefully thought about what exactly the program is doing. There are three types of bugs that can happen with your program:

- **Syntax Errors** are a type of bug that comes from typos in your program. When the Python interpreter sees a syntax error, it is because your code is not written in proper Python language. A Python program with even a single syntax error will not run.
- **Runtime Errors** are bugs that happen while the program is running (that is, executing). The program will work up until it reaches the line of code with the error, and then the program terminates with an error message (this is called **crashing**). The Python interpreter will display something called a "traceback" and show the line where the problem happens.
- **Semantic Errors** are the trickiest bugs to fix. This bug does not crash the program, and the program may appear to work fine. However, it is not doing what the programmer intended for the program to do. For example, if the programmer wants the variable total to be the sum of the values in variables a, b, and c but writes total = a + b * c, then the value in total will be wrong. This won't cause the program to crash immediately, but may or may not cause some other code to crash later on because of the unexpected value in total.

Finding bugs in our program can be hard, if you even notice them at all! When running your program, you may discover that sometimes functions are not called when they are suppose to be, or maybe they are called too many times. You may code the condition for a while loop wrong, so that it loops the wrong number of times. (A loop in your program that never exits is a kind of bug is called an **infinite loop**. In order to stop this program, you can press Ctrl-C in the interactive shell.) Any of these things could mistakenly happen in your code if you are not careful.

It can be hard to figure out how your code could be producing a bug because all the lines of code get executed very quickly and the values in variables change so often. A **debugger** is a program that lets you step through your code one line at a time (in the same order that Python executes them), and shows what values are stored in all of the variables. A debugger lets you look at how each line of code affects your program. This can be very helpful to figure out what exactly the program is doing.

A video tutorial on using the debugger that comes with IDLE can be found on this book's website at *http://inventwithpython.com/videos/*

Starting the Debugger

In IDLE, go ahead and open the Dragon Realm game that you made in the last chapter. In the interactive shell, click on **File** and then **Open**, and then select *dragon.py* (or whatever you named the file when you saved it).

After opening the *dragon.py* file, click on the **Debug** menu item at the top of the interactive shell, and then click **Debugger** to make the Debug Control window appear (Figure 7-1).

Figure 7-1: The Debug Control window.

Now when you run the Dragon Realm game (by pressing F5 or clicking **Run**, then **Run Module** in the file editor window's top menu), the debugger program will be activated. This is called running a program "under a debugger". In the Debug Control window, check the **Source** and **Globals** checkboxes. Then run the program by pressing F5 in the file editor window (Figure 7-2).

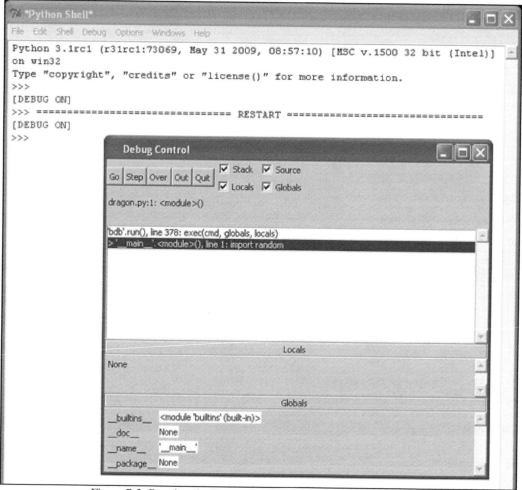

Figure 7-2: Running the Dragon Realm game under the debugger.

When you run Python programs with the debugger activated, the program will stop before it executes the first line of code. If you click on the file editor window's title bar (and you have checked the **Source** checkbox in the Debug Control window), the first line of code is highlighted in gray. Also, the Debug Control window shows that you are on line 1, which is the `import random` line.

The debugger lets you execute one line or code at a time (called "stepping"). To execute a single instruction, click the **Step** button in the Debug Window. Go ahead and click the Step button once. This will cause the Python interpreter to execute the `import random` instruction, and then stop before it executes the next instruction. The Debug Control window will change to show that you are now on line 2, the `import time` line.

Stepping

Here is a summary of what happens when you click the Step button when you run the Dragon Realm game under a debugger. A detailed description is below it.

1. Click the Step button twice to run the two `import` lines.
2. Click the Step button three more times to execute the three `def` statements.
3. Click the Step button again to define the `playAgain` variable.
4. Click Go to run the rest of the program, or click Quit to terminate the program.

Stepping is the process of executing one instruction of the program at a time. Doing this lets you see what happens after running a single line of code, which can help you figure out where a bug first appears in your programs.

The Debug Control window will show you what line is *about* to be executed when you click the **Step** button in the Debug Control window. This window will also tell you what line number it is on and show you the line of code itself. Remember to have the

Click the Step button twice to run the two `import` lines.

Click the Step button again to run the `import time` instruction. The debugger will execute this `import` statment and then move to line 4. The debugger skipped line 3 because it is a blank line. Notice that you can only step forward with the debugger, you cannot go backwards.

Click the Step button three more times to execute the three `def` statements.

Click the Step button three more times. This will execute the three `def` statements to define these functions. As you define these functions, they will appear in the Globals area of the Debug Control window.

The text next to the function names in the Global area will look something like "<function checkCave at 0x012859B0>". The module names also have confusing looking text next to them, such as "<module 'random' from 'C:\\Python31\\lib\\random.pyc'>". This is detailed information is useful to advanced Python programmers, but you don't need to know what it means to debug your programs. Just seeing that the functions and modules are there in the Global area will tell you if the function has been defined or the module has been imported. You can also ignore the `__builtins__`, `__doc__`, and `__name__` lines in the Global area. (Those are variables that appear in every Python program.)

Click the Step button again to define the `playAgain` variable.

The debugger will now be (after clicking Step four times) at line 35, the `playAgain = 'yes'` line. When you click Step to execute this line, the `playAgain` variable will be created and will show up in the Global area. Next to it will be the value stored in this variable, which is the string `'yes'`. The debugger lets you see the values of all the variables in the program as the run program runs. This can be very useful if you need to fix your programs.

The **Global area** in the Debug Control window is where all the global variables are stored. Remember, global variables are the variables that are created outside of any functions (that is, in the global scope). There is also a **Local area**, which shows you the local scope variables and their values. The local area will only have variables in it when the program execution is inside of a function. Since we are still in the global scope, this area is blank.

The Python debugger (and almost all debuggers) only lets you step forward in your program. Once you have executed an instruction, you cannot step backwards and undo the instruction.

The Go and Quit Buttons

If you get tired of clicking the step button over and over again, and just want the program to run normally, click the **Go** button at the top of the Debug Control window. This will tell the program to run as if you didn't have the debugger turned on.

If you ever want to terminate the program while it is running, just click the **Quit** button at the top of the Debug Control window. The program will immediately exit. This can be handy if you want to stop the program and start debugging it from the beginning again.

Stepping Into, Over, and Out

Start the Dragon Realm program with the debugger, and keep stepping (by clicking the Step button in the Debug Control window) until the debugger is at line 38 (the call to `displayIntro()` line). When you click Step again, the debugger will jump into this function call and appear on line 5 (the first line in the def-block of the `displayIntro()` function. The kind of stepping we have been doing is called **stepping into**, because it will step into function calls.

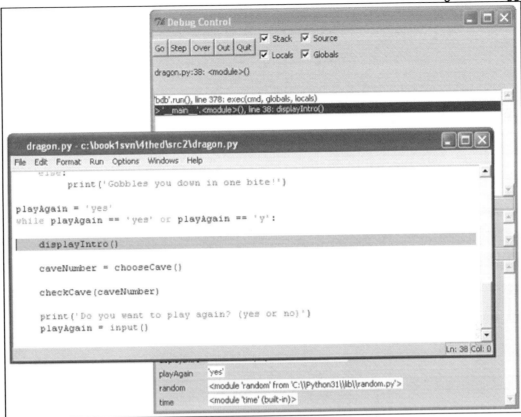

Figure 7-3: Keep stepping until you reach line 38.

If you click Step a few more times, you will see the output of the print() function call appear in the interactive shell window one at a time. When you step over the last print() function call in the displayIntro() function, the debugger will jump back to the first line (line 40) after function call.

Click Step one more time to step into the chooseCave() function. Keep stepping through the code until you execute the function call input() call. The program will wait until you type a response into the shell, just like when you run the program normally. If you try clicking the Step button now, nothing will happen because the program is waiting for a keyboard response.

Enter a response by clicking back on the interactive shell window and type which cave you want to enter. You have to click on the bottom line in the shell before typing. If you are typing but nothing appears on the screen (and the blinking cursor is not below the Which cave will you go into? (1 or 2) text), then you have not clicked on the last line of the shell window.

Once you press the Enter key to enter your response, the debugger will continue to step lines of code again. Instead of clicking Step, try clicking the **Out** button on the Debug Control window. This is called **stepping out**, because it will cause the debugger to step over as many lines as it needs to until it jumps out of the function that it was in. After it jumps out, the execution will be on the line after the line that called the function. For example, if you were inside the `displayIntro()` function on line 6, clicking Out would have the debugger keep stepping until the function was over and returned to the line after the call to `displayIntro()`. Stepping out can save you from having to click Step over and over again to jump out of the function.

If you are not inside a function (that is, you are in the global scope) and you click Out, the debugger will execute all the remaining lines in the program (exactly as if you clicked the Go button).

The last kind of stepping is done by the **Over** button in the Debug Control window, and it is for stepping over function calls. **Stepping over** means that the debugger will not step into function calls. Instead, the debugger executes all the code inside the function at once and only stop at the line after the function call. This is useful if you do not want to step through every single line inside the function. (Think of Stepping Over as the same as Stepping Into and then immediately Stepping Out.)

You now know what the five buttons at the top of the Debug Control window do. Here's a recap of what each button does:

- **Go** - Executes the rest of the code as normal, or until it reaches a break point. (Break points are described later.)
- **Step** - Step one line of code. If the line is a function call, the debugger will *step into* the function.
- **Over** - Step one line of code. If the line is a function call, the debugger will not step into the function, but instead *step over* the call.
- **Out** - Keeps stepping over lines of code until the debugger leaves the function it was in when Out was clicked. This *steps out* of the function.
- **Quit** - Immediately terminates the program.

Find the Bug

Using the debugger is a good way to figure out what is causing bugs in your program. As an example, here is a small program that has a bug in it. The program comes up with a random addition problem for the user to solve. In the interactive shell window, click on File, then New Window to open a new file editor window. Type this program into that window, and save the program as *buggy.py*.

```
buggy.py
1. import random
2. number1 = random.randint(1, 10)
3. number2 = random.randint(1, 10)
4. print('What is ' + str(number1) + ' + ' + str(number2) +
   '?')
5. answer = input()
6. if answer == number1 + number2:
7.     print('Correct!')
```

```
8. else:
9.     print('Nope! The answer is ' + str(number1 + number2))
```

Type the program in exactly as it is above, even if you can already tell what the bug is. Then trying running the program by pressing F5. This is a simple arithmetic game that comes up with two random numbers and asks you to add them. Here's what it might look like when you run the program:

```
What is 5 + 1?
6
Nope! The answer is 6
```

That's not right! This program has a semantic bug in it. Even if the user types in the correct answer, the program says they are wrong.

You could look at the code and think hard about where it went wrong. That works sometimes. But you might figure out the cause of the bug quicker if you run the program under the debugger. At the top of the interactive shell window, click on **Debug**, then **Debugger** (if there is no check already by the Debugger menu item) to display the Debug Control window. In the Debug Control window, make sure the all four checkboxes (Stack, Source, Locals, and Globals) are checked. This makes the Debug Control window provide the most information. Then press F5 in the file editor window to run the program under the debugger.

The debugger starts at the `import random` line. Nothing special happens here, so just click **Step** to execute it. You should see the `random` module added to the bottom of the Debug Control window in the Globals area.

Click Step again to run line 2. A new file editor window will pop open showing the `random.py` file. Remember that the `randint()` function is inside the `random` module. When you stepped into the function, you stepped into the `random` module because that is where the `randint` function is. The functions that come with Python's modules almost never have bugs in their code, so you can just click **Out** to step out of the `randint()` function and back to your program. After you have stepped out, you can close the `random` module's window.

Line 3 is also a call to the `randint()` function. We don't need to step through this code, so just click **Over** to step over this function call. The `randint()` function's code is still executed, it is just executed all at once so that we don't have to step through it.

Line 4 is a `print()` call to show the player the random numbers. But since we are using the debugger, we know what numbers the program will print even before it prints them! Just look at the Globals area of the Debug Control window. You can see the `number1` and `number2` variables, and next to them are the integer values stored in those variables. When

I ran the debugger, it looked like Figure 7-4.

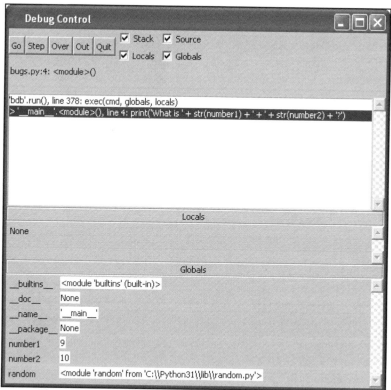

Figure 7-4: number1 is set to 9 and number2 is set to 10.

The number1 variable has the value 9 and the number2 variable has the value 10. When you click Step, the program will display the string in the print() call with these values. (Of course, we use the str() function so that we can concatenate the string version of these integers.)

Clicking on Step on line 5 will cause the debugger to wait until the player enters a response. Go ahead and type in the correct answer (in my case, 19) into the interactive shell window. The debugger will resume and move down to line 6.

Line 6 is an if statement. The condition is that the value in answer must match the sum of number1 and number2. If the condition is True, then the debugger will move to line 7. If the condition is False, the debugger will move to line 9. Click Step one more time to find out where it goes.

The debugger is now on line 9! What happened? The condition in the if statement must have been False. Take a look at the values for number1, number2, and answer. Notice that number1 and number2 are integers, so their sum would have also been an integer. But answer is a string. That means that the answer == number1 + number2 condition would have evaluated to '19' == 19. A string value and an integer value will always not equal each other, so the condition would have evaluated to False.

That is the bug in the program. The bug is that we use `answer` when we should be using `int(answer)`. Go ahead and change line 6 to use `int(answer) == number1 + number2` instead of `answer == number1 + number2`, and run the program again.

```
What is 2 + 3?
5
Correct!
```

This time, the program worked correctly. Run it one more time and enter a wrong answer on purpose to make sure the program doesn't tell us we gave the correct answer. We have now debugged this program. Remember, the computer will run your programs exactly as you type them, even if what you type is not what you intend.

Break Points

Stepping through the code one line at a time might still be too slow. Often you will want the program to run at normal speed until it reaches a certain line. You can do this with break points. A **break point** is set on a line when you want the debugger to take control once execution reaches that line. So if you think there is a problem with your code on, say, line 17, just set a break point on line 17 (or maybe a few lines before that) and when execution reaches that line, the debugger will stop execution. Then you can step through a few lines to see what is happening. Then you can click Go to let the program execute until it reaches the end (or another break point).

To set a break point, right-click on the line that you want a break point on and select "Set Breakpoint" from the menu that appears. The line will be highlighted with yellow to indicate a break point is on that line. You can set break points on as many lines as you want. To remove the break point, click on the line and select "Clear Breakpoint" from the menu that appears.

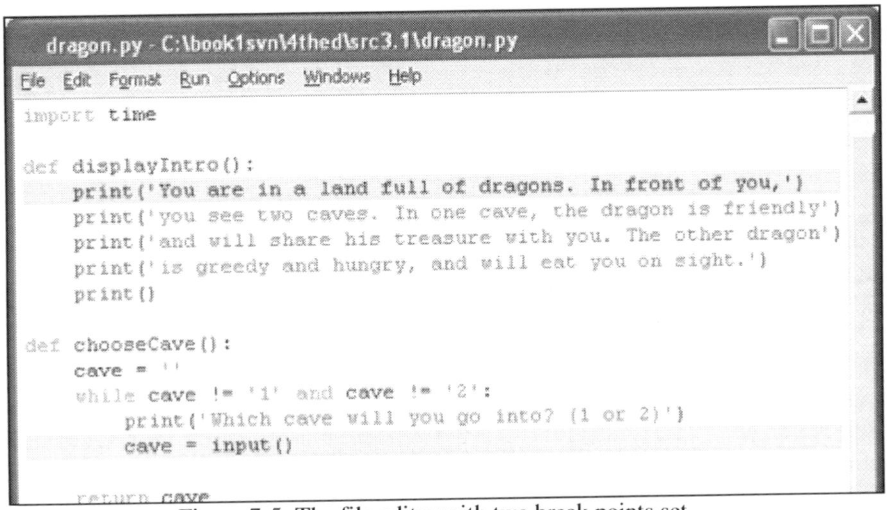

Figure 7-5: The file editor with two break points set.

Example of Using Break Points

Let's try debugging a program with break points. Here is a program that simulates coin flips by calling `random.randint(0, 1)`. Each time this function call returns the integer 1, we will consider that "heads" and increment a variable called `heads`. We will also increment a variable called `flips` to keep track of how many times we do this "coin flip".

The program will do "coin flips" one thousand times. This would take a person over an hour to do, but the computer can do it in one second! Type in the following code into the file editor and save it as *coinFlips.py*. You can also download this code from *http://inventwithpython.com/coinFlips.py*

---

coinFlips.py
This code can be downloaded from *http://inventwithpython.com/coinFlips.py*
If you get errors after typing this code in, compare it to the book's code with the online diff tool at *http://inventwithpython.com/diff* or email the author at al@inventwithpython.com

```
 1. import random
 2. print('I will flip a coin 1000 times. Guess how many
       times it will come up heads. (Press enter to begin)')
 3. input()
 4. flips = 0
 5. heads = 0
 6. while flips < 1000:
 7.     if random.randint(0, 1) == 1:
 8.         heads = heads + 1
 9.     flips = flips + 1
10.
11.     if flips == 900:
12.         print('900 flips and there have been ' + str
    (heads) + ' heads.')
13.     if flips == 100:
14.         print('At 100 tosses, heads has come up ' + str
    (heads) + ' times so far.')
15.     if flips == 500:
16.         print('Half way done, and heads has come up ' +
    str(heads) + ' times.')
17.
18. print()
19. print('Out of 1000 coin tosses, heads came up ' + str
    (heads) + ' times!')
20. print('Were you close?')
```

The program runs pretty fast. It probably spent more time waiting for the user to press the Enter key than it did doing the coin flips. Let's say we wanted to see it do coin flips one by one. On the interactive shell's window, click on Debug and then Debugger at the top menu to bring up the Debug Control window. Then press F5 to run the program.

The program starts in the debugger on line 1. Press Step three times in the Debug Control window to execute the first three lines (that is, lines 1, 2, and 3). You'll notice the buttons become disabled because the input() function has been called and the interactive shell window is waiting for the player to type something. Click on the interactive shell window and press Enter. (Be sure to click beneath the text in the shell window, otherwise IDLE might not receive your keystrokes.) After entering text for the input() call, the Step buttons will become enabled again.

You can click Step a few more times, but you'll find that it would take quite a while to get through the entire program. Instead, set a break point on lines 12, 14, and 16 (Figure 7-6).

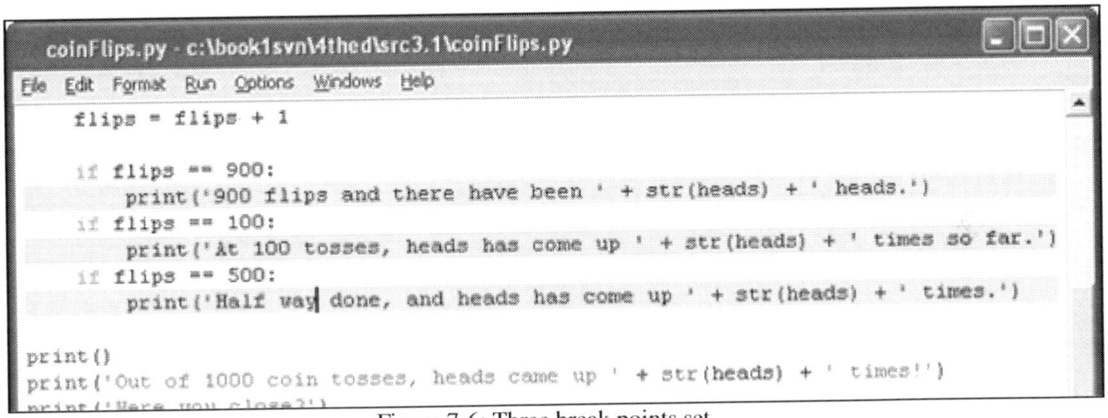

Figure 7-6: Three break points set.

After setting the breakpoints, click Go in the Debug Control window. The program will run at its normal speed until it reaches flip 100. On that flip, the condition for the if statement on line 13 is True. This causes line 14 (where we have a break point set) to execute, which tells the debugger to stop the program and take over. Look at the Debug Control window in the Globals section to see what the value of flips and heads are.

Click Go again and the program will continue until it reaches the next break point on line 16. Again, see how the values in flips and heads have changed. You can click Go one more time to continue the execution until it reaches the next break point.

And if you click Go again, the execution will continue until the next break point is reached, which is on line 12. You probably noticed that the print() functions on lines 12, 14 and 16 are called in a different order than they appear in the source code. That is because they are called in the order that their if statement's condition becomes True. Using the debugger can help make it clear why this is.

Summary

Writing programs is only part of the work for making games. The next part is making sure the code we wrote actually works. Debuggers let us step through the code one line at a time, while examining which lines execute (and in what order) and what values the variables contain. When this is too slow, we can set break points and click Go to let the program run normally until it reaches a break point.

Using the debugger is a great way to understand what exactly a program is doing. While this book provides explanations of all the games in it, the debugger can help you find out more on your own.

Chapter 8
Flow Charts

Topics Covered In This Chapter:

- How to play Hangman.
- ASCII art
- Designing our game by drawing a flow chart before programming.

In this chapter, we will make the design for a Hangman game. This game is more complicated than our previous game, but it is also much more fun. Because the game is advanced, we should first carefully plan it out by creating a diagram called a flow chart (explained later). In the next chapter, we will actually write out the code for Hangman.

In case you've never played Hangman before, let's first learn the rules for Hangman.

How to Play "Hangman"

In case you don't know, Hangman is a game for two people that's usually played using paper and pencil. One player thinks of a word, and then draws a blank on the page for each letter in the word. Then the second player tries to guess letters that might be in the word. If they guess correctly, the first player writes the letter in the proper blank. If they guess incorrectly, the first player draws a single body part of the hanging man. If the second player can guess all the letters in the word before the hangman has been completely drawn, they win. But if they can't figure it out in time, the man is hanged and they lose the game!

Sample Run of "Hangman"

Here is an example of what the player might see when they run the Hangman program we will write later. The text that the player enters in shown in bold.

```
H A N G M A N

    +---+
    |   |
        |
        |
        |
        |
=========
Missed letters:

_ _ _
Guess a letter.
a

    +---+
    |   |
        |
        |
        |
        |
=========
Missed letters:
_ a _
Guess a letter.
o

    +---+
    |   |
    O   |
        |
        |
        |
=========

Missed letters: o
_ a _
Guess a letter.
r

    +---+
    |   |
    O   |
    |   |
        |
        |
=========

Missed letters: or
_ a _
```

```
Guess a letter.
t

    +---+
    |   |
    O   |
    |   |
        |
        |
    =========
Missed letters: or
_ a t
Guess a letter.
a
You have already guessed that letter. Choose again.
Guess a letter.
c
Yes! The secret word is "cat"! You have won!
Do you want to play again? (yes or no)
no
```

ASCII Art

The graphics for hangman are all made out of keyboard characters printed on the screen. This type of graphics is called **ASCII art** (pronounced "ask-ee"), because keyboard characters (such as letters, numbers, and also all the other signs on the keyboard) are called ASCII characters. ASCII stands for American Standard Code for Information Interchange (we'll learn more about it in the Caesar Cipher chapter). Here are a couple cats done in ASCII art:

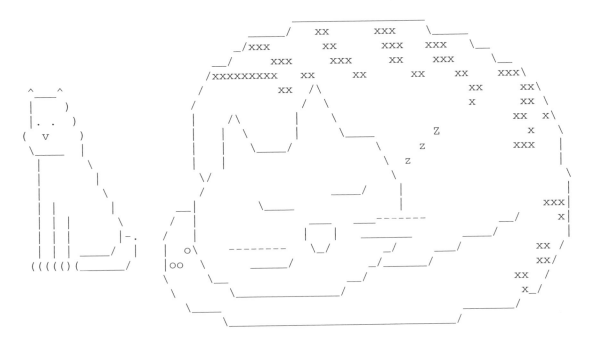

Designing a Program with a Flowchart

This game is a bit more complicated than the ones we've seen so far, so let's take a moment to think about how it's put together. First we'll create a flow chart (like the one at the end of the Dragon Realm chapter) to help us visualize what this program will do. This chapter will go over what flow charts are and why they are useful. The next chapter will go over the source code to the Hangman game. A **flow chart** is a diagram that shows a series of steps as a number of boxes connected with arrows. Each box represents a step, and the arrows show how one step leads to other steps. You can trace through the flow chart by putting your finger on the "Start" box of the flow chart and following the arrows to other boxes until you get to the "End" box. You can only move from one box to another in the direction of the arrow. You can never go backwards (unless there is a second arrow going back, like in the "Player already guessed this letter" box below.) Here is the complete flow chart for the Hangman game (Figure 8-1).

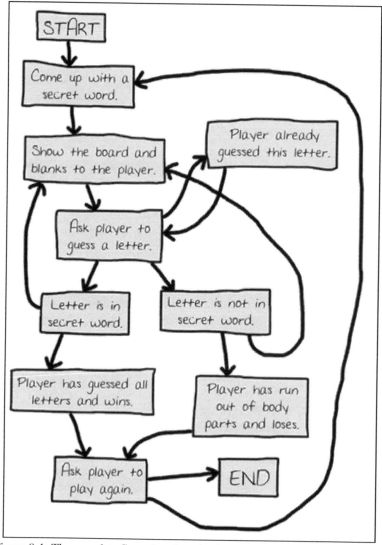

Figure 8-1: The complete flow chart for what happens in the Hangman game.

Of course, we don't *have* to make a flow chart. We could just start writing code. But often, once we start programming, we will think of things that need to be added or changed that we hadn't considered before. We may end up having to change or delete a lot of code that we had already written, which would be a waste of effort. To avoid this, it's always best to think carefully, and plan how the program will work before we start writing it.

The following flow chart is provided as an example of what flow charts look like and how to make them. For now, since you're just using the source code from this book, you don't need to draw a flow chart before writing code. The program is already written, so you don't have to plan anything out. But when you make your own games, a flow chart can be very handy.

Creating the Flow Chart

Keep in mind, your flow charts don't always have to look exactly like this one. As long as you understand the flow chart you made, it will be helpful when you start coding. We'll begin with a flow chart that only has a "Start" and an "End" box, as shown in Figure 8-2:

Figure 8-2: Begin your flow chart with a Start and End box.

Now let's think about what happens when we play Hangman. First, one player (the computer in this case) thinks of a secret word. Then the second player (the person running the program) will guess letters. Let's add boxes for these events, as shown in Figure 8-3. (The boxes that are new to each flow chart have a dashed outline around them.) The arrows show the order that the program should move. That is, first the program should come up with a secret word, and after that it should ask the player to guess a letter.

Figure 8-3: Draw out the first two steps of Hangman as boxes with descriptions.

But the game doesn't end after the player guesses one letter. It needs to check to see if that letter is in the secret word or not.

Branching from a Flowchart Box

There are two possibilities: the letter will either be in the word or it won't be. This means we need to add *two* new boxes to our flowchart. From the "Ask player to guess a letter" box, we can only move to the "Letter is in secret word" box *or* the "Letter is not in secret word" box. This will create a branch (that is, a split) in the flow chart, as show in Figure 8-4:

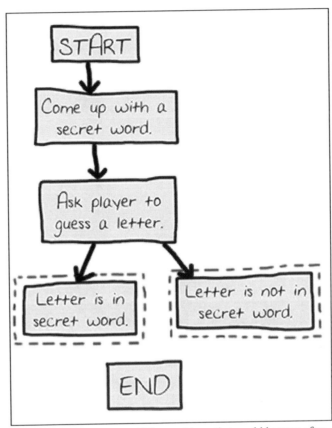

Figure 8-4: There are two different things that could happen after the player guesses, so have two arrows going to separate boxes.

If the letter is in the secret word, we need to check to see if the player has guessed all the letters, which would mean they've won the game. But, if the letter is not in the secret word, another body part is added to the hanging man.

We can add boxes for those cases too. We **don't** need an arrow from the "Letter is in secret word" box to the "Player has run out of body parts and loses" box, because it's impossible to lose as long as you are only guessing correct letters. Also, it's impossible to win as long as you are guessing only incorrect letters, so we don't need to draw that arrow either. Our flow chart now looks like Figure 8-5.

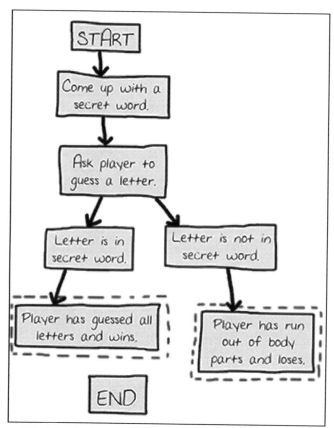

Figure 8-5: After the branch, the steps continue on their separate paths.

Ending or Restarting the Game

Once the player has won or lost, we'll ask them if they want to play again with a new secret word. If the player doesn't want to play again, the program will end. If the program doesn't end, we think of a new secret word, as shown in Figure 8-6:

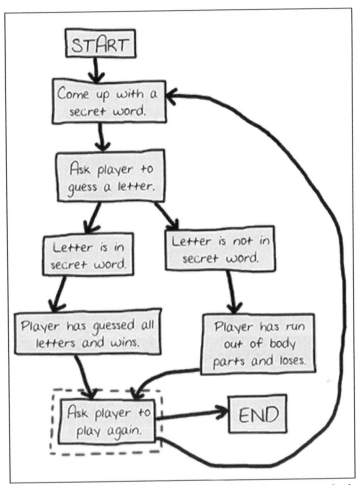

Figure 8-6: The game ends if the player doesn't want to play again, or the game goes back to the beginning.

Guessing Again

This flow chart might look like it is finished, but there's something we're forgetting: the player doesn't guess a letter just once. They have to keep guessing letters over and over until they either win or lose. We need to draw two new arrows so the flow chart shows this, as shown in Figure 8-7.

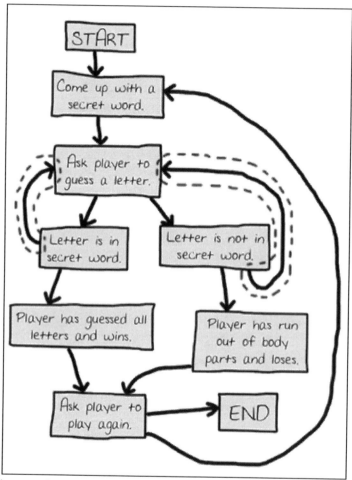

Figure 8-7: The game does not always end after a guess. The new arrows (outlined) show that the player can guess again.

We are forgetting something else, as well. What if the player guesses a letter that they've guessed before? Rather than have them win or lose in this case, we'll allow them to guess a different letter instead, as shown in Figure 8-8.

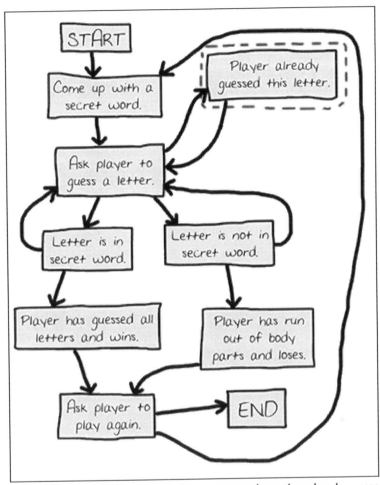

Figure 8-8: Adding a step in case the player guesses a letter they already guessed.

Offering Feedback to the Player

We also need some way to show the player how they're doing. In order to do this, we'll show them the hangman board, as well as the secret word (with blanks for the letters they haven't guessed yet). These visuals will let them see how close they are to winning or losing the game.

We'll need to update this information every time the player guesses a letter. We can add a "Show the board and blanks to the player." box to the flow chart between the "Come up with a secret word" box and the "Ask player to guess a letter" box, as shown in Figure 8-9. This box will remind us that we need to show the player an updated hangman board so they can see which letters they have guessed correctly and which letters are not in the secret word.

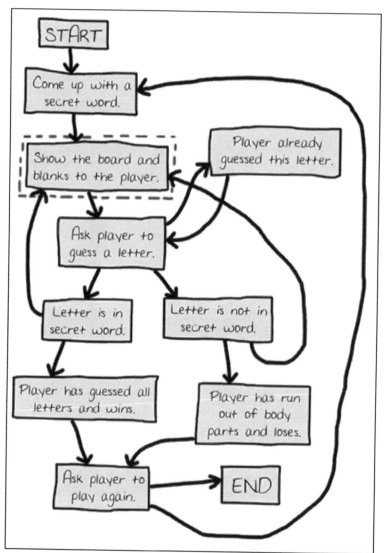

Figure 8-9: Adding "Show the board and blanks to the player." to give the player feedback.

That looks good! This flow chart completely maps out everything that can possibly happen in Hangman, and in what order. Of course this flow chart is just an example-you won't really need to use it, because you're just using the source code that's given here. But when you design your own games, a flow chart can help you remember everything you need to code.

Summary: The Importance of Planning Out the Game

It may seem like a lot of work to sketch out a flow chart about the program first. After all, people want to play games, not look at flowcharts! But it is much easier to make changes and notice problems by thinking about how the program works before writing the code for it.

If you jump in to write the code first, you may discover problems that require you to change the code you've already written. Every time you change your code, you are taking a chance that you create bugs by changing too little or too much. It is much better to know what you want to build before you build it.

Chapter 9

Hangman

Topics Covered In This Chapter:

- Methods
- The `append()` list method
- The `lower()` and `upper()` string methods
- The `reverse()` list method
- The `split()` string method
- The `range()` function
- The `list()` function
- `for` loops
- elif statements
- The `startswith()` and `endswith()` string methods.
- The dictionary data type.
- key-value pairs
- The `keys()` and `values()` dictionary methods
- Multiple variable assignment, such as a, b, c = [1, 2, 3]

This game introduces many new concepts. But don't worry; we'll experiment with these programming concepts in the interactive shell first. Some data types such as strings and lists have functions that are associated with their values called methods. We will learn several different methods that can manipulate strings and lists for us. We will also learn about a new type of loop called a `for` loop and a new type of data type called a dictionary. Once you understand these concepts, it will be much easier to understand the game in this chapter: Hangman.

You can learn more from Wikipedia: *http://en.wikipedia.org/wiki/Hangman_(game)*

Hangman's Source Code

This chapter's game is a bit longer than our previous games. You can either type in the code below directly into the file editor (which I recommend) or you can obtain the code from this book's website. To grab the code from the web, in a web browser go to the URL *http://inventwithpython.com/chapter9* and follow the instructions for downloading the source code.

hangman.py

This code can be downloaded from *http://inventwithpython.com/hangman.py*

If you get errors after typing this code in, compare it to the book's code with the online diff tool at *http://inventwithpython.com/diff* or email the author at al@inventwithpython.com

```
 1. import random
 2. HANGMANPICS = ['''
 3.
 4.    +---+
 5.    |   |
 6.        |
 7.        |
 8.        |
 9.        |
10. =========''', '''
11.
12.    +---+
13.    |   |
14.    O   |
15.        |
16.        |
17.        |
18. =========''', '''
19.
20.    +---+
21.    |   |
22.    O   |
23.    |   |
24.        |
25.        |
26. =========''', '''
27.
28.    +---+
29.    |   |
30.    O   |
31.   /|   |
32.        |
33.        |
34. =========''', '''
35.
36.    +---+
37.    |   |
```

```
38.     O   |
39.    /|\  |
40.        |
41.        |
42.  ========''', '''
43.
44.     +---+
45.     |   |
46.     O   |
47.    /|\  |
48.    /    |
49.        |
50.  ========''', '''
51.
52.     +---+
53.     |   |
54.     O   |
55.    /|\  |
56.    / \  |
57.        |
58.  ========''']
59.  words = 'ant baboon badger bat bear beaver camel cat clam
     cobra cougar coyote crow deer dog donkey duck eagle
     ferret fox frog goat goose hawk lion lizard llama mole
     monkey moose mouse mule newt otter owl panda parrot
     pigeon python rabbit ram rat raven rhino salmon seal
     shark sheep skunk sloth snake spider stork swan tiger
     toad trout turkey turtle weasel whale wolf wombat
     zebra'.split()
60.
61.  def getRandomWord(wordList):
62.      # This function returns a random string from the
     passed list of strings.
63.      wordIndex = random.randint(0, len(wordList) - 1)
64.      return wordList[wordIndex]
65.
66.  def displayBoard(HANGMANPICS, missedLetters,
     correctLetters, secretWord):
67.      print(HANGMANPICS[len(missedLetters)])
68.      print()
69.
70.      print('Missed letters:', end=' ')
71.      for letter in missedLetters:
72.          print(letter, end=' ')
73.      print()
74.
75.      blanks = '_' * len(secretWord)
76.
77.      for i in range(len(secretWord)): # replace blanks
     with correctly guessed letters
78.          if secretWord[i] in correctLetters:
79.              blanks = blanks[:i] + secretWord[i] + blanks
     [i+1:]
80.
```

```
81.        for letter in blanks: # show the secret word with
    spaces in between each letter
82.            print(letter, end=' ')
83.        print()
84.
85. def getGuess(alreadyGuessed):
86.     # Returns the letter the player entered. This
    function makes sure the player entered a single letter,
    and not something else.
87.     while True:
88.         print('Guess a letter.')
89.         guess = input()
90.         guess = guess.lower()
91.         if len(guess) != 1:
92.             print('Please enter a single letter.')
93.         elif guess in alreadyGuessed:
94.             print('You have already guessed that letter.
    Choose again.')
95.         elif guess not in 'abcdefghijklmnopqrstuvwxyz':
96.             print('Please enter a LETTER.')
97.         else:
98.             return guess
99.
100. def playAgain():
101.     # This function returns True if the player wants to
    play again, otherwise it returns False.
102.     print('Do you want to play again? (yes or no)')
103.     return input().lower().startswith('y')
104.
105.
106. print('H A N G M A N')
107. missedLetters = ''
108. correctLetters = ''
109. secretWord = getRandomWord(words)
110. gameIsDone = False
111.
112. while True:
113.     displayBoard(HANGMANPICS, missedLetters,
    correctLetters, secretWord)
114.
115.     # Let the player type in a letter.
116.     guess = getGuess(missedLetters + correctLetters)
117.
118.     if guess in secretWord:
119.         correctLetters = correctLetters + guess
120.
121.         # Check if the player has won
122.         foundAllLetters = True
123.         for i in range(len(secretWord)):
124.             if secretWord[i] not in correctLetters:
125.                 foundAllLetters = False
126.                 break
127.         if foundAllLetters:
```

```
128.            print('Yes! The secret word is "' +
    secretWord + '"! You have won!')
129.            gameIsDone = True
130.        else:
131.            missedLetters = missedLetters + guess
132.
133.            # Check if player has guessed too many times and
    lost
134.            if len(missedLetters) == len(HANGMANPICS) - 1:
135.                displayBoard(HANGMANPICS, missedLetters,
    correctLetters, secretWord)
136.                print('You have run out of guesses!\nAfter '
    + str(len(missedLetters)) + ' missed guesses and ' + str
    (len(correctLetters)) + ' correct guesses, the word was
    "' + secretWord + '"')
137.                gameIsDone = True
138.
139.    # Ask the player if they want to play again (but only
    if the game is done).
140.    if gameIsDone:
141.        if playAgain():
142.            missedLetters = ''
143.            correctLetters = ''
144.            gameIsDone = False
145.            secretWord = getRandomWord(words)
146.        else:
147.            break
```

How the Code Works

```
1. import random
```

The Hangman program is going to randomly select a secret word from a list of secret words. This means we will need the random module imported.

```
2. HANGMANPICS = ['''
3.
4.    +---+
5.    |   |
6.        |
7.        |
8.        |
9.        |
10. =========''', '''
```

...the rest of the code is too big to show here...

This "line" of code is a simple variable assignment, but it actually stretches over several real lines in the source code. The actual "line" doesn't end until line 58. To help you understand what this code means, you should learn about multi-line strings and lists:

Multi-line Strings

Ordinarily when you write strings in your source code, the string has to be on one line. However, if you use three single-quotes instead of one single-quote to begin and end the string, the string can be on several lines:

```
>>> fizz = '''Dear Alice,
I will return home at the end of the month. I will
see you then.
Your friend,
Bob'''
>>> print(fizz)
Dear Alice,
I will return home at the end of the month. I will
see you then.
Your friend,
Bob
>>>
```

If we didn't have multi-line strings, we would have to use the \n escape character to represent the new lines. But that can make the string hard to read in the source code, like in this example:

```
>>> fizz = 'Dear Alice,\nI will return home at the
end of the month. I will see you then.\nYour
friend,\nBob'
>>> print(fizz)
Dear Alice,
I will return home at the end of the month. I will
see you then.
Your friend,
Bob
>>>
```

Multi-line strings do not have to keep the same indentation to remain in the same block. Within the multi-line string, Python ignores the indentation rules it normally has for where blocks end.

```
def writeLetter():
    # inside the def-block
    print('''Dear Alice,
How are you? Write back to me soon.

Sincerely,
  Bob''') # end of the multi-line string and print
() call
    print('P.S. I miss you.') # still inside the
def-block

writeLetter() # This is the first line outside the
def-block.
```

Constant Variables

You may have noticed that HANGMANPICS's name is in all capitals. This is the programming convention for constant variables. **Constants** are variables whose values do not change throughout the program. Although we can change HANGMANPICS just like any other variable, the all-caps reminds the programmer to not write code that does so.

Constant variables are helpful for providing descriptions for values that have a special meaning. Since the multi-string value never changes, there is no reason we couldn't copy this multi-line string each time we needed that value. The HANGMANPICS variable never varies. But it is much shorter to type HANGMANPICS than it is to type that large multi-line string.

Also, there are cases where typing the value by itself may not be obvious. If we set a variable eggs = 72, we may forget why we were setting that variable to the integer 72. But if we define a constant variable DOZEN = 12, then we could set eggs = DOZEN * 6 and by just looking at the code know that the eggs variable was set to six dozen.

Like all conventions, we don't *have* to use constant variables, or even put the names of constant variables in all capitals. But doing it this way makes it easier for other programmers to understand how these variables are used. (It even can help you if you are looking at code you wrote a long time ago.)

Lists

I will now tell you about a new data type called a **list**. A list value can contain several other values in it. Try typing this into the shell: ['apples', 'oranges', 'HELLO WORLD']. This is a list value that contains three string values. Just like any other value, you can store this list in a variable. Try typing spam = ['apples', 'oranges', 'HELLO WORLD'], and then type spam to view the contents of spam.

```
>>> spam = ['apples', 'oranges', 'HELLO WORLD']
>>> spam
['apples', 'oranges', 'HELLO WORLD']
>>>
```

Lists are a good way to store several different values into one variable. The individual values inside of a list are also called **items**. Try typing: `animals = ['aardvark',` `'anteater', 'antelope', 'albert']` to store various strings into the variable `animals`. The square brackets can also be used to get an item from a list. Try typing `animals[0]`, or `animals[1]`, or `animals[2]`, or `animals[3]` into the shell to see what they evaluate to.

```
>>> animals = ['aardvark', 'anteater', 'antelope',
'albert']
>>> animals[0]
'aardvark'
>>> animals[1]
'anteater'
>>> animals[2]
'antelope'
>>> animals[3]
'albert'
>>>
```

The number between the square brackets is the **index**. In Python, the first index is the number 0 instead of the number 1. So the first item in the list is at index 0, the second item is at index 1, the third item is at index 2, and so on. Lists are very good when we have to store lots and lots of values, but we don't want variables for each one. Otherwise we would have something like this:

```
>>> animals1 = 'aardvark'
>>> animals2 = 'anteater'
>>> animals3 = 'antelope'
>>> animals4 = 'albert'
>>>
```

This makes working with all the strings as a group very hard, especially if you have hundreds or thousands (or even millions) of different strings that you want stored in a list. Using the square brackets, you can treat items in the list just like any other value. Try typing `animals[0] + animals[2]` into the shell:

```
>>> animals[0] + animals[2]
'aardvarkantelope'
>>>
```

Because `animals[0]` evaluates to the string `'aardvark'` and `animals[2]` evaluates to the string `'antelope'`, then the expression `animals[0] + animals[2]` is the same as `'aardvark' + 'antelope'`. This string concatenation evaluates to `'aardvarkantelope'`.

What happens if we enter an index that is larger than the list's largest index? Try typing `animals[4]` or `animals[99]` into the shell:

```
>>> animals = ['aardvark', 'anteater', 'antelope',
'albert']
>>> animals[4]
Traceback (most recent call last):
File "", line 1, in
animals[4]
IndexError: list index out of range
>>> animals[99]
Traceback (most recent call last):
File "", line 1, in
animals[99]
IndexError: list index out of range
>>>
```

If you try accessing an index that is too large, you will get an **index error**.

Changing the Values of List Items with Index Assignment

You can also use the square brackets to change the value of an item in a list. Try typing `animals[1] = 'ANTEATER'`, then type `animals` to view the list.

```
>>> animals = ['aardvark', 'anteater', 'antelope',
'albert']
>>> animals[1] = 'ANTEATER'
>>> animals
['aardvark', 'ANTEATER', 'antelope', 'albert']
>>>
```

The second item in the `animals` list has been overwritten with a new string.

110

List Concatenation

You can join lists together into one list with the + operator, just like you can join strings. When joining lists, this is known as **list concatenation**. Try typing `[1, 2, 3, 4] + ['apples', 'oranges'] + ['Alice', 'Bob']` into the shell:

```
>>> [1, 2, 3, 4] + ['apples', 'oranges'] +
['Alice', 'Bob']
[1, 2, 3, 4, 'apples', 'oranges', 'Alice', 'Bob']
>>>
```

Notice that lists do not have to store values of the same data types. The example above has a list with both integers and strings in it. Remember, when you do list concatenation, you must add together two list values. `['apples'] + ['oranges']` will evaluate to `['apples', 'oranges']`. But `['apples'] + 'oranges'` will result in an error because you are adding a list value and string value instead of two list values. If you want to add non-list values to a list, use the `append()` method (which is described later).

The `in` Operator

The `in` operator makes it easy to see if a value is inside a list or not. Expressions that use the `in` operator return a Boolean value: `True` if the value is in the list and `False` if the value is not in the list. Try typing `'antelope' in animals` into the shell:

```
>>> animals = ['aardvark', 'anteater', 'antelope',
'albert']
>>> 'antelope' in animals
True
>>>
```

The expression `'antelope' in animals` returns `True` because the string `'antelope'` can be found in the list, `animals`. (It is located at index 2.)

But if we type the expression `'ant' in animals`, this will return `False` because the string `'ant'` does not exist in the list. We can try the expression `'ant' in ['beetle', 'wasp', 'ant']`, and see that it will return `True`.

```
>>> animals = ['aardvark', 'anteater', 'antelope',
'albert']
>>> 'antelope' in animals
True
>>> 'ant' in animals
```

111

```
False
>>> 'ant' in ['beetle', 'wasp', 'ant']
True
>>>
```

The `in` operator also works for strings as well as lists. You can check if one string exists in another the same way you can check if a value exists in a list. Try typing `'hello' in 'Alice said hello to Bob.'` into the shell. This expression will evaluate to `True`.

```
>>> 'hello' in 'Alice said hello to Bob.'
True
>>>
```

Removing Items from Lists with `del` Statements

You can remove items from a list with a `del` statement. ("del" is short for "delete.") Try creating a list of numbers by typing: `spam = [2, 4, 6, 8, 10]` and then `del spam[1]`. Type `spam` to view the list's contents:

```
>>> spam = [2, 4, 6, 8, 10]
>>> del spam[1]
>>> spam
[2, 6, 8, 10]
>>>
```

Notice that when you deleted the item at index 1, the item that used to be at index 2 became the new value at index 1. The item that used to be at index 3 moved to be the new value at index 2. Everything above the item that we deleted moved down one index. We can type `del spam[1]` again and again to keep deleting items from the list:

```
>>> spam = [2, 4, 6, 8, 10]
>>> del spam[1]
>>> spam
[2, 6, 8, 10]
>>> del spam[1]
>>> spam
[2, 8, 10]
>>> del spam[1]
>>> spam
```

```
[2, 10]
>>>
```

Just remember that `del` is a statement, not a function or an operator. It does not evaluate to any return value.

Lists of Lists

Lists are a data type that can contain other values as items in the list. But these items can also be other lists. Let's say you have a list of groceries, a list of chores, and a list of your favorite pies. You can put all three of these lists into another list. Try typing this into the shell:

```
>>> groceries = ['eggs', 'milk', 'soup', 'apples',
'bread']
>>> chores = ['clean', 'mow the lawn', 'go grocery
shopping']
>>> favoritePies = ['apple', 'frumbleberry']
>>> listOfLists = [groceries, chores,
favoritePies]
>>> listOfLists
[['eggs', 'milk', 'soup', 'apples', 'bread'],
['clean', 'mow the lawn', 'go grocery shopping'],
['apple', 'frumbleberry']]
>>>
```

You could also type the following and get the same values for all four variables:

```
>>> listOfLists = [['eggs', 'milk', 'soup',
'apples', 'bread'], ['clean', 'mow the lawn', 'go
grocery shopping'], ['apple', 'frumbleberry']]
>>> groceries = listOfLists[0]
>>> chores = listOfLists[1]
>>> favoritePies = listOfLists[2]
>>> groceries
['eggs', 'milk', 'soup', 'apples', 'bread']
>>> chores
['clean', 'mow the lawn', 'go grocery shopping']
>>> favoritePies
['apple', 'frumbleberry']
>>>
```

To get an item inside the list of lists, you would use *two* sets of square brackets like this: `listOfLists[1][2]` which would evaluate to the string `'go grocery shopping'`. This is because `listOfLists[1]` evaluates to the list `['clean', 'mow the lawn', 'go grocery shopping'][2]`. That finally evaluates to `'go grocery shopping'`.

Here is another example of a list of lists, along with some of the indexes that point to the items in the list of lists named x. The red arrows point to indexes of the inner lists themselves. The image is also flipped on its side to make it easier to read:

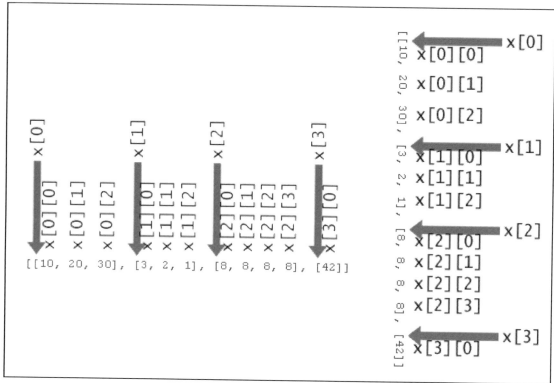

Figure 9-1: The indexes of a list of lists.

Methods

Methods are just like functions, but they are always attached to a value. For example, all string values have a `lower()` method, which returns a copy of the string value in lowercase. You cannot just call `lower()` by itself and you do not pass a string argument to `lower()` by itself (as in `lower('Hello')`). You must attach the method call to a specific string value using a period.

The `lower()` and `upper()` String Methods

Try entering `'Hello world!'.lower()` into the interactive shell to see an example of this method:

```
>>> 'Hello world'.lower()
'hello world!'
>>>
```

There is also an upper() method for strings, which changes all the characters in a string to uppercase. Try entering 'Hello world'.upper() into the shell:

```
>>> 'Hello world'.upper()
'HELLO WORLD! '
>>>
```

Because the upper() method returns a string, you can call a method on *that* string as well. Try typing 'Hello world!'.upper().lower() into the shell:

```
>>> 'Hello world'.upper().lower()
'hello world!'
>>>
```

'Hello world!'.upper() evaluates to the string 'HELLO WORLD!', and then we call that string's lower() method. This returns the string 'hello world!', which is the final value in the evaluation. The order is important. 'Hello world!'.lower().upper() is not the same as 'Hello world!'.upper().lower():

```
>>> 'Hello world'.lower().upper()
'HELLO WORLD!'
>>>
```

Remember, if a string is stored in a variable, you can call a string method on that variable. Look at this example:

```
>>> fizz = 'Hello world'
>>> fizz.upper()
'HELLO WORLD'
>>>
```

The reverse() and append() List Methods

The list data type also has methods. The reverse() method will reverse the order of the items in the list. Try entering spam = [1, 2, 3, 4, 5, 6, 'meow', 'woof'], and then spam.reverse() to reverse the list. Then enter spam to view the contents of the variable.

```
>>> spam = [1, 2, 3, 4, 5, 6, 'meow', 'woof']
>>> spam.reverse()
>>> spam
['woof', 'meow', 6, 5, 4, 3, 2, 1]
>>>
```

The most common list method you will use is append(). This method will add the value you pass as an argument to the end of the list. Try typing the following into the shell:

```
>>> eggs = []
>>> eggs.append('hovercraft')
>>> eggs
['hovercraft']
>>> eggs.append('eels')
>>> eggs
['hovercraft', 'eels']
>>> eggs.append(42)
>>> eggs
['hovercraft', 'eels', 42]
>>>
```

Though string and list data types have methods, integers do not happen to have any methods.

The Difference Between Methods and Functions

You may be wondering why Python has methods, since they seem to act just like functions. Some data types have methods. Methods are functions associated with values of that data type. For example, string methods are functions that can be called on any string. If you have the string value 'Hello', you could call the string method upper() like this: 'Hello'.upper(). Or if the string 'Hello' were stored in a variable named spam, it would look like this: spam.upper()

You cannot call string methods on values of other data types. For example, [1, 2, 'apple'].upper() would cause an error because [1, 2, 'apple'] is a list and upper() is a string method.

The values of data types that have methods are also called objects. Object-oriented programming is a bit advanced for this book, and you don't need to understand it to make games. Just understand that objects are another name for a values of data types that have methods. For example, all strings and lists are objects.

The `split()` List Method

Line 59 is a very long line of code, but it is really just a simple assignment statement. This line also uses the `split()` method, which is a method for the string data type (just like the `lower()` and `upper()` methods).

```
59. words = 'ant baboon badger bat bear beaver camel cat clam
    cobra cougar coyote crow deer dog donkey duck eagle
    ferret fox frog goat goose hawk lion lizard llama mole
    monkey moose mouse mule newt otter owl panda parrot
    pigeon python rabbit ram rat raven rhino salmon seal
    shark sheep skunk sloth snake spider stork swan tiger
    toad trout turkey turtle weasel whale wolf wombat
    zebra'.split()
```

As you can see, this line is just one very long string, full of words separated by spaces. And at the end of the string, we call the `split()` method. The `split()` method changes this long string into a list, with each word making up a single list item. The "split" occurs wherever a space occurs in the string. The reason we do it this way, instead of just writing out the list, is that it is easier for us to type as one long string. If we created it as a list to begin with, we would have to type: `['ant', 'baboon', 'badger',` ... and so on, with quotes and commas for every single word.

For an example of how the `split()` string method works, try typing this into the shell:

```
>>> 'My very energetic mother just served us nine
pies'.split()
['My', 'very', 'energetic', 'mother', 'just',
'served', 'us', 'nine', 'pies']
>>>
```

The result is a list of nine strings, one string for each of the words in the original string. The spaces are dropped from the items in the list. Once we've called `split()`, the `words` list will contain all the possible secret words that can be chosen by the computer for our Hangman game. You can also add your own words to the string, or remove any you don't want to be in the game. Just make sure that the words are separated by spaces.

How the Code Works

Starting on line 61, we define a new function called `getRandomWord()`, which has a single parameter named `wordList`. We will call this function when we want to pick a single secret word from a list of secret words.

```
61. def getRandomWord(wordList):
```

```
62.        # This function returns a random string from the
      passed list of strings.
63.        wordIndex = random.randint(0, len(wordList) - 1)
64.        return wordList[wordIndex]
```

The function getRandomWord() is passed a list of strings as the argument for the wordList parameter. On line 63, we will store a random index for this list in the wordIndex variable. We do this by calling randint() with two arguments. Remember that arguments in a function call are separated by commas, so the first argument is 0 and the second argument is len(wordList) - 1. The second argument is an expression that is first evaluated. len(wordList) will return the integer size of the list passed to getRandomWord(), and then we subtract one.

The reason we need the - 1 is because the indexes for lists start at 0, not 1. If we have a list of three items, the index of the first item is 0, the index of the second item is 1, the index of the third item is 2. The length of this list is 3, but the index 3 is after the last index. This is why we subtract 1 from the length.

For example, if we passed ['apple', 'orange', grape'] as an argument to getRandomWord(), then len(wordList) would return the integer 3 and the expression 3 - 1 would evaluate to the integer 2.

That means that wordIndex would contain the return value of randint(0, 2), which means wordIndex would equal 0, 1, or 2. On line 64, we would return the element in wordList at the integer index stored in wordIndex.

Let's pretend we did send ['apple', 'orange', grape'] as the argument to getRandomWord() and that randint(0, 2) returned the integer 2. That would mean that line 64 would become return wordList[2], which would evaluate to return 'grape'. This is how the getRandomWord() returns a random string in the wordList list. The following code entered into the interactive shell demonstrates this:

```
>>> wordIndex = 2
>>> print(wordIndex)
2
>>> print(['apple', 'orange', 'grape'][wordIndex])
grape
>>>
```

And remember, we can pass any list of strings we want to the getRandomWord() function, which is what makes it so useful for our Hangman game.

Displaying the Board to the Player

Next we need to create another function which will print the hangman board on the screen, along with how many letters the player has correctly (and incorrectly) guessed.

```
66. def displayBoard(HANGMANPICS, missedLetters,
    correctLetters, secretWord):
67.     print(HANGMANPICS[len(missedLetters)])
68.     print()
```

This code defines a new function named `displayBoard()`. This function has four parameters. This function will implement the code for the "Show the board and blanks to the player" box in our flow chart. Here is what each parameter means:

- `HANGMANPICS` - This is a list of multi-line strings that will display the board as ASCII art. We will always pass the global `HANGMANPICS` variable as the argument for this parameter.
- `missedLetters` - This is a string made up of the letters the player has guessed that are not in the secret word.
- `correctLetters` - This is a string made up of the letters the player has guessed that are in the secret word.
- `secretWord` - This string is the secret word that the player is trying to guess..

The first `print()` function call will display the board. `HANGMANPICS` will be a list of strings for each possible board. `HANGMANPICS[0]` shows an empty gallows, `HANGMANPICS[1]` shows the head (this happens when the player misses one letter), `HANGMANPICS[2]` shows a head and body (this happens when the player misses two letters), and so on until `HANGMANPICS[6]` when the full hangman is shown and the player loses.

The number of letters in `missedLetters` will tell us how many incorrect guesses the player has made. We can call `len(missedLetters)` to find out this number. This number can also be used as the index to the `HANGMANPICS` list, which will allow us to print the correct board for the number of incorrect guesses. So, if `missedLetters` is `'aetr'` then `len('aetr')` will return 4 and we will display the string `HANGMANPICS[4]`. This is what `HANGMANPICS[len(missedLetters)]` evaluates to. This line shows the correct hangman board to the player.

```
70.     print('Missed letters:', end=' ')
71.     for letter in missedLetters:
72.         print(letter, end=' ')
73.     print()
```

Line 71 is a new type of loop, called a `for` loop. A `for` loop is kind of like a `while` loop. Line 72 is the entire body of the `for` loop. The `range()` function is often used with `for` loops. I will explain both in the next two sections.

Remember that the keyword argument end=' ' uses only one = sign (like =), not two (like ==).

The `range()` and `list()` Functions

The `range()` function is easy to understand. You can call it with either one or two integer arguments. When called with one argument, `range()` will return a range object of integers from 0 up to (but not including) the argument. This range object can be converted to the more familiar list data type with the `list()` function. Try typing `list(range(10))` into the shell:

```
>>> list(range(10))
[0, 1, 2, 3, 4, 5, 6, 7, 8, 9]
>>>
```

The `list()` function is very similar to the `str()` or `int()` functions. It just converts the object it is passed into a list. It's very easy to generate huge lists with the `range()` function. Try typing in `list(range(10000))` into the shell:

```
>>> list(range(10000))
[0, 1, 2, 3, 4, 5, 6, 7, 8, 9, 10, 11, 12, 13, 14,
15,...
        ...The text here has been skipped for
brevity...
...9989, 9990, 9991, 9992, 9993, 9994, 9995, 9996,
9997, 9998, 9999]
>>>
```

The list is so huge, that it won't even all fit onto the screen. But we can save the list into the variable just like any other list by entering this:

```
>>> spam = list(range(10000))
>>>
```

If you pass two arguments to `range()`, the list of integers it returns is from the first argument up to (but not including) the second argument. Try typing `list(range(10, 20))` into the shell:

```
>>> list(range(10, 20))
[10, 11, 12, 13, 14, 15, 16, 17, 18, 19]
>>>
```

The `range()` is a very useful function, because we often use it in `for` loops (which are much like the `while` loops we have already seen).

`for` Loops

The `for` loop is very good at looping over a list of values. This is different from the `while` loop, which loops as long as a certain condition is true. A `for` statement begins with the `for` keyword, followed by a variable name, followed by the `in` keyword, followed by a sequence (such as a list or string) or a range object (returned by the `range()` function), and then a colon. Each time the program execution goes through the loop (that is, on each **iteration** through the loop) the variable in the `for` statement takes on the value of the next item in the list.

For example, you just learned that the `range()` function will return a list of integers. We will use this list as the `for` statement's list. In the shell, type `for i in range(10):` and press Enter. Nothing will happen, but the shell will indent the cursor and change the prompt from >>> to . . . because it is waiting for you to type in the for-block. Type `print(i)` and press Enter. Then, to tell the interactive shell you are done typing in the for-block, press Enter again to enter a blank line. The shell will then execute your `for` statement and block:

```
>>> for i in range(10):
...      print(i)
...
0
1
2
3
4
5
6
7
8
9
>>>
```

Notice that with `for` loops, you do not need to convert the range object returned by the `range()` function into a list with `list()`. `for` loops do this for us automatically.

The `for` loop executes the code inside the for-block once for each item in the list. Each time it executes the code in the for-block, the variable `i` is assigned the next value of the next item in the list. If we used the `for` statement with the list [0, 1, 2, 3, 4, 5, 6, 7, 8, 9] instead of `range(10)`, it would have been the same:

```
>>> for i in [0, 1, 2, 3, 4, 5, 6, 7, 8, 9]:
...     print(i)
...
0
1
2
3
4
5
6
7
8
9
>>>
```

The `for` statement automatically converts the range object returned by `range()` into a list, so there is no need to put something like list(range(10)) in the `for` statemet, just use `range(10)`.

Try typing this into the shell: `for thing in ['cats', 'pasta', 'programming', 'spam']:` and press Enter, then type `print('I really like ' + thing)` and press Enter, and then press Enter again to tell the shell to end the for-block. The output should look like this:

```
>>> for thing in ['cats', 'pasta', 'programming',
'spam']:
...     print('I really like ' + thing)
...
I really like cats
I really like pasta
I really like programming
I really like spam
>>
```

And remember, because strings are also a sequence data type just like lists, you can use them in `for` statements as well. This example uses a single character from the string on each iteration:

```
>>> for i in 'Hello world!':
...     print(i)
...
H
e
l
l
o

w
o
r
l
d
!
>>>
```

A `while` Loop Equivalent of a `for` Loop

The `for` loop is very similar to the `while` loop, but when you only need to iterate over items in a list, using a `for` loop is much less code to type. You can make a `while` loop that acts the same way as a `for` loop by adding extra code:

```
>>> sequence = ['cats', 'pasta', 'programming',
'spam']
>>> index = 0
>>> while (index < len(sequence)):
...     thing = sequence[index]
...     print('I really like ' + thing)
...     index = index + 1
...
I really like cats
I really like pasta
I really like programming
I really like spam
>>>
```

But using the `for` statement automatically does all this extra code for us and makes programming easier since we have less to type. Our Hangman game will use `for` loops so you can see how useful they are in real games.

One more thing about `for` loops, is that the `for` statement has the `in` keyword in it. But when you use the `in` keyword in a `for` statement, Python does not treat it like the `in` operator you would use in something like `42 in [0, 42, 67]`. The `in` keyword in `for` statements is just used to separate the variable and the list it gets its values from.

The rest of the `displayBoard()` function displays the missed letters and creates the string of the secret word with all the unguessed letters as blanks.

```
print('Missed letters:', end=' ')
for letter in missedLetters:
    print(letter, end=' ')
print()
```

This `for` loop on line 71 will display all the missed guesses that the player has made. When you play Hangman on paper, you usually write down these letters off to the side so you know not to guess them again. On each iteration of the loop the value of `letter` will be each letter in `missedLetters` in turn. Remember that the `end=' '` will replace the newline character that is printed after the string with a single space character.

If `missedLetters` was `'ajtw'` then this `for` loop would display a j t w.

Slices and Slicing

If we want to get a shorter copy of some of the items in a list, we can use list slicing. **Slicing** creates a duplicate list out of some or all of the items in another list. In code, we can create a slice of a list by specifying two indexes (the beginning and end) and a colon. For example, type the following into the interactive shell:

```
>>> spam = ['apples', 'oranges', 'pears',
'bananas']
>>> eggs = spam[1:3]
>>> eggs
['oranges', 'pears']
```

The expression `spam[0:2]` evaluates to a list that contains all the items from index 0 up to (but not including) index 2 in `spam`. We store this smaller list in the variable `eggs`.

If you leave out the first index, Python will automatically think you want to specify index 0 for the first index:

```
>>> spam = ['apples', 'oranges', 'pears',
'bananas']
>>> spam[:3]
['apples', 'oranges', 'pears']
```

If you leave out the second index, Python will automatically think you want to specify the rest of the list:

```
>>> spam = ['apples', 'oranges', 'pears',
'bananas']
>>> spam[1:]
['oranges', 'pears', 'bananas']
```

Slicing is a simple way to get a subset of the items in a list. You can also use slices with strings in the same way you use them with lists. Each character in the string is like an item in the list. Try typing the following into the shell:

```
>>> myName = 'Zophie the Fat Cat'
>>> myName[4:12]
'ie the F'
>>> myName[:10]
'Zophie the'
>>> myName[7:]
'the Fat Cat'
>>>
```

Slices are used in the next part of the code we look at.

Displaying the Secret Word with Blanks

So by this point we have shown the player the hangman board and the missed letters. Now we want to print the secret word, except we want blank lines for the letters. We can use the _ character (called the underscore character) for this. But we should print the letters in the secret word that the player has guessed, and use _ characters for the letters the player has not guessed yet. We can first create a string with nothing but one underscore for each letter in the secret word. Then we can replace the blanks for each letter in correctLetters. So if the secret word was 'otter' then the blanked out string would be '_____' (five _ characters). If correctLetters was the string 'rt' then we would want to change the blanked string to '_tt_r'. Here is the code that does that:

```
75.        blanks = '_' * len(secretWord)
76.
77.        for i in range(len(secretWord)): # replace blanks
    with correctly guessed letters
78.            if secretWord[i] in correctLetters:
79.                blanks = blanks[:i] + secretWord[i] + blanks
    [i+1:]
80.
```

```
81.      for letter in blanks: # show the secret word with
      spaces in between each letter
```

Line 75 creates the blanks variable full of _ underscores using string replication. Remember that the * operator can also be used on a string and an integer, so the expression 'hello' * 3 evaluates to 'hellohellohello'. This will make sure that blanks has the same number of underscores as secretWord has letters.

Then we use a for loop to go through each letter in secretWord and replace the underscore with the actual letter if it exists in correctLetters. Line 79 may look confusing. It seems that we are using the square brackets with the blanks and secretWord variables. But wait a second, blanks and secretWord are strings, not lists. And the len() function also only takes lists as parameters, not strings. But in Python, many of the things you can do to lists you can also do to strings such as replication, indexing, and slicing.

Replacing the Underscores with Correctly Guessed Letters

```
77.      for i in range(len(secretWord)): # replace blanks
      with correctly guessed letters
78.          if secretWord[i] in correctLetters:
79.              blanks = blanks[:i] + secretWord[i] + blanks
      [i+1:]
```

Let's pretend the value of secretWord is 'otter' and the value in correctLetters is 'tr'. Then len(secretWord) will return 5. Then range(len(secretWord)) becomes range(5), which in turn returns the list [0, 1, 2, 3, 4].

Because the value of i will take on each value in [0, 1, 2, 3, 4], then the for loop code is equivalent to this:

```
if secretWord[0] in correctLetters:
blanks = blanks[:0] + secretWord[0] + blanks[1:]
if secretWord[1] in correctLetters:
blanks = blanks[:1] + secretWord[1] + blanks[2:]
if secretWord[2] in correctLetters:
blanks = blanks[:2] + secretWord[2] + blanks[3:]
if secretWord[3] in correctLetters:
blanks = blanks[:3] + secretWord[3] + blanks[4:]
if secretWord[4] in correctLetters:
blanks = blanks[:4] + secretWord[4] + blanks[5:]
```

(By the way, writing out the code like this is called **loop unrolling**.)

126

If you are confused as to what the value of something like `secretWord[0]` or `blanks[3:]` is, then look at this picture. It shows the value of the `secretWord` and `blanks` variables, and the index for each letter in the string.

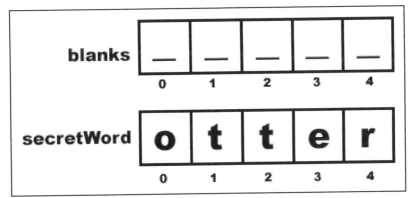

Figure 9-2: The indexes of the `blanks` and `secretWord` strings.

If we replace the list slices and the list indexes with the values that they represent, the unrolled loop code would be the same as this:

```
if 'o' in 'tr': # False, blanks == '_____'
    blanks = '' + 'o' + '____' # This line is
skipped.
if 't' in 'tr': # True, blanks == '_____'
    blanks = '_' + 't' + '___' # This line is
executed.
if 't' in 'tr': # True, blanks == '_t___'
    blanks = '_t' + 't' + '__' # This line is
executed.
if 'e' in 'tr': # False, blanks == '_tt__'
    blanks = '_tt' + 'e' + '_' # This line is
skipped.
if 'r' in 'tr': # True, blanks == '_tt__'
    blanks = '_tt_' + 'r' + '' # This line is
executed.
# blanks now has the value '_tt_r'
```

The above three code examples all do the *same thing* (at least, they do when `secretWord` is `'otter'` and `correctLetters` is `'tr'`. The first box is the actual code we have in our game. The second box shows code that does the same thing except without a `for` loop. The third box is the same as the second box, except we have evaluated many of the expressions in the second box.

The next few lines of code display the new value of `blanks` with spaces in between each letter.

```
81.        for letter in blanks: # show the secret word with
       spaces in between each letter
82.            print(letter, end=' ')
83.        print()
```

This `for` loop will print out each character in the string `blanks`. Remember that by now, `blanks` may have some of its underscores replaced with the letters in `secretWord`. The `end` keyword argument in line 82's `print()` call makes the `print()` function put a space character at the end of the string instead of a newline character. This is the end of the `displayBoard()` function.

Get the Player's Guess

The `getGuess()` function we create next will be called whenever we want to let the player type in a letter to guess. The function returns the letter the player guessed as a string. Further, `getGuess()` will make sure that the player types a valid letter before returning from the function.

```
85. def getGuess(alreadyGuessed):
86.     # Returns the letter the player entered. This
       function makes sure the player entered a single letter,
       and not something else.
```

The `getGuess()` function has a string parameter called `alreadyGuessed` which should be passed a string that contains the letters the player has already guessed, and will ask the player to guess a single letter. This single letter will be the return value for this function.

```
87.     while True:
88.         print('Guess a letter.')
89.         guess = input()
90.         guess = guess.lower()
```

We will use a `while` loop because we want to keep asking the player for a letter until they enter text that is a single letter they have not guessed previously. Notice that the condition for the `while` loop is simply the Boolean value `True`. That means the only way execution will ever leave this loop is by executing a `break` statement (which leaves the loop) or a `return` statement (which leaves the entire function). Such a loop is called an **infinite loop**, because it will loop forever (unless it reaches a `break` statement).

The code inside the loop asks the player to enter a letter, which is stored in the variable `guess`. If the player entered a capitalized letter, it will be converted to lowercase on line 90.

elif ("Else If") Statements

Take a look at the following code:

```
if catName == 'Fuzzball':
    print('Your cat is fuzzy.')
else:
    print('Your cat is not very fuzzy at all.')
```

We've seen code like this before and it's rather simple. If the catName variable is equal to the string 'Fuzzball', then the if statement's condition is True and we tell the user that her cat is fuzzy. If catName is anything else, then we tell the user her cat is not fuzzy.

But what if we wanted something else besides "fuzzy" and "not fuzzy"? We could put another if and else statement inside the first else block like this:

```
if catName == 'Fuzzball':
    print('Your cat is fuzzy.')
else:
    if catName == 'Spots'
        print('Your cat is spotted.')
    else:
        print('Your cat is neither fuzzy nor
spotted.')
```

But if we wanted more things, then the code starts to have a lot of indentation:

```
if catName == 'Fuzzball':
    print('Your cat is fuzzy.')
else:
    if catName == 'Spots'
        print('Your cat is spotted.')
    else:
        if catName == 'FattyKitty'
            print('Your cat is fat.')
        else:
            if catName == 'Puff'
                print('Your cat is puffy.')
            else:
                print('Your cat is neither fuzzy
nor spotted nor fat nor puffy.')
```

Typing all those spaces means you have more chances of making a mistake with the indentation. So Python has the `elif` keyword. Using `elif`, the above code looks like this:

```
if catName == 'Fuzzball':
    print('Your cat is fuzzy.')
elif catName == 'Spots'
    print('Your cat is spotted.')
elif catName == 'FattyKitty'
    print('Your cat is fat.')
elif catName == 'Puff'
    print('Your cat is puffy.')
else:
    print('Your cat is neither fuzzy nor spotted
nor fat nor puffy.')
```

If the condition for the `if` statement is `False`, then the program will check the condition for the first `elif` statement (which is `catName == 'Spots'`). If that condition is `False`, then the program will check the condition of the next `elif` statement. If *all* of the conditions for the `if` and `elif` statements are `False`, then the code in the `else` block executes.

But if one of the `elif` conditions are `True`, the elif-block code is executed and then execution jumps down to the first line past the else-block. So *only one* of the blocks in this if-elif-else statement will be executed. You can also leave off the else-block if you don't need one, and just have an if-else statement.

Making Sure the Player Entered a Valid Guess

```
91.         if len(guess) != 1:
92.             print('Please enter a single letter.')
93.         elif guess in alreadyGuessed:
94.             print('You have already guessed that letter.
    Choose again.')
95.         elif guess not in 'abcdefghijklmnopqrstuvwxyz':
96.             print('Please enter a LETTER.')
97.         else:
98.             return guess
```

The `guess` variable contains the text the player typed in for their letter guess. We need to make sure they typed in one and only one lowercase letter. If they didn't, we should loop back and ask them again. The `if` statement's condition checks that the text is one and only one letter. If it is not, then we execute the if-block code, and then execution jumps down past the else-block. But since there is no more code after this if-elif-else statement, execution loops back to line 87.

If the condition for the `if` statement is `False`, we check the `elif` statement's condition on line 93. This condition is `True` if the letter exists inside the `alreadyGuessed` variable (remember, this is a string that has every letter the player has already guessed). If this condition is `True`, then we display the error message to the player, and jump down past the else-block. But then we would be at the end of the while-block, so execution jumps back up to line 87.

If the condition for the `if` statement and the `elif` statement are both `False`, then we check the second `elif` statement's condition on line 95. If the player typed in a number or a funny character (making `guess` have a value like `'5'` or `'!'`), then guess would not exist in the string `'abcdefghijklmnopqrstuvwxyz'`. If this is the case, the `elif` statement's condition is `True`.

Figure 9-3 is an example of `elif` statements. Unless these three conditions are all `False`, the code will not return and the loop will keep asking for a letter. But when all three of the conditions are `False`, then the else-block's `return` statement will run and we will exit this loop and function.

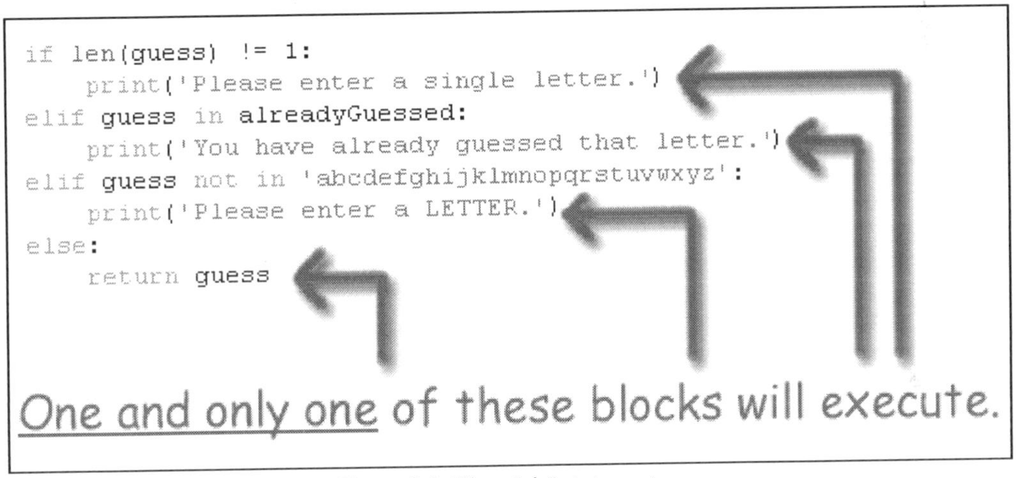

```
if len(guess) != 1:
    print('Please enter a single letter.')
elif guess in alreadyGuessed:
    print('You have already guessed that letter.')
elif guess not in 'abcdefghijklmnopqrstuvwxyz':
    print('Please enter a LETTER.')
else:
    return guess
```

One and only one of these blocks will execute.

Figure 9-3: The `elif` statement.

Asking the Player to Play Again

```
100. def playAgain():
101.     # This function returns True if the player wants to
     play again, otherwise it returns False.
102.     print('Do you want to play again? (yes or no)')
103.     return input().lower().startswith('y')
```

The `playAgain()` function has just a `print()` function call and a `return` statement. The `return` statement has an expression that looks complicated, but we can break it down. Once we evaluate this expression to a value, that value will be returned from this function.

The expression on line 103 doesn't have any operators, but it does have a function call and two method calls. The function call is `input()` and the method calls are `lower()` and `startswith('y')`. Remember that method calls are function calls that are attached by a period to the *value* on their *left*. `lower()` is attached to the return value of `input()`.

`input()` returns a string of the text that the user typed in. Here's a step by step look at how Python evaluates this expression if the user types in YES.

```
input().lower().startswith('y')

          ⬇

'YES'.lower().startswith('y')

          ⬇

'yes'.startswith('y')

          ⬇

True
```

The point of the `playAgain()` function is to let the player type in yes or no to tell our program if they want to play another round of Hangman. If the player types in YES, then the return value of `input()` is the string `'YES'`. And `'YES'.lower()` returns the lowercase version of the attached string. So the return value of `'YES'.lower()` is `'yes'`.

But there's the second method call, `startswith('y')`. This function returns `True` if the associated string begins with the string parameter between the parentheses, and `False` if it doesn't. The return value of `'yes'.startswith('y')` is `True`.

Now we have evaluated this expression! We can see that what this does is let the player type in a response, we lowercase the response, check if it begins with the letter `'y'` or `'Y'`, and then return `True` if it does and `False` if it doesn't. Whew!

On a side note, there is also a `endswith(someString)` string method that will return `True` if the string ends with the string in `someString` and `False` if it doesn't. `endswith()` is sort of like the opposite of `startswith()`.

Review of the Functions We Defined

That's all the functions we are creating for this game!

- `getRandomWord(wordList)` will take a list of strings passed to it as a parameter, and return one string from it. That is how we will choose a word for the player to guess.

- `displayBoard(HANGMANPICS, missedLetters, correctLetters, secretWord)` will show the current state of the board, including how much of the secret word the player has guessed so far and the wrong letters the player has guessed. This function needs four parameters passed to work correctly. `HANGMANPICS` is a list of strings that hold the ASCII art for each possible hangman board. `correctLetters` and `missedLetters` are strings made up of the letters that the player has guessed that are in and not in the secret word. And `secretWord` is the secret word the player is trying to guess. This function has no return value.
- `getGuess(alreadyGuessed)` takes a string of letters the player has already guessed and will keep asking the player for a letter that is a letter that he hasn't already guessed. (That is, a letter that is not in `alreadyGuessed`.) This function returns the string of the acceptable letter the player guessed.
- `playAgain()` is a function that asks if the player wants to play another round of Hangman. This function returns `True` if the player does and `False` if the player doesn't.

We'll now start the code for the main part of the game, which will call the above functions as needed. As a refresher, look back at our flow chart in Figure 9-4.

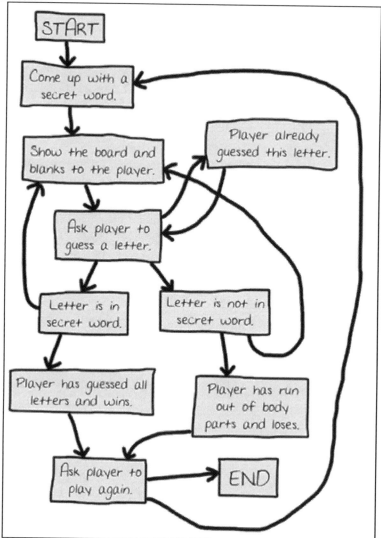

Figure 9-4: The complete flow chart of Hangman.

The Main Code for Hangman

We need to write code that does everything in this flow chart, and does it in the correct order. The main part of the code starts at line 106. Everything previous was just function definitions and a very large variable assignment for HANGMANPICS.

Setting Up the Variables

```
106. print('H A N G M A N')
107. missedLetters = ''
108. correctLetters = ''
109. secretWord = getRandomWord(words)
110. gameIsDone = False
```

Line 106 is the first actual line that executes in our game. We start by assigning a blank string for `missedLetters` and `correctLetters`, because the player has not guessed any missed or correct letters yet. Then we call `getRandomWord(words)`, where `words` is a variable with the huge list of possible secret words we assigned on line 59. The return value of `getRandomWord(words)` is one of these words, and we save it to the `secretWord` variable. Then we also set a variable named `gameIsDone` to `False`. We will set `gameIsDone` to `True` when we want to signal that the game is over and the program should ask the player if they want to play again.

Setting the values of these variables is what we do before the player starts guessing letters.

Displaying the Board to the Player

```
112. while True:
113.     displayBoard(HANGMANPICS, missedLetters,
        correctLetters, secretWord)
```

The `while` loop's condition is always `True`, which means we will always loop forever until a `break` statement is encountered. We will execute a `break` statement when the game is over (either because the player won or the player lost).

Line 113 calls our `displayBoard()` function, passing it the list of hangman ASCII art pictures and the three variables we set on lines 107, 108, and 109. The execution moves to the start of `displayBoard()` at line 66. Based on how many letters the player has correctly guessed and missed, this function displays the appropriate hangman board to the player.

Letting the Player Enter Their Guess

```
115.     # Let the player type in a letter.
116.     guess = getGuess(missedLetters + correctLetters)
```

If you look at our flow chart, you see only one arrow going from the "Show the board and the blanks to the player." box to the "Ask a player to guess a letter." box. Since we have already written a function to get the guess from the player, let's call that function. Remember that the function needs all the letters in `missedLetters` and `correctLetters` combined, so we will pass as an argument a string that is a concatenation of both of those strings. This argument is needed by `getGuess()` because the function has code to check if the player types in a letter that they have already guessed.

Checking if the Letter is in the Secret Word

```
118.     if guess in secretWord:
```

```
119.            correctLetters = correctLetters + guess
```

Now let's see if the single letter in the guess string exists in secretWord. If it does exist, then we should concatenate the letter in guess to the correctLetters string. Next we can check if we have guessed all of the letters and won.

Checking if the Player has Won

```
121.            # Check if the player has won
122.            foundAllLetters = True
123.            for i in range(len(secretWord)):
124.                if secretWord[i] not in correctLetters:
125.                    foundAllLetters = False
126.                    break
```

How do we know if the player has guessed every single letter in the secret word? Well, correctLetters has each letter that the player correctly guessed and secretWord is the secret word itself. We can't just check if correctLetters == secretWord because consider this situation: if secretWord was the string 'otter' and correctLetters was the string 'orte', then correctLetters == secretWord would be False even though the player has guessed each letter in the secret word.

The player simply guessed the letters out of order and they still win, but our program would incorrectly think the player hasn't won yet. Even if they did guess the letters in order, correctLetters would be the string 'oter' because the player can't guess the letter t more than once. The expression 'otter' == 'oter' would evaluate to False even though the player guessed all the letters.

The only way we can be sure the player won is to go through each letter in secretWord and see if it exists in correctLetters. If, and only if, every single letter in secretWord exists in correctLetters will the player have won.

Note that this is different than checking if every letter in correctLetters is in secretWord. If correctLetters was the string 'ot' and secretWord was 'otter', it would be true that every letter in 'ot' is in 'otter', but that doesn't mean the player has guessed the secret word and won.

So how can we do this? We can loop through each letter in secretWord and if we find a letter that does not exist in correctLetters, we know that the player has not guessed all the letters. This is why we create a new variable named foundAllLetters and set it to the Boolean value True. We start out assuming that we have found all the letters, but will change foundAllLetters to False when we find a letter in secretWord that is not in correctLetters.

The `for` loop will go through the numbers 0 up to (but not including) the length of the word. Remember that `range(5)` will evaluate to the list `[0, 1, 2, 3, 4]`. So on line 123, the program executes all the code inside the for-block five times. The first time it executes with the variable `i` set to 0, the second time set to 1, then 2, then 3, then finally 4.

We use `range(len(secretWord))` so that `i` can be used to access each letter in the secret word. So if the first letter in `secretWord` (which is located at `secretWord[0]`) is not in `correctLetters`, we know we can set `foundAllLetters` to `False`. Also, because we don't have to check the rest of the letters in `secretWord`, we can just break out of this loop. Otherwise, we loop back to line 123 and check the next letter.

If `foundAllLetters` manages to stay set to `True`, then it will keep the original `True` value we gave it. Either way, the value in `foundAllLetters` is accurate by the time we get past this `for` loop and run line 127.

```
129.            if foundAllLetters:
130.                print('Yes! The secret word is "' +
        secretWord + '"! You have won!')
131.                gameIsDone = True
```

This is a simple check to see if we found all the letters. If we have found every letter in the secret word, we should tell the player that they have won. We will also set the `gameIsDone` variable to `True`. We will check this variable to see if we should let the player guess again or if the player is done guessing.

When the Player Guesses Incorrectly

```
130.    else:
```

This is the start of the else-block. Remember, the code in this block will execute if the condition was `False`. But which condition? To find out, point your finger at the start of the `else` keyword and move it straight up. You will see that the `else` keyword's indentation is the same as the `if` keyword's indentation on line 118. So if the condition on line 118 was `False`, then we will run the code in this else-block. Otherwise, we skip down past the else-block to line 140.

```
131.        missedLetters = missedLetters + guess
```

Because the player's guessed letter was wrong, we will add it to the `missedLetters` string. This is like what we did on line 119 when the player guessed correctly.

```
133.            # Check if player has guessed too many times and
        lost
```

```
134.            if len(missedLetters) == len(HANGMANPICS) - 1:
135.                displayBoard(HANGMANPICS, missedLetters,
       correctLetters, secretWord)
136.                print('You have run out of guesses!\nAfter '
       + str(len(missedLetters)) + ' missed guesses and ' + str
       (len(correctLetters)) + ' correct guesses, the word was
       "' + secretWord + '"')
137.                gameIsDone = True
```

Think about how we know when the player has guessed too many times. When you play Hangman on paper, this is when the drawing of the hangman is finished. We draw the hangman on the screen with `print()` calls, based on how many letters are in `missedLetters`. Remember that each time the player guesses wrong, we add (or as a programmer would say, concatenate) the wrong letter to the string in `missedLetters`. So the length of `missedLetters` (or, in code, `len(missedLetters)`) can tell us the number of wrong guesses.

At what point does the player run out of guesses and lose? Well, the HANGMANPICS list has 7 pictures (really, they are ASCII art strings). So when `len(missedLetters)` equals 6, we know the player has lost because the hangman picture will be finished. (Remember that HANGMANPICS[0] is the first item in the list, and HANGMANPICS[6] is the last one. This is because the index of a list with 7 items goes from 0 to 6, not 1 to 7.)

So why do we have `len(missedLetters) == len(HANGMANPICS) - 1` as the condition on line 134, instead of `len(missedLetters) == 6`? Pretend that we add another string to the HANGMANPICS list (maybe a picture of the full hangman with a tail, or a third mutant arm). Then the last picture in the list would be at HANGMANPICS[7]. So not only would we have to change the HANGMANPICS list with a new string, but we would also have to remember to change line 134 to `len(missedLetters) == 7`. This might not be a big deal for a small program like Hangman, but when you start writing larger programs you may have to change several different lines of code all over your program just to make a single change in the program's behavior. This way, if we want to make the game harder or easier, we just have to add or remove ASCII art strings to HANGMANPICS and change nothing else.

A second reason we user `len(HANGMANPICS) - 1` is so that when we read the code in this program later, we know why this program behaves the way it does. If you wrote `len(missedLetters) == 6` and then looked at the code two weeks later, you may wonder what is so special about the number 6. You may have forgotten that 6 is the last index in the HANGMANPICS list. Of course, you could write a comment to remind yourself, like:

```
if len(missedLetters) == 6: # 6 is the last index
in the HANGMANPICS list
```

But it is easier to just use `len(HANGMANPICS) - 1` instead.

So, when the length of the `missedLetters` string is equal to `len(HANGMANPICS)` – 1, we know the player has run out of guesses and has lost the game. We print a long string telling the user what the secret word was, and then set the `gameIsDone` value to the Boolean value `True`. This is how we will tell ourselves that the game is done and we should start over.

Remember that when we have \n in a string, that represents the newline character. That is how the one `print()` call on line 136 displays several lines of text.

```
139.       # Ask the player if they want to play again (but only
        if the game is done).
140.     if gameIsDone:
141.       if playAgain():
142.         missedLetters = ''
143.         correctLetters = ''
144.         gameIsDone = False
145.         secretWord = getRandomWord(words)
```

If the player won or lost after guessing their letter, then our code would have set the `gameIsDone` variable to `True`. If this is the case, we should ask the player if they want to play again. We already wrote the `playAgain()` function to handle getting a yes or no from the player. This function returns a Boolean value of `True` if the player wants to play another game of Hangman, and `False` if they've had enough.

If the player does want to play again, we will reset the values in `missedLetters` and `correctLetters` to blank strings, set `gameIsDone` to `False`, and then choose a new secret word by calling `getRandomWord()` again, passing it the list of possible secret words.

This way, when we loop back to the beginning of the loop (on line 112) the board will be back to the start (remember we decide which hangman picture to show based on the length of `missedLetters`, which we just set as the blank string) and the game will be just as the first time we entered the loop. The only difference is we will have a new secret word, because we programmed `getRandomWord()` to return a randomly chosen word each time we call it.

There is a small chance that the new secret word will be the same as the old secret word, but this is just a coincidence. Let's say you flipped a coin and it came up heads, and then you flipped the coin again and it also came up heads. Both coin flips were random, it was just a coincidence that they came up the same both times. Accordingly, you may get the same word return from `getRandomWord()` twice in a row, but this is just a coincidence.

```
146.     else:
147.       break
```

If the player typed in 'no' when asked if they wanted to play again, then they return value of the call to the playAgain() function would be False and the else-block would have executed. This else-block only has one line, a break statement. This causes the execution to jump to the end of the loop that was started on line 112. But because there is no more code after the loop, the program terminates.

Making New Changes to the Hangman Program

This program was much bigger than the Dragon Realm program, but this program is also more sophisticated. It really helps to make a flow chart or small sketch to remember how you want everything to work. Take a look at the flow chart a few pages back in Figure 9-4 and try to find the lines of code that represent each block.

Let's look at some ways we can improve our Hangman game.

After you have played Hangman a few times, you might think that six guesses aren't enough to get many of the words. We can easily give the player more guesses by adding more multi-line strings to the HANGMANPICS list. It's easy, just change the] square bracket on line 58 to a ,''' comma and three quotes (see line 57 below). Then add the following:

```
58. ==========''', '''
59.
60.    +----+
61.    |    |
62.   [O    |
63.   /|\   |
64.   / \   |
65.        |
66. ==========''', '''
67.
68.    +----+
69.    |    |
70.   [O]   |
71.   /|\   |
72.   / \   |
73.        |
74. ==========''']
```

We have added two new multi-line strings to the HANGMANPICS list, one with the hangman's left ear drawn, and the other with both ears drawn. Because our program will tell the player they have lost when the number of guesses is the same as the number of strings in HANGMANPICS (minus one), this is the only change we need to make.

We can also change the list of words by changing the words on line 59. Instead of animals, we could have colors:

```
59. words = 'red orange yellow green blue indigo violet white
       black brown'.split()
```

Or shapes:

```
59. words = 'square triangle rectangle circle ellipse rhombus
       trapazoid chevron pentagon hexagon septagon
       octogon'.split()
```

Or fruits:

```
59. words = 'apple orange lemon lime pear watermelon grape
       grapefruit cherry banana cantalope mango strawberry
       tomato'.split()
```

Dictionaries

With some modification, we can change our code so that our Hangman game can use all of these words as separate sets. We can tell the player which set the secret word is from (like "animal", "color", "shape", or "fruit"). This way, the player isn't guessing animals all the time.

To make this change, we will introduce a new data type called a **dictionary**. A dictionary is a collection of many values much like a list is, but instead of accessing the items in the dictionary with an integer index, you access them with an index (for dictionaries, the indexes are called **keys**) of any data type (but most often strings).

Try typing the following into the shell:

```
>>> stuff = {'hello':'Hello there, how are you?',
'chat':'How is the weather?', 'goodbye':'It was
nice talking to you!'}
>>>
```

Those are curly braces { and }. On the keyboard they are on the same key as the square braces [and]. We use curly braces to type out a dictionary value in Python. The values in between them are **key-value pairs**. The keys are the things on the left of the colon and the values are on the right of the colon. You can access the values (which are like items in lists) in the dictionary by using the key (which are like indexes in lists). Try typing into the shell stuff['hello'] and stuff['chat'] and stuff['goodbye']:

```
>>> stuff['hello']
'Hello there, how are you?'
```

```
>>> stuff['chat']
'How is the weather?'
>>> stuff['goodbye']
'It was nice talking to you!'
>>>
```

Getting the Size of Dictionaries with `len()`

You see, instead of putting an integer index in between the square brackets, you put a string key. This will evaluate to the value for that key. You can get the size (that is, how many key-value pairs in the dictionary) with the `len()` function. Try typing `len (stuff)` into the shell:

```
>>> len(stuff)
3
>>>
```

The list version of this dictionary would have only the values, and look something like this:

```
listStuff = ['Hello there, how are you?', 'How is
the weather?', 'It was nice talking to you!']
```

The list doesn't have any keys, like `'hello'` and `'chat'` and `'goodbye'` in the dictionary. We have to use integer indexes 0, 1, and 2.

The Difference Between Dictionaries and Lists

Dictionaries are different from lists because they are **unordered**. The first item in a list named `listStuff` would be `listStuff[0]`. But there is no "first" item in a dictionary, because dictionaries do not have any sort of order. Try typing this into the shell:

```
>>> favorites1 = {'fruit':'apples', 'number':42,
'animal':'cats'}
>>> favorites2 = {'animal':'cats', 'number':42,
'fruit':'apples'}
>>> favorites1 == favorites2
True
>>>
```

As you can see, the expression `favorites1 == favorites2` evaluates to `True` because dictionaries are unordered, and they are considered to be the same if they have the same key-value pairs in them. Lists are ordered, so a list with the same values in them but in a different order are not the same. Try typing this into the shell:

```
>>> listFavs1 = ['apples', 'cats', 42]
>>> listFavs2 = ['cats', 42, 'apples']
>>> listFavs1 == listFavs2
False
>>>
```

As you can see, the two lists `listFavs1` and `listFavs2` are not considered to be the same because order matters in lists.

You can also use integers as the keys for dictionaries. Dictionaries can have keys of any data type, not just strings. But remember, because 0 and '0' are different values, they will be different keys. Try typing this into the shell:

```
>>> myDict = {'0':'a string', 0:'an integer'}
>>> myDict[0]
'an integer'
>>> myDict['0']
'a string'
>>>
```

You might think that using a `for` loop is hard with dictionaries because they do not have integer indexes. But actually, it's easy. Try typing the following into the shell. (Here's a hint, in IDLE, you do not have to type spaces to start a new block. IDLE does it for you. To end the block, just insert a blank line by just hitting the Enter key. Or you could start a new file, type in this code, and then press F5 to run the program.)

```
>>> favorites = {'fruit':'apples',
'animal':'cats', 'number':42}
>>> for i in favorites:
...     print(i)

fruit
number
animal
>>> for i in favorites:
...     print(favorites[i])

apples
42
```

```
cats
>>>
```

As you can see, if you just use a dictionary in a `for` loop, the variable `i` will take on the values of the dictionary's keys, not its values. But if you have the dictionary and the key, you can get the value as we do above with `favorites[i]`. But remember that because dictionaries are unordered, you cannot predict which order the `for` loop will execute in. Above, we typed the `'animal'` key as coming before the `'number'` key, but the `for` loop printed out `'number'` before `'animal'`.

Dictionaries also have two useful methods, `keys()` and `values()`. These will return values of a type called `dict_keys` and `dict_values`, respectively. Those data types are beyond the scope of this book, but you can easily convert them to lists with the `list()` function (just like `str()` converts a value to a string value). Then you will have an ordered list of the key [...] value. Try typing the following into the shel [...]

```
>>> favori
'animal':'
>>> list(f
['fruit',
>>> list(f
['apples',
>>>
```

Using these methods [...] a dictionary can be very helpful. Do not for [...] s and `dict_keys` with the `dict_keys` f [...] your program.

Sets of Words for Hangman

We will make changes to our original Hangman program. These changes can be downloaded from *http://inventwithpython.com/hangman2.py*

So how can we use dictionaries in our game? First, let's change the list `words` into a dictionary whose keys are strings and values are lists of strings. (Remember that the string method `split()` evaluates to a list.

```
59. words = {'Colors':'red orange yellow green blue indigo
        violet white black brown'.split(),
60. 'Shapes':'square triangle rectangle circle ellipse
        rhombus trapezoid chevron pentagon hexagon septagon
        octogon'.split(),
```

```
61.    'Fruits':'apple orange lemon lime pear watermelon grape
           grapefruit cherry banana cantalope mango strawberry
           tomato'.split(),
62.    'Animals':'bat bear beaver cat cougar crab deer dog
           donkey duck eagle fish frog goat leech lion lizard monkey
           moose mouse otter owl panda python rabbit rat shark sheep
           skunk squid tiger turkey turtle weasel whale wolf wombat
           zebra'.split()}
```

This code is put across multiple lines in the file, even though the Python interpreter thinks of it as just one "line of code." (The line of code doesn't end until the final } curly brace.)

The `random.choice()` Function

Now we will have to change our `getRandomWord()` function so that it chooses a random word from a dictionary of lists of strings, instead of from a list of strings. Here is what the function originally looked like:

```
61. def getRandomWord(wordList):
62.     # This function returns a random string from the
    passed list of strings.
63.     wordIndex = random.randint(0, len(wordList) - 1)
64.     return wordList[wordIndex]
```

Change the code in this function so that it looks like this:

```
64. def getRandomWord(wordDict):
65.     # This function returns a random string from the
    passed dictionary of lists of strings, and the key also.
66.     # First, randomly select a key from the dictionary:
67.     wordKey = random.choice(list(wordDict.keys()))
68.
69.     # Second, randomly select a word from the key's list
    in the dictionary:
70.     wordIndex = random.randint(0, len(wordDict[wordKey])
    - 1)
71.
72.     return [wordDict[wordKey][wordIndex], wordKey]
```

Line 61 just changes the name of the parameter to something a little more descriptive. Now instead of choosing a random word from a list of strings, first we choose a random key from the dictionary and then we choose a random word from the key's list of strings. Line 65 calls a new function in the `random` module named `choice()`. The `choice()` function has one parameter, a list. The return value of `choice()` is an item randomly selected from this list each time it is called.

Remember that `randint(a, b)` will return a random integer between (and including) the two integers a and b and `choice(a)` returns a random item from the list a. Look at these two lines of code, and figure out why they do the exact same thing:

```
random.randint(0, 9)
random.choice(list(range(0, 10)))
```

Line 64 (line 70 in the new code) has also been changed. Now instead of returning the string `wordList[wordIndex]`, we are returning a list with two items. The first item is `wordDict[wordKey][wordIndex]`. The second item is `wordKey`. We return a list because we actually want the `getRandomWord()` to return two values, so putting those two values in a list and returning the list is the easiest way to do this.

Evaluating a Dictionary of Lists

`wordDict[wordKey][wordIndex]` may look kind of complicated, but it is just an expression you can evaluate one step at a time like anything else. First, imagine that `wordKey` had the value `'Fruits'` (which was chosen on line 65) and `wordIndex` has the value 5 (chosen on line 68). Here is how `wordDict[wordKey][wordIndex]` would evaluate:

```
wordDict[wordKey][wordIndex]
        ⬇
wordDict['Fruits'][5]
        ⬇
['apple', 'orange', 'lemon', 'lime', 'pear',
'watermelon', 'grape', 'grapefruit', 'cherry',
'banana', 'cantalope', 'mango', 'strawberry',
'tomato'][5]
        ⬇
'watermelon'
```

In the above case, the item in the list this function returns would be the string `'watermelon'`. (Remember that indexes start at 0, so `[5]` refers to the 6th item in the list.)

There are just three more changes to make to our program. The first two are on the lines that we call the `getRandomWord()` function. The function is called on lines 109 and 145 in the original program:

```
108.            correctLetters = ''
```

```
109.                    secretWord = getRandomWord(words)
110.                    gameIsDone = False


...


144.                    gameIsDone = False
145.                    secretWord = getRandomWord(words)
146.            else:
```

Because the getRandomWord() function now returns a list of two items instead of a string, secretWord will be assigned a list, not a string. We would then have to change the code as follows:

```
108. correctLetters = ''
109. secretWord = getRandomWord(words)
110. secretKey = secretWord[1]
111. secretWord = secretWord[0]
112. gameIsDone = False


...


144. gameIsDone = False
145. secretWord = getRandomWord(words)
146. secretKey = secretWord[1]
147. secretWord = secretWord[0]
148. else:
```

With the above changes, secretWord is first a list of two items. Then we add a new variable named secretKey and set it to the second item in secretWord. Then we set secretWord itself to the first item in the secretWord list. That means that secretWord will then be a string.

Multiple Assignment

But there is an easier way by doing a little trick with assignment statements. Try typing the following into the shell:

```
>>> a, b, c = ['apples', 'cats', 42]
>>> a
'apples'
>>> b
'cats'
>>> c
```

```
42
>>>
```

The trick is to put the same number of variables (delimited by commas) on the left side of the = sign as are in the list on the right side of the = sign. Python will automatically assign the first item's value in the list to the first variable, the second item's value to the second variable, and so on. But if you do not have the same number of variables on the left side as there are items in the list on the right side, the Python interpreter will give you an error.

```
>>> a, b, c, d = ['apples', 'cats', 42]

Traceback (most recent call last):
  File "<pyshell#8>", line 1, in <module>
    a, b, c, d = ['apples', 'cats', 42, 10,
'hello']
ValueError: too many values to unpack

>>> a, b, c, d = ['apples', 'cats']

Traceback (most recent call last):
  File "<pyshell#9>", line 1, in <module>
    a, b, c = ['apples', 'cats']
ValueError: need more than 2 values to unpack
>>>
```

So we should change our code in Hangman to use this trick, which will mean our program uses fewer lines of code.

```
108. correctLetters = ''
109. secretWord, secretKey = getRandomWord(words)
110. gameIsDone = False

...

144. gameIsDone = False
145. secretWord, secretKey = getRandomWord(words)
146. else:
```

Printing the Word Category for the Player

The last change we will make is to add a simple print() call to tell the player which set of words they are trying to guess. This way, when the player plays the game they will know if the secret word is an animal, color, shape, or fruit. Add this line of code after line 112. Here is the original code:

```
112. while True:
113.     displayBoard(HANGMANPICS, missedLetters,
     correctLetters, secretWord)
```

Add the line so your program looks like this:

```
112. while True:
113.     print('The secret word is in the set: ' + secretKey)
114.     displayBoard(HANGMANPICS, missedLetters,
     correctLetters, secretWord)
```

Now we are done with our changes. Instead of just a single list of words, the secret word will be chosen from many different lists of words. We will also tell the player which set of words the secret word is from. Try playing this new version. You can easily change the `words` dictionary on line 59 to include more sets of words.

Summary

We're done with Hangman. This has been a long chapter, and several new concepts have been introduced. But Hangman has been our most advanced game yet. As your games get more and more complex, it'll be a good idea to sketch out a flow chart on paper of what happens in your program.

Methods are just like functions, except that are associated with values. Methods return values just like functions return values.

`for` loops iterate over the items in a list. The `range()` function is often used with `for` loops because it is an easy way to create lists of sequential numbers.

Else-if statements (which use the `elif` keyword) will execute their block if their condition is `True` and the previous `if` and `elif` conditions are `False`

Dictionaries are very similar to lists except that they can use any value for an index. The indexes in dictionaries are called keys. Keys can be strings, integers, or any value of any data type.

Chapter 10
Tic Tac Toe

Topics Covered In This Chapter:

- Artificial Intelligence
- List References
- Short-Circuit Evaluation
- The None Value

We will now create a Tic Tac Toe game where the player plays against a simple artificial intelligence. An **artificial intelligence** (or **AI**) is a computer program that can intelligently respond to the player's moves. This game doesn't introduce any complicated new concepts. We will see that the artificial intelligence that plays Tic Tac Toe is really just a few lines of code.

Tic Tac Toe is a simple game to play with a paper and pencil between two people. One player is X and the other player is O. On a simple nine square grid (which we call the board), the players take turns placing their X or O) on the board. If a player gets three of their marks on the board in a row, column or one of the two diagonals, they win.

Most games of Tic Tac Toe end in a draw, which happens when the board is filled up with neither player having three marks in a row. Instead of a second human player, our artificial intelligence will make moves against the user. You can learn more about Tic Tac Toe from Wikipedia: *http://en.wikipedia.org/wiki/Tic-tac-toe*

While this chapter may not introduce many new programming concepts, it does make use of our existing programming knowledge to make an intelligent Tic Tac Toe player. Let's get started by looking at a sample run of the program. The player makes their move by entering the number of the space they wish to go. These numbers are in the same places as the number keys on your keyboard's keypad (see Figure 10-2).

Sample Run of Tic Tac Toe

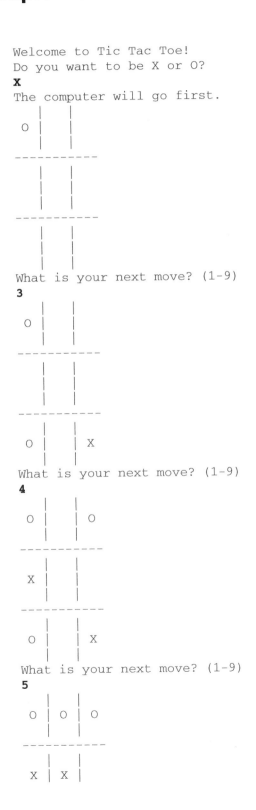

```
Welcome to Tic Tac Toe!
Do you want to be X or O?
X
The computer will go first.
     |   |
   O |   |
     |   |
  -----------
     |   |
     |   |
     |   |
  -----------
     |   |
     |   |
     |   |
What is your next move? (1-9)
3
     |   |
   O |   |
     |   |
  -----------
     |   |
     |   |
     |   |
  -----------
     |   |
   O |   | X
     |   |
What is your next move? (1-9)
4
     |   |
   O |   | O
     |   |
  -----------
     |   |
   X |   |
     |   |
  -----------
     |   |
   O |   | X
     |   |
What is your next move? (1-9)
5
     |   |
   O | O | O
     |   |
  -----------
     |   |
   X | X |
```

```
      |   |
 -----------
      |   |
  O   |   | X
      |   |
```

The computer has beaten you! You lose.
Do you want to play again? (yes or no)
no

Source Code of Tic Tac Toe

In a new file editor window, type in this source code and save it as *tictactoe.py*. Then run the game by pressing F5. You do not need to type in this program before reading this chapter. You can also download the source code by visiting the website at the URL *http://inventwithpython.com/chapter10* and following the instructions on the webpage.

---

tictactoe.py

This code can be downloaded from *http://inventwithpython.com/tictactoe.py*
If you get errors after typing this code in, compare it to the book's code with the online diff tool at *http://inventwithpython.com/diff* or email the author at al@inventwithpython.com

```python
1. # Tic Tac Toe
2.
3. import random
4.
5. def drawBoard(board):
6.     # This function prints out the board that it was
   passed.
7.
8.     # "board" is a list of 10 strings representing the
   board (ignore index 0)
9.     print('   |   |')
10.    print(' ' + board[7] + ' | ' + board[8] + ' | ' +
   board[9])
11.    print('   |   |')
12.    print('-----------')
13.    print('   |   |')
14.    print(' ' + board[4] + ' | ' + board[5] + ' | ' +
   board[6])
15.    print('   |   |')
16.    print('-----------')
17.    print('   |   |')
18.    print(' ' + board[1] + ' | ' + board[2] + ' | ' +
   board[3])
19.    print('   |   |')
20.
21. def inputPlayerLetter():
22.     # Let's the player type which letter they want to be.
```

```
23.         # Returns a list with the player's letter as the
    first item, and the computer's letter as the second.
24.     letter = ''
25.     while not (letter == 'X' or letter == 'O'):
26.         print('Do you want to be X or O?')
27.         letter = input().upper()
28.
29.     # the first element in the list is the player's
    letter, the second is the computer's letter.
30.     if letter == 'X':
31.         return ['X', 'O']
32.     else:
33.         return ['O', 'X']
34.
35. def whoGoesFirst():
36.     # Randomly choose the player who goes first.
37.     if random.randint(0, 1) == 0:
38.         return 'computer'
39.     else:
40.         return 'player'
41.
42. def playAgain():
43.     # This function returns True if the player wants to
    play again, otherwise it returns False.
44.     print('Do you want to play again? (yes or no)')
45.     return input().lower().startswith('y')
46.
47. def makeMove(board, letter, move):
48.     board[move] = letter
49.
50. def isWinner(bo, le):
51.     # Given a board and a player's letter, this function
    returns True if that player has won.
52.     # We use bo instead of board and le instead of letter
    so we don't have to type as much.
53.     return ((bo[7] == le and bo[8] == le and bo[9] == le)
    or # across the top
54.     (bo[4] == le and bo[5] == le and bo[6] == le) or #
    across the middle
55.     (bo[1] == le and bo[2] == le and bo[3] == le) or #
    across the bottom
56.     (bo[7] == le and bo[4] == le and bo[1] == le) or #
    down the left side
57.     (bo[8] == le and bo[5] == le and bo[2] == le) or #
    down the middle
58.     (bo[9] == le and bo[6] == le and bo[3] == le) or #
    down the right side
59.     (bo[7] == le and bo[5] == le and bo[3] == le) or #
    diagonal
60.     (bo[9] == le and bo[5] == le and bo[1] == le)) #
    diagonal
61.
62. def getBoardCopy(board):
```

```
 63.         # Make a duplicate of the board list and return it
       the duplicate.
 64.         dupeBoard = []
 65.
 66.         for i in board:
 67.             dupeBoard.append(i)
 68.
 69.         return dupeBoard
 70.
 71.  def isSpaceFree(board, move):
 72.         # Return true if the passed move is free on the
       passed board.
 73.         return board[move] == ' '
 74.
 75.  def getPlayerMove(board):
 76.         # Let the player type in his move.
 77.         move = ' '
 78.         while move not in '1 2 3 4 5 6 7 8 9'.split() or not
       isSpaceFree(board, int(move)):
 79.             print('What is your next move? (1-9)')
 80.             move = input()
 81.         return int(move)
 82.
 83.  def chooseRandomMoveFromList(board, movesList):
 84.         # Returns a valid move from the passed list on the
       passed board.
 85.         # Returns None if there is no valid move.
 86.         possibleMoves = []
 87.         for i in movesList:
 88.             if isSpaceFree(board, i):
 89.                 possibleMoves.append(i)
 90.
 91.         if len(possibleMoves) != 0:
 92.             return random.choice(possibleMoves)
 93.         else:
 94.             return None
 95.
 96.  def getComputerMove(board, computerLetter):
 97.         # Given a board and the computer's letter, determine
       where to move and return that move.
 98.         if computerLetter == 'X':
 99.             playerLetter = 'O'
100.         else:
101.             playerLetter = 'X'
102.
103.         # Here is our algorithm for our Tic Tac Toe AI:
104.         # First, check if we can win in the next move
105.         for i in range(1, 10):
106.             copy = getBoardCopy(board)
107.             if isSpaceFree(copy, i):
108.                 makeMove(copy, computerLetter, i)
109.                 if isWinner(copy, computerLetter):
110.                     return i
111.
```

```
112.        # Check if the player could win on his next move, and
      block them.
113.        for i in range(1, 10):
114.            copy = getBoardCopy(board)
115.            if isSpaceFree(copy, i):
116.                makeMove(copy, playerLetter, i)
117.                if isWinner(copy, playerLetter):
118.                    return i
119.
120.        # Try to take one of the corners, if they are free.
121.        move = chooseRandomMoveFromList(board, [1, 3, 7, 9])
122.        if move != None:
123.            return move
124.
125.        # Try to take the center, if it is free.
126.        if isSpaceFree(board, 5):
127.            return 5
128.
129.        # Move on one of the sides.
130.        return chooseRandomMoveFromList(board, [2, 4, 6, 8])
131.
132. def isBoardFull(board):
133.        # Return True if every space on the board has been
      taken. Otherwise return False.
134.        for i in range(1, 10):
135.            if isSpaceFree(board, i):
136.                return False
137.        return True
138.
139.
140. print('Welcome to Tic Tac Toe!')
141.
142. while True:
143.        # Reset the board
144.        theBoard = [' '] * 10
145.        playerLetter, computerLetter = inputPlayerLetter()
146.        turn = whoGoesFirst()
147.        print('The ' + turn + ' will go first.')
148.        gameIsPlaying = True
149.
150.        while gameIsPlaying:
151.            if turn == 'player':
152.                # Player's turn.
153.                drawBoard(theBoard)
154.                move = getPlayerMove(theBoard)
155.                makeMove(theBoard, playerLetter, move)
156.
157.                if isWinner(theBoard, playerLetter):
158.                    drawBoard(theBoard)
159.                    print('Hooray! You have won the game!')
160.                    gameIsPlaying = False
161.                else:
162.                    if isBoardFull(theBoard):
163.                        drawBoard(theBoard)
```

```
164.                        print('The game is a tie!')
165.                        break
166.                    else:
167.                        turn = 'computer'
168.
169.            else:
170.                # Computer's turn.
171.                move = getComputerMove(theBoard,
        computerLetter)
172.                makeMove(theBoard, computerLetter, move)
173.
174.                if isWinner(theBoard, computerLetter):
175.                    drawBoard(theBoard)
176.                    print('The computer has beaten you! You
        lose.')
177.                    gameIsPlaying = False
178.                else:
179.                    if isBoardFull(theBoard):
180.                        drawBoard(theBoard)
181.                        print('The game is a tie!')
182.                        break
183.                    else:
184.                        turn = 'player'
185.
186.        if not playAgain():
187.            break
```

Designing the Program

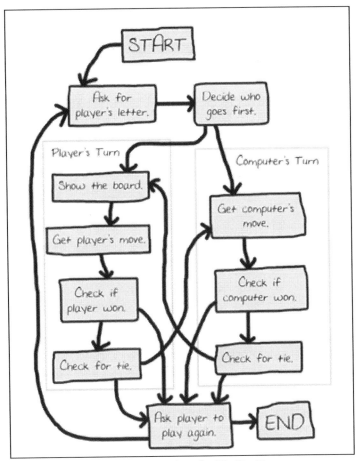

Figure 10-1: Flow chart for Tic Tac Toe

Tic Tac Toe is a very easy and short game to play on paper. In our Tic Tac Toe computer game, we'll let the player choose if they want to be X or O, randomly choose who goes first, and then let the player and computer take turns making moves on the board. Figure 10-1 is what a flow chart of Tic Tac Toe could look like.

You can see a lot of the boxes on the left side of the chart are what happens during the player's turn. The right side of the chart shows what happens on the computer's turn. The player has an extra box for drawing the board because the computer doesn't need the board printed on the screen. After the player or computer makes a move, we check if they won or caused a tie, and then the game switches turns. After the game is over, we ask the player if they want to play again.

Representing the Board as Data

First, we need to figure out how we are going to represent the board as a variable. On paper, the Tic Tac Toe board is drawn as a pair of horizontal lines and a pair of vertical lines, with either an X, O, or empty space in each of the nine spaces.

In our program, we are going to represent the Tic Tac Toe board as a list of strings. Each string will represent one of the nine positions on the board. We will give a number to each of the spaces on the board. To make it easier to remember which index in the list is for which piece, we will mirror the numbers on the keypad of our keyboard. See Figure 10-2.

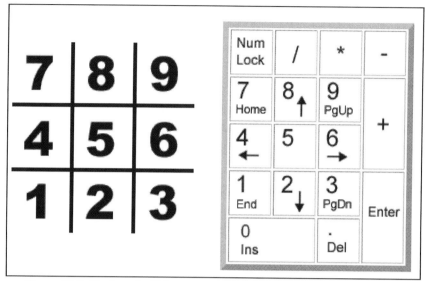

Figure 10-2: The board will be numbered like the keyboard's number pad.

The strings will either be 'X' for the X player, 'O' for the O player, or a space string ' ' to mark a spot on the board where no one has marked yet. The index of the string in the list will also be the number of the space on the board.

So if we had a list with ten strings named board, then board[7] would be the top-left square on the board (either an X, O, or blank space). board[5] would be the very center. When the player types in which place they want to move, they will type a number from 1 to 9. (Because there is no 0 on the keypad, we will just ignore the string at index 0 in our list.)

Game AI

When we talk about how our AI behaves, we will be talking about which types of spaces on the board it will move on. Just to be clear, we will label three types of spaces on the Tic Tac Toe board: corners, sides, and the center. Figure 10-3 is a chart of what each space is:

The AI for this game will follow a simple algorithm. An **algorithm** is a series of instructions to compute something. This is a loose definition of algorithm. A single program can make use of several different algorithms. An algorithm, like a complete program, can be represented with a flow chart. In the case of our Tic Tac Toe AI's algorithm, the series of steps will determine which is the best place to move. (See Figure 10-4.) There is nothing in the code that says, "These lines are an algorithm." like there is with a function's def-block. We just consider the AI algorithm as all the code that is used in our program that determines the AI's next move.

Our algorithm will have the following steps:

1. First, see if there is a move the computer can make that will win the game. If there is, take that move. Otherwise, go to step 2.

2. See if there is a move the player can make that will cause the computer to lose the game. If there is, we should move there to block the player. Otherwise, go to step 3.

3. Check if any of the corner spaces (spaces 1, 3, 7, or 9) are free. (We always want to take a corner piece instead of the center or a side piece.) If no corner piece is free, then go to step 4.

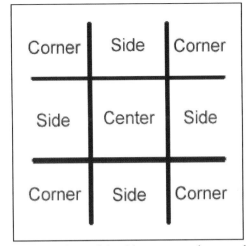

Figure 10-3: Locations of the side, corner, and center places.

4. Check if the center is free. If so, move there. If it isn't, then go to step 5.

5. Move on any of the side pieces (spaces 2, 4, 6, or 8). There are no more steps, because if we have reached step 5 the side spaces are the only spaces left.

This all takes place in the "Get computer's move." box on our flow chart. We could add this information to our flow chart like this:

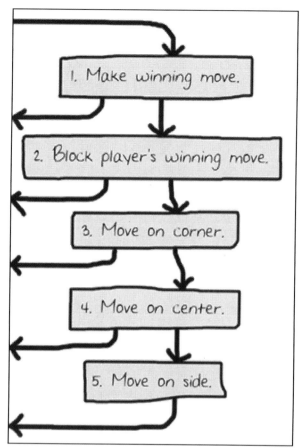

Figure 10-4: The five steps of the "Get computer's move" algorithm.
The arrows leaving go to the "Check if computer won" box.

We will implement this algorithm as code in our getComputerMove() function, and
the other functions that getComputerMove() calls.

How the Code Works: Lines 1 to 81

Now that we know about how we want the program to work, let's look at what each line
does.

The Start of the Program

```
1. # Tic Tac Toe
2.
3. import random
```

The first couple of lines are a comment and importing the random module so we can
use the randint() function in our game.

Printing the Board on the Screen

```
5. def drawBoard(board):
6.     # This function prints out the board that it was
    passed.
7.
8.     # "board" is a list of 10 strings representing the
    board (ignore index 0)
9.     print('   |   |')
10.    print(' ' + board[7] + ' | ' + board[8] + ' | ' +
    board[9])
11.    print('   |   |')
12.    print('-----------')
13.    print('   |   |')
14.    print(' ' + board[4] + ' | ' + board[5] + ' | ' +
    board[6])
15.    print('   |   |')
16.    print('-----------')
17.    print('   |   |')
18.    print(' ' + board[1] + ' | ' + board[2] + ' | ' +
    board[3])
19.    print('   |   |')
```

This function will print out the game board, marked as directed by the board parameter. Remember that our board is represented as a list of ten strings, where the string at index 1 is the mark on space 1 on the Tic Tac Toe board. (And remember that we ignore the string at index 0, because the spaces are labeled with numbers 1 to 9.) Many of our functions will work by passing the board as a list of ten strings to our functions. Be sure to get the spacing right in the strings, otherwise the board will look funny when it is printed on the screen.

Just as an example, here are some values that the board parameter could have (on the left side of the table) and what the drawBoard() function would print out (on the right):

Table 10-1: Examples of values of board and output from drawBoard(board) calls.

board value	drawBoard(board) output
| [' ', ' ', ' ', ' ', 'X', 'O', ' ', 'X', ' ', 'O'] | ```
  |   |
X |   | O
  |   |
-----------
  |   |
X | O |
  |   |
-----------
  |   |
  |   |
  |   |
``` |
```

[' ', 'O', 'O', ' ', ' ',
'X', ' ', ' ', ' ', ' ']
	<pre>	|
		
			|
			  ---------- 	
			
				X |
				
					|
					  ---------- 	
					  O
						O |
						
							|</pre>

[' ', ' ', ' ', ' ', ' ',
' ', ' ', ' ', ' ', ' ']
	<pre>	|
		
			|
			  ---------- 	
			
				|
				
					|
					  ---------- 	
					
						|
						
							|</pre>

[' ', 'X', 'X', 'X', 'X',
'X', 'X', 'X', 'X', 'X']
	<pre> X	X	X
			
				|
				  ---------- 	
				  X
					X	X
						
							|
							  ---------- 	
							  X
								X	X
									
										|</pre>

['0', '1', '2', '3', '4',
'5', '6', '7', '8', '9']
	<pre> 7	8	9
			
				|
				  ---------- 	
				  4
					5	6
						
							|
							  ---------- 	
							  1
								2	3
									
										|</pre>

The second to last board filled with X's could not possibly have happened (unless the X player skipped all of the O player's turns!) And the last board has strings of digits instead of X and O, which are invalid strings for the board. But the `drawBoard()` function doesn't care. It just prints the `board` parameter that it was passed. Computer programs only do exactly what you tell them, even if you tell them the wrong things to do. We will just make sure these invalid strings are not put into the passed list in the first place.

Letting the Player be X or O

```
21. def inputPlayerLetter():
22.     # Let's the player type which letter they want to be.
23.     # Returns a list with the player's letter as the
    first item, and the computer's letter as the second.
24.     letter = ''
25.     while not (letter == 'X' or letter == 'O'):
26.         print('Do you want to be X or O?')
27.         letter = input().upper()
```

The `inputPlayerLetter()` is a simple function. It asks if the player wants to be X or O, and will keep asking the player (with the `while` loop) until the player types in an X or O. Notice on line 26 that we automatically change the string returned by the call to `input()` to uppercase letters with the `upper()` string method.

The `while` loop's condition contains parentheses, which means the expression inside the parentheses is evaluated first. If the `letter` variable was set to `'X'`, the expression would evaluate like this:

```
while not (letter == 'X' or letter == 'O'):

            ⬇

while not ('X' == 'X' or 'X' == 'O'):

            ⬇

while not (True or False):

            ⬇

while not (True):

            ⬇

while not True:

            ⬇

while False:
```

As you can see, if `letter` has the value `'X'` or `'O'`, then the loop's condition will be `False` and lets the program execution continue.

```
29.        # the first element in the list is the player's
      letter, the second is the computer's letter.
30.    if letter == 'X':
31.        return ['X', 'O']
32.    else:
33.        return ['O', 'X']
```

This function returns a list with two items. The first item (that is, the string at index 0) will be the player's letter, and the second item (that is, the string at index 1) will be the computer's letter. This `if-else` statement chooses the appropriate list to return.

Deciding Who Goes First

```
35. def whoGoesFirst():
36.     # Randomly choose the player who goes first.
37.     if random.randint(0, 1) == 0:
38.         return 'computer'
39.     else:
40.         return 'player'
```

The `whoGoesFirst()` function does a virtual coin flip to determine who goes first, the computer or the player. Instead of flipping an actual coin, this code gets a random number of either 0 or 1 by calling the `random.randint()` function. If this function call returns a 0, the `whoGoesFirst()` function returns the string `'computer'`. Otherwise, the function returns the string `'player'`. The code that calls this function will use the return value to know who will make the first move of the game.

Asking the Player to Play Again

```
42. def playAgain():
43.     # This function returns True if the player wants to
      play again, otherwise it returns False.
44.     print('Do you want to play again? (yes or no)')
45.     return input().lower().startswith('y')
```

The `playAgain()` function asks the player if they want to play another game. The function returns `True` if the player types in `'yes'` or `'YES'` or `'y'` or anything that begins with the letter Y. For any other response, the function returns `False`. The order of the method calls on line 45 is important. The return value from the call to the `input()` function is a string that has its `lower()` method called on it. The `lower()` method returns another string (the lowercase string) and that string has its `startswith()` method called on it, passing the argument `'y'`.

There is no loop, because we assume that if the user entered anything besides a string that begins with `'y'`, they want to stop playing. So, we only ask the player once.

Placing a mark on the Board

```
47. def makeMove(board, letter, move):
48.     board[move] = letter
```

The makeMove() function is very simple and only one line. The parameters are a list with ten strings named board, one of the player's letters (either 'X' or 'O') named letter, and a place on the board where that player wants to go (which is an integer from 1 to 9) named move.

But wait a second. You might think that this function doesn't do much. It seems to change one of the items in the board list to the value in letter. But because this code is in a function, the board parameter will be forgotten when we exit this function and leave the function's scope.

Actually, this is not the case. This is because lists (and dictionaries) are special when you pass them as arguments to functions. This is because you pass a reference to the list (or dictionary) and not the list itself. Let's learn about the difference between lists and list references.

List References

Try entering the following into the shell:

```
>>> spam = 42
>>> cheese = spam
>>> spam = 100
>>> spam
100
>>> cheese
42
```

This makes sense from what we know so far. We assign 42 to the spam variable, and then we copy the value in spam and assign it to the variable cheese. When we later change the value in spam to 100, this doesn't affect the value in cheese. This is because spam and cheese are different variables that store different values.

But lists don't work this way. When you assign a list to a variable with the = sign, you are actually assigning a list reference to the variable. A **reference** is a value that points to some bit of data, and a **list reference** is a value that points to a list. Here is some code that will make this easier to understand. Type this into the shell:

```
>>> spam = [0, 1, 2, 3, 4, 5]
>>> cheese = spam
>>> cheese[1] = 'Hello!'
>>> spam
[0, 'Hello!', 2, 3, 4, 5]
>>> cheese
[0, 'Hello!', 2, 3, 4, 5]
```

This looks odd. The code only changed the cheese list, but it seems that both the cheese and spam lists have changed.

Notice that the line cheese = spam copies the *list reference* in spam to cheese, instead of copying the *list value* itself. This is because the value stored in the spam variable is a list *reference*, and not the list *value* itself. This means that the values stored in both spam and cheese refer to the same list. There is only one list because the list was not copied, the reference to the list was copied. So when you modify cheese in the cheese[1] = 'Hello!' line, you are modifying the same list that spam refers to. This is why spam seems to have the same list value that cheese does.

Remember that variables are like boxes that contain values. List variables don't actually contain lists at all, they contain references to lists. Here are some pictures that explain what happens in the code you just typed in:

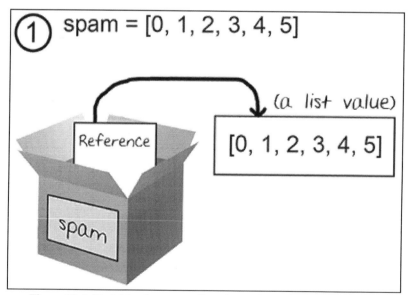

Figure 10-5: Variables do no store lists, but rather references to lists.

On the first line, the actual list is not contained in the spam variable but a reference to the list. The list itself is not stored in any variable.

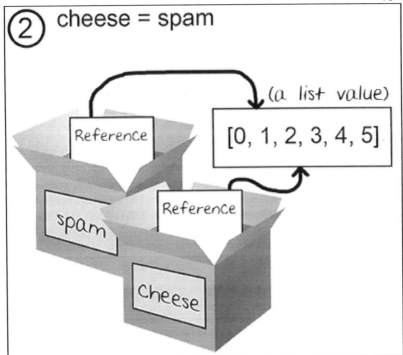

Figure 10-6: Two variables store two references to the same list.

When you assign the reference in spam to cheese, the cheese variable contains a copy of the reference in spam. Now both cheese and spam refer to the same list.

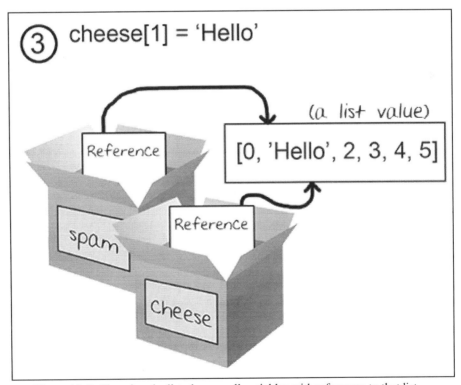

Figure 10-7: Changing the list changes all variables with references to that list.

When you alter the list that cheese refers to, the list that spam refers to is also changed because they are the same list. If you want spam and cheese to store two different lists, you have to create two different lists instead of copying a reference:

```
>>> spam = [0, 1, 2, 3, 4, 5]
>>> cheese = [0, 1, 2, 3, 4, 5]
```

In the above example, spam and cheese have two different lists stored in them (even though these lists are identical in content). Now if you modify one of the lists, it will not affect the other because spam and cheese have references to two different lists:

```
>>> spam = [0, 1, 2, 3, 4, 5]
>>> cheese = [0, 1, 2, 3, 4, 5]
>>> cheese[1] = 'Hello!'
>>> spam
[0, 1, 2, 3, 4, 5]
>>> cheese
[0, 'Hello!', 2, 3, 4, 5]
```

Figure 10-8 shows how the two references point to two different lists:

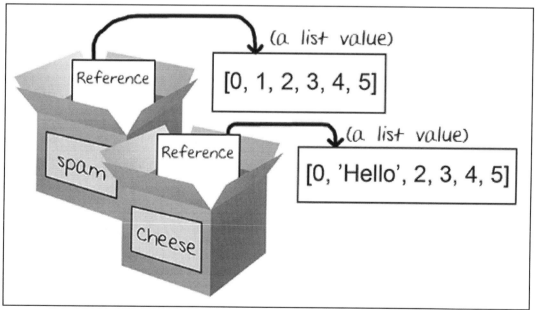

Figure 10-8: Two variables each storing references to two different lists.

Dictionaries work in the same way. Dictionaries do not store values, they store references to values. These are called **dictionary references** (or you can call both dictionary references and list references by the plain name, "reference".)

Using List References in `makeMove()`

Let's go back to the `makeMove()` function:

```
47. def makeMove(board, letter, move):
48.     board[move] = letter
```

When we pass a list value as the argument for the `board` parameter, the function's local variable is a copy of the reference, not a copy of the list itself. The `letter` and `move` parameters are copies of the string and integer values that we pass. Since they are copies, if we modify `letter` or `move` in this function, the original variables we used when we called `makeMove()` would not be modified. Only the copies would be modified.

But a copy of the reference still refers to the same list that the original reference refers to. So if we make changes to `board` in this function, the original list is modified. When we exit the `makeMove()` function, the copy of the reference is forgotten along with the other parameters. But since we were actually changing the original list, those changes remain after we exit the function. This is how the `makeMove()` function modifies the list that a reference of is passed.

Checking if the Player Has Won

```
50. def isWinner(bo, le):
51.     # Given a board and a player's letter, this function
    returns True if that player has won.
52.     # We use bo instead of board and le instead of letter
    so we don't have to type as much.
53.     return ((bo[7] == le and bo[8] == le and bo[9] == le)
    or # across the top
54.     (bo[4] == le and bo[5] == le and bo[6] == le) or #
    across the middle
55.     (bo[1] == le and bo[2] == le and bo[3] == le) or #
    across the bottom
56.     (bo[7] == le and bo[4] == le and bo[1] == le) or #
    down the left side
57.     (bo[8] == le and bo[5] == le and bo[2] == le) or #
    down the middle
58.     (bo[9] == le and bo[6] == le and bo[3] == le) or #
    down the right side
59.     (bo[7] == le and bo[5] == le and bo[3] == le) or #
    diagonal
60.     (bo[9] == le and bo[5] == le and bo[1] == le)) #
    diagonal
```

Lines 53 to 60 in the `isWinner()` function are actually one very long `if` statement. We use `bo` and `le` for the board and letter parameters so that we have less to type in this function. (This is a trick programmers sometimes use to reduce the amount they need to type. Be sure to add a comment that explains this though, otherwise you may forget what bo and le are supposed to mean.)

There are eight possible ways to win at Tic Tac Toe. You can have a line across the top, middle, and bottom. Or you can have a line down the left, middle, or right. And you can have either of the two diagonals. Note that each line of the condition checks if the three spaces are equal to the letter provided (combined with the and operator) and we use the or operator to combine the eight different ways to win. This means only one of the eight ways must be true in order for us to say that the player who owns letter in le is the winner.

Let's pretend that le is 'O', and the board looks like this:

If the board looks like that, then bo must be equal to [' ', 'O', 'O', 'O', ' ', 'X', ' ', 'X', ' ', ' ']. Here is how the expression after the return keyword on line 53 would evaluate:

Here is the expression as it is in the code:

```
53.     return ((bo[7] == le and bo[8] == le and bo[9] == le) or
54.     (bo[4] == le and bo[5] == le and bo[6] == le) or
55.     (bo[1] == le and bo[2] == le and bo[3] == le) or
56.     (bo[7] == le and bo[4] == le and bo[1] == le) or
57.     (bo[8] == le and bo[5] == le and bo[2] == le) or
58.     (bo[9] == le and bo[6] == le and bo[3] == le) or
59.     (bo[7] == le and bo[5] == le and bo[3] == le) or
60.     (bo[9] == le and bo[5] == le and bo[1] == le))
```

First Python will replace the variable bo with the value inside of it:

```
53.     return (('X' == 'O' and ' ' == 'O' and ' ' == 'O') or
54.     (' ' == 'O' and 'X' == 'O' and ' ' == 'O') or
55.     ('O' == 'O' and 'O' == 'O' and 'O' == 'O') or
56.     ('X' == 'O' and ' ' == 'O' and 'O' == 'O') or
57.     (' ' == 'O' and 'X' == 'O' and 'O' == 'O') or
```

```
58.         (' ' == 'O' and ' ' == 'O' and 'O' == 'O') or
59.         ('X' == 'O' and 'X' == 'O' and 'O' == 'O') or
60.         (' ' == 'O' and 'X' == 'O' and 'O' == 'O'))
```

Next, Python will evaluate all those == comparisons inside the parentheses to a Boolean value:

```
53.     return ((False and False and False) or
54.     (False and False and False) or
55.     (True and True and True) or
56.     (False and False and True) or
57.     (False and False and True) or
58.     (False and False and True) or
59.     (False and False and True) or
60.     (False and False and True))
```

Then the Python interpreter will evaluate all those expressions inside the parentheses:

```
53.     return ((False) or
54.     (False) or
55.     (True) or
56.     (False) or
57.     (False) or
58.     (False) or
59.     (False) or
60.     (False))
```

Since now there is only one value inside the parentheses, we can get rid of them:

```
53.     return (False or
54.     False or
55.     True or
56.     False or
57.     False or
58.     False or
59.     False or
60.     False)
```

Now we evaluate the expression that is connecter by all those or operators:

```
53.     return (True)
```

> Once again, we get rid of the parentheses, and we are left with one value:
>
> ```
> 53.     return True
> ```

So given those values for bo and le, the expression would evaluate to True. Remember that the value of le matters. If le is 'O' and X has won the game, the isWinner() would return False.

Duplicating the Board Data

```
62. def getBoardCopy(board):
63.     # Make a duplicate of the board list and return it
    the duplicate.
64.     dupeBoard = []
65.
66.     for i in board:
67.         dupeBoard.append(i)
68.
69.     return dupeBoard
```

The getBoardCopy() function is here so that we can easily make a copy of a given 10-string list that represents a Tic Tac Toe board in our game. There are times that we will want our AI algorithm to make temporary modifications to a temporary copy of the board without changing the original board. In that case, we call this function to make a copy of the board's list. The actual new list is created on line 64, with the blank list brackets [].

Line 64 actually creates a brand new list and stores a reference to it in dupeBoard. But the list stored in dupeBoard is just an empty list. The for loop will go through the board parameter, appending a copy of the string values in the original board to our duplicate board. Finally, after the loop, we will return the dupeBoard variable's reference to the duplicate board. So you can see how the getBoardCopy() function is building up a copy of the original board and returning a reference to this new board, and not the original one.

Checking if a Space on the Board is Free

```
71. def isSpaceFree(board, move):
72.     # Return true if the passed move is free on the
    passed board.
73.     return board[move] == ' '
```

This is a simple function that, given a Tic Tac Toe board and a possible move, will return if that move is available or not. Remember that free spaces on our board lists are marked as a single space string.

Letting the Player Enter Their Move

```
75. def getPlayerMove(board):
76.     # Let the player type in his move.
77.     move = ' '
78.     while move not in '1 2 3 4 5 6 7 8 9'.split() or not
    isSpaceFree(board, int(move)):
79.         print('What is your next move? (1-9)')
80.         move = input()
81.     return int(move)
```

The `getPlayerMove()` function asks the player to enter the number for the space they wish to move. The function makes sure that they enter a space that is a valid space (an integer 1 through 9). It also checks that the space that is not already taken, given the Tic Tac Toe board passed to the function in the `board` parameter.

The two lines of code inside the `while` loop simply ask the player to enter a number from 1 to 9. The loop's condition will keep looping, that is, it will keep asking the player for a space, as long as the condition is `True`. The condition is `True` if either of the expressions on the *left* or *right* side of the `or` keyword is `True`.

The expression on the *left* side checks if the move that the player entered is equal to `'1'`, `'2'`, `'3'`, and so on up to `'9'` by creating a list with these strings (with the `split()` method) and checking if move is in this list. `'1 2 3 4 5 6 7 8 9'.split()` evaluates to be the same as `['1', '2', '3', '4', '5', '6', '7', '8', '9']`, but it easier to type.

The expression on the *right* side checks if the move that the player entered is a free space on the board. It checks this by calling the `isSpaceFree()` function we just wrote. Remember that `isSpaceFree()` will return `True` if the move we pass is available on the board. Note that `isSpaceFree()` expects an integer for `move`, so we use the `int()` function to evaluate an integer form of `move`.

We add the `not` operators to both sides so that the condition will be `True` when both of these requirements are unfulfilled. This will cause the loop to ask the player again and again until they enter a proper move.

Finally, on line 81, we will return the integer form of whatever move the player entered. Remember that `input()` returns a string, so we will want to use the `int()` function to evaluate the string as an integer.

Short-Circuit Evaluation

You may have noticed there is a possible problem in our `getPlayerMove()` function. What if the player typed in `'X'` or some other non-integer string? The `move not in '1 2 3 4 5 6 7 8 9'.split()` expression on the left side of `or` would return

False as expected, and then we would evaluate the expression on the right side of the or operator. But when we pass 'X' (which would be the value in move) to the int() function, int('X') would give us an error. It gives us this error because the int() function can only take strings of number characters, like '9' or '0', not strings like 'X'.

As an example of this kind of error, try entering this into the shell:

```
>>> int('42')
42
>>> int('X')

Traceback (most recent call last):
  File "<pyshell#3>", line 1, in <module>
    int('X')
ValueError: invalid literal for int() with base
10: 'X'
```

But when you play our Tic Tac Toe game and try entering 'X' for your move, this error doesn't happen. The reason is because the while loop's condition is being short-circuited.

What **short-circuiting** means is that because the expression on the left side of the or keyword (move not in '1 2 3 4 5 6 7 8 9'.split()) evaluates to True, the Python interpreter knows that the entire expression will evaluate to True. It doesn't matter if the expression on the right side of the or keyword evaluates to True or False, because only one value on the side of the or operator needs to be True.

Think about it: The expression True or False evaluates to True and the expression True or True also evaluates to True. If the value on the left side is True, it doesn't matter what the value is on the right side. So Python stops checking the rest of the expression and doesn't even bother evaluating the not isSpaceFree(board, int (move)) part. This means the int() and the isSpaceFree() functions are never called as long as move not in '1 2 3 4 5 6 7 8 9'.split() is True.

This works out well for us, because if the expression on the right side is True then move is not a string in number form. That would cause int() to give us an error. The only times move not in '1 2 3 4 5 6 7 8 9'.split() evaluates to False are when move is not a single-digit string. In that case, the call to int() would not give us an error.

An Example of Short-Circuit Evaluation

Here's a short program that gives a good example of short-circuiting. Open a new file in the IDLE editor and type in this program, save it as *truefalsefizz.py*, then press F5 to run it. Don't add the numbers down the left side of the program, those just appear in this book to make the program's explanation easier to understand. The function calls in **bold** are the function calls that are evaluated.

truefalsefizz.py

This code can be downloaded from *http://inventwithpython.com/truefalsefizz.py*

If you get errors after typing this code in, compare it to the book's code with the online diff tool at *http://inventwithpython.com/diff* or email the author at al@inventwithpython.com

```
 1. def TrueFizz(message):
 2.     print(message)
 3.     return True
 4.
 5. def FalseFizz(message):
 6.     print(message)
 7.     return False
 8.
 9. if FalseFizz('Cats') or TrueFizz('Dogs'):
10.    print('Step 1')
11.
12. if TrueFizz('Hello') or TrueFizz('Goodbye'):
13.     print('Step 2')
14.
15. if TrueFizz('Spam') and TrueFizz('Cheese'):
16.     print('Step 3')
17.
18. if FalseFizz('Red') and TrueFizz('Blue'):
19.     print('Step 4')
```

When you run this program, you can see the output (the letters on the left side have been added to make the output's explanation easier to understand):

```
A. Cats
B. Dogs
C. Step 1
D. Hello
E. Step 2
F. Spam
G. Cheese
H. Step 3
I. Red
```

This small program has two functions: `TrueFizz()` and `FalseFizz()`. `TrueFizz()` will display a message and return the value `True`, while `FalseFizz()` will display a message and return the value `False`. This lets us determine if these functions are being called, or if these functions are being skipped due to short-circuiting.

The First `if` Statement (Cats and Dogs)

The first `if` statement on line 9 in our small program will first evaluate `TrueFizz()`. We know this happens because `Cats` is printed to the screen (on line A in the output). The entire expression could still be `True` if the expression to the right of the or keyword is `True`. So the call `TrueFizz('Dogs')` on line 9 is evaluated, `Dogs` is printed to the screen (on line B in the output) and `True` is returned. On line 9, the `if` statement's condition evaluates to `False or True`, which in turn evaluates to `True`. `'Step 1'` is then printed to the screen. No short-circuiting took place for this expression's evaluation.

The Second `if` Statement (Hello and Goodbye)

The second `if` statement on line 12 also has short-circuiting. This is because when we call `TrueFizz('Hello')` on line 12, it prints `Hello` (see line D in the output) and returns `True`. The Python interpreter doesn't call `TrueFizz('Goodbye')` because it doesn't matter what is on the right side of the or keyword. You can tell it is not called because `Goodbye` is not printed to the screen. The `if` statement's condition is `True`, so `'Step 2'` is printed to the screen (see line E).

The Third `if` Statement (Spam and Cheese)

The third `if` statement on line 15 does not have short-circuiting. The call to `TrueFizz('Spam')` returns `True`, but we do not know if the entire condition is `True` or `False` because of the and operator. So Python will call `TrueFizz('Cheese')`, which prints `Cheese` and returns `True`. The `if` statement's condition is evaluated to `True and True`, which in turn evaluates to `True`. Because the condition is `True`, `'Step 3'` is printed to the screen (see line H).

The Fourth `if` Statement (Red and Blue)

The fourth `if` statement on line 18 does have short-circuiting. The `FalseFizz('Red')` call prints `Red` (see line I in the output) and returns `False`. Because the left side of the and keyword is `False`, it does not matter if the right side is `True or False`, the condition will evaluate to `False` anyway. So `TrueFizz('Blue')` is not called and `Blue` does not appear on the screen. Because the `if` statement's condition evaluated to `False`, `'Step 4'` is also not printed to the screen.

Short-circuiting can happen for any expression that includes the Boolean operators and and or. It is important to remember that this can happen; otherwise you may find that some function calls in the expression are never called and you will not understand why.

How the Code Works: Lines 83 to 94

Choosing a Move from a List of Moves

```
83. def chooseRandomMoveFromList(board, movesList):
84.     # Returns a valid move from the passed list on the
    passed board.
85.     # Returns None if there is no valid move.
86.     possibleMoves = []
87.     for i in movesList:
88.         if isSpaceFree(board, i):
89.             possibleMoves.append(i)
```

The chooseRandomMoveFromList() function will be of use to us when we are implementing the code for our AI. The first parameter board is the 10-string list that represents a Tic Tac Toe board. The second parameter movesList is a list of integers that represent possible moves. For example, if movesList is [1, 3, 7, 9], that means we should return the number for one of the corner spaces on the board.

The chooseRandomMoveFromList() function will then choose one of those moves from the possibleMoves list. It also makes sure that the move that it chooses is not already taken. To do this, we create a blank list and assign it to possibleMoves. The for loop will go through the list of moves passed to this function in movesList. If that move is available (which we figure out with a call to isSpaceFree()), then we add it to possibleMoves with the append() method.

```
91.     if len(possibleMoves) != 0:
92.         return random.choice(possibleMoves)
93.     else:
94.         return None
```

At this point, the possibleMoves list has all of the moves that were in movesList that are also free spaces on the board represented by board. If the list is not empty, then there is at least one possible move that can be made on the board.

This list might be empty. For example, if movesList was [1, 3, 7, 9] but the board represented by the board parameter had all the corner spaces already taken, the possibleMoves list would have been empty.

If possibleMoves is empty, then len(possibleMoves) will evaluate to 0 and the code in the else-block will execute. Notice that it returns something called None.

The None Value

None is a special value that you can assign to a variable. The **None value** represents the lack of a value. None is the only value of the data type NoneType. (Just like the Boolean data type has only two values, the NoneType data type has only one value, None.) It can be very useful to use the None value when you need a value that means "does not exist". For example, say you had a variable named quizAnswer which holds the user's answer to some True-False pop quiz question. You could set quizAnswer to None if the user skipped the question and did not answer it. Using None would be better because if you set it to True or False before assigning the value of the user's answer, it may look like the user gave an answer the question even though they didn't.

Calls to functions that do not return anything (that is, they exit by reaching the end of the function and not from a return statement) will evaluate to None. The None value is written **without** quotes and with a capital "N" and lowercase "one".

How the Code Works: Lines 96 to 187

Creating the Computer's Artificial Intelligence

```
 96. def getComputerMove(board, computerLetter):
 97.     # Given a board and the computer's letter, determine
     where to move and return that move.
 98.     if computerLetter == 'X':
 99.         playerLetter = 'O'
100.     else:
101.         playerLetter = 'X'
```

The getComputerMove() function is where our AI will be coded. The arguments are a Tic Tac Toe board (in the board parameter) and which letter the computer is (either 'X' or 'O' in the computerLetter parameter). The first few lines simply assign the other letter to a variable named playerLetter. This lets us use the same code, no matter who is X and who is O. This function will return the integer 1 to 9 that represents which space the computer will move.

Remember how our algorithm works: First, see if there is a move the computer can make that will win the game. If there is, take that move. Otherwise, go to the second step.

Second, see if there is a move the player can make that will cause the computer to lose the game. If there is, we should move there to block the player. Otherwise, go to the third step.

Third, check if any of the corner spaces (spaces 1, 3, 7, or 9) are free. (We always want to take a corner piece instead of the center or a side piece.) If no corner piece is free, then go to the fourth step.

Fourth, check if the center is free. If so, move there. If it isn't, then go to the fifth step.

Fifth, move on any of the side pieces (spaces 2, 4, 6, or 8). There are no more steps, because if we have reached this step then the side spaces are the only spaces left.

The Computer Checks if it Can Win in One Move

```
103.        # Here is our algorithm for our Tic Tac Toe AI:
104.        # First, check if we can win in the next move
105.        for i in range(1, 10):
106.            copy = getBoardCopy(board)
107.            if isSpaceFree(copy, i):
108.                makeMove(copy, computerLetter, i)
109.                if isWinner(copy, computerLetter):
110.                    return i
```

More than anything, if the computer can win in the next move, the computer should immediately make that winning move. We will do this by trying each of the nine spaces on the board with a for loop. The first line in the loop (line 106) makes a copy of the board list. We want to make a move on the copy of the board, and then see if that move results in the computer winning. We don't want to modify the original Tic Tac Toe board, which is why we make a call to getBoardCopy(). We check if the space we will move is free, and if so, we move on that space and see if this results in winning. If it does, we return that space's integer.

If moving on none of the spaces results in winning, then the loop will finally end and we move on to line 112.

The Computer Checks if the Player Can Win in One Move

```
112.        # Check if the player could win on his next move, and
     block them.
113.        for i in range(1, 10):
114.            copy = getBoardCopy(board)
115.            if isSpaceFree(copy, i):
116.                makeMove(copy, playerLetter, i)
117.                if isWinner(copy, playerLetter):
118.                    return i
```

At this point, we know we cannot win in one move. So we want to make sure the human player cannot win in one more move. The code is very similar, except on the copy of the board, we place the player's letter before calling the isWinner() function. If there is a position the player can move that will let them win, the computer should move there to block that move.

If the human player cannot win in one more move, the for loop will eventually stop and execution continues on to line 120.

Checking the Corner, Center, and Side Spaces (in that Order)

```
120.        # Try to take one of the corners, if they are free.
121.        move = chooseRandomMoveFromList(board, [1, 3, 7, 9])
122.        if move != None:
123.            return move
```

Our call to chooseRandomMoveFromList() with the list of [1, 3, 7, 9] will ensure that it returns the integer for one of the corner spaces. (Remember, the corner spaces are represented by the integers 1, 3, 7, and 9.) If all the corner spaces are taken, our chooseRandomMoveFromList() function will return the None value. In that case, we will move on to line 125.

```
125.        # Try to take the center, if it is free.
126.        if isSpaceFree(board, 5):
127.            return 5
```

If none of the corners are available, we will try to move on the center space if it is free. If the center space is not free, the execution moves on to line 129.

```
129.        # Move on one of the sides.
130.        return chooseRandomMoveFromList(board, [2, 4, 6, 8])
```

This code also makes a call to chooseRandomMoveFromList(), except we pass it a list of the side spaces ([2, 4, 6, 8]). We know that this function will not return None, because the side spaces are the only spaces we have not yet checked. This is the end of the getComputerMove() function and our AI algorithm.

Checking if the Board is Full

```
132. def isBoardFull(board):
133.     # Return True if every space on the board has been
     taken. Otherwise return False.
134.     for i in range(1, 10):
135.         if isSpaceFree(board, i):
136.             return False
137.     return True
```

The last function we will write is isBoardFull(), which returns True if the 10-string list board argument it was passed has an 'X' or 'O' in every index (except for index 0, which is just a placeholder that we ignore). If there is at least one space in board that is set to a single space ' ' then it will return False.

The `for` loop will let us check spaces 1 through 9 on the Tic Tac Toe board. (Remember that `range(1, 10)` will make the `for` loop iterate over the integers 1, 2, 3, 4, 5, 6, 7, 8, and 9.) As soon as it finds a free space in the board (that is, when `isSpaceFree(board, i)` returns `True`), the `isBoardFull()` function will return `False`.

If execution manages to go through every iteration of the loop, we will know that none of the spaces are free. So at that point (on line 137), we will execute `return True`.

The Start of the Game

```
140. print('Welcome to Tic Tac Toe!')
```

Line 140 is the first line that isn't inside of a function, so it is the first line of code that is executed when we run this program.

```
142. while True:
143.     # Reset the board
144.     theBoard = [' '] * 10
```

This `while` loop has `True` for the condition, so that means we will keep looping in this loop until we encounter a `break` statement. Line 144 sets up the main Tic Tac Toe board that we will use, named `theBoard`. It is a 10-string list, where each string is a single space `' '`. Remember the little trick using the multiplication operator with a list to replicate it: `[' '] * 10`. That evaluates to `[' ', ' ', ' ', ' ', ' ', ' ', ' ', ' ', ' ', ' ']`, but is shorter for us to type `[' '] * 10`.

Deciding the Player's Mark and Who Goes First

```
145.     playerLetter, computerLetter = inputPlayerLetter()
```

The `inputPlayerLetter()` function lets the player type in whether they want to be X or O. The function returns a 2-string list, either `['X', 'O']` or `['O', 'X']`. We use the multiple assignment trick here that we learned in the Hangman chapter. If `inputPlayerLetter()` returns `['X', 'O']`, then `playerLetter` is set to `'X'` and `computerLetter` is set to 'O'. If `inputPlayerLetter()` returns `['O', 'X']`, then `playerLetter` is set to 'O' and `computerLetter` is set to 'X'.

```
146.     turn = whoGoesFirst()
147.     print('The ' + turn + ' will go first.')
148.     gameIsPlaying = True
```

The `whoGoesFirst()` function randomly decides who goes first, and returns either the string `'player'` or the string `'computer'`. On line 147, we tell the player who will go first. The `gameIsPlayer` variable is what we will use to keep track of whether the game has been won, lost, tied or if it is the other player's turn.

Running the Player's Turn

```
150.        while gameIsPlaying:
```

This is a loop that will keep going back and forth between the player's turn and the computer's turn, as long as `gameIsPlaying` is set to `True`.

```
151.            if turn == 'player':
152.                # Player's turn.
153.                drawBoard(theBoard)
154.                move = getPlayerMove(theBoard)
155.                makeMove(theBoard, playerLetter, move)
```

The turn variable was originally set by the `whoGoesFirst()` call on line 146). It is either set to `'player'` or `'computer'`. If `turn` contains the string `'computer'`, then the condition is `False` and execution will jump down to line 169.

The first thing we do when it is the player's turn (according to the flow chart we drew at the beginning of this chapter) is show the board to the player. Calling the `drawBoard()` and passing the `theBoard` variable will print the board on the screen. We then let the player type in his move by calling our `getPlayerMove()` function, and set the move on the board by calling our `makeMove()` function.

```
157.            if isWinner(theBoard, playerLetter):
158.                drawBoard(theBoard)
159.                print('Hooray! You have won the game!')
160.                gameIsPlaying = False
```

Now that the player has made his move, our program should check if they have won the game with this move. If the `isWinner()` function returns `True`, we should show them the winning board (the previous call to `drawBoard()` shows the board *before* they made the winning move) and print a message telling them they have won.

Then we set `gameIsPlaying` to `False` so that execution does not continue on to the computer's turn.

```
161.            else:
162.                if isBoardFull(theBoard):
163.                    drawBoard(theBoard)
164.                    print('The game is a tie!')
165.                    break
```

If the player did not win with his last move, then maybe his last move filled up the entire board and we now have a tie. In this else-block, we check if the board is full with a call to the `isBoardFull()` function. If it returns `True`, then we should draw the board by calling `drawBoard()` and tell the player a tie has occurred. The `break` statement will break us out of the `while` loop we are in and jump down to line 186.

Running the Computer's Turn

```
166.                else:
167.                    turn = 'computer'
```

If the player has not won or tied the game, then we should just set the `turn` variable to `'computer'` so that when this `while` loop loops back to the start it will execute the code for the computer's turn.

```
169.            else:
```

If the `turn` variable was not set to `'player'` for the condition on line 151, then we know it is the computer's turn and the code in this else-block will execute. This code is very similar to the code for the player's turn, except the computer does not need the board printed on the screen so we skip calling the `drawBoard()` function.

```
170.                # Computer's turn.
171.                move = getComputerMove(theBoard,
        computerLetter)
172.                makeMove(theBoard, computerLetter, move)
```

The code above is almost identical to the code for the player's turn on lines 154 and 155.

```
174.                if isWinner(theBoard, computerLetter):
175.                    drawBoard(theBoard)
176.                    print('The computer has beaten you! You
        lose.')
177.                    gameIsPlaying = False
```

We want to check if the computer won with its last move. The reason we call `drawBoard()` here is because the player will want to see what move the computer made to win the game. We then set `gameIsPlaying` to `False` so that the game does not continue. Notice that lines 174 to 177 are almost identical to lines 157 to 160.

```
178.                else:
179.                    if isBoardFull(theBoard):
180.                        drawBoard(theBoard)
181.                        print('The game is a tie!')
```

```
182.                        break
```

The lines of code above are identical to the code on lines 162 to 165. The only difference is this is a check for a tied game after the computer has moved, instead of the player.

```
183.              else:
184.                  turn = 'player'
```

If the game is neither won nor tied, it then becomes the player's turn. There are no more lines of code inside the `while` loop, so execution would jump back to the `while` statement on line 150.

```
186.       if not playAgain():
187.          break
```

These lines of code are located immediately after the while-block started by the `while` statement on line 150. Remember, we would only exit out of that `while` loop if it's condition (the `gameIsPlaying` variable) was `False`. `gameIsPlaying` is set to `False` when the game has ended, so at this point we are going to ask the player if they want to play again.

Remember, when we evaluate the condition in this `if` statement, we call the `playAgain()` function which will let the user type in if they want to play or not. `playAgain()` will return `True` if the player typed something that began with a `'y'` like `'yes'` or `'y'`. Otherwise `playAgain()` will return `False`.

If `playAgain()` returns `False`, then the `if` statement's condition is `True` (because of the `not` operator that reverses the Boolean value) and we execute the break statement. That breaks us out of the `while` loop that was started on line 142. But there are no more lines of code after that while-block, so the program terminates.

Summary: Creating Game-Playing Artificial Intelligences

Creating a program that can play a game comes down to carefully considering all the possible situations the AI can be in and how it should respond in each of those situations. Our Tic Tac Toe AI is fairly simple because there are not many possible moves in Tic Tac Toe compared to a game like chess or checkers.

Our AI simply blocks the players move if the player is about to win. If the player is not about to win, it checks if any possible move can allow itself to win. Then the AI simply chooses any available corner space, then the center space, then the side spaces. This is a simple algorithm for the computer to follow.

The key to implementing our AI is by making copies of the board data and simulating moves on the copy. That way, the AI code can see if a move will result in a win or loss. Then the AI can make that move on the real board. This type of simulation is very effective at predicting what is a good move or not.

Chapter 11
Bagels

Topics Covered In This Chapter:

- Hard-coding
- Augmented Assignment Operators, +=, -=, *=, /=
- The random.shuffle() Function
- The sort() List Method
- The join() List Method
- String Interpolation (also called String Formatting)
- Conversion Specifier %s
- Nested Loops

In this chapter you will learn a few new methods and functions that come with Python. You will also learn about augmented assignment operators and string interpolation. These concepts don't let you do anything you couldn't do before, but they are nice shortcuts that make typing your code easier.

Bagels is a simple game you can play with a friend. Your friend thinks up a random 3-digit number with no repeating digits, and you try to guess what the number is. After each guess, your friend gives you clues on how close your guess was. If the friend tells you "bagels", that means that none of the three digits you guessed is in the secret number. If your friend tells you "pico", then one of the digits is in the secret number, but your guess has the digit in the wrong place. If your friend tells you "fermi", then your guess has a correct digit in the correct place. Of course, even if you get a pico or fermi clue, you still don't know which digit in your guess is the correct one.

You can also get multiple clues after each guess. Say the secret number is 456, and your guess is 546. The clue you get from your friend would be "fermi pico pico" because one digit is correct and in the correct place (the digit 6), and two digits are in the secret number but in the wrong place (the digits 4 and 5).

Sample Run

```
I am thinking of a 3-digit number. Try to guess what it is.
Here are some clues:
When I say:    That means:
  Pico         One digit is correct but in the wrong position.
  Fermi        One digit is correct and in the right position.
  Bagels       No digit is correct.
I have thought up a number. You have 10 guesses to get it.
Guess #1:
123
Fermi
Guess #2:
453
Pico
Guess #3:
425
Fermi
Guess #4:
326
Bagels
Guess #5:
489
Bagels
Guess #6:
075
Fermi Fermi
Guess #7:
015
Fermi Pico
Guess #8:
175
You got it!
Do you want to play again? (yes or no)
no
```

Bagel's Source Code

---

bagels.py

This code can be downloaded from *http://inventwithpython.com/bagels.py*

If you get errors after typing this code in, compare it to the book's code with the online diff tool at *http://inventwithpython.com/diff* or email the author at al@inventwithpython.com

```
1. import random
2. def getSecretNum(numDigits):
```

```
3.         # Returns a string that is numDigits long, made up of
    unique random digits.
4.         numbers = list(range(10))
5.         random.shuffle(numbers)
6.         secretNum = ''
7.         for i in range(numDigits):
8.             secretNum += str(numbers[i])
9.         return secretNum
10.
11. def getClues(guess, secretNum):
12.         # Returns a string with the pico, fermi, bagels clues
    to the user.
13.         if guess == secretNum:
14.             return 'You got it!'
15.
16.         clue = []
17.
18.         for i in range(len(guess)):
19.             if guess[i] == secretNum[i]:
20.                 clue.append('Fermi')
21.             elif guess[i] in secretNum:
22.                 clue.append('Pico')
23.         if len(clue) == 0:
24.             return 'Bagels'
25.
26.         clue.sort()
27.         return ' '.join(clue)
28.
29. def isOnlyDigits(num):
30.         # Returns True if num is a string made up only of
    digits. Otherwise returns False.
31.         if num == '':
32.             return False
33.
34.         for i in num:
35.             if i not in '0 1 2 3 4 5 6 7 8 9'.split():
36.                 return False
37.
38.         return True
39.
40. def playAgain():
41.         # This function returns True if the player wants to
    play again, otherwise it returns False.
42.         print('Do you want to play again? (yes or no)')
43.         return input().lower().startswith('y')
44.
45. NUMDIGITS = 3
46. MAXGUESS = 10
47.
48. print('I am thinking of a %s-digit number. Try to guess
    what it is.' % (NUMDIGITS))
49. print('Here are some clues:')
50. print('When I say:    That means:')
```

```
51.  print('  Pico          One digit is correct but in the
     wrong position.')
52.  print('  Fermi         One digit is correct and in the
     right position.')
53.  print('  Bagels        No digit is correct.')
54.
55.  while True:
56.      secretNum = getSecretNum(NUMDIGITS)
57.      print('I have thought up a number. You have %s
     guesses to get it.' % (MAXGUESS))
58.
59.      numGuesses = 1
60.      while numGuesses <= MAXGUESS:
61.          guess = ''
62.          while len(guess) != NUMDIGITS or not isOnlyDigits
     (guess):
63.              print('Guess #%s: ' % (numGuesses))
64.              guess = input()
65.
66.          clue = getClues(guess, secretNum)
67.          print(clue)
68.          numGuesses += 1
69.
70.          if guess == secretNum:
71.              break
72.          if numGuesses > MAXGUESS:
73.              print('You ran out of guesses. The answer was
     %s.' % (secretNum))
74.
75.      if not playAgain():
76.          break
```

Designing the Program

Here is a flow chart for this program. The flow chart in Figure 11-1 describes the basic events of what happens in this game, and in what order they can happen.

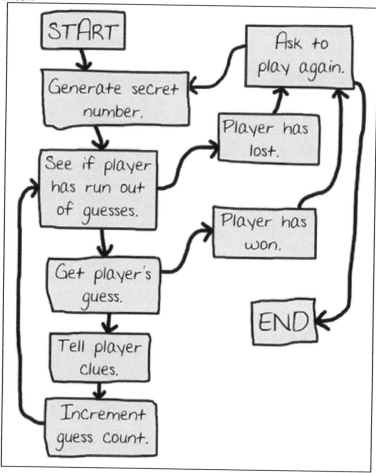

Figure 11-1: Flow chart for the Bagels game.

And here is the source code for our game. Start a new file and type the code in, and then save the file as *bagels.py*. We will design our game so that it is very easy to change the size of the secret number. It can be 3 digits or 5 digits or 30 digits. We will do this by using a constant variable named NUMDIGITS instead of hard-coding the integer 3 into our source code.

Hard-coding means writing a program in a way that it changing the behavior of the program requires changing a lot of the source code. For example, we could hard-code a name into a print() function call like: print('Hello, Albert'). Or we could use this line: print('Hello, ' + name) which would let us change the name that is printed by changing the name variable name the program is running.

How the Code Works: Lines 1 to 9

At the start of the program we import the random module and also create a function for generating a random secret number for the player to guess. The process of creating this number isn't hard, and also guarantees that it only has unique digits in it.

```
1. import random
```

This game imports the `random` module so we can use the module's random number functions.

Shuffling a Unique Set of Digits

```
2. def getSecretNum(numDigits):
3.     # Returns a string that is numDigits long, made up of
   unique random digits.
4.     numbers = list(range(10))
5.     random.shuffle(numbers)
```

Our first function is named `getSecretNum()`, which will generate the random secret number. Instead of having the code only produce 3-digit numbers, we use a parameter named `numDigits` to tell us how many digits the secret number should have. (This way, we can make the game produce secret numbers with four or six digits, for example, just by passing 4 or 6 as `numDigits`.)

You may have noticed that the return value of our call to `range()` was in turn passed to a function called `list()`. The `list()` function returns a list value of the value passed to it, much like the `str()` function returns a string form or the `int()` function returns an integer form. The reason we do this is because the `range()` function technically does not return a list but something called an iterator object. Iterators are a topic that you don't need to know at this point, so they aren't covered in this book.

Just about every time we use the `range()` function it is in a `for` loop. Iterators are fine to use in `for` loops (just like lists and strings are), but if we ever want to store a list of integers in a variable, be sure to convert the return value of `range()` to a list with the `list()` function first. (Just like we do on line 4.)

The `random.shuffle()` Function

First, we create a list of integers 0 to 9 by calling `list(range(10))` and store a reference to this list in numbers. Then we call a function in the random module named `shuffle()`. The only parameter to `random.shuffle()` is a reference to a list. The `shuffle()` function will randomly change the order of all the items in the list.

Notice that `random.shuffle()` does not return a value. It changes the list you pass it "in place" (just like our `makeMove()` function in the Tic Tac Toe chapter modified the list it was passed in place, rather than return a new list with the change). It would actually be incorrect to write `numbers = random.shuffle(numbers)`.

Try experimenting with the `random.shuffle()` function by entering the following code into the interactive shell:

```
>>> import random
>>> spam = list(range(10))
>>> print(spam)
[0, 1, 2, 3, 4, 5, 6, 7, 8, 9]
>>> random.shuffle(spam)
>>> print(spam)
[3, 0, 5, 9, 6, 8, 2, 4, 1, 7]
>>> random.shuffle(spam)
>>> print(spam)
[1, 2, 5, 9, 4, 7, 0, 3, 6, 8]
>>> random.shuffle(spam)
>>> print(spam)
[9, 8, 3, 5, 4, 7, 1, 2, 0, 6]
>>>
```

Every time you pass a list reference to random.shuffle(), afterwards the list it references will have all the same items but in a different order. The reason we do this is because we want the secret number to have unique values. The Bagels game is much more fun if you don't have duplicate numbers in the secret number, such as '244' or '333'.

Getting the Secret Number from the Shuffled Digits

```
6.      secretNum = ''
7.      for i in range(numDigits):
8.          secretNum += str(numbers[i])
9.      return secretNum
```

The secret number will be a string of the first three digits (because we'll pass 3 for the numDigits parameter) of the shuffled list of integers. For example, if the shuffled list is [9, 8, 3, 5, 4, 7, 1, 2, 0, 6] then we want the string returned by getSecretNum() to be '983'.

The secretNum variable starts out as a blank string. We then loop a number of times equal to the integer value in numDigits. On each iteration through the loop, a new integer is pulled from the shuffled list, converted to a string, and concatenated to the end of secretNum. So if numDigits is 3, the loop will iterate three times and three random digits will be concatenated as strings.

For example, if numbers refers to the list [9, 8, 3, 5, 4, 7, 1, 2, 0, 6], then on the first iteration, numbers[0] (that is, 9) will be passed to str(), which in turn returns '9' which is concatenated to the end of secretNum. On the second iteration, the same happens with numbers[1] (that is, 8) and on the third iteration the same happens with numbers[2] (that is, 3). The final value of secretNum that is returned is '983'.

You may notice that secretNum in this function is a string, not an integer. This may seem odd, but remember that our secret number could be something like '012'. If we stored this as an integer, it would be 12 (without the leading zero) which would make it harder to work with in our program.

Augmented Assignment Operators

The += operator on line 8 is new. This is one of the augmented assignment operators. Normally, if you wanted to add or concatenate a value to a variable, you would use code that looked like this:

```
spam = 42
spam = spam + 10
eggs = 'Hello '
eggs = eggs + 'world!'
```

After running the above code, spam would have the value 52 and eggs would have the value 'Hello world!'. The augmented assignment operators are a shortcut that frees you from retyping the variable name. The following code does the exact same thing as the above code:

```
spam = 42
spam += 10              # Like spam = spam + 10
eggs = 'Hello '
eggs += 'world!' # Like eggs = eggs + 'world!'
```

There are other augmented assignment operators. -= will subtract a value from an integer. *= will multiply the variable by a value. /= will divide a variable by a value. Notice that these augmented assignment operators do the same math operations as the -, *, and / operators. Augmented assignment operators are a neat shortcut.

How the Code Works: Lines 11 to 24

We also need a way of figuring out which clues to show to the player.

```
11. def getClues(guess, secretNum):
12.     # Returns a string with the pico, fermi, bagels clues
    to the user.
13.     if guess == secretNum:
14.         return 'You got it!'
```

The getClues() function will return a string with the fermi, pico, and bagels clues, depending on what it is passed for the guess and secretNum parameters. The most obvious and easiest step is to check if the guess is the exact same as the secret number. In that case, we can just return 'You got it!'.

```
16.      clue = []
17.
18.      for i in range(len(guess)):
19.          if guess[i] == secretNum[i]:
20.              clue.append('Fermi')
21.          elif guess[i] in secretNum:
22.              clue.append('Pico')
```

If the guess is not the exact same as the secret number, we need to figure out what clues to give the player. First we'll set up a list named clue, which we will add the strings 'Fermi' and 'Pico' as needed. We will combine the strings in this list into a single string to return.

We do this by looping through each possible index in guess and secretNum (we make sure both strings are the same size before we call getClues()). We will assume that guess and secretNum are the same size. As the value of i changes from 0 to 1 to 2, and so on, the if statement checks if the first, second, third, etc. letter of guess is the same as the number in the same position in secretNum. If so, we will add a string 'Fermi' to clue.

If that condition is False we will check if the number at the ith position in guess exists anywhere in secretNum. If this condition is True we know that the number is somewhere in the secret number but not in the same position. This is why we add the 'Pico' to clue.

```
23.      if len(clue) == 0:
24.          return 'Bagels'
```

If we go through the entire for loop above and never add anything to the clue list, then we know that there are no correct digits at all in guess. In this case, we should just return the string 'Bagels' as our only clue.

The `sort()` List Method

```
26.        clue.sort()
```

Lists have a method named `sort()` that rearranges the items in the list to be in alphanumerical order (this means in alphabetical order, but numbers are also in order). Try entering the following into the interactive shell:

```
>>> spam = [5, 'bat', 3, 1, 4, 'cat', 2, 'ape']
>>> spam.sort()
>>> spam
[1, 2, 3, 4, 5, 'ape', 'bat', 'cat']
```

Notice that the `sort()` method does not *return* a sorted list, but rather just sorts the list it is called on "in place". This is much like how the `reverse()` method works. You would never want to use this line of code: `return spam.sort()` because that would return the value `None` (which is what `sort()` returns). Instead you would want a separate line `spam.sort()` and then the line `return spam`.

The reason we want to sort the `clue` list is because we might return extra clues that we did not intend based on the order of the clues. If `clue` referenced the list `['Pico', 'Fermi', 'Pico']`, then that would tell us that the center digit of our guess is in the correct position. Since the other two clues are both Pico, then we know that all we have to do is swap the first and third digit and we have the secret number. But if the clues are always sorted in alphabetical order, the player can't be sure which number the Fermi clue refers to (which is what we want for this game).

The `join()` String Method

```
27.        return ' '.join(clue)
```

The `join()` string method returns a string of each item in the list argument joined together. The string that the method is called on (on line 27, this is a single space, `' '`) appears in between each item in the list. So the string that is returned on line 27 is each string in `clue` combined together with a single space in between each string.

For an example, enter the following into the interactive shell:

```
>>> 'x'.join(['hello', 'world'])
'helloxworld'
>>> 'ABCDEF'.join(['x', 'y', 'z'])
```

```
'xABCDEFyABCDEFz'
>>> ' '.join(['My', 'name', 'is', 'Zophie'])
'My name is Zophie'
```

The `join()` string method is sort of like the opposite of the `split()` string method. While `split()` returns a list from a split up string, `join()` returns a string from a combined list.

How the Code Works: Lines 29 to 53

We need a couple more functions for our game to use. The first is a function that will tell us if the guess that the player entered is a valid integer. Remember that the `input()` function returns a string of whatever the player typed in. If the player enters in anything but numbers for their guess, we want to ask the player again for a proper guess.

The second function is something we've seen before in previous games. We want a function that will ask the player if they want to play the game again and from the player's response, figure out if it was a Yes or No answer.

Checking if a String Only has Numbers

```
29. def isOnlyDigits(num):
30.     # Returns True if num is a string made up only of
    digits. Otherwise returns False.
31.     if num == '':
32.         return False
```

The `isOnlyDigits()` is a small function that will help us determine if the player entered a guess that was only made up of numbers. To do this, we will check each individual letter in the string named num and make sure it is a number.

Line 31 does a quick check to see if we were sent the blank string, and if so, we return `False`.

```
34.     for i in num:
35.         if i not in '0 1 2 3 4 5 6 7 8 9'.split():
36.             return False
37.
38.     return True
```

We use a `for` loop on the string num. The value of `i` will have a single character from the num string on each iteration. Inside the for-block, we check if `i` does not exist in the list returned by `'0 1 2 3 4 5 6 7 8 9'.split()`. If it doesn't, we know that there is a character in num that is something besides a number. In that case, we should return the value `False`.

If execution continues past the `for` loop, then we know that every character in `num` is a number because we did not return out of the function. In that case, we return the value `True`.

Finding out if the Player Wants to Play Again

```
40. def playAgain():
41.     # This function returns True if the player wants to
    play again, otherwise it returns False.
42.     print('Do you want to play again? (yes or no)')
43.     return input().lower().startswith('y')
```

The `playAgain()` function is the same one we used in Hangman and Tic Tac Toe. The long expression on line 43 will evaluate to either `True` or `False`. The return value from the call to the `input()` function is a string that has its `lower()` method called on it. The `lower()` method returns another string (the lowercase string) and that string has its `startswith()` method called on it, passing the argument `'y'`.

The Start of the Game

```
45. NUMDIGITS = 3
46. MAXGUESS = 10
47.
48. print('I am thinking of a %s-digit number. Try to guess
    what it is.' % (NUMDIGITS))
49. print('Here are some clues:')
50. print('When I say:    That means:')
51. print('  Pico         One digit is correct but in the
    wrong position.')
52. print('  Fermi        One digit is correct and in the
    right position.')
53. print('  Bagels       No digit is correct.')
```

This is the actual start of the program. Instead of hard-coding three digits as the size of the secret number, we will use the constant variable `NUMDIGITS`. And instead of hard-coding a maximum of ten guesses that the player can make, we will use the constant variable `MAXGUESS`. (This is because if we increase the number of digits the secret number has, we also might want to give the player more guesses. We put the variable names in all capitals to show they are meant to be constant.)

The `print()` function calls will tell the player the rules of the game and what the Pico, Fermi, and Bagels clues mean. Line 48's `print()` call has `% (NUMDIGITS)` added to the end and `%s` inside the string. This is a technique know as string interpolation.

String Interpolation

String interpolation is another shortcut, like augmented assignment operators. Normally, if you want to use the string values inside variables in another string, you have to use the + concatenation operator:

```
>>> name = 'Alice'
>>> event = 'party'
>>> where = 'the pool'
>>> day = 'Saturday'
>>> time = '6:00pm'
>>> print('Hello, ' + name + '. Will you go to the
' + event + ' at ' + where + ' this ' + day + ' at
' + time + '?')
Hello, Alice. Will you go to the party at the pool
this Saturday at 6:00pm?
>>>
```

As you can see, it can be very hard to type a line that concatenates several strings together. Instead, you can use **string interpolation**, which lets you put placeholders like %s (these placeholders are called **conversion specifiers**), and then put all the variable names at the end. Each %s is replaced with the value in the variable at the end of the line. For example, the following code does the same thing as the above code:

```
>>> name = 'Alice'
>>> event = 'party'
>>> where = 'the pool'
>>> day = 'Saturday'
>>> time = '6:00pm'
>>> print('Hello, %s. Will you go to the %s at %s
this %s at %s?' % (name, event, where, day, time))
Hello, Alice. Will you go to the party at the pool
this Saturday at 6:00pm?
>>>
```

String interpolation can make your code much easier to type and read, rather than using several + concatenation operators.

The final line has the print() call with a string with conversion specifiers, followed by the % sign, followed by a set of parentheses with the variables in them. The first variable name will be used for the first %s, the second variable with the second %s and so on. The Python interpreter will give you an error if you do not have the same number of %s conversion specifiers as you have variables.

Another benefit of using string interpolation instead of string concatenation is that interpolation works with any data type, not just strings. All values are automatically converted to the string data type. (This is what the s in %s stands for.) If you typed this code into the shell, you'd get an error:

```
>>> spam = 42
>>> print('Spam == ' + spam)
Traceback (most recent call last):
  File "<stdin>", line 1, in <module>
TypeError: Can't convert 'int' object to str
implicitly
>>>
```

You get this error because string concatenation can only combine two strings, and spam is an integer. You would have to remember to put str(spam) in there instead. But with string interpolation, you can have any data type. Try entering this into the shell:

```
>>> spam = 42
>>> print('Spam == %s' % (spam))
Spam == 42
>>>
```

As you can see, using string interpolation instead of string concatenation is much easier because you don't have to worry about the data type of the variable. Also, string interpolation can be done on any strings, not just strings used in print() function calls.

String interpolation is also known as **string formatting**.

How the Code Works: Lines 55 to 76

Now that the program has displayed the rules to Bagels to the player, the program will randomly create a secret number and then enter a loop where it repeatedly asks for the player's guesses until she has either correctly guessed the secret number, or has run out of guesses. After that, we will ask the player if she wants to play again.

Creating the Secret Number

```
55. while True:
56.     secretNum = getSecretNum(NUMDIGITS)
57.     print('I have thought up a number. You have %s
    guesses to get it.' % (MAXGUESS))
58.
59.     numGuesses = 1
```

```
60.         while numGuesses <= MAXGUESS:
```

We start with a `while` loop that has a condition of `True`, meaning it will loop forever until we execute a `break` statement. Inside the infinite loop, we get a secret number from our `getSecretNum()` function (passing it `NUMDIGITS` to tell how many digits we want the secret number to have) and assign it to `secretNum`. Remember that `secretNum` is a string, not an integer.

We tell the player how many digits is in our secret number by using string interpolation instead of string concatenation. We set a variable `numGuesses` to 1, to denote that this is the first guess. Then we enter a new `while` loop which will keep looping as long as `numGuesses` is less than or equal to `MAXGUESS`.

Getting the Player's Guess

Notice that this second `while` loop on line 60 is inside another `while` loop that started on line 55. Whenever we have these loops-inside-loops, we call them **nested loops**. You should know that any `break` or `continue` statements will only `break` or `continue` out of the innermost loop, and not any of the outer loops.

```
61.             guess = ''
62.             while len(guess) != NUMDIGITS or not isOnlyDigits
    (guess):
63.                 print('Guess #%s: ' % (numGuesses))
64.                 guess = input()
```

The `guess` variable will hold the player's guess. We will keep looping and asking the player for a guess until the player enters a guess that has the same number of digits as the secret number and is made up only of digits. This is what the `while` loop that starts on line 62 is for. We set `guess` as the blank string on line 61 so that the `while` loop's condition is `False` the first time, ensuring that we enter the loop at least once.

Getting the Clues for the Player's Guess

```
66.             clue = getClues(guess, secretNum)
67.             print(clue)
68.             numGuesses += 1
```

After execution gets past the `while` loop on line 62, we know that `guess` contains a valid guess. We pass this and the secret number in `secretNum` to our `getClues()` function. It returns a string that contains our clues, which we will display to the player. We then increment `numGuesses` by 1 using the augmented assignment operator for addition.

Checking if the Player Won or Lost

```
70.        if guess == secretNum:
71.            break
72.        if numGuesses > MAXGUESS:
73.            print('You ran out of guesses. The answer was
       %s.' % (secretNum))
```

If `guess` is the same value as `secretNum`, then we know the player has correctly guessed the secret number and we can break out of this loop (the `while` loop that was started on line 60). If not, then execution continues to line 72, where we check to see if the player ran out of guesses. If so, then we tell the player that they have lost and what the secret number was. We know that the condition for the `while` loop on line 55 will be `False`, so there is no need for a `break` statement.

At this point, execution jumps back to the `while` loop on line 60 where we let the player have another guess. If the player ran out of guesses (or we broke out of the loop with the `break` statement on line 71), then execution would proceed past the loop and to line 75.

Asking the Player to Play Again

```
75.    if not playAgain():
76.        break
```

After leaving the `while` loop that starts on line 60, we ask the player if want to play again by calling our `playAgain()` function. If `playAgain()` returns `False`, then we should break out of the `while` loop that was started on line 55. Since there is no more code after this loop, the program terminates.

If `playAgain()` returned `True`, then we would not execute the `break` statement and execution would jump back to line 55. A new secret number would be generated so that the player can play a new game.

Summary: Getting Good at Bagels

Bagels is a fairly simple game to program but can be difficult to win at. But if you keep playing, you will eventually discover better ways to guess and make use of the clues the game gives you.

This chapter introduced a few new functions and methods (`random.shuffle()`, `sort()`, and `join()`), along with a couple handy shortcuts. Using the augmented assignment operators involve less typing when you want to change a variable's relative value (such as in `spam = spam + 1`, which can be shortend to `spam += 1`). String interpolation can make your code much more readable by placing `%s` (called a conversion specifier) inside the string instead of using many string concatenation operations.

The `join()` string method is passed a list of strings that will be concatenated together, with the original associated string in between them. For example, `'X'.join( ['hello', 'world', 'yay'] )` will evaluate to the string, `'helloXworldXyay'`.

The `sort()` list method will rearrange the items in the list to be in alphabetical order.

The `append()` list method will add a value to the end of the associated list. If `spam` contains the list `['a', 'b', 'c']`, then calling `spam.append('d')` will change the list in `spam` to be `['a', 'b', 'c', 'd']`.

The next chapter is not about programming directly, but will be necessary for the games we want to create in the later chapters of this book. We will learn about the math concepts of Cartesian coordinates and negative numbers. These will be used in the Sonar, Reversi, and Dodger games, but Cartesian coordinates and negative numbers are used in almost all games (especially graphical games). If you already know about these concepts, give the next chapter a brief read anyway just to freshen up. Let's dive in!

Chapter 12
Cartesian Coordinates

Topics Covered In This Chapter:

- Cartesian coordinate systems.
- The X-axis and Y-axis.
- The Commutative Property of Addition.
- Absolute values and the abs() function.

This chapter does not introduce a new game, but instead goes over some simple mathematical concepts that we will use in the rest of the games in this book.

When you look at 2D games (such as Tetris or old Super Nintendo or Sega Genesis games) you can see that most of the graphics on the screen can move left or right (the first dimension) and up or down (the second dimension, hence 2D). In order for us to create games that have objects moving around two dimensions (such as the two dimensional computer screen), we need a system that can translate a place on the screen to integers that our program can deal with.

This is where Cartesian coordinate systems come in. The coordinates can point to a very specific point on the screen so that our program can keep track of different areas on the screen.

Negative numbers are often used with Cartesian coordinate systems as well. The second half of this chapter will explain how we can do math with negative numbers.

You may already know about Cartesian coordinate systems and negative numbers from math class. In that case, you can just give this chapter a quick read anyway to refresh yourself.

Grids and Cartesian Coordinates

A problem in many games is how to talk about exact points on the board. A common way of solving this is by marking each individual row and column on a board with a letter and a number. Figure 12-1 is a chess board that has each row and each column marked.

In chess, the knight piece looks like a horse head. The white knight is located at the point e, 6 and the black knight is located at point a, 4. We can also see that every space on row 7 and every space in column c is empty.

A grid with labeled rows and columns like the chess board is a Cartesian coordinate system. By using a row label and column label, we can give a coordinate that is for one and only one space on the board. This can

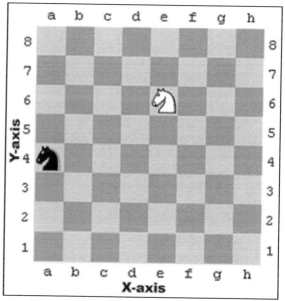

Figure 12-1: A sample chessboard with a black knight at a, 4 and a white knight at e, 6.

really help us describe to a computer the exact location we want. If you have learned about Cartesian coordinate systems in math class, you may know that usually we have numbers for both the rows and columns. This is handy, because otherwise after the 26th column we would run out of letters. That board would look like Figure 12-2.

The numbers going left and right that describe the columns are part of the **X-axis**. The numbers going up and down that describe the rows are part of the **Y-axis**. When we describe coordinates, we always say the X-coordinate first, followed by the Y-coordinate. That means the white knight in the above picture is located at the coordinate 5, 6 (and not 6, 5). The black knight is located at the coordinate 1, 4 (not to be confused with 4, 1).

Notice that for the black knight to move to the white knight's position, the black knight must move up two spaces, and then to the right by four spaces. (Or move right four spaces and then move up two spaces.) But we don't need to look at the board to figure this out. If we know the white knight is located at 5, 6 and the black knight is located

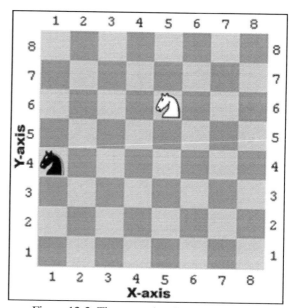

Figure 12-2: The same chessboard but with numeric coordinates for both rows and columns.

at 1, 4, then we can just use subtraction to figure out this information.

Subtract the black knight's X-coordinate and white knight's X-coordinate: 5 - 1 = 4. That means the black knight has to move along the X-axis by four spaces.

Subtract the black knight's Y-coordinate and white knight's Y-coordinate: 6 - 4 = 2. That means the black knight has to move along the Y-axis by two spaces.

Negative Numbers

Another concept that Cartesian coordinates use is negative numbers. **Negative numbers** are numbers that are smaller than zero. We put a minus sign in front of a number to show that it is a negative number. -1 is smaller than 0. And -2 is smaller than -1. And -3 is smaller than -2. If you think of regular numbers (called **positive numbers**) as starting from 1 and increasing, you can think of negative numbers as starting from -1 and decreasing. 0 itself is not positive or negative. In this picture, you can see the positive numbers increasing to the right and the negative numbers decreasing to the left:

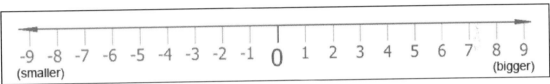

Figure 12-3: A number line.

The number line is really useful for doing subtraction and addition with negative numbers. The expression 4 + 3 can be thought of as the white knight starting at position 4 and moving 3 spaces over to the right (addition means increasing, which is in the right direction).

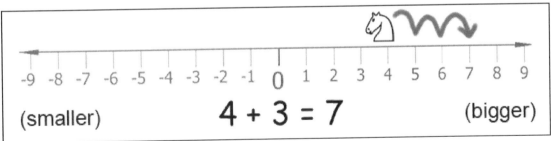

Figure 12-4: Moving the white knight to the right adds to the coordinate.

As you can see, the white knight ends up at position 7. This makes sense, because 4 + 3 is 7.

Subtraction can be done by moving the white knight to the left. Subtraction means decreasing, which is in the left direction. 4 - 6 would be the white knight starting at position 4 and moving 6 spaces to the left, like in Figure 12-5:

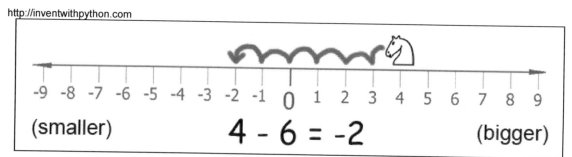

Figure 12-5: Moving the white knight to the left subtracts from the coordinate.

The white knight ends up at position -2. That means 4 - 6 equals -2.

If we add or subtract a negative number, the white knight would move in the *opposite* direction. If you add a negative number, the knight moves to the *left*. If you subtract a negative number, the knight moves to the *right*. The expression -6 - -4 would be equal to -2. The knight starts at -6 and moves to the *right* by 4 spaces. Notice that -6 - -4 has the same answer as -6 + 4.

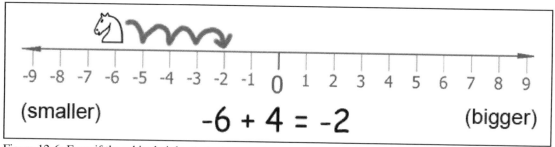

Figure 12-6: Even if the white knight starts at a negative coordinate, moving right still adds to the coordinate.

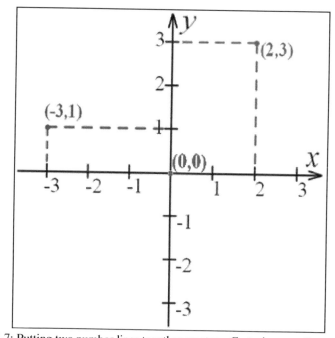

Figure 12-7: Putting two number lines together creates a Cartesian coordinate system.

The number line is the same as the X-axis. If we made the number line go up and down instead of left and right, it would model the Y-axis. Adding a positive number (or subtracting a negative number) would move the knight up the number line, and subtracting a positive number (or adding a negative number) would move the knight down. When we put these two number lines together, we have a Cartesian coordinate system like in Figure 12-7. The 0, 0 coordinate has a special name: the **origin**.

Math Tricks

Subtracting negative numbers or adding negative numbers seems easy when you have a number line in front of you, but it can be easy when you only have the numbers too. Here are three tricks you can do to make evaluating these expressions by yourself easier to do.

Trick 1: "A Minus Eats the Plus Sign on its Left"

The first is if you are adding a negative number, for example; 4 + -2. The first trick is "a minus eats the plus sign on its left". When you see a minus sign with a plus sign on the left, you can replace the plus sign with a minus sign. The answer is still the same, because adding a negative value is the same as subtracting a positive value. 4 + -2 and 4 - 2 both evaluate to 2.

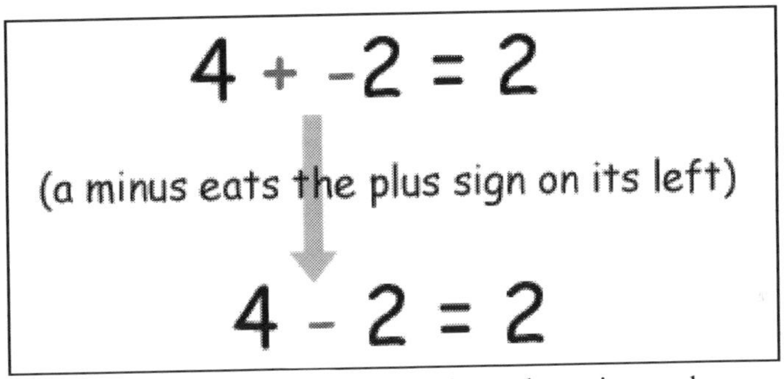

$$4 + -2 = 2$$

(a minus eats the plus sign on its left)

$$4 - 2 = 2$$

Figure 12-8: Trick 1 - Adding a positive and negative number.

Trick 2: "Two Minuses Combine Into a Plus"

The second trick is if you are subtracting a negative number, for example, 4 - -2. The second trick is "two minuses combine into a plus". When you see the two minus signs next to each other without a number in between them, they can combine into a plus sign. The answer is still the same, because subtracting a negative value is the same as adding a positive value.

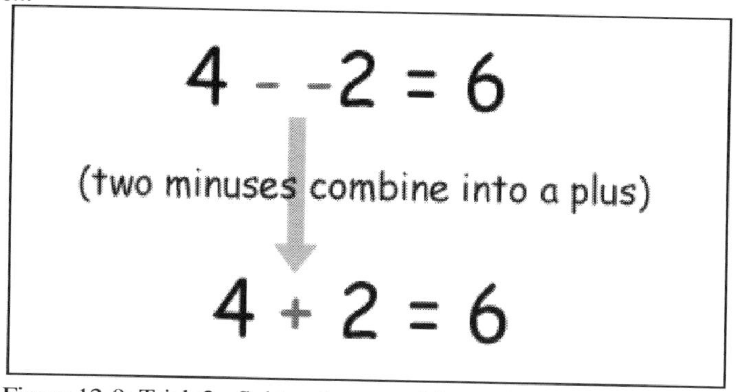

$$4 - -2 = 6$$

(two minuses combine into a plus)

$$4 + 2 = 6$$

Figure 12-9: Trick 2 - Subtracting a positive and negative number.

Trick 3: The Commutative Property of Addition

A third trick is to remember that when you add two numbers like 6 and 4, it doesn't matter what order they are in. (This is called the **commutative property** of addition.) That means that 6 + 4 and 4 + 6 both equal the same value, 10. If you count the boxes in the figure below, you can see that it doesn't matter what order you have the numbers for addition.

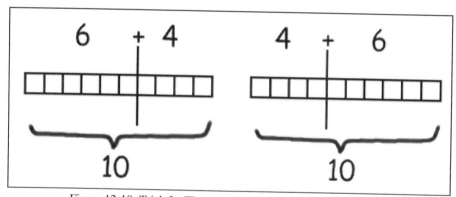

Figure 12-10: Trick 3 - The commutative property of addition.

Say you are adding a negative number and a positive number, like -6 + 8. Because you are adding numbers, you can swap the order of the numbers without changing the answer. -6 + 8 is the same as 8 + -6. But when you look at 8 + -6, you see that the minus sign can eat the plus sign to its left, and the problem becomes 8 - 6 = 2. But this means that -6 + 8 is also 2! We've rearranged the problem to have the same answer, but made it easier for us to solve without using a calculator or the computer.

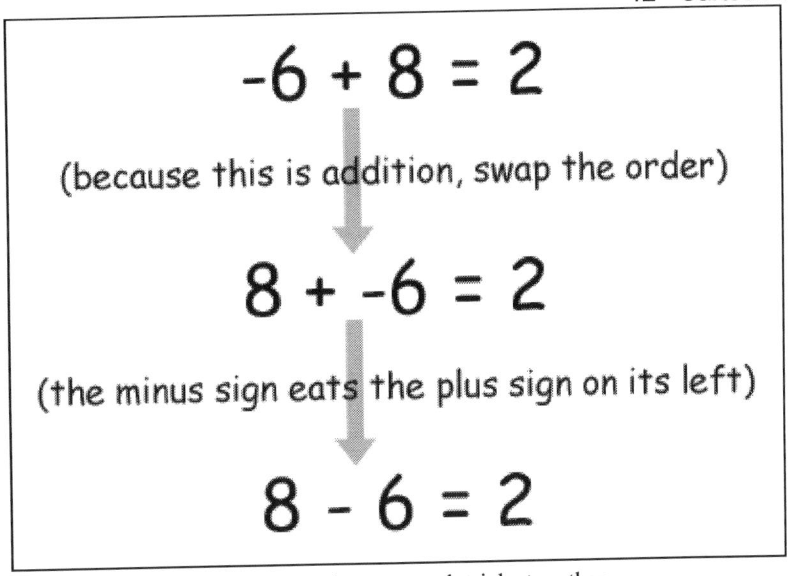

$$-6 + 8 = 2$$

(because this is addition, swap the order)

$$8 + -6 = 2$$

(the minus sign eats the plus sign on its left)

$$8 - 6 = 2$$

Figure 12-11: Using our math tricks together.

Of course, you can always use the interactive shell as a calculator to evaluate these expressions. It is still very useful to know the above three tricks when adding or subtracting negative numbers. After all, you won't always be in front of a computer with Python all the time!

```
>>> 4 + -2
2
>>> -4 + 2
-2
>>> -4 + -2
-6
>>> 4 - -2
6
>>> -4 - 2
-6
>>> -4 - -2
-2
>>>
```

Absolute Values and the `abs()` Function

The **absolute value** of a number is the number without the negative sign in front of it. This means that positive numbers do not change, but negative numbers become positive. For example, the absolute value of -4 is 4. The absolute value of -7 is 7. The absolute value of 5 (which is positive) is just 5.

We can find how far away two things on a number line are from each other by taking the absolute value of their difference. Imagine that the white knight is at position 4 and the black knight is at position -2. To find out the distance between them, you would find the difference by subtracting their positions and taking the absolute value of that number.

It works no matter what the order of the numbers is. -2 - 4 (that is, negative two minus four) is -6, and the absolute value of -6 is 6. However, 4 - -2 (that is, four minus negative two) is 6, and the absolute value of 6 is 6. Using the absolute value of the difference is a good way of finding the distance between two points on a number line (or axis).

The abs() function can be used to return the absolute value of an integer. The abs() function is a built-in function, so you do not need to import any modules to use it. Pass it an integer or float value and it will return the absolute value:

```
>>> abs(-5)
5
>>> abs(42)
42
>>> abs(-10.5)
10.5
```

Coordinate System of a Computer Monitor

It is common that computer monitors use a coordinate system that has the origin (0, 0) at the top left corner of the screen, which increases going down and to the right. There are no negative coordinates. This is because text is printed starting at the top left, and is printed going to the right and downwards. Most computer graphics use this coordinate system, and we will use it in our games. Also it is common to assume that monitors can display 80 text characters per row and 25 text characters per column (look at Figure 12-12). This used to be the maximum screen size that monitors could support. While today's monitors can usually display much more text, we will not assume that the user's screen is bigger than 80 by 25.

Figure 12-12: The Cartesian coordinate system on a computer monitor.

Summary: Using this Math in Games

This hasn't been too much math to learn for programming. In fact, most programming does not require understanding a lot of math. Up until this chapter, we have been getting by on simple addition and multiplication.

Cartesian coordinate systems are needed to describe exactly where in a two dimensional area a certain position is. Coordinates are made up of two numbers: the X-coordinate and the Y-coordinate. The X-axis runs left and right and the Y-axis runs up and down. On a computer screen (and in most computer programming), the X-axis starts at 0 at the left side and increases on the way to the right. The Y-axis starts at 0 on the top of the screen and increases on the way down.

The three tricks we learned in this chapter make it very easy to add positive and negative integers. The first trick is that a minus sign will eat the plus sign on its left. The second trick is that two minuses next to each other will combine into a plus sign. And the third trick is that you can swap the position of the numbers you are adding. This is called the commutative property of addition.

For the rest of the book, we will use the concepts we learned in this chapter in our games because they have two dimensional areas in them. All graphical games require understanding how Cartesian coordinates work.

Chapter 13
Sonar Treasure Hunt

Topics Covered In This Chapter:

- Data structures.
- The `remove()` list method.
- The `isdigit()` string method.
- The `sys.exit()` function.

The game in this chapter only introduces a couple new helpful methods that come with Python, the `remove()` list method and the `isdigit()` string method. But this is the first program which will make use of Cartesian coordinates and the mathematical concepts we learned in chapter 11. This program will also use make use of data structures (which is really just a fancy way of saying variables that contain lists of lists.) As our games become more complicated, we will need to store our data in well-organized ways.

Sonar is a technology that ships use to locate objects under the sea. In this chapter's game, the player places sonar devices at various places in the ocean to locate sunken treasure chests. The sonar devices (in our game) can tell the player how far away a treasure chest is from the sonar device, but not in what direction. But by placing multiple sonar devices down, the player can figure out where exactly the treasure chest is.

There are three chests to collect, but the player has only sixteen sonar devices to use to find them. Imagine that we could not see the treasure chest in the following picture. Because each sonar device can only find the distance but not direction, the possible places the treasure could be is anywhere in a ring around the sonar device (see Figure 13-1).

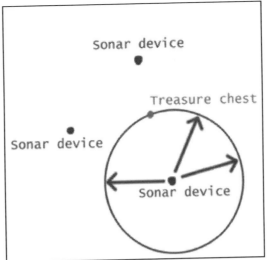

Figure 13-1: The first sonar device shows a ring
of possible places the treasure could be located.

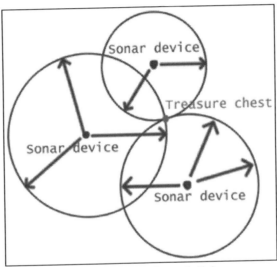

Figure 13-2: Combining the rings of all three sonar
devices shows only one possible place for the treasure.

But if we have multiple sonar devices working together, we can narrow it down to an
exact place where all the rings intersect each other. (See Figure 13-2)

Sample Run

```
S O N A R !

Would you like to view the instructions? (yes/no)
no
                  1         2         3         4         5
        01234567890123456789012345678901234567890123456789
  0  `~~~`~~~`~`~ ~~~~`~`~`~~~~`~`~~~~`~`~`~~`~``~`~``~`~~~~`` 0
  1  ~`~~~`~``~~~~`~`~ ~`~~~~`~`~~~~`~``~~~~~`~``~`~~`~`~~~~`  1
  2  `~`~``~`~~~`~`~~~~`~`~~`~`~`~``~~~~~~~`~~`~``~~~~~``~~`~``` 2
```

213

```
 3 `~`~~~`~`~`~`~~`~`~`~`~`~`~~~~`~`~~~`~`~`~`~`~`~~~~``~`~       3
 4 ``~`~`~`~`~~`~`~`~`~`~`~~`~`~`~`~`~`~~`~`~`~`~~``~`~``       4
 5 ~~~`~`~`~`~`~`~`~`~`~`~`~~`~`~`~`~`~`~`~`~`~`~`~`~`       5
 6 `~~`~`~`~`~`~`~`~`~`~`~`~`~`~`~`~`~`~`~`~`~`~`~~~      6
 7 ``~`~`~`~`~`~`~`~`~`~`~`~`~`~`~`~`~`~`~`~`~`~~~     7
 8 `~`~`~`~`~`~`~`~`~`~`~`~`~`~`~`~`~`~`~`~`~~~`     8
 9 ~`~`~`~`~`~`~`~`~`~`~`~`~`~`~`~`~`~`~`~`~~~`      9
10 ``~`~`~`~`~`~`~`~`~`~`~`~`~`~`~`~`~`~`~`~~~`~ 10
11 ``~`~`~`~`~`~`~`~`~`~`~`~`~`~`~`~`~`~`~`~`~`~ 11
12 ~~~`~`~`~`~`~`~`~`~`~`~`~`~`~`~`~`~`~`~`~~~~`~ 12
13 `~~`~`~`~`~`~`~`~`~`~`~`~`~~~~~~`~`~`~``~`~~~~` 13
14 ``~~`~`~`~`~`~`~`~`~`~`~`~~~~`~`~`~`~~~`````~ 14

   012345678901234567890123456789012345678901234567890123456789
            1         2         3         4         5
You have 16 sonar devices left. 3 treasure chests remaining.
Where do you want to drop the next sonar device? (0-59 0-14) (or
type quit)
```
10 10
```
            1         2         3         4         5
   012345678901234567890123456789012345678901234567890123456789

 0 `~~~`~~~`~`~`~~`~~~~`~~~~`~``~`~`~`~~`~`~`~`~`~~~`~~~`` 0
 1 ~`~`~`~~`~~~`~`~`~`~`~`~~~~`~~~~~`~`~`~`~`~`~`~`~`~ 1
 2 `~`~`~`~`~`~`~`~~~~~~`~`~`~~~~`~`~`~`~`~`~`~`~~ 2
 3 `~`~`~`~`~`~`~`~`~`~`~`~`~`~`~`~`~`~`~`~`~`~`~`~ 3
 4 ~`~`~`~`~`~`~`~`~`~`~`~`~`~`~`~`~`~`~`~`~`~`~`~ 4
 5 ~~`~`~`~`~`~`~`~`~`~`~`~`~`~`~`~`~`~`~`~`~`~~~` 5
 6 `~`~`~`~`~`~`~`~`~`~~~~`~`~`~`~`~`~`~`~`~`~~~~ 6
 7 `~`~`~`~`~`~`~`~`~~`~`~`~`~`~`~`~`~`~`~`~~~~ 7
 8 `~`~`~`~`~`~`~`~`~`~`~`~`~`~`~`~`~`~`~`~~~` 8
 9 ~`~`~`~`~`~`~`~`~`~`~`~`~`~`~`~`~`~`~`~`~ 9
10 ```~`~`~`~`~5`~`~`~`~`~`~`~`~`~`~`~`~~~ 10
11 ``~`~`~`~`~`~`~`~`~`~`~`~`~`~`~`~`~`~`` 11
12 ~~~`~`~`~`~`~`~`~`~`~~~~`~`~`~`~`~`~`~`~ 12
13 `~~`~`~`~`~`~`~`~`~`~`~~~~~~`~`~`~`~`~~~~ 13
14 `~~`~`~`~`~`~`~`~`~~`~`~`~`~`~`~`~~~`~`~`~`~~ 14

   012345678901234567890123456789012345678901234567890123456789
            1         2         3         4         5
Treasure detected at a distance of 5 from the sonar device.
You have 15 sonar devices left. 3 treasure chests remaining.
Where do you want to drop the next sonar device? (0-59 0-14) (or
type quit)
```
15 6
```
            1         2         3         4         5
   012345678901234567890123456789012345678901234567890123456789

 0 `~~~`~~~`~`~~`~~`~~`~~~~`~`~~~`~`~~`~`~~~~`` 0
 1 ~`~~~`~~~~`~`~`~`~`~~~`~`~~~~`~`~~~~ 1
 2 `~`~`~`~`~`~`~`~`~~~~~~`~`~`~`~`~`~`~ 2
 3 `~`~`~`~`~`~`~`~`~`~`~`~`~`~`~`~`~`~ 3
 4 `~`~`~`~`~`~`~`~`~`~`~`~`~`~`~`~`~`~ 4
 5 ~~`~`~`~`~`~`~`~`~`~`~`~`~`~`~`~`~~~~ 5
 6 `~~`~``~`~~~~`~4~~~`~`~``~`~`~`~``~`` 6
 7 `~`~`~`~`~`~`~`~`~`~`~`~`~`~`~`~~~ 7
 8 `~`~`~`~`~`~`~`~`~`~`~`~`~`~`~~~~` 8
 9 ~`~`~`~`~`~`~`~`~`~`~`~`~`~`~~~`~` 9
10 ``~`~``~`~`~5`~`~`~`~`~`~`~`~`~~~ 10
11 ```~`~`~`~`~`~`~`~`~`~`~`~`~`~~~~ 11
12 ~~~`~`~`~`~`~`~`~`~`~`~`~`~`~`~~~ 12
13 `~`~`~`~`~`~`~`~`~`~`~`~`~`~`~~~~~ 13
14 `~~`~`~`~`~`~`~`~~`~`~`~`~`~`~`~~~~ 14

```

```
            0123456789012345678901234567890123456789012345678901234567 89
                     1         2         3         4         5
Treasure detected at a distance of 4 from the sonar device.
You have 14 sonar devices left. 3 treasure chests remaining.
Where do you want to drop the next sonar device? (0-59 0-14) (or
type quit)
```
15 10
```
                     1         2         3         4         5
            0123456789012345678901234567890123456789012345678901234567 89

   0  `~~~`~~~`~`~~`~~~~` ~`~~~~~`~`~~~`~`~`~~~`~`~~``~`~~~``   0
   1  ~`~~~``~~`~~~`~~`~`~~`~`~~~`~`~~~`~`~`~~`~~`~~~`            1
   2  `~~~`~~`~~`~~~`~~~~~`~`~~`~~~~`~`~~~`~~`~~`~~``             2
   3  ``~~``~~`~~~`~`~~~`~~~~~`~`~~~`~~`~~~~`~`~~~~`              3
   4  ``~``~~`~~~`~~~`~`~~~`~~`~~~`~~`~~~`~`~~`~`~~~`             4
   5  ~~`~~`~`~~~`~`~~`~~~`~`~~~`~`~~`~~`~~`~`~~`~`~`~            5
   6  ``~~`~~~`~~~~~O~~~`~~`~~~`~`~~`~~~`~~`~~~`~`~~`~            6
   7  `~`~~`~~~`~~`~~~`~`~~~`~`~~`~~~`~~~`~~`~`~~`~~`~            7
   8  `~`~~~`~`~~~`~~`~~~`~~`~~~`~`~~`~~~`~`~`~~~``~`             8
   9  ~`~`~~`~`~`~~`~`~`~~`~~`~~`~~`~~`~~`~`~~~`~`~` 10
   10 ``~`~``~O~`~`O~~`~~`~~`~`~~`~~`~~~`~~~`~`~`` 11
   11 `~`~`~`~~~`~~`~~`~`~`~~`~~`~`~~`~~`~~`~`~~`~`~ 12
   12 ~~~`~`~~`~~~~~`~~~~`~`~`~~`~`~`~~`~`~``~`~~~~ 13
   13 `~~`~~`~`~~`~~`~~`~~`~~`~~`~~`~~`~~~`~~`~~~`~ 14
   14 `~~`~`~`~`~~~`~`~~`~`~~`~`~~`~`~~`~~~`~`~~``
```
```
            0123456789012345678901234567890123456789012345678901234567 89
                     1         2         3         4         5
You have found a sunken treasure chest!
You have 13 sonar devices left. 2 treasure chests remaining.
Where do you want to drop the next sonar device? (0-59 0-14) (or
type quit)
```

...skipped over for brevity....

```
                     1         2         3         4         5
            0123456789012345678901234567890123456789012345678901234567 89

   0  `~~~`~~~`~`~~`~~~~`~``~~~~`~`~~~`~`~`~~~`~`~~``  0
   1  ~`~~~``~`~~~~`~`~~`~`~`~~`~~~`~~`~~~~`~`~~`~~~`  1
   2  `~`~`~``~~~`~`~~`~``~~`~~~O~~~O~~`~`~~`~`~~~~~`~~~`~`~`~~`  2
   3  ``~3~~``8~`~`~`~`~~`~~`~`~~~`O~`~~~`~~~~`~  3
   4  `~~`~~`~``~`~~`~~``~`~~O`~~O``~~`~~~`~~~~`  4
   5  ~~``~~~`~~`~~`~``~`~~`~~`~~`~~~`~~`~~`~~~~  5
   6  `~`~~`~``~~~~O~~~`~~~~`~~`~~`~~`O`~~`~~~  6
   7  `~~`~~`~~`~~`~~`~~~`~`~~~`~`~`~~``~~`~~`~~  7
   8  `~~`~~`~~`~~`~~`~~~`~~~`~`~O`~``O`~`~~`~~~~  8
   9  ~`~`~~`~`~`~~`~`~O~`~~~~`~``~`~~`~~`~~~` 10
   10 ``~`~`~`~O~`~O~~`~~`~~~`~~`~~`~~`~~~`~~~~ 11
   11 `~`~`~`~~~`~~`~~`~`~`~~`~~`~`~~`~~`~`~`~~`~`~ 12
   12 ~~~`~`~~`~~~~~`~~~~`~`~`~~`~`~`~~`~`~``~`~~~~ 13
   13 `~~`~~`~`~~`~~`~~`~~`~~`~~`~~`~~`~~~`~~`~~~`~ 14
   14 `~~`~`~`~`~~~`~`~~`~`~~`~`~~`~`~~`~~~`~`~~``
```
```
            0123456789012345678901234567890123456789012345678901234567 89
                     1         2         3         4         5
Treasure detected at a distance of 4 from the sonar device.
We've run out of sonar devices! Now we have to turn the ship around
and head
for home with treasure chests still out there! Game over.
```

215

```
        The remaining chests were here:
        0, 4
   Do you want to play again? (yes or no)
   no
```

Sonar's Source Code

Knowing about Cartesian coordinates, number lines, negative numbers, and absolute values will help us out with our Sonar game. If you do not think you understand these concepts, go back to chapter 12. Below is the source code for the game. Type it into a new file, then save the file as *sonar.py* and run it by pressing the F5 key. You do not need to understand the code to type it in or play the game, the source code will be explained later.

Also, you can download the source code from the book's website at the URL *http://inventwithpython.com/chapter13*.

---

sonar.py

This code can be downloaded from *http://inventwithpython.com/sonar.py*
If you get errors after typing this code in, compare it to the book's code with the online diff tool at *http://inventwithpython.com/diff* or email the author at al@inventwithpython.com

```python
 1. # Sonar
 2.
 3. import random
 4. import sys
 5.
 6. def drawBoard(board):
 7.     # Draw the board data structure.
 8.
 9.     hline = '    ' # initial space for the numbers down
    the left side of the board
10.     for i in range(1, 6):
11.         hline += (' ' * 9) + str(i)
12.
13.     # print the numbers across the top
14.     print(hline)
15.     print('  ' + ('0123456789' * 6))
16.     print()
17.
18.     # print each of the 15 rows
19.     for i in range(15):
20.         # single-digit numbers need to be padded with an
    extra space
21.         if i < 10:
22.             extraSpace = ' '
23.         else:
24.             extraSpace = ''
25.         print('%s%s %s %s' % (extraSpace, i, getRow
    (board, i), i))
26.
```

```
27.        # print the numbers across the bottom
28.        print()
29.        print('   ' + ('0123456789' * 6))
30.        print(hline)
31.
32.
33. def getRow(board, row):
34.        # Return a string from the board data structure at a
    certain row.
35.        boardRow = ''
36.        for i in range(60):
37.            boardRow += board[i][row]
38.        return boardRow
39.
40. def getNewBoard():
41.        # Create a new 60x15 board data structure.
42.        board = []
43.        for x in range(60): # the main list is a list of 60
    lists
44.            board.append([])
45.            for y in range(15): # each list in the main list
    has 15 single-character strings
46.                # use different characters for the ocean to
    make it more readable.
47.                if random.randint(0, 1) == 0:
48.                    board[x].append('~')
49.                else:
50.                    board[x].append('`')
51.        return board
52.
53. def getRandomChests(numChests):
54.        # Create a list of chest data structures (two-item
    lists of x, y int coordinates)
55.        chests = []
56.        for i in range(numChests):
57.            chests.append([random.randint(0, 59),
    random.randint(0, 14)])
58.        return chests
59.
60. def isValidMove(x, y):
61.        # Return True if the coordinates are on the board,
    otherwise False.
62.        return x >= 0 and x <= 59 and y >= 0 and y <= 14
63.
64. def makeMove(board, chests, x, y):
65.        # Change the board data structure with a sonar device
    character. Remove treasure chests
66.        # from the chests list as they are found. Return
    False if this is an invalid move.
67.        # Otherwise, return the string of the result of this
    move.
68.        if not isValidMove(x, y):
69.            return False
70.
```

```
71.          smallestDistance = 100 # any chest will be closer
       than 100.
72.      for cx, cy in chests:
73.          if abs(cx - x) > abs(cy - y):
74.              distance = abs(cx - x)
75.          else:
76.              distance = abs(cy - y)
77.
78.          if distance < smallestDistance: # we want the
       closest treasure chest.
79.              smallestDistance = distance
80.
81.      if smallestDistance == 0:
82.          # xy is directly on a treasure chest!
83.          chests.remove([x, y])
84.          return 'You have found a sunken treasure chest!'
85.      else:
86.          if smallestDistance < 10:
87.              board[x][y] = str(smallestDistance)
88.              return 'Treasure detected at a distance of %s
       from the sonar device.' % (smallestDistance)
89.          else:
90.              board[x][y] = 'O'
91.              return 'Sonar did not detect anything. All
       treasure chests out of range.'
92.
93.
94. def enterPlayerMove():
95.      # Let the player type in her move. Return a two-item
       list of int xy coordinates.
96.      print('Where do you want to drop the next sonar
       device? (0-59 0-14) (or type quit)')
97.      while True:
98.          move = input()
99.          if move.lower() == 'quit':
100.             print('Thanks for playing!')
101.             sys.exit()
102.
103.         move = move.split()
104.         if len(move) == 2 and move[0].isdigit() and move
    [1].isdigit() and isValidMove(int(move[0]), int(move
    [1])):
105.             return [int(move[0]), int(move[1])]
106.         print('Enter a number from 0 to 59, a space, then
    a number from 0 to 14.')
107.
108.
109. def playAgain():
110.     # This function returns True if the player wants to
    play again, otherwise it returns False.
111.     print('Do you want to play again? (yes or no)')
112.     return input().lower().startswith('y')
113.
114.
```

```
115. def showInstructions():
116.     print('''Instructions:
117. You are the captain of the Simon, a treasure-hunting
        ship. Your current mission
118. is to find the three sunken treasure chests that are
        lurking in the part of the
119. ocean you are in and collect them.
120.
121. To play, enter the coordinates of the point in the ocean
        you wish to drop a
122. sonar device. The sonar can find out how far away the
        closest chest is to it.
123. For example, the d below marks where the device was
        dropped, and the 2's
124. represent distances of 2 away from the device. The 4's
        represent
125. distances of 4 away from the device.
126.
127.     444444444
128.     4       4
129.     4 22222 4
130.     4 2   2 4
131.     4 2 d 2 4
132.     4 2   2 4
133.     4 22222 4
134.     4       4
135.     444444444
136. Press enter to continue...''')
137.     input()
138.
139.     print('''For example, here is a treasure chest (the
        c) located a distance of 2 away
140. from the sonar device (the d):
141.
142.     22222
143.     c   2
144.     2 d 2
145.     2   2
146.     22222
147.
148. The point where the device was dropped will be marked
        with a 2.
149.
150. The treasure chests don't move around. Sonar devices can
        detect treasure
151. chests up to a distance of 9. If all chests are out of
        range, the point
152. will be marked with O
153.
154. If a device is directly dropped on a treasure chest, you
        have discovered
155. the location of the chest, and it will be collected. The
        sonar device will
156. remain there.
```

```
157.
158. When you collect a chest, all sonar devices will update
       to locate the next
159. closest sunken treasure chest.
160. Press enter to continue...''')
161.     input()
162.     print()
163.
164.
165. print('S O N A R !')
166. print()
167. print('Would you like to view the instructions?
       (yes/no)')
168. if input().lower().startswith('y'):
169.     showInstructions()
170.
171. while True:
172.     # game setup
173.     sonarDevices = 16
174.     theBoard = getNewBoard()
175.     theChests = getRandomChests(3)
176.     drawBoard(theBoard)
177.     previousMoves = []
178.
179.     while sonarDevices > 0:
180.         # Start of a turn:
181.
182.         # show sonar device/chest status
183.         if sonarDevices > 1: extraSsonar = 's'
184.         else: extraSsonar = ''
185.         if len(theChests) > 1: extraSchest = 's'
186.         else: extraSchest = ''
187.         print('You have %s sonar device%s left. %s
     treasure chest%s remaining.' % (sonarDevices,
     extraSsonar, len(theChests), extraSchest))
188.
189.         x, y = enterPlayerMove()
190.         previousMoves.append([x, y]) # we must track all
     moves so that sonar devices can be updated.
191.
192.         moveResult = makeMove(theBoard, theChests, x, y)
193.         if moveResult == False:
194.             continue
195.         else:
196.             if moveResult == 'You have found a sunken
     treasure chest!':
197.                 # update all the sonar devices currently
     on the map.
198.                 for x, y in previousMoves:
199.                     makeMove(theBoard, theChests, x, y)
200.             drawBoard(theBoard)
201.             print(moveResult)
202.
203.         if len(theChests) == 0:
```

220

```
204.             print('You have found all the sunken treasure
       chests! Congratulations and good game!')
205.             break
206.
207.         sonarDevices -= 1
208.
209.     if sonarDevices == 0:
210.         print('We\'ve run out of sonar devices! Now we
       have to turn the ship around and head')
211.         print('for home with treasure chests still out
       there! Game over.')
212.         print('    The remaining chests were here:')
213.         for x, y in theChests:
214.             print('    %s, %s' % (x, y))
215.
216.     if not playAgain():
217.         sys.exit()
```

Designing the Program

Sonar is kind of complicated, so it might be better to type in the game's code and play it a few times first to understand what is going on. After you've played the game a few times, you can kind of get an idea of the sequence of events in this game.

The Sonar game uses lists of lists and other complicated variables. These complicated variables are known as **data structures**. Data structures will let us store arrangements of values in a single variable to represent something (such as the locations of the treasure chests in Sonar). We will use data structures for the locations of the treasure chests and dropped sonar devices. One example of a data structure was the board variable in the Tic Tac Toe chapter.

It is also helpful to write out the things we need our program to do, and come up with some function names that will handle these actions. Remember to name functions after what they specifically do. Otherwise we might end up forgetting a function, or typing in two different functions that do the same thing.

Table 13-1: A list of each function the Sonar game needs.

What the code should do.	The function that will do it.
Prints the game board on the screen based on the board data structure it is passed, including the coordinates along the top, bottom, and left and right sides.	drawBoard()
Create a fresh board data structure.	getNewBoard()
Create a fresh chests data structure that has a number of chests randomly scattered across the game board.	getRandomChests()

Check that the XY coordinates that are passed to this function are located on the game board or not.	`isValidMove()`
Let the player type in the XY coordinates of his next move, and keep asking until they type in the coordinates correctly.	`enterPlayerMove()`
Place a sonar device on the game board, and update the `board` data structure then return a string that describes what happened.	`makeMove()`
Ask the player if they want to play another game of Sonar.	`playAgain()`
Print out instructions for the game.	`showInstructions()`

These might not be all of the functions we need, but a list like this is a good idea to help you get started with programming your own games. For example, when designing the `drawBoard()` function in the Sonar game, we find out we also need a function that does what `getRow()` does. Writing out a function once and then calling it twice is preferable to writing out the code twice. The whole point of functions is to reduce duplicate code down to one place, so if we ever need to make changes to that code we only need to change one place in our program.

How the Code Works: Lines 1 to 38

```
1. # Sonar
2.
3. import random
4. import sys
```

Here we import two modules, `random` and `sys`. The `sys` module contains the `exit()` function, which causes the program to immediately terminate. We will call this function later in our program.

Drawing the Game Board

```
6. def drawBoard(board):
```

The back tick (`) and tilde (~) characters are located next to the 1 key on your keyboard. They resemble the waves of the ocean. Somewhere in this ocean are three treasure chests, but you don't know where. You can figure it out by planting sonar devices, and tell the game program where by typing in the X and Y coordinates (which are printed on the four sides of the screen.)

The `drawBoard()` function is the first function we will define for our program. The sonar game's board is an ASCII-art ocean with coordinates going along the X- and Y-axis, and looks like this:

```
                     1         2         3         4         5
           012345678901234567890123456789012345678901234567890123456789

       0   ~~~`\`\~~~`\`~~~~`\~`~`~`~`~~`~~~`~~~`~\`\\`\`~~`~`\~`~`    0
       1   `~`~`~`\\`~~`~~`~`~`\\`~\`~~~`\\\`\\`~\`~~`~`~~`~~`    1
       2   `\`~~~~`~`~~`\\`~~`~~`\`~`~`~`~`\\\`\\`~~`~~~~~~`\\`    2
       3   ~~~~`~`\`~~`~`~~`~~`~`~`~`~`~`\`~`~`~`~~`~~`~~`~    3
       4   ~`\`~~~~`~~`~~~`~`~`~`~`\\`~`~`~`~~~~~`~`\\`~    4
       5   `~`~`~`\~`~~`~~`~`\\\`~`~`~`~~`~~`\`\~~`\\`    5
       6   `~~~`~`~`~`~~`~~`\\\`~`~`~~`~~~`\\`~~`~~`~~`~    6
       7   `~`~`~~~~`~`~~`~~`~`~`~~`~`~~`\\`~~~~~`~`~~~`    7
       8   ~~`~`~`~~`~`\\`~~`~~`~`~`~`~`\`~~~~~`~`\`~~~~`\\    8
       9   `\`~`~`~`~~`~~`~~`~`~`~`~`~`~`~~`~`\\`\\`    9
      10   `~~~`\`\~~`~~`~`~`~~`~~~`\\`~`\~~~~`~~~`~~`~    10
      11   ~~`~`~\`~~`~~`~`~`~~`~`~`~\`~`\\\`~~`\~~~`~~`~    11
      12   ~~`~~~~`~~`~~~`~~`~~`\\`~`~`~\\\`~~`\\`~`\`~~~~    12
      13   `\`\\`~~`~~`\\`~`~`~~~~`~`~`~`~`\`~`~`~`\\`~~~    13
      14   ~~~`\`~`\~`\\`~`~`~`~`~`~`~`~`~`~`~~~~    14

           012345678901234567890123456789012345678901234567890123456789
                     1         2         3         4         5
```

We will split up the drawing in the `drawBoard()` function into four steps. First, we create a string variable of the line with 1, 2, 3, 4, and 5 spaced out with wide gaps (to mark the coordinates for 10, 20, 30, 40, and 50). Second, we use that string to display the X-axis coordinates along the top of the screen. Third, we print each row of the ocean along with the Y-axis coordinates on both sides of the screen. And fourth, we print out the X-axis again at the bottom. Having the coordinates on all sides makes it easier for the player to move their finger along the spaces to see where exactly they want to plan a sonar device.

Drawing the X-coordinates Along the Top

```
 7.        # Draw the board data structure.
 8.
 9.        hline = '     '  # initial space for the numbers down
     the left side of the board
10.        for i in range(1, 6):
11.            hline += (' ' * 9) + str(i)
```

Let's look again at the top part of the board, this time with plus signs instead of blank spaces so we can count the spaces easier:

```
+++++++++++++1+++++++++2+++++++++3 # first line
+++0123456789012345678901234567890123456789 # second line

+0 ~~`~`~ `~~~``~~~~``~`~`~`~`~`~~ ~~~~`` `~`~` 0 # third line
```

Figure 13-3: The spacing we use for printing the top of the game board.

The numbers on the first line which mark the tens position all have nine spaces in between them, and there are thirteen spaces in front of the 1. We are going to create a string with this line and store it in a variable named `hline`.

```
13.        # print the numbers across the top
14.        print(hline)
15.        print('   ' + ('0123456789' * 6))
16.        print()
```

To print the numbers across the top of the sonar board, we first print the contents of the `hline` variable. Then on the next line, we print three spaces (so that this row lines up correctly), and then print the string
`'0123456789012345678901234567890123456789012345678901234567890123456789'`
But this is tedious to type into the source, so instead we type (`'0123456789' * 6`) which evaluates to the same string.

Drawing the Rows of the Ocean

```
18.        # print each of the 15 rows
19.        for i in range(15):
20.            # single-digit numbers need to be padded with an
    extra space
21.            if i < 10:
22.                extraSpace = ' '
23.            else:
24.                extraSpace = ''
25.            ·print('%s%s %s %s' % (extraSpace, i, getRow
    (board, i), i))
```

Now we print the each row of the board, including the numbers down the side to label the Y-axis. We use the `for` loop to print rows 0 through 14 on the board, along with the row numbers on either side of the board.

We have a small problem. Numbers with only one digit (like 0, 1, 2, and so on) only take up one space when we print them out, but numbers with two digits (like 10, 11, and 12) take up two spaces. This means the rows might not line up and would look like this:

```
8 ~~`~`~~```~``~~``~~~``~~`~`~~`~`~```~```~~``~~~~~`~`~~~~` 8
9 ```~`~`~~`~~``~`~`````~``~~~`~```~`~``~~`~~~~~`~```~~~~``` 9
```

```
10 `~~~~``~`~`~```~`~`~~``~`~~~~`~`~``~`~```~~````` `~`~`~`````` 10
11 ~~`~`~~`~``~`~~~``````~~~~~~~~```~~```~`~~``~`~~~~`~~~`~ 11
```

The solution is easy. We just add a space in front of all the single-digit numbers. The `if-else` statement that starts on line 21 does this. We will print the variable `extraSpace` when we print the row, and if `i` is less than 10 (which means it will have only one digit), we assign a single space string to `extraSpace`. Otherwise, we set `extraSpace` to be a blank string. This way, all of our rows will line up when we print them.

The `getRow()` function will return a string representing the row number we pass it. Its two parameters are the board data structure stored in the `board` variable and a row number. We will look at this function next.

Drawing the X-coordinates Along the Bottom

```
27.     # print the numbers across the bottom
28.     print()
29.     print('    ' + ('0123456789' * 6))
30.     print(hline)
```

This code is similar to lines 13 to 16. This will print the X-axis coordinates along the bottom of the screen.

Getting the State of a Row in the Ocean

```
33. def getRow(board, row):
34.     # Return a string from the board data structure at a
    certain row.
35.     boardRow = ''
36.     for i in range(60):
37.         boardRow += board[i][row]
38.     return boardRow
```

This function constructs a string called `boardRow` from the characters stored in `board`. First we set `boardRow` to the blank string. The row number (which is the Y coordinate) is passed as a parameter. The string we want is made by concatenating `board[0][row]`, `board[1][row]`, `board[2][row]`, and so on up to `board[59][row]`. (This is because the row is made up of 60 characters, from index 0 to index 59.)

The `for` loop iterates from integers 0 to 59. On each iteration the next character in the board data structure is copied on to the end of `boardRow`. By the time the loop is done, `boardRow` is fully formed, so we return it.

How the Code Works: Lines 40 to 62

Now that we have a function to print a given board data structure to the string, let's turn to the other functions that we will need. At the start of the game, we will need to create a new game board data structure (kind of like a blank Tic Tac Toe board) and also place treasure chests randomly around the board. We should also create a function that can tell if the coordinates entered by the player are a valid move or not.

Creating a New Game Board

```
40. def getNewBoard():
41.     # Create a new 60x15 board data structure.
42.     board = []
43.     for x in range(60): # the main list is a list of 60 lists
44.         board.append([])
```

At the start of each new game, we will need a fresh board data structure. The board data structure is a list of lists of strings. The first list represents the X coordinate. Since our game's board is 60 characters across, this first list needs to contain 60 lists. So we create a for loop that will append 60 blank lists to it.

```
45.         for y in range(15): # each list in the main list has 15 single-character strings
46.             # use different characters for the ocean to make it more readable.
47.             if random.randint(0, 1) == 0:
48.                 board[x].append('~')
49.             else:
50.                 board[x].append('`')
```

But board is more than just a list of 60 blank lists. Each of the 60 lists represents the Y coordinate of our game board. There are 15 rows in the board, so each of these 60 lists must have 15 characters in them. We have another for loop to add 15 single-character strings that represent the ocean. The "ocean" will just be a bunch of '~' and '`' strings, so we will randomly choose between those two. We can do this by generating a random number between 0 and 1 with a call to random.randint(). If the return value of random.randint() is 0, we add the '~' string. Otherwise we will add the '`' string.

This is like deciding which character to use by tossing a coin. And since the return value from random.randint() will be 0 about half the time, half of the ocean characters will be '~' and the other half will be '`'. This will give our ocean a random, choppy look to it.

Remember that the board variable is a list of 60 lists that have 15 strings. That means to get the string at coordinate 26, 12, we would access board[26][12], and not board[12][26]. The X coordinate is first, then the Y coordinate.

Figure 13-4 is the picture to demonstrate the indexes of a list of lists named x. The red arrows point to indexes of the inner lists themselves. The image is also flipped on its side to make it easier to read:

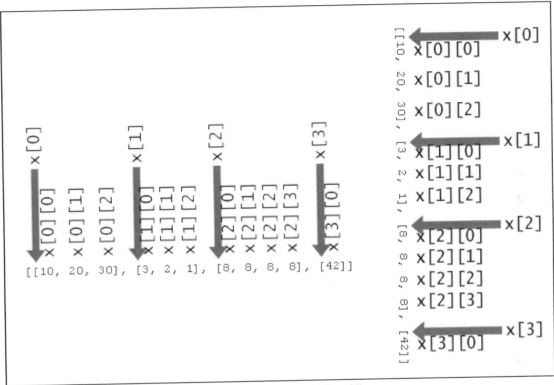

Figure 13-4: The indexes of a list of lists.

```
51.        return board
```

Finally, we return the board variable. Remember that in this case, we are returning a reference to the list that we made. Any changes we made to the list (or the lists inside the list) in our function will still be there outside of the function.

Creating the Random Treasure Chests

```
53. def getRandomChests(numChests):
54.     # Create a list of chest data structures (two-item
    lists of x, y int coordinates)
55.     chests = []
56.     for i in range(numChests):
57.         chests.append([random.randint(0, 59),
    random.randint(0, 14)])
```

```
58.        return chests
```

Another task we need to do at the start of the game is decide where the hidden treasure chests are. We will represent the treasure chests in our game as a list of lists of two integers. These two integers will be the X and Y coordinates. For example, if the chest data structure was [[2, 2], [2, 4], [10, 0]], then this would mean there are three treasure chests, one at 2, 2, another at 2, 4, and a third one at 10, 0.

We will pass the numChests parameter to tell the function how many treasure chests we want it to generate. We set up a for loop to iterate this number of times, and on each iteration we append a list of two random integers. The X coordinate can be anywhere from 0 to 59, and the Y coordinate can be from anywhere between 0 and 14. The expression [random.randint(0, 59), random.randint(0, 14)] that is passed to the append method will evaluate to something like [2, 2] or [2, 4] or [10, 0]. This data structure is then returned.

Determining if a Move is Valid

```
60. def isValidMove(x, y):
61.     # Return True if the coordinates are on the board,
    otherwise False.
62.     return x >= 0 and x <= 59 and y >= 0 and y <= 14
```

The player will type in X and Y coordinates of where they want to drop a sonar device. But they may not type in coordinates that do not exist on the game board. The X coordinates must be between 0 and 59, and the Y coordinate must be between 0 and 14. This function uses a simple expression that uses and operators to ensure that each part of the condition is True. If just one is False, then the entire expression evaluates to False. This Boolean value is returned by the function.

How the Code Works: Lines 64 to 91

Placing a Move on the Board

```
64. def makeMove(board, chests, x, y):
65.     # Change the board data structure with a sonar device
    character. Remove treasure chests
66.     # from the chests list as they are found. Return
    False if this is an invalid move.
67.     # Otherwise, return the string of the result of this
    move.
68.     if not isValidMove(x, y):
69.         return False
```

In our Sonar game, the game board is updated to display a number for each sonar device dropped. The number shows how far away the closest treasure chest is. So when the player makes a move by giving the program an X and Y coordinate, we will change the board based on the positions of the treasure chests. This is why our makeMove() function takes four parameters: the game board data structure, the treasure chests data structures, and the X and Y coordinates.

This function will return the False Boolean value if the X and Y coordinates if was passed do not exist on the game board. If isValidMove() returns False, then makeMove() will return False.

If the coordinates land directly on the treasure, makeMove() will return the string 'You have found a sunken treasure chest!'. If the XY coordinates are within a distance of 9 or less of a treasure chest, we return the string 'Treasure detected at a distance of %s from the sonar device.' (where %s is the distance). Otherwise, makeMove() will return the string 'Sonar did not detect anything. All treasure chests out of range.'.

```
71.     smallestDistance = 100 # any chest will be closer
    than 100.
72.     for cx, cy in chests:
73.         if abs(cx - x) > abs(cy - y):
74.             distance = abs(cx - x)
75.         else:
76.             distance = abs(cy - y)
77.
78.         if distance < smallestDistance: # we want the
    closest treasure chest.
79.             smallestDistance = distance
```

Given the XY coordinates of where the player wants to drop the sonar device, and a list of XY coordinates for the treasure chests (in the chests list of lists), we will need an algorithm to find out which treasure chest is closest.

An Algorithm for Finding the Closest Treasure Chest

While the x and y variables are just integers (say, 5 and 0), together they represent the location on the game board (which is a Cartesian coordinate system) where the player guessed. The chests variable may have a value such as [[5, 0], [0, 2], [4, 2]], that value represents the locations of three treasure chests. Even though these variables are a bunch of numbers, we can visualize it like this:

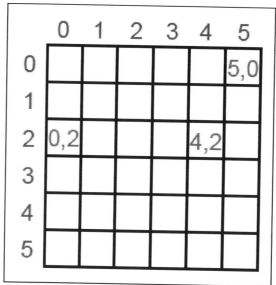

Figure 13-5: The places on the board that [[5, 0], [0, 2], [4, 2]] represents.

We figure out the distance from the sonar device located at 0, 2 with "rings" and the distances around it:

	0	1	2	3	4	5
0	2	2	2	3	4	5,2
1	1	1	2	3	4	5
2	0,0	1	2	3	4,0	5
3	1	1	2	3	4	5
4	2	2	2	3	4	5
5	3	3	3	3	4	5

Figure 13-6: The board marked with distances from the 0, 2 position.

But how do we translate this into code for our game? We need a way to represent distance as an expression. Notice that the distance from an XY coordinate is always the larger of two values: the absolute value of the difference of the two X coordinates and the absolute value of the difference of the two Y coordinates.

That means we should subtract the sonar device's X coordinate and a treasure chest's X coordinate, and then take the absolute value of this number. We do the same for the sonar device's Y coordinate and a treasure chest's Y coordinate. The larger of these two values is the distance. Let's look at our example board with rings above to see if this algorithm is correct.

The sonar's X and Y coordinates are 3 and 2. The first treasure chest's X and Y coordinates (first in the list `[[5, 0], [0, 2], [4, 2]]` that is) are 5 and 0.

For the X coordinates, 3 - 5 evaluates to -2, and the absolute value of -2 is 2.

For the Y coordinates, 2 - 1 evaluates to 1, and the absolute value of 1 is 1.

Comparing the two absolute values 2 and 1, the larger value is 2 so that should be the distance between the sonar device and the treasure chest at coordinates 5, 1. We can look at the board and see that this algorithm works, because the treasure chest at 5,1 is in the sonar device's 2nd ring. Let's quickly compare the other two chests to see if his distances work out correctly also.

The `abs()` function returns the absolute value of the number we pass to it. Let's find the distance from the sonar device at 3,2 and the treasure chest at 0,2: `abs(3 - 0)` evaluates to 3. `abs(2 - 2)` evaluates to 0. 3 is larger than 0, so the distance from the sonar device at 3,2 and the treasure chest at 0,2 is 3. We can look at the board and see this is true.

Let's find the distance from the sonar device at 3,2 and the last treasure chest at 4,2. `abs(3 - 4)` evaluates to 1. `abs(2 - 2)` evaluates to 0. 1 is larger than 0, so the distance from the sonar device at 3,2 and the treasure chest at 4,2 is 1. We look at the board and see this is true also.

All three distances worked out correctly, so it seems our algorithm works. The distances from the sonar device to the three sunken treasure chests are 2, 3, and 1. On each guess, we want to know the distance from the sonar device to the closest of the three treasure chest distances. To do this we use a variable called `smallestDistance`. Let's look at the code again:

```
71.      smallestDistance = 100 # any chest will be closer
    than 100.
72.      for cx, cy in chests:
73.          if abs(cx - x) > abs(cy - y):
74.              distance = abs(cx - x)
75.          else:
76.              distance = abs(cy - y)
77.
78.          if distance < smallestDistance: # we want the
    closest treasure chest.
79.              smallestDistance = distance
```

You can also use multiple assignment in `for` loops. Remember, the assignment statement `a, b = [5, 10]` will assign 5 to a and 10 to b. Also, the `for` loop `for i in [0, 1, 2, 3, 4]` will assign the i variable the values 0 and 1 and so on for each iteration.

`for cx, cy in chests:` combines both of these principles. Because `chests` is a list where each item in the list is itself a list of two integers, the first of these integers is assigned to cx and the second integer is assigned to cy. So if chests has the value [[5, 0], [0, 2], [4, 2]], cx will have the value 5 and cy will have the value 0 on the first iteration through the loop.

Line 73 determines which is larger: the absolute value of the difference of the X coordinates, or the absolute value of the difference of the Y coordinates. (abs (cx - x) < abs (cy - y) seems like much easier way to say that, doesn't it?). The if-else statement assigns the larger of the values to the distance variable.

So on each iteration of the for loop, the distance variable holds the distance of a treasure chest's distance from the sonar device. But we want the shortest (that is, smallest) distance of all the treasure chests. This is where the smallestDistance variable comes in. Whenever the distance variable is smaller than smallestDistance, then the value in distance becomes the new value of smallestDistance.

We give smallestDistance the impossibly high value of 100 at the beginning of the loop so that at least one of the treasure chests we find will be put into smallestDistance. By the time the for loop has finished, we know that smallestDistance holds the shortest distance between the sonar device and all of the treasure chests in the game.

```
81.        if smallestDistance == 0:
82.            # xy is directly on a treasure chest!
83.            chests.remove([x, y])
84.            return 'You have found a sunken treasure chest!'
```

The only time that smallestDistance is equal to 0 is when the sonar device's XY coordinates are the same as a treasure chest's XY coordinates. This means the player has correctly guessed the location of a treasure chest. We should remove this chest's two-integer list from the chests data structure with the remove() list method.

The remove() List Method

The remove() list method will remove the first occurrence of the value passed as a parameter from the list. For example, try typing the following into the interactive shell:

```
>>> x = [42, 5, 10, 42, 15, 42]
>>> x.remove(10)
>>> x
[42, 5, 42, 15, 42]
```

You can see that the 10 value has been removed from the x list. The remove() method removes the first occurrence of the value you pass it, and only the first. For example, type the following into the shell:

```
>>> x = [42, 5, 10, 42, 15, 42]
>>> x.remove(42)
>>> x
[5, 10, 42, 15, 42]
```

Notice that only the first 42 value was removed, but the second and third ones are still there. The `remove()` method will cause an error if you try to remove a value that is not in the list:

```
>>> x = [5, 42]
>>> x.remove(10)
Traceback (most recent call last):
  File "<stdin>", line 1, in <module>
ValueError: list.remove(x): x not in list
>>>
```

After removing the found treasure chest from the `chests` list, we return the string `'You have found a sunken treasure chest!'` to tell the caller that the guess was correct. Remember that any changes made to the list in a function will exist outside the function as well.

```
85.       else:
86.           if smallestDistance < 10:
87.               board[x][y] = str(smallestDistance)
88.               return 'Treasure detected at a distance of %s
      from the sonar device.' % (smallestDistance)
89.           else:
90.               board[x][y] = 'O'
91.               return 'Sonar did not detect anything. All
      treasure chests out of range.'
```

The `else` block executes if `smallestDistance` was not 0, which means the player did not guess an exact location of a treasure chest. We return two different strings, depending on if the sonar device was placed within range of any of the treasure chests. If it was, we mark the board with the string version of `smallestDistance`. If not, we mark the board with a `'O'`.

How the Code Works: Lines 94 to 162

The last few functions we need are to let the player enter their move on the game board, ask the player if he wants to play again (this will be called at the end of the game), and print the instructions for the game on the screen (this will be called at the beginning of the game).

Getting the Player's Move

```
 94. def enterPlayerMove():
 95.     # Let the player type in her move. Return a two-item
         list of int xy coordinates.
 96.     print('Where do you want to drop the next sonar
         device? (0-59 0-14) (or type quit)')
 97.     while True:
 98.         move = input()
 99.         if move.lower() == 'quit':
100.             print('Thanks for playing!')
101.             sys.exit()
```

This function collects the XY coordinates of the player's next move. It has a `while` loop so that it will keep asking the player for her next move. The player can also type in `quit` in order to quit the game. In that case, we call the `sys.exit()` function which immediately terminates the program.

```
103.         move = move.split()
104.         if len(move) == 2 and move[0].isdigit() and move
     [1].isdigit() and isValidMove(int(move[0]), int(move
     [1])):
105.             return [int(move[0]), int(move[1])]
106.         print('Enter a number from 0 to 59, a space, then
     a number from 0 to 14.')
```

Assuming the player has not typed in `'quit'`, we call the `split()` method on `move` and set the list it returns as the new value of `move`. What we expect `move` to be is a list of two numbers. These numbers will be strings, because the `split()` method returns a list of strings. But we can convert these to integers with the `int()` function.

If the player typed in something like `'1 2 3'`, then the list returned by `split()` would be `['1', '2', '3']`. In that case, the expression `len(move) == 2` would be `False` and the entire expression immediately evaluates to `False` (because of short-circuiting as described in chapter 10.)

If the list returned by `split()` does have a length of 2, then it will have a `move[0]` and `move[1]`. We call the string method `isdigit()` on those strings. `isdigit()` will return `True` if the string consists solely of numbers. Otherwise it returns `False`. Try typing the following into the interactive shell:

```
>>> '42'.isdigit()
True
>>> 'forty'.isdigit()
False
>>> ''.isdigit()
False
>>> 'hello'.isdigit()
False
>>> x = '10'
>>> x.isdigit()
True
>>>
```

As you can see, both `move[0].isdigit()` and `move[1].isdigit()` must be `True` for the whole condition to be `True`. The final part of this expression calls our `move[1]` function to check if the XY coordinates exist on the board. If all these expressions are `True`, then this function returns a two-integer list of the XY coordinates. Otherwise, the player will be asked to enter coordinates again.

Asking the Player to Play Again

```
109. def playAgain():
110.     # This function returns True if the player wants to
     play again, otherwise it returns False.
111.     print('Do you want to play again? (yes or no)')
112.     return input().lower().startswith('y')
```

The `playAgain()` function will ask the player if they want to play again, and will keep asking until the player types in a string that begins with `'y'`.

Printing the Game Instructions for the Player

```
115. def showInstructions():
116.     print('''Instructions:
117. You are the captain of the Simon, a treasure-hunting
     ship. Your current mission
118. is to find the three sunken treasure chests that are
     lurking in the part of the
119. ocean you are in and collect them.
120.
121. To play, enter the coordinates of the point in the ocean
     you wish to drop a
```

```
122.  sonar device. The sonar can find out how far away the
      closest chest is to it.
123.  For example, the d below marks where the device was
      dropped, and the 2's
124.  represent distances of 2 away from the device. The 4's
      represent
125.  distances of 4 away from the device.
126.
127.     444444444
128.     4       4
129.     4 22222 4
130.     4 2   2 4
131.     4 2 d 2 4
132.     4 2   2 4
133.     4 22222 4
134.     4       4
135.     444444444
136.  Press enter to continue...''')
137.     input()
```

The showInstructions() is just a couple of print() calls that print multi-line
strings. The input() function just gives the player a chance to press Enter before printing
the next string. This is because the screen can only show 25 lines of text at a time.

```
139.      print('''For example, here is a treasure chest (the
      c) located a distance of 2 away
140.  from the sonar device (the d):
141.
142.     22222
143.     c   2
144.     2 d 2
145.     2   2
146.     22222
147.
148.  The point where the device was dropped will be marked
      with a 2.
149.
150.  The treasure chests don't move around. Sonar devices can
      detect treasure
151.  chests up to a distance of 9. If all chests are out of
      range, the point
152.  will be marked with O
153.
154.  If a device is directly dropped on a treasure chest, you
      have discovered
155.  the location of the chest, and it will be collected. The
      sonar device will
156.  remain there.
157.
158.  When you collect a chest, all sonar devices will update
      to locate the next
159.  closest sunken treasure chest.
```

```
160. Press enter to continue...''')
161.     input()
162.     print()
```

This is the rest of the instructions in one multi-line string. After the player presses Enter, the function returns. These are all of the functions we will define for our game. The rest of the program is the main part of our game.

How the Code Works: Lines 165 to 217

Now that we are done writing all of the functions our game will need, let's start the main part of the program.

The Start of the Game

```
165. print('S O N A R !')
166. print()
167. print('Would you like to view the instructions?
     (yes/no)')
168. if input().lower().startswith('y'):
169.     showInstructions()
```

The expression `input().lower().startswith('y')` asks the player if they want to see the instructions, and evaluates to `True` if the player typed in a string that began with `'y'` or `'Y'`. If so, `showInstructions()` is called.

```
171. while True:
172.     # game setup
173.     sonarDevices = 16
174.     theBoard = getNewBoard()
175.     theChests = getRandomChests(3)
176.     drawBoard(theBoard)
177.     previousMoves = []
```

This `while` loop is the main loop for this game. Here are what the variables are for:

Table 13-2: Variables used in the main game loop.

Variable	Description
sonarDevices	The number of sonar devices (and turns) the player has left.
theBoard	The board data structure we will use for this game.
theChests	The list of chest data structures. `getRandomChests()` will return a list of three treasure chests at random places on the board.
previousMoves	A list of all the XY moves that the player has made in the game.

Displaying the Game Status for the Player

```
179.        while sonarDevices > 0:
180.            # Start of a turn:
181.
182.            # show sonar device/chest status
183.            if sonarDevices > 1: extraSsonar = 's'
184.            else: extraSsonar = ''
185.            if len(theChests) > 1: extraSchest = 's'
186.            else: extraSchest = ''
187.            print('You have %s sonar device%s left. %s
    treasure chest%s remaining.' % (sonarDevices,
    extraSsonar, len(theChests), extraSchest))
```

This `while` loop executes as long as the player has sonar devices remaining. We want to print a message telling the user how many sonar devices and treasure chests are left. But there is a problem. If there are two or more sonar devices left, we want to print `'2 sonar devices'`. But if there is only one sonar device left, we want to print `'1 sonar device'` left. We only want the plural form of "devices" if there are multiple sonar devices. The same goes for `'2 treasure chests'` and `'1 treasure chest'`.

Notice on lines 183 through 186 that we have code after the `if` and `else` statements' colon. This is perfectly valid Python. Instead of having a block of code after the statement, instead you can just use the rest of the same line to make your code more concise. (Of course, this means you can only have one line of code.) This applies to any statement that uses colons, including `while` and `for` loops.

So we have two string variables named `extraSsonar` and `extraSchest`, which are set to `' '` (space) if there are multiple sonar devices or treasures chests. Otherwise, they are blank. We use them in the `while` statement on line 187.

Getting the Player's Move

```
189.        x, y = enterPlayerMove()
190.        previousMoves.append([x, y]) # we must track all
    moves so that sonar devices can be updated.
191.
192.        moveResult = makeMove(theBoard, theChests, x, y)
193.        if moveResult == False:
194.            continue
```

Line 189 uses the multiple assignment trick. `enterPlayerMove()` returns a two-item list. The first item will be stored in the `x` variable and the second will be stored in the `y` variable. We then put these two variables into another two-item list, which we store in the `previousMoves` list with the `append()` method. This means `previousMoves` is a list of XY coordinates of each move the player makes in this game.

The x and y variables, along with theBoard and theChests (which represent the current state of the game board) are all sent to the makeMove() function. As we have already seen, this function will make the necessary modifications to the game board. If makeMove() returns the value False, then there was a problem with the x and y values we passed it. The continue statement will send the execution back to the start of the while loop that began on line 179 to ask the player for XY coordinates again.

Finding a Sunken Treasure Chest

```
195.          else:
196.              if moveResult == 'You have found a sunken
      treasure chest!':
197.                  # update all the sonar devices currently
      on the map.
198.                  for x, y in previousMoves:
199.                      makeMove(theBoard, theChests, x, y)
200.              drawBoard(theBoard)
201.              print(moveResult)
```

If makeMove() did not return the value False, it would have returned a string that tells us what were the results of that move. If this string was 'You have found a sunken treasure chest!', then that means we should update all the sonar devices on the board so they detect the next closest treasure chest on the board. We have the XY coordinates of all the sonar devices currently on the board stored in previousMoves. So we can just pass all of these XY coordinates to the makeMove() function again to have it redraw the values on the board.

We don't have to worry about this call to makeMove() having errors, because we already know all the XY coordinates in previousMoves are valid. We also know that this call to makeMove() won't find any new treasure chests, because they would have already been removed from the board when that move was first made.

The for loop on line 198 also uses the same multiple assignment trick for x and y because the items in previousMoves list are themselves two-item lists. Because we don't print anything here, the player doesn't realize we are redoing all of the previous moves. It just appears that the board has been entirely updated.

Checking if the Player has Won

```
203.          if len(theChests) == 0:
204.              print('You have found all the sunken treasure
      chests! Congratulations and good game!')
205.              break
```

Remember that the makeMove() function modifies the theChests list we send it. Because theChests is a list, any changes made to it inside the function will persist after

239

execution returns from the function. makeMove() removes items from theChests when treasure chests are found, so eventually (if the player guesses correctly) all of the treasure chests will have been removed. (Remember, by "treasure chest" we mean the two-item lists of the XY coordinates inside the theChests list.)

When all the treasure chests have been found on the board and removed from theChests, the theChests list will have a length of 0. When that happens, we display a congratulations to the player, and then execute a break statement to break out of this while loop. Execution will then move down to line 209 (the first line after the while-block.)

Checking if the Player has Lost

```
207.            sonarDevices -= 1
```

This is the last line of the while loop that started on line 179. We decrement the sonarDevices variable because the player has used one. If the player keeps missing the treasure chests, eventually sonarDevices will be reduced to 0. After this line, execution jumps back up to line 179 so we can re-evaluate the while statement's condition (which is sonarDevices > 0). If sonarDevices is 0, then the condition will be False and execution will continue outside the while-block on line 209.

But until then, the condition will remain True and the player can keep making guesses.

```
209.      if sonarDevices == 0:
210.          print('We\'ve run out of sonar devices! Now we
      have to turn the ship around and head')
211.          print('for home with treasure chests still out
      there! Game over.')
212.          print('    The remaining chests were here:')
213.          for x, y in theChests:
214.              print('    %s, %s' % (x, y))
```

Line 209 is the first line outside the while loop. By this point the game is over. But how do we tell if the player won or not? The only two places where the program execution would have left the while loop is on line 179 if the condition failed. In that case, sonarDevices would be 0 and the player would have lost.

The second place is the break statement on line 205. That statement is executed if the player has found all the treasure chests before running out of sonar devices. In that case, sonarDevices would be some value greater than 0.

Lines 210 to 212 will tell the player they've lost. The for loop on line 213 will go through the treasure chests remaining in theChests and show their location to the player so that they can know where the treasure chests had been lurking.

Asking the Player to Play Again, and the `sys.exit()` Function

```
216.        if not playAgain():
217.            sys.exit()
```

Win or lose, we call the `playAgain()` function to let the player type in whether they want to keep playing or not. If not, then `playAgain()` returns `False`. The `not` operator changes this to `True`, making the `if` statement's condition `True` and the `sys.exit()` function is executed. This will cause the program to terminate.

Otherwise, execution jumps back to the beginning of the `while` loop on line 171.

Summary: Review of our Sonar Game

Remember how our Tic Tac Toe game numbered the spaces on the Tic Tac Toe board 1 through 9? This sort of coordinate system might have been okay for a board with less than ten spaces. But the Sonar board has nine hundred spaces! The Cartesian coordinate system we learned in the last chapter really makes all these spaces manageable, especially when our game needs to find the distance between two points on the board.

Locations in games that use a Cartesian coordinate system are often stored in a list of lists so that the first index is the x-coordinate and the second index is the y-coordinate. This make accessing a coordinates look like `board[x][y]`.

These data structures (such as the ones used for the ocean and locations of the treasure chests) make it possible to have complicated concepts represented as data in our program, and our game programs become mostly about modifying these data structures.

In the next chapter, we will be representing letters as numbers using their ASCII numbers. (This is the same ASCII term we used in "ASCII art" previously.) By representing text as numbers, we can perform mathematically operations on them which will encrypt or decrypt secret messages.

Chapter 14

Caesar Cipher

Topics Covered In This Chapter:

- Cryptography and ciphers
- Encrypting and decrypting
- Ciphertext, plaintext, keys, and symbols
- The Caesar Cipher
- ASCII ordinal values
- The chr() and ord() functions
- The isalpha() string method
- The isupper() and islower() string methods
- Cryptanalysis
- The brute force technique

The program in this chapter is not really a game, but it is fun to play with nonetheless. Our program will convert normal English into a secret code, and also convert secret codes back into regular English again. Only someone who is knowledgeable about secret codes will be able to understand our secret messages.

Because this program manipulates text in order to convert it into secret messages, we will learn several new functions and methods that come with Python for manipulating strings. We will also learn how programs can do math with text strings just as it can with numbers.

About Cryptography

The science of writing secret codes is called **cryptography**. Cryptography has been used for thousands of years to send secret messages that only the recipient could understand, even if someone captured the messenger and read the coded message. A secret code system is called a **cipher**. There are thousands of different ciphers that have been used, each using different techniques to keep the messages a secret.

In cryptography, we call the message that we want to be secret the **plaintext**. The plaintext could look something like this:

```
Hello there! The keys to the house are hidden under the
reddish flower pot.
```

When we convert the plaintext into the encoded message, we call this **encrypting** the plaintext. The plaintext is encrypted into the **ciphertext**. The ciphertext looks like random letters (also called **garbage data**), and we cannot understand what the original plaintext was by just looking at the ciphertext. Here is an example of some ciphertext:

```
Ckkz fkx kj becqnejc kqp pdeo oaynap iaoowca!
```

But if we know about the cipher used to encrypt the message, we can **decrypt** the ciphertext back to the plaintext. (Decryption is the opposite of encryption.)

Many ciphers also use keys. **Keys** are secret values that let you decrypt ciphertext that was encrypted using a specific cipher. Think of the cipher as being like a door lock. Although all the door locks of the same type are built the same, but a particular lock will only unlock if you have the key made for that lock.

The Caesar Cipher

When we encrypt a message using a cipher, we will choose the key that is used to encrypt and decrypt this message. The key for our Caesar Cipher will be a number from 1 to 26. Unless you know the key (that is, know the number), you will not be able to decrypt the encrypted message.

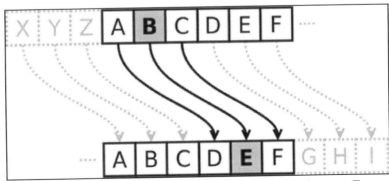

Figure 14-1: Shifting over letters by three spaces. Here, B becomes E.

The **Caesar Cipher** was one of the earliest ciphers ever invented. In this cipher, you encrypt a message by taking each letter in the message (in cryptography, these letters are called **symbols** because they can be letters, numbers, or any other sign) and replacing it with a "shifted" letter. If you shift the letter A by one space, you get the letter B. If you shift the letter A by two spaces, you get the letter C. Figure 14-1 is a picture of some letters shifted over by 3 spaces.

To get each shifted letter, draw out a row of boxes with each letter of the alphabet. Then draw a second row of boxes under it, but start a certain number of spaces over. When you get to the leftover letters at the end, wrap around back to the start of the boxes. Here is an example with the letters shifted by three spaces:

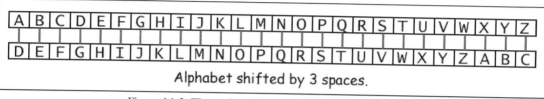

Alphabet shifted by 3 spaces.

Figure 14-2: The entire alphabet shifted by three spaces.

The number of spaces we shift is the key in the Caesar Cipher. The example above shows the letter translations for the key 3.

Using a key of 3, if we encrypt the plaintext "Howdy", then the "H" becomes "K". The letter "o" becomes "r". The letter "w" becomes "z". The letter "d" becomes "g". And the letter "y" becomes "b". The ciphertext of "Hello" with key 3 becomes "Krzgb".

We will keep any non-letter characters the same. In order to decrypt "Krzgb" with the key 3, we just go from the bottom boxes back to the top. The letter "K" becomes "H", the letter "r" becomes "o", the letter "z" becomes "w", the letter "g" becomes "d", and the letter "b" becomes "y" to form "Howdy".

You can find out more about the Caesar Cipher from Wikipedia at *http://en.wikipedia.org/wiki/Caesar_cipher*

ASCII, and Using Numbers for Letters

How do we implement this shifting of the letters in our program? We can do this by representing each letter as a number (called an **ordinal**), and then adding or subtracting from this number to form a new number (and a new letter). **ASCII** (pronounced "ask-ee" and stands for American Standard Code for Information Interchange) is a code that connects each character to a number between 32 and 127. The numbers less than 32 refer to "unprintable" characters, so we will not be using them.

The capital letters "A" through "Z" have the ASCII numbers 65 through 90. The lowercase letters "a" through "z" have the ASCII numbers 97 through 122. The numeric digits "0" through "9" have the ASCII numbers 48 through 57.

Table 14-1: The ASCII Table

32	(space)	48	0	64	@	80	P	96	`	112	p
33	!	49	1	65	A	81	Q	97	a	113	q
34	"	50	2	66	B	82	R	98	b	114	r
35	#	51	3	67	C	83	S	99	c	115	s
36	$	52	4	68	D	84	T	100	d	116	t
37	%	53	5	69	E	85	U	101	e	117	u
38	&	54	6	70	F	86	V	102	f	118	v
39	'	55	7	71	G	87	W	103	g	119	w
40	(	56	8	72	H	88	X	104	h	120	x
41	)	57	9	73	I	89	Y	105	i	121	y
42	*	58	:	74	J	90	Z	106	j	122	z
43	+	59	;	75	K	91	[	107	k	123	{
44	,	60	<	76	L	92	\	108	l	124	l
45	-	61	=	77	M	93	]	109	m	125	}
46	.	62	>	78	N	94	^	110	n	126	~
47	/	63	?	79	O	95	_	111	o		

So if we wanted to shift "A" by three spaces, we first convert it to a number (65). Then we add 3 to 65, to get 68. Then we convert the number 68 back to a letter ("D"). We will use the chr() and ord() functions to convert between letters and numbers.

For example, the letter "A" is represented by the number 65. The letter "m" is represented by the number 109. A table of all the ASCII characters from 32 to 12 is in Table 14-1.

The chr() and ord() Functions

The chr() function (pronounced "char", short for "character") takes an integer ASCII number for the parameter and returns the single-character string. The ord() function (short for "ordinal") takes a single-character string for the parameter, and returns the integer ASCII value for that character. Try typing the following into the interactive shell:

```
>>> chr(65)
'A'
>>> ord('A')
65
```

```
>>> chr(65+8)
'I'
>>> chr(52)
'4'
>>> chr(ord('F'))
'F'
>>> ord(chr(68))
68
>>>
```

On the third line, chr(65+8) evaluates to chr(73). If you look at the ASCII table, you can see that 73 is the ordinal for the capital letter "I". On the fifth line, chr(ord('F')) evaluates to chr(70) which evaluates to 'F'. Feeding the result of ord() to chr() will evaluate to the same as the original argument. The same goes for feeding the result of chr() to ord(), as shown by the sixth line.

Using chr() and ord() will come in handy for our Caesar Cipher program. They are also helpful when we need to convert strings to numbers and numbers to strings.

Sample Run of Caesar Cipher

Here is a sample run of the Caesar Cipher program, encrypting a message:

```
Do you wish to encrypt or decrypt a message?
encrypt
Enter your message:
The sky above the port was the color of television, tuned to a
dead channel.
Enter the key number (1-26)
13
Your translated text is:
Gur fxl nobir gur cbeg jnf gur pbybe bs gryrivfvba, gharq gb n
qrnq punaary.
Now we will run the program and decrypt the text that we just
encrypted.
Do you wish to encrypt or decrypt a message?
decrypt
Enter your message:
Gur fxl nobir gur cbeg jnf gur pbybe bs gryrivfvba, gharq gb n
qrnq punaary.
Enter the key number (1-26)
13
Your translated text is:
The sky above the port was the color of television, tuned to a
dead channel.
```

On this run we will try to decrypt the text that was encrypted, but we will use the wrong key. Remember that if you do not know the correct key, the decrypted text will just be garbage data.

```
Do you wish to encrypt or decrypt a message?
decrypt
Enter your message:
Gur fxl nobir gur cbeg jnf gur pbybe bs gryrivfvba, gharq gb n
qrnq punaary.
Enter the key number (1-26)
15
Your translated text is:
Rfc qiw yzmtc rfc nmpr uyq rfc amjmp md rcjctgqgml, rslcb rm y
bcyb afyllcj.
```

Caesar Cipher's Source Code

Here is the source code for the Caesar Cipher program. If you don't want to type all of this code in, you can visit this book's website at the URL *http://inventwithpython.com/chapter14* and follow the instructions to download the source code. After you type this code in, save the file as *cipher.py*

cipher.py

This code can be downloaded from *http://inventwithpython.com/cipher.py*
If you get errors after typing this code in, compare it to the book's code with the online diff tool at *http://inventwithpython.com/diff* or email the author at al@inventwithpython.com

```python
1. # Caesar Cipher
2.
3. MAX_KEY_SIZE = 26
4.
5. def getMode():
6.     while True:
7.         print('Do you wish to encrypt or decrypt a message?')
8.         mode = input().lower()
9.         if mode in 'encrypt e decrypt d'.split():
10.            return mode
11.        else:
12.            print('Enter either "encrypt" or "e" or "decrypt" or "d".')
13.
14. def getMessage():
15.     print('Enter your message:')
16.     return input()
17.
18. def getKey():
19.     key = 0
```

```
20.        while True:
21.            print('Enter the key number (1-%s)' %
       (MAX_KEY_SIZE))
22.            key = int(input())
23.            if (key >= 1 and key <= MAX_KEY_SIZE):
24.                return key
25.
26. def getTranslatedMessage(mode, message, key):
27.        if mode[0] == 'd':
28.            key = -key
29.        translated = ''
30.
31.        for symbol in message:
32.            if symbol.isalpha():
33.                num = ord(symbol)
34.                num += key
35.
36.                if symbol.isupper():
37.                    if num > ord('Z'):
38.                        num -= 26
39.                    elif num < ord('A'):
40.                        num += 26
41.                elif symbol.islower():
42.                    if num > ord('z'):
43.                        num -= 26
44.                    elif num < ord('a'):
45.                        num += 26
46.
47.                translated += chr(num)
48.            else:
49.                translated += symbol
50.        return translated
51.
52. mode = getMode()
53. message = getMessage()
54. key = getKey()
55.
56. print('Your translated text is:')
57. print(getTranslatedMessage(mode, message, key))
```

How the Code Works: Lines 1 to 34

This code is much shorter compared to our other games. The encryption and decryption processes are the just the reverse of the other, and even then they still share much of the same code. Let's look at how each line works.

```
1. # Caesar Cipher
2.
3. MAX_KEY_SIZE = 26
```

The first line is simply a comment. The Caesar Cipher is one cipher of a type of ciphers called simple substitution ciphers. **Simple substitution ciphers** are ciphers that replace one symbol in the plaintext with one (and only one) symbol in the ciphertext. So if a "G" was substituted with "Z" in the cipher, every single "G" in the plaintext would be replaced with (and only with) a "Z".

MAX_KEY_SIZE is a variable that stores the integer 26 in it. MAX_KEY_SIZE reminds us that in this program, the key used in our cipher should be between 1 and 26.

Deciding to Encrypt or Decrypt

```
 5. def getMode():
 6.     while True:
 7.         print('Do you wish to encrypt or decrypt a
    message?')
 8.         mode = input().lower()
 9.         if mode in 'encrypt e decrypt d'.split():
10.             return mode
11.         else:
12.             print('Enter either "encrypt" or "e" or
    "decrypt" or "d".')
```

The getMode() function will let the user type in if they want to encrypt or decrypt the message. The return value of input() (which then has the lower() method called on it, which returns the lowercase version of the string) is stored in mode. The if statement's condition checks if the string stored in mode exists in the list returned by 'encrypt e decrypt d'.split(). This list is ['encrypt', 'e', 'decrypt', 'd'], but it is easier for the programmer to just type in 'encrypt e decrypt d'.split() and not type in all those quotes and commas. But you can use whatever is easiest for you; they both evaluate to the same list value.

This function will return the first character in mode as long as mode is equal to 'encrypt', 'e', 'decrypt', or 'd'. This means that getMode() will return the string 'e' or the string 'd'.

Getting the Message from the Player

```
14. def getMessage():
15.     print('Enter your message:')
16.     return input()
```

The getMessage() function simply gets the message to encrypt or decrypt from the user and uses this string as its return value.

Getting the Key from the Player

```
18. def getKey():
19.     key = 0
20.     while True:
21.         print('Enter the key number (1-%s)' %
    (MAX_KEY_SIZE))
22.         key = int(input())
23.         if (key >= 1 and key <= MAX_KEY_SIZE):
24.             return key
```

The getKey() function lets the player type in key they will use to encrypt or decrypt the message. The while loop ensures that the function only returns a valid key. A valid key here is one that is between the integer values 1 and 26 (remember that MAX_KEY_SIZE will only have the value 26 because it is constant). It then returns this key. Remember that on line 22 that key was set to the integer version of what the user typed in, and so getKey() returns an integer.

Encrypt or Decrypt the Message with the Given Key

```
26. def getTranslatedMessage(mode, message, key):
27.     if mode[0] == 'd':
28.         key = -key
29.     translated = ''
```

getTranslatedMessage() is the function that does the encrypting and decrypting in our program. It has three parameters. mode sets the function to encryption mode or decryption mode. message is the plaintext (or ciphertext) to be encrypted (or decrypted). key is the key that is used in this cipher.

The first line in the getTranslatedMessage() function determines if we are in encryption mode or decryption mode. If the first letter in the mode variable is the string 'd', then we are in decryption mode. The only difference between the two modes is that in decryption mode, the key is set to the negative version of itself. If key was the integer 22, then in decryption mode we set it to -22. The reason for this will be explained later.

translated is the string that will hold the end result: either the ciphertext (if we are encrypting) or the plaintext (if we are decrypting). We will only be concatenating strings to this variable, so we first store the blank string in translated. (A variable must be defined with some string value first before a string can be concatenated to it.)

The `isalpha()` String Method

The `isalpha()` string method will return `True` if the string is an uppercase or lowercase letter from A to Z. If the string contains any non-letter characters, then `isalpha()` will return `False`. Try typing the following into the interactive shell:

```
>>> 'Hello'.isalpha()
True
>>> 'Forty two'.isalpha()
False
>>> 'Fortytwo'.isalpha()
True
>>> '42'.isalpha()
False
>>> ''.isalpha()
False
>>>
```

As you can see, `'Forty two'.isalpha()` will return `False` because `'Forty two'` has a space in it, which is a non-letter character. `'Fortytwo'.isalpha()` returns `True` because it does not have this space. `'42'.isalpha()` returns `False` because both `'4'` and `'2'` are non-letter characters. And `''.isalpha()` is `False` because `isalpha()` only returns `True` if the string has only letter characters and is not blank.

We will use the `isalpha()` method in our program in the next few lines.

```
31.     for symbol in message:
32.         if symbol.isalpha():
33.             num = ord(symbol)
34.             num += key
```

Line 31's `for` loop iterates over each letter (remember in cryptography they are called symbols) in the `message` string. In a `for` loop, strings are treated just like lists of single-character strings. If `message` had the string `'Hello'`, then `for symbol in 'Hello'` would be the same as `for symbol in ['H', 'e', 'l', 'l', 'o']`. On each iteration through this loop, `symbol` will have the value of a letter in `message`.

The reason we have the `if` statement on line 32 is because we will only encrypt/decrypt letters in the message. Numbers, signs, punctuation marks, and everything else will stay in their untranslated form. The `num` variable will hold the integer ordinal value of the letter stored in `symbol`. Line 34 then "shifts" the value in `num` by the value in `key`.

251

The `isupper()` and `islower()` String Methods

The `isupper()` and `islower()` string methods (which are on line 36 and 41) work in a way that is very similar to the `isdigit()` and `isalpha()` methods. `isupper()` will return `True` if the string it is called on contains at least one uppercase letter and no lowercase letters. `islower()` returns `True` if the string it is called on contains at least one lowercase letter and no uppercase letters. Otherwise these methods return `False`. The existence of non-letter characters like numbers and spaces does not affect the outcome. Although strings that do not have any letters, including blank strings, will also return `False`. Try typing the following into the interactive shell:

```
>>> 'HELLO'.isupper()
True
>>> 'hello'.isupper()
False
>>> 'hello'.islower()
True
>>> 'Hello'.islower()
False
>>> 'LOOK OUT BEHIND YOU!'.isupper()
True
>>> '42'.isupper()
False
>>> '42'.islower()
False
>>> ''.isupper()
False
>>> ''.islower()
False
>>>
```

How the Code Works: Lines 36 to 57

The process of encrypting (or decrypting) each letter is fairly simple. We want to apply the same Python code to every letter character in the string, which is what the next several lines of code do.

Encrypting or Decrypting Each Letter

```
36.            if symbol.isupper():
37.                if num > ord('Z'):
38.                    num -= 26
39.                elif num < ord('A'):
```

```
40.                        num += 26
```

This code checks if the symbol is an uppercase letter. If so, there are two special cases we need to worry about. What if `symbol` was `'Z'` and `key` was 4? If that were the case, the value of `num` here would be the character `'^'` (The ordinal of `'^'` is 94). But ^ isn't a letter at all. We wanted the ciphertext to "wrap around" to the beginning of the alphabet.

The way we can do this is to check if `key` has a value larger than the largest possible letter's ASCII value (which is a capital "Z"). If so, then we want to **subtract** 26 (because there are 26 letters in total) from `num`. After doing this, the value of `num` is 68, which is the ASCII value for `'D'`.

```
41.             elif symbol.islower():
42.                 if num > ord('z'):
43.                     num -= 26
44.                 elif num < ord('a'):
45.                     num += 26
```

If the symbol is a lowercase letter, the program runs code that is very similar to lines 36 through 40. The only difference is that we use `ord('z')` and `ord('a')` instead of `ord('Z')` and `ord('A')`.

If we were in decrypting mode, then `key` would be negative. Then we would have the special case where `num -= 26` might be less than the smallest possible value (which is `ord('A')`, that is, 65). If this is the case, we want to **add** 26 to `num` to have it "wrap around".

```
47.                 translated += chr(num)
48.             else:
49.                 translated += symbol
```

The `translated` string will be appended with the encrypted/decrypted character. If the symbol was not an uppercase or lowercase letter, then the else-block on line 48 would have executed instead. All the code in the else-block does is append the original, untranslated symbol to the `translated` string. This means that spaces, numbers, punctuation marks, and other characters will not be encrypted or decrypted.

```
50.     return translated
```

The last line in the `getTranslatedMessage()` function returns the translated string.

The Start of the Program

```
52. mode = getMode()
53. message = getMessage()
54. key = getKey()
55.
56. print('Your translated text is:')
57. print(getTranslatedMessage(mode, message, key))
```

This is the main part of our program. We call each of the three functions we have defined above in turn to get the mode, message, and key that the user wants to use. We then pass these three values as arguments to getTranslatedMessage(), whose return value (the translated string) is printed to the user.

Brute Force

That's the entire Caesar Cipher. However, while this cipher may fool some people who don't understand cryptography, it won't keep a message secret from someone who knows cryptanalysis. While cryptography is the science of making codes, **cryptanalysis** is the science of breaking codes.

```
Do you wish to encrypt or decrypt a message?
encrypt
Enter your message:
Doubts may not be pleasant, but certainty is absurd.
Enter the key number (1-26)
8
Your translated text is:
Lwcjba uig vwb jm xtmiaivb, jcb kmzbiqvbg qa ijaczl.
```

The whole point of cryptography is that so if someone else gets their hands on the encrypted message, they cannot figure out the original unencrypted message from it. Let's pretend we are the code breaker and all we have is the encrypted text:

Lwcjba uig vwb jm xtmiaivb, jcb kmzbiqvbg qa ijaczl.

One method of cryptanalysis is called brute force. **Brute force** is the technique of trying every single possible key. If the cryptanalyst knows the cipher that the message uses (or at least guesses it), they can just go through every possible key. Because there are only 26 possible keys, it would be easy for a cryptanalyst to write a program than prints the decrypted ciphertext of every possible key and see if any of the outputs make sense. Let's add a brute force feature to our program.

Adding the Brute Force Mode to Our Program

First, change lines 7, 9, and 12 (which are in the `getMode()` function) to look like the following (the changes are in bold):

```
 5. def getMode():
 6.     while True:
 7.         print('Do you wish to encrypt or decrypt or brute
    force a message?')
 8.         mode = input().lower()
 9.         if mode in 'encrypt e decrypt d brute b'.split():
10.             return mode[0]
11.         else:
12.             print('Enter either "encrypt" or "e" or
    "decrypt" or "d" or "brute" or "b".')
```

This will let us select "brute force" as a mode for our program. Then modify and add the following changes to the main part of the program:

```
52. mode = getMode()
53. message = getMessage()
54. if mode[0] != 'b':
55.     key = getKey()
56.
57. print('Your translated text is:')
58. if mode[0] != 'b':
59.     print(getTranslatedMessage(mode, message, key))
60. else:
61.     for key in range(1, MAX_KEY_SIZE + 1):
62.         print(key, getTranslatedMessage('decrypt',
    message, key))
```

These changes make our program ask the user for a key if they are not in "brute force" mode. If they are not in "brute force" mode, then the original `getTranslatedMessage()` call is made and the translated string is printed.

However, otherwise we are in "brute force" mode, and we run a `getTranslatedMessage()` loop that iterates from 1 all the way up to `MAX_KEY_SIZE` (which is 26). Remember that when the `range()` function returns a list of integers up to but not including the second parameter, which is why we have + 1. This program will print out every possible translation of the message (including the key number used in the translation). Here is a sample run of this modified program:

```
Do you wish to encrypt or decrypt or brute force a
message?
brute
Enter your message:
Lwcjba uig vwb jm xtmiaivb, jcb kmzbiqvbg qa ijaczl.
Your translated text is:
1 Kvbiaz thf uva il wslhzhua, iba jlyahpuaf pz hizbyk.
2 Juahzy sge tuz hk vrkgygtz, haz ikxzgotze oy ghyaxj.
3 Itzgyx rfd sty gj uqjfxfsy, gzy hjwyfnsyd nx fgxzwi.
4 Hsyfxw qec rsx fi tpiewerx, fyx givxemrxc mw efwyvh.
5 Grxewv pdb qrw eh sohdvdqw, exw fhuwdlqwb lv devxug.
6 Fqwdvu oca pqv dg rngcucpv, dwv egtvckpva ku cduwtf.
7 Epvcut nbz opu cf qmfbtbou, cvu dfsubjouz jt bctvse.
8 Doubts may not be pleasant, but certainty is absurd.
9 Cntasr lzx mns ad okdzrzms, ats bdqszhmsx hr zartqc.
10 Bmszrq kyw lmr zc njcyqylr, zsr acpryglrw gq yzqspb.
11 Alryqp jxv klq yb mibxpxkq, yrq zboqxfkqv fp xyproa.
12 Zkqxpo iwu jkp xa lhawowjp, xqp yanpwejpu eo wxoqnz.
13 Yjpwon hvt ijo wz kgzvnvio, wpo xzmovdiot dn vwnpmy.
14 Xiovnm gus hin vy jfyumuhn, von wylnuchns cm uvmolx.
15 Whnuml ftr ghm ux iextltgm, unm vxkmtbgmr bl tulnkw.
16 Vgmtlk esq fgl tw hdwsksfl, tml uwjlsaflq ak stkmjv.
17 Uflskj drp efk sv gcvrjrek, slk tvikrzekp zj rsjliu.
18 Tekrji cqo dej ru fbuqiqdj, rkj suhjqydjo yi qrikht.
19 Sdjqih bpn cdi qt eatphpci, qji rtgipxcin xh pqhjgs.
20 Rciphg aom bch ps dzsogobh, pih qsfhowbhm wg opgifr.
21 Qbhogf znl abg or cyrnfnag, ohg pregnvagl vf nofheq.
22 Pagnfe ymk zaf nq bxqmemzf, ngf oqdfmuzfk ue mnegdp.
23 Ozfmed xlj yze mp awpldlye, mfe npceltyej td lmdfco.
24 Nyeldc wki xyd lo zvokckxd, led mobdksxdi sc klcebn.
25 Mxdkcb vjh wxc kn yunjbjwc, kdc lnacjrwch rb jkbdam.
26 Lwcjba uig vwb jm xtmiaivb, jcb kmzbiqvbg qa ijaczl.
```

After looking over each row, you can see that the 8th message is not garbage, but plain English! The cryptanalyst can deduce that the original key for this encrypted text must have been 8. This brute force would have been difficult to do back in the days of Caesars and the Roman Empire, but today we have computers that can quickly go through millions or even billions of keys in a short time. You can even write a program that can recognize when it has found a message in English, so you don't have read through all the garbage text.

Summary: Reviewing Our Caesar Cipher Program

Computers are very good at doing mathematics. When we create a system to translate some piece of information into numbers (such as we do with text and ASCII or with space and coordinate systems), computer programs can process these numbers very quickly and efficiently.

But while our Caesar cipher program here can encrypt messages that will keep them secret from people who have to figure it out with pencil and paper, it won't keep it secret from people who know how to get computers to process information for them. (Our brute force mode proves this.) And there are other cryptographic ciphers that are so advanced that nobody knows how to decrypt the secret messages they make. (Except for the people with the key of course!)

A large part of figuring out how to write a program is figuring out how to represent the information you want to manipulate as numbers. I hope this chapter has especially shown you how this can be done. The next chapter will present our final game, Reversi (also known as Othello). The AI that plays this game will be much more advanced than the AI that played Tic Tac Toe in chapter 9. In fact, the AI is so good, that you'll find that most of the time you will be unable to beat it!

Chapter 15
Reversi

Topics Covered In This Chapter:

- The `bool()` Function
- Evaluating Non-Boolean Values as Booleans

How to Play Reversi

In this chapter we will make a game called Reversi. Reversi (also called Othello) is a board game that is played on a grid (so we will use a Cartesian coordinate system with XY coordinates, like we did with Sonar.) It is a game played with two players. Our version of the game will have a computer AI that is more advanced than the AI we made for Tic Tac Toe. In fact, this AI is so good that it will probably beat you almost every time you play. (I know I lose whenever I play against it!)

If you would like to see a video of Reversi being played, there is a demonstration on this book's website. Go to the URL *http://inventwithpython.com/videos* and find the "Reversi Demo Video" video.

Reversi has an 8 x 8 board with tiles that are black on one side and white on the other (our game will use O's and X's though). The starting board looks like Figure 15-1. Each player takes turn placing down a new tile of their color. Any of the opponent's tiles that are between the new tile and the other tiles of that color is flipped. The goal of the game is to have as many of the tiles with your color as possible. For example, Figure 15-2 is what it looks like if the white player places a new white tile on space 5, 6.

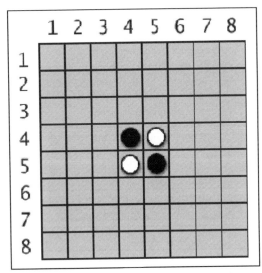

Figure 15-1: The starting Reversi board
has two white tiles and two black tiles.

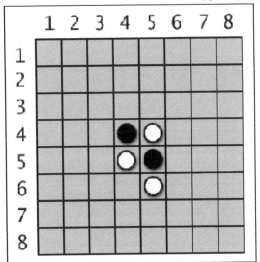

Figure 15-2: White places a new tile.

The black tile at 5, 5 is in between the new white tile and the existing white tile at 5, 4. That black tile is flipped over and becomes a new white tile, making the board look like Figure 15-3. Black makes a similar move next, placing a black tile on 4, 6 which flips the white tile at 4, 5. This results in a board that looks like Figure 15-4.

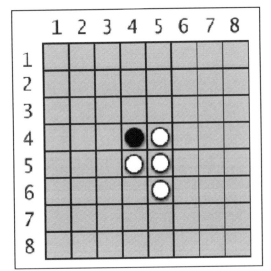

Figure 15-3: White's move will
flip over one of black's tiles.

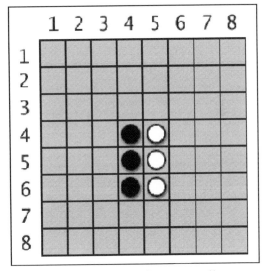

Figure 15-4: Black places a new tile,
which flips over one of white's tiles.

Tiles in all directions are flipped as long as they are in between the player's new tile and existing tile. In Figure 15-5, the white player places a tile at 3, 6 and flips black tiles in both directions (marked by the lines.) The result is in Figure 15-6.

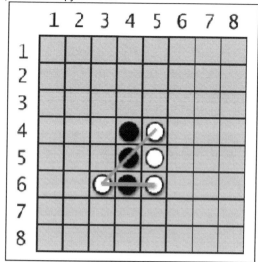
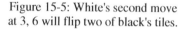

Figure 15-5: White's second move at 3, 6 will flip two of black's tiles.

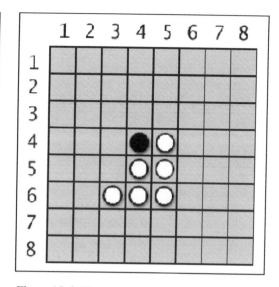

Figure 15-6: The board after white's second move.

As you can see, each player can quickly grab a majority of the tiles on the board in just one or two moves. Players must always make a move that captures at least one tile. The game ends when a player either cannot make a move, or the board is completely full. The player with the most tiles of their color wins.

The basic strategy of Reversi is to look at which move would turn over the most tiles. But you should also consider taking a move that will not let your opponent recapture many tiles after your move. Placing a tile on the sides or, even better, the corners is good because there is less chance that those tiles will end up between your opponent's tiles. The AI we make for this game will simply look for any corner moves they can take. If there are no corner moves available, then the computer will select the move that claims the most tiles.

You can learn more about Reversi from Wikipedia: *http://en.wikipedia.org/wiki/Reversi*

Sample Run

Notice that our version of Reversi doesn't use black and white tiles because the text that our program creates will always be the same color. Instead, we will use X's and O's to represent the human and computer players.

```
Welcome to Reversi!
Do you want to be X or O?
x
The player will go first.
    1   2   3   4   5   6   7   8
  +---+---+---+---+---+---+---+---+
  |   |   |   |   |   |   |   |   |
```

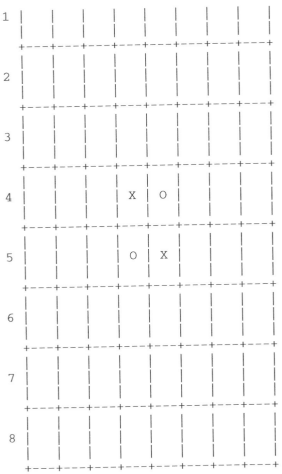

```
1 |   |   |   |   |   |   |   |   |
  |   |   |   |   |   |   |   |   |
  +---+---+---+---+---+---+---+---+
  |   |   |   |   |   |   |   |   |
2 |   |   |   |   |   |   |   |   |
  |   |   |   |   |   |   |   |   |
  +---+---+---+---+---+---+---+---+
  |   |   |   |   |   |   |   |   |
3 |   |   |   |   |   |   |   |   |
  |   |   |   |   |   |   |   |   |
  +---+---+---+---+---+---+---+---+
  |   |   |   |   |   |   |   |   |
4 |   |   |   | X | O |   |   |   |
  |   |   |   |   |   |   |   |   |
  +---+---+---+---+---+---+---+---+
  |   |   |   |   |   |   |   |   |
5 |   |   |   | O | X |   |   |   |
  |   |   |   |   |   |   |   |   |
  +---+---+---+---+---+---+---+---+
  |   |   |   |   |   |   |   |   |
6 |   |   |   |   |   |   |   |   |
  |   |   |   |   |   |   |   |   |
  +---+---+---+---+---+---+---+---+
  |   |   |   |   |   |   |   |   |
7 |   |   |   |   |   |   |   |   |
  |   |   |   |   |   |   |   |   |
  +---+---+---+---+---+---+---+---+
  |   |   |   |   |   |   |   |   |
8 |   |   |   |   |   |   |   |   |
  |   |   |   |   |   |   |   |   |
  +---+---+---+---+---+---+---+---+
```

You have 2 points. The computer has 2 points.
Enter your move, or type quit to end the game, or hints to turn
off/on hints.

53

```
    1   2   3   4   5   6   7   8
  +---+---+---+---+---+---+---+---+
  |   |   |   |   |   |   |   |   |
1 |   |   |   |   |   |   |   |   |
  |   |   |   |   |   |   |   |   |
  +---+---+---+---+---+---+---+---+
  |   |   |   |   |   |   |   |   |
2 |   |   |   |   |   |   |   |   |
  |   |   |   |   |   |   |   |   |
  +---+---+---+---+---+---+---+---+
  |   |   |   |   |   |   |   |   |
3 |   |   |   | X |   |   |   |   |
  |   |   |   |   |   |   |   |   |
  +---+---+---+---+---+---+---+---+
  |   |   |   |   |   |   |   |   |
4 |   |   | X | X |   |   |   |   |
  |   |   |   |   |   |   |   |   |
  +---+---+---+---+---+---+---+---+
  |   |   |   |   |   |   |   |   |
5 |   |   | O | X |   |   |   |   |
  |   |   |   |   |   |   |   |   |
  +---+---+---+---+---+---+---+---+
```

You have 4 points. The computer has 1 points.
Press Enter to see the computer's move.

...skipped for brevity...

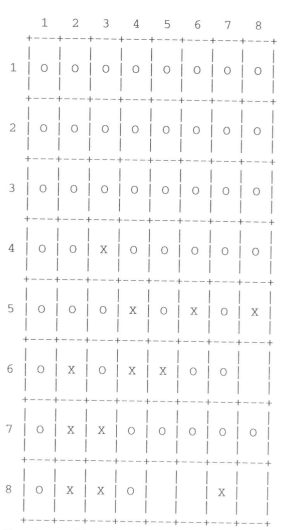

You have 12 points. The computer has 48 points.
Enter your move, or type quit to end the game, or hints to turn
off/on hints.

```
X scored 15 points. O scored 46 points.
You lost. The computer beat you by 31 points.
Do you want to play again? (yes or no)
no
```

As you can see, the AI was pretty good at beating me. To help the player out, we'll program our game to provide hints. If the player types 'hints' as their move, they can toggle the hints mode on and off. When hints mode is on, all the possible moves the player can make will show up on the board as '.' characters, like this:

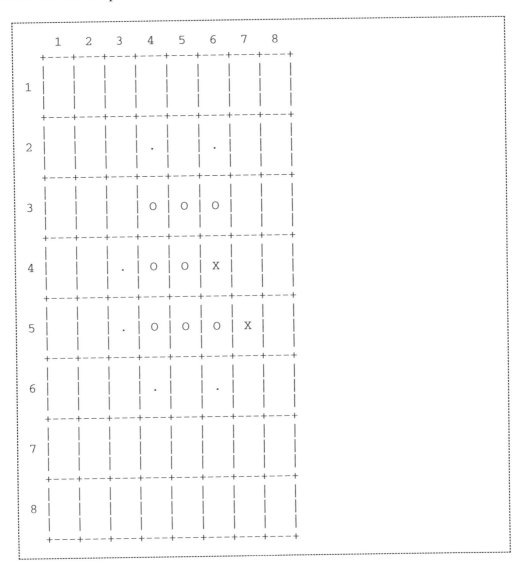

Reversi's Source Code

Reversi is a mammoth program compared to our previous games. It comes in over 300 lines long! (But don't worry, many of these lines are just comments or blank lines to space out the code and make it more readable.) As always, you don't have to type in the program before reading this chapter. And you can also download the program by going to this book's website at the URL, *http://inventwithpython.com/chapter15* and following the instructions online.

As with our other programs, we will first create several functions to carry out Reversi-related tasks that the main section of our program will call. Roughly the first 250 lines of code are for these helper functions, and the last 50 lines of code implement the Reversi game itself.

reversi.py

This code can be downloaded from *http://inventwithpython.com/reversi.py*
If you get errors after typing this code in, compare it to the book's code with the online diff tool at *http://inventwithpython.com/diff* or email the author at al@inventwithpython.com

```
1. # Reversi
2.
3. import random
4. import sys
5.
6. def drawBoard(board):
7.     # This function prints out the board that it was
    passed. Returns None.
8.     HLINE = '    +---+---+---+---+---+---+---+---+'
9.     VLINE = '    |   |   |   |   |   |   |   |   |'
10.
11.     print('    1   2   3   4   5   6   7   8')
12.     print(HLINE)
13.     for y in range(8):
14.         print(VLINE)
15.         print(y+1, end=' ')
16.         for x in range(8):
17.             print('| %s' % (board[x][y]), end=' ')
18.         print('|')
19.         print(VLINE)
20.         print(HLINE)
21.
22.
23. def resetBoard(board):
24.     # Blanks out the board it is passed, except for the
    original starting position.
25.     for x in range(8):
26.         for y in range(8):
27.             board[x][y] = ' '
28.
29.     # Starting pieces:
30.     board[3][3] = 'X'
31.     board[3][4] = 'O'
32.     board[4][3] = 'O'
33.     board[4][4] = 'X'
34.
35.
```

```
36. def getNewBoard():
37.     # Creates a brand new, blank board data structure.
38.     board = []
39.     for i in range(8):
40.         board.append([' '] * 8)
41.
42.     return board
43.
44.
45. def isValidMove(board, tile, xstart, ystart):
46.     # Returns False if the player's move on space xstart,
    ystart is invalid.
47.     # If it is a valid move, returns a list of spaces
    that would become the player's if they made a move here.
48.     if board[xstart][ystart] != ' ' or not isOnBoard
    (xstart, ystart):
49.         return False
50.
51.     board[xstart][ystart] = tile # temporarily set the
    tile on the board.
52.
53.     if tile == 'X':
54.         otherTile = 'O'
55.     else:
56.         otherTile = 'X'
57.
58.     tilesToFlip = []
59.     for xdirection, ydirection in [[0, 1], [1, 1], [1,
    0], [1, -1], [0, -1], [-1, -1], [-1, 0], [-1, 1]]:
60.         x, y = xstart, ystart
61.         x += xdirection # first step in the direction
62.         y += ydirection # first step in the direction
63.         if isOnBoard(x, y) and board[x][y] == otherTile:
64.             # There is a piece belonging to the other
    player next to our piece.
65.             x += xdirection
66.             y += ydirection
67.             if not isOnBoard(x, y):
68.                 continue
69.             while board[x][y] == otherTile:
70.                 x += xdirection
71.                 y += ydirection
72.                 if not isOnBoard(x, y): # break out of
    while loop, then continue in for loop
73.                     break
74.             if not isOnBoard(x, y):
75.                 continue
76.             if board[x][y] == tile:
77.                 # There are pieces to flip over. Go in
    the reverse direction until we reach the original space,
    noting all the tiles along the way.
78.                 while True:
79.                     x -= xdirection
80.                     y -= ydirection
```

```
81.                            if x == xstart and y == ystart:
82.                                break
83.                            tilesToFlip.append([x, y])
84.
85.        board[xstart][ystart] = ' ' # restore the empty space
86.        if len(tilesToFlip) == 0: # If no tiles were flipped,
    this is not a valid move.
87.            return False
88.        return tilesToFlip
89.
90.
91. def isOnBoard(x, y):
92.     # Returns True if the coordinates are located on the
    board.
93.     return x >= 0 and x <= 7 and y >= 0 and y <=7
94.
95.
96. def getBoardWithValidMoves(board, tile):
97.     # Returns a new board with . marking the valid moves
    the given player can make.
98.     dupeBoard = getBoardCopy(board)
99.
100.    for x, y in getValidMoves(dupeBoard, tile):
101.        dupeBoard[x][y] = '.'
102.    return dupeBoard
103.
104.
105. def getValidMoves(board, tile):
106.    # Returns a list of [x,y] lists of valid moves for
    the given player on the given board.
107.    validMoves = []
108.
109.    for x in range(8):
110.        for y in range(8):
111.            if isValidMove(board, tile, x, y) != False:
112.                validMoves.append([x, y])
113.    return validMoves
114.
115.
116. def getScoreOfBoard(board):
117.    # Determine the score by counting the tiles. Returns
    a dictionary with keys 'X' and 'O'.
118.    xscore = 0
119.    oscore = 0
120.    for x in range(8):
121.        for y in range(8):
122.            if board[x][y] == 'X':
123.                xscore += 1
124.            if board[x][y] == 'O':
125.                oscore += 1
126.    return {'X':xscore, 'O':oscore}
127.
128.
129. def enterPlayerTile():
```

```
130.        # Let's the player type which tile they want to be.
131.        # Returns a list with the player's tile as the first
      item, and the computer's tile as the second.
132.        tile = ''
133.        while not (tile == 'X' or tile == 'O'):
134.            print('Do you want to be X or O?')
135.            tile = input().upper()
136.
137.        # the first element in the tuple is the player's
      tile, the second is the computer's tile.
138.        if tile == 'X':
139.            return ['X', 'O']
140.        else:
141.            return ['O', 'X']
142.
143.
144. def whoGoesFirst():
145.        # Randomly choose the player who goes first.
146.        if random.randint(0, 1) == 0:
147.            return 'computer'
148.        else:
149.            return 'player'
150.
151.
152. def playAgain():
153.        # This function returns True if the player wants to
      play again, otherwise it returns False.
154.        print('Do you want to play again? (yes or no)')
155.        return input().lower().startswith('y')
156.
157.
158. def makeMove(board, tile, xstart, ystart):
159.        # Place the tile on the board at xstart, ystart, and
      flip any of the opponent's pieces.
160.        # Returns False if this is an invalid move, True if
      it is valid.
161.        tilesToFlip = isValidMove(board, tile, xstart,
      ystart)
162.
163.        if tilesToFlip == False:
164.            return False
165.
166.        board[xstart][ystart] = tile
167.        for x, y in tilesToFlip:
168.            board[x][y] = tile
169.        return True
170.
171.
172. def getBoardCopy(board):
173.        # Make a duplicate of the board list and return the
      duplicate.
174.        dupeBoard = getNewBoard()
175.
176.        for x in range(8):
```

```
177.              for y in range(8):
178.                  dupeBoard[x][y] = board[x][y]
179.
180.      return dupeBoard
181.
182.
183. def isOnCorner(x, y):
184.      # Returns True if the position is in one of the four
     corners.
185.      return (x == 0 and y == 0) or (x == 7 and y == 0) or
     (x == 0 and y == 7) or (x == 7 and y == 7)
186.
187.
188. def getPlayerMove(board, playerTile):
189.      # Let the player type in their move.
190.      # Returns the move as [x, y] (or returns the strings
     'hints' or 'quit')
191.      DIGITS1TO8 = '1 2 3 4 5 6 7 8'.split()
192.      while True:
193.          print('Enter your move, or type quit to end the
     game, or hints to turn off/on hints.')
194.          move = input().lower()
195.          if move == 'quit':
196.              return 'quit'
197.          if move == 'hints':
198.              return 'hints'
199.
200.          if len(move) == 2 and move[0] in DIGITS1TO8 and
     move[1] in DIGITS1TO8:
201.              x = int(move[0]) - 1
202.              y = int(move[1]) - 1
203.              if isValidMove(board, playerTile, x, y) ==
     False:
204.                  continue
205.              else:
206.                  break
207.          else:
208.              print('That is not a valid move. Type the x
     digit (1-8), then the y digit (1-8).')
209.              print('For example, 81 will be the top-right
     corner.')
210.
211.      return [x, y]
212.
213.
214. def getComputerMove(board, computerTile):
215.      # Given a board and the computer's tile, determine
     where to
216.      # move and return that move as a [x, y] list.
217.      possibleMoves = getValidMoves(board, computerTile)
218.
219.      # randomize the order of the possible moves
220.      random.shuffle(possibleMoves)
221.
```

```
222.        # always go for a corner if available.
223.        for x, y in possibleMoves:
224.            if isOnCorner(x, y):
225.                return [x, y]
226.
227.        # Go through all the possible moves and remember the
     best scoring move
228.        bestScore = -1
229.        for x, y in possibleMoves:
230.            dupeBoard = getBoardCopy(board)
231.            makeMove(dupeBoard, computerTile, x, y)
232.            score = getScoreOfBoard(dupeBoard)[computerTile]
233.            if score > bestScore:
234.                bestMove = [x, y]
235.                bestScore = score
236.        return bestMove
237.
238.
239. def showPoints(playerTile, computerTile):
240.        # Prints out the current score.
241.        scores = getScoreOfBoard(mainBoard)
242.        print('You have %s points. The computer has %s
     points.' % (scores[playerTile], scores[computerTile]))
243.
244.
245.
246. print('Welcome to Reversi!')
247.
248. while True:
249.        # Reset the board and game.
250.        mainBoard = getNewBoard()
251.        resetBoard(mainBoard)
252.        playerTile, computerTile = enterPlayerTile()
253.        showHints = False
254.        turn = whoGoesFirst()
255.        print('The ' + turn + ' will go first.')
256.
257.        while True:
258.            if turn == 'player':
259.                # Player's turn.
260.                if showHints:
261.                    validMovesBoard = getBoardWithValidMoves
     (mainBoard, playerTile)
262.                    drawBoard(validMovesBoard)
263.                else:
264.                    drawBoard(mainBoard)
265.                showPoints(playerTile, computerTile)
266.                move = getPlayerMove(mainBoard, playerTile)
267.                if move == 'quit':
268.                    print('Thanks for playing!')
269.                    sys.exit() # terminate the program
270.                elif move == 'hints':
271.                    showHints = not showHints
272.                    continue
```

```
273.              else:
274.                  makeMove(mainBoard, playerTile, move[0],
     move[1])
275.
276.                  if getValidMoves(mainBoard, computerTile) ==
     []:
277.                      break
278.                  else:
279.                      turn = 'computer'
280.
281.          else:
282.              # Computer's turn.
283.              drawBoard(mainBoard)
284.              showPoints(playerTile, computerTile)
285.              input('Press Enter to see the computer\'s
     move.')
286.              x, y = getComputerMove(mainBoard,
     computerTile)
287.              makeMove(mainBoard, computerTile, x, y)
288.
289.              if getValidMoves(mainBoard, playerTile) ==
     []:
290.                  break
291.              else:
292.                  turn = 'player'
293.
294.      # Display the final score.
295.      drawBoard(mainBoard)
296.      scores = getScoreOfBoard(mainBoard)
297.      print('X scored %s points. O scored %s points.' %
     (scores['X'], scores['O']))
298.      if scores[playerTile] > scores[computerTile]:
299.          print('You beat the computer by %s points!
     Congratulations!' % (scores[playerTile] - scores
     [computerTile]))
300.      elif scores[playerTile] < scores[computerTile]:
301.          print('You lost. The computer beat you by %s
     points.' % (scores[computerTile] - scores[playerTile]))
302.      else:
303.          print('The game was a tie!')
304.
305.      if not playAgain():
306.          break
```

How the Code Works

The Game Board Data Structure

Before we get into the code, we should talk about the board data structure. This data structure is a list of lists, just like the one in our previous Sonar game. The list is created so that board[x][y] will represent the character on space located at position x on the X-

270

axis (going left/right) and position y on the Y-axis (going up/down). This character can either be a ' ' space character (to represent a blank space), a '.' period character (to represent a possible move in hint mode), or an 'X' or 'O' (to represent a player's tile). Whenever you see a parameter named board, that parameter variable is meant to be this list of lists board data structure.

Importing Other Modules

```
1. # Reversi
2.
3. import random
4. import sys
```

We import the random module for its randint() and choice() functions and the sys module for its exit() function.

Drawing the Board Data Structure on the Screen

```
 6. def drawBoard(board):
 7.     # This function prints out the board that it was
        passed. Returns None.
 8.     HLINE = '    +---+---+---+---+---+---+---+---+'
 9.     VLINE = '    |   |   |   |   |   |   |   |   |'
10.
11.     print('    1   2   3   4   5   6   7   8')
12.     print(HLINE)
```

The drawBoard() function will print out the current game board based on the data structure in board. Notice that each square of the board looks like this:

```
+---+
|   |
| X |
|   |
+---+
```

Since we are going to print the string with the horizontal line (and plus signs at the intersections) over and over again, we will store that in a constant variable named HLINE. There are also lines above and below the very center of X or O tile that are nothing but '|' characters (called "pipe" characters) with three spaces in between. We will store this string in a constant named VLINE.

Line 11 is the first print() function call executed, and it prints out the labels for the X-axis along the top of the board. Line 12 prints the top horizontal line of the board.

```
13.        for y in range(8):
14.            print(VLINE)
15.            print(y+1, end=' ')
16.            for x in range(8):
17.                print('| %s' % (board[x][y]), end=' ')
18.            print('|')
19.            print(VLINE)
20.            print(HLINE)
```

Printing each row of spaces on the board is fairly repetitive, so we can use a loop here. We will loop eight times, once for each row. Line 15 prints the label for the Y-axis on the left side of the board, and has an end=' ' keyword argument at the end of it to print a single space instead of a new line. This is so we can have another loop (which again loops eight times, once for each space) print out each space (along with the 'X', 'O', or ' ' character for that space depending on what is stored in board.)

The print() function call inside the inner loop also has an end=' ' keyword argument at the end of it, meaning a space character is printed instead of a newline character. This produces the second space in the pipe-space-tile-space string that we print out, over and over for eight times. That will produce a single line on the screen that looks like '| X | X | X | X | X | X | X | X ' (that is, if each of the board[x] [y] values were 'X'). After the inner loop is done, the print() function call on line 18 prints out the final ' | ' character along with a newline (since it does not end with an end keyword argument).

(The print() call forces us to always print a newline character or a space at the end of everything we print. If we do not want this last character, then we can always use the sys.stdout.write() function, which has a single string parameter that it prints out. Be sure to import sys first before calling this function.)

The code inside the outer for loop from line 14 to line 20 prints out an entire row of the board like this:

```
 |   |   |   |   |   |   |   |   |
 | X | X | X | X | X | X | X | X |
 |   |   |   |   |   |   |   |   |
 +---+---+---+---+---+---+---+---+
```

When the for loop on line 13 prints the row eight times, it forms the entire board (of course, some of the spaces on the board will have 'O' or ' ' instead of 'X'):

```
 |   |   |   |   |   |   |   |   |
 | X | X | X | X | X | X | X | X |
 |   |   |   |   |   |   |   |   |
 +---+---+---+---+---+---+---+---+
 |   |   |   |   |   |   |   |   |
 | X | X | X | X | X | X | X | X |
```

```
|   |   |   |   |   |   |   |   |
+---+---+---+---+---+---+---+---+
|   |   |   |   |   |   |   |   |
| X | X | X | X | X | X | X | X |
|   |   |   |   |   |   |   |   |
+---+---+---+---+---+---+---+---+
|   |   |   |   |   |   |   |   |
| X | X | X | X | X | X | X | X |
|   |   |   |   |   |   |   |   |
+---+---+---+---+---+---+---+---+
|   |   |   |   |   |   |   |   |
| X | X | X | X | X | X | X | X |
|   |   |   |   |   |   |   |   |
+---+---+---+---+---+---+---+---+
|   |   |   |   |   |   |   |   |
| X | X | X | X | X | X | X | X |
|   |   |   |   |   |   |   |   |
+---+---+---+---+---+---+---+---+
|   |   |   |   |   |   |   |   |
| X | X | X | X | X | X | X | X |
|   |   |   |   |   |   |   |   |
+---+---+---+---+---+---+---+---+
|   |   |   |   |   |   |   |   |
| X | X | X | X | X | X | X | X |
|   |   |   |   |   |   |   |   |
+---+---+---+---+---+---+---+---+
|   |   |   |   |   |   |   |   |
| X | X | X | X | X | X | X | X |
|   |   |   |   |   |   |   |   |
+---+---+---+---+---+---+---+---+
```

Resetting the Game Board

An important thing to remember is that the coordinates that we print out to the player are from 1 to 8, but the indexes in the board data structure are from 0 to 7.

```
23. def resetBoard(board):
24.     # Blanks out the board it is passed, except for the
    original starting position.
25.     for x in range(8):
26.         for y in range(8):
27.             board[x][y] = ' '
```

Here we use a loop inside a loop to set the board data structure to be all single-space strings to make a blank Reversi board. We will call the resetBoard() function whenever we start a new game and want to remove the tiles from a previous game.

Setting Up the Starting Pieces

```
29.     # Starting pieces:
30.     board[3][3] = 'X'
31.     board[3][4] = 'O'
32.     board[4][3] = 'O'
```

```
33.        board[4][4] = 'X'
```

When we start a new game of Reversi, it isn't enough to have a completely blank board. At the very beginning, each player has two tiles already laid down in the very center, so we will also have to set those.

We do not have to return the board variable, because board is a reference to a list. Even when we make changes inside the local function's scope, these changes happen to the original list that was passed as an argument. (Remember, this is one way list variables are different from non-list variables.)

Creating a New Game Board Data Structure

```
36. def getNewBoard():
37.     # Creates a brand new, blank board data structure.
38.     board = []
39.     for i in range(8):
40.         board.append([' '] * 8)
41.
42.     return board
```

The getNewBoard() function creates a new board data structure and returns it. Line 38 creates the outer list and stores a reference to this list in board. Line 40 creates the inner lists using list replication. ([' '] * 8 evaluates to be the same as [' ', ' ', ' ', ' ', ' ', ' ', ' ', ' '] but with less typing.) The for loop here runs line 40 eight times to create the eight inner lists. The spaces represent a completely empty game board.

What board ends up being is a list of eight lists, and each of those eight lists themselves has eight strings. The result is sixty four (8 x 8 = 64) strings. Each string is (right now) a single space character.

Checking if a Move is Valid

```
45. def isValidMove(board, tile, xstart, ystart):
46.     # Returns False if the player's move on space xstart,
    ystart is invalid.
47.     # If it is a valid move, returns a list of spaces
    that would become the player's if they made a move here.
48.     if board[xstart][ystart] != ' ' or not isOnBoard
    (xstart, ystart):
49.         return False
50.
51.     board[xstart][ystart] = tile # temporarily set the
    tile on the board.
52.
53.     if tile == 'X':
```

```
54.            otherTile = 'O'
55.        else:
56.            otherTile = 'X'
57.
58.        tilesToFlip = []
```

`isValidMove()` is one of the more complicated functions. Given a board data structure, the player's tile, and the XY coordinates for player's move, this function should return `True` if the Reversi game rules allow a move to those coordinates and `False` if they don't.

The easiest check we can do to disqualify a move is to see if the XY coordinates are on the game board or if the space at XY is not empty. This is what the `if` statement on line 48 checks for. `isOnBoard()` is a function we will write that makes sure both the X and Y coordinates are between 0 and 7. We do this on line 48 and 49.

For the purposes of this function, we will go ahead and copy the XY coordinate pointed to by `xstart` and `ystart` with the player's tile. We set this place on the board back to a space before we leave this function.

The player's tile (either the human player or the computer player) has been passed to us, but we will need to be able to identify the other player's tile. If the player's tile is `'X'` then obviously the other player's tile is `'O'`, and vice versa.

Finally, if the given XY coordinate ends up as a valid position, we will return a list of all the opponent's tiles that would be flipped by this move.

```
59.    for xdirection, ydirection in [[0, 1], [1, 1], [1,
    0], [1, -1], [0, -1], [-1, -1], [-1, 0], [-1, 1]]:
```

The `for` loop iterates through a list of lists which represent directions you can move on the game board. The game board is a Cartesian coordinate system with an X and Y direction. There are eight directions you can move: up, down, left, right, and the four diagonal directions. Each of the eight 2-item lists in the list on line 59 represents one of these directions. We will move around the board in a direction by adding the first value in the two-item list to our X coordinate, and the second value to our Y coordinate.

Because the X coordinates increase as you go to the right, you can "move" to the right by adding 1 to the X coordinate. Moving to the left is the opposite: you would subtract 1 (or add -1) from the X coordinate. We can move up, down, left, and right by adding or subtracting to only one coordinate at a time. But to move diagonally, we need to add or subtract to both coordinates. For example, adding 1 to the X coordinate to move right and adding -1 to the Y coordinate to move up would result in moving to the up-right diagonal direction.

Checking Each of the Eight Directions

Here is a diagram to make it easier to remember which two-item list represents which direction:

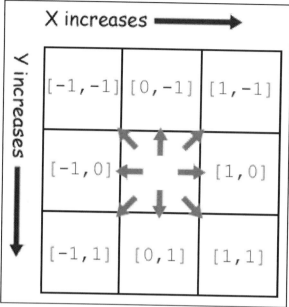

Figure 15-7: Each two-item list represents one of the eight directions.

```
59.        for xdirection, ydirection in [[0, 1], [1, 1], [1,
   0], [1, -1], [0, -1], [-1, -1], [-1, 0], [-1, 1]]:
60.            x, y = xstart, ystart
61.            x += xdirection # first step in the direction
62.            y += ydirection # first step in the direction
```

Line 60 sets an x and y variable to be the same value as xstart and ystart, respectively. We will change x and y to "move" in the direction that xdirection and ydirection dictate. xstart and ystart will stay the same so we can remember which space we originally intended to check. (Remember, we need to set this place back to a space character, so we shouldn't overwrite the values in them.)

We make the first step in the direction as the first part of our algorithm.

```
63.            if isOnBoard(x, y) and board[x][y] == otherTile:
64.                # There is a piece belonging to the other
   player next to our piece.
65.                x += xdirection
66.                y += ydirection
67.                if not isOnBoard(x, y):
68.                    continue
```

Remember, in order for this to be a valid move, the first step in this direction must be 1) on the board and 2) must be occupied by the other player's tile. Otherwise there is no chance to flip over any of the opponent's tiles. In that case, the `if` statement on line 63 is not `True` and execution goes back to the `for` statement for the next direction.

But if the first space does have the other player's tile, then we should keep proceeding in that direction until we reach on of our own tiles. If we move off of the board, then we should continue back to the `for` statement to try the next direction.

```
69.                 while board[x][y] == otherTile:
70.                     x += xdirection
71.                     y += ydirection
72.                     if not isOnBoard(x, y): # break out of
    while loop, then continue in for loop
73.                         break
74.                 if not isOnBoard(x, y):
75.                     continue
```

The `while` loop on line 69 ensures that `x` and `y` keep going in the current direction as long as we keep seeing a trail of the other player's tiles. If `x` and `y` move off of the board, we break out of the `for` loop and the flow of execution moves to line 74. What we really want to do is break out of the `while` loop but continue in the `for` loop. But if we put a `continue` statement on line 73, that would only continue to the `while` loop on line 69.

Instead, we recheck `not isOnBoard(x, y)` on line 74 and then continue from there, which goes to the next direction in the `for` statement on line 59. It is important to know that `break` and `continue` will only break or continue in the loop they are called from, and not an outer loop that contain the loop they are called from.

Finding Out if There are Pieces to Flip Over

```
76.                 if board[x][y] == tile:
77.                     # There are pieces to flip over. Go in
    the reverse direction until we reach the original space,
    noting all the tiles along the way.
78.                     while True:
79.                         x -= xdirection
80.                         y -= ydirection
81.                         if x == xstart and y == ystart:
82.                             break
83.                         tilesToFlip.append([x, y])
```

If the `while` loop on line 69 stopped looping because the condition was `False`, then we have found a space on the board that holds our own tile or a blank space. Line 76 checks if this space on the board holds one of our tiles. If it does, then we have found a valid move. We will then start a new `while` loop, this time subtracting `x` and `y` to move in the opposite direction we were originally going. We note each space between our tiles on the board by appending the space to the tilesToFlip list.

We break out of the while loop once x and y have returned to the original position (which was still stored in xstart and ystart).

```
85.        board[xstart][ystart] = ' ' # restore the empty space
86.        if len(tilesToFlip) == 0: # If no tiles were flipped,
    this is not a valid move.
87.            return False
88.        return tilesToFlip
```

We perform this check in all eight directions, and afterwards the tilesToFlip list will contain the XY coordinates all of our opponent's tiles that would be flipped if the player moved on xstart, ystart. Remember, the isValidMove() function is only checking to see if the original move was valid, it does not actually change the data structure of the game board.

If none of the eight directions ended up flipping at least one of the opponent's tiles, then tilesToFlip would be an empty list and this move would not be valid. In that case, isValidMove() should return False. Otherwise, we should return tilesToFlip.

Checking for Valid Coordinates

```
91. def isOnBoard(x, y):
92.     # Returns True if the coordinates are located on the
    board.
93.        return x >= 0 and x <= 7 and y >= 0 and y <=7
```

isOnBoard() is a function called from isValidMove(), and is just shorthand for the rather complicated Boolean expression that returns True if both x and y are in between 0 and 7. This function lets us make sure that the coordinates are actually on the game board.

Getting a List with All Valid Moves

```
 96. def getBoardWithValidMoves(board, tile):
 97.     # Returns a new board with . marking the valid moves
    the given player can make.
 98.     dupeBoard = getBoardCopy(board)
 99.
100.     for x, y in getValidMoves(dupeBoard, tile):
101.         dupeBoard[x][y] = '.'
102.     return dupeBoard
```

`getBoardWithValidMoves()` is used to return a game board data structure that has '.' characters for all valid moves on the board. This is used by the hints mode to display to the player a board with all possible moves marked on it.

Notice that this function creates a duplicate game board data structure instead of modifying the one passed to it in the `board` parameter. Line 100 calls `getValidMoves()`, which returns a list of XY coordinates with all the legal moves the player could make. The board copy is then marked with a period in those spaces. How `getValidMoves()` works is described next.

```
105. def getValidMoves(board, tile):
106.     # Returns a list of [x,y] lists of valid moves for
     the given player on the given board.
107.     validMoves = []
108.
109.     for x in range(8):
110.         for y in range(8):
111.             if isValidMove(board, tile, x, y) != False:
112.                 validMoves.append([x, y])
113.     return validMoves
```

The `getValidMoves()` function returns a list of two-item lists that hold the XY coordinates for all valid moves for tile's player, given a particular game board data structure in `board`.

This function uses two loops to check every single XY coordinate (all sixty four of them) by calling `isValidMove()` on that space and checking if it returns `False` or a list of possible moves (in which case it is a valid move). Each valid XY coordinate is appended to the list, `validMoves`.

The `bool()` Function

Remember how you could use the `int()` and `str()` functions to get the integer and string value of other data types? For example, `str(42)` would return the string `'42'`, and `int('100')` would return the integer `100`.

There is a similar function for the Boolean data type, `bool()`. Most other data types have one value that is considered the `False` value for that data type, and every other value is consider `True`. The integer `0`, the floating point number `0.0`, the empty string, the empty list, and the empty dictionary are all considered to be `False` when used as the condition for an `if` or loop statement. All other values are `True`. Try entering the following into the interactive shell:

```
>>> bool(0)
False
>>> bool(0.0)
```

```
False
>>> bool('')
False
>>> bool([])
False
>>> bool({})
False
>>> bool(1)
True
>>> bool('Hello')
True
>>> bool([1, 2, 3, 4, 5])
True
>>> bool({'spam':'cheese', 'fizz':'buzz'})
True
>>>
```

Whenever you have a condition, imagine that the entire condition is placed inside a call to bool() as the parameter. Conditions are automatically interpreted as Boolean values. This is similar to how print() can be passed non-string values and will automatically interpret them as strings when they print.

This is why the condition on line 111 works correctly. The call to the isValidMove() function either returns the Boolean value False or a non-empty list. If you imagine that the entire condition is placed inside a call to bool(), then the condition False becomes bool(False) (which, of course, evalutes to False). And a condition of a non-empty list placed as the parameter to bool() will return True. This is why the return value of isValidMove() can be used as a condition.

Getting the Score of the Game Board

```
116. def getScoreOfBoard(board):
117.     # Determine the score by counting the tiles. Returns
      a dictionary with keys 'X' and 'O'.
118.     xscore = 0
119.     oscore = 0
120.     for x in range(8):
121.         for y in range(8):
122.             if board[x][y] == 'X':
123.                 xscore += 1
124.             if board[x][y] == 'O':
125.                 oscore += 1
126.     return {'X':xscore, 'O':oscore}
```

The getScoreOfBoard() function uses nested for loops to check all 64 spaces on the board (8 rows times 8 columns per row is 64 spaces) and see which tile (if any) is on them. For each `'X'` tile, the code increments `xscore`. For each `'O'` tile, the code increments `oscore`.

Notice that this function does not return a two-item list of the scores. A two-item list might be a bit confusing, because you may forget which item is for X and which item is for O. Instead the function returns a dictionary with keys `'X'` and `'O'` whose values are the scores.

Getting the Player's Tile Choice

```
129. def enterPlayerTile():
130.     # Let's the player type which tile they want to be.
131.     # Returns a list with the player's tile as the first
     item, and the computer's tile as the second.
132.     tile = ''
133.     while not (tile == 'X' or tile == 'O'):
134.         print('Do you want to be X or O?')
135.         tile = input().upper()
```

This function asks the player which tile they want to be, either `'X'` or `'O'`. The `for` loop will keep looping until the player types in `'X'` or `'O'`.

```
137.     # the first element in the tuple is the player's
     tile, the second is the computer's tile.
138.     if tile == 'X':
139.         return ['X', 'O']
140.     else:
141.         return ['O', 'X']
```

The `enterPlayerTile()` function then returns a two-item list, where the player's tile choice is the first item and the computer's tile is the second. We use a list here instead of a dictionary so that the assignment statement calling this function can use the multiple assignment trick. (See line 252.)

Determining Who Goes First

```
144. def whoGoesFirst():
145.     # Randomly choose the player who goes first.
146.     if random.randint(0, 1) == 0:
147.         return 'computer'
148.     else:
149.         return 'player'
```

The `whoGoesFirst()` function randomly selects who goes first, and returns either the string `'computer'` or the string `'player'`.

Asking the Player to Play Again

```
152. def playAgain():
153.     # This function returns True if the player wants to
     play again, otherwise it returns False.
154.     print('Do you want to play again? (yes or no)')
155.     return input().lower().startswith('y')
```

We have used the playAgain() in our previous games. If the player types in something that begins with 'y', then the function returns True. Otherwise the function returns False.

Placing Down a Tile on the Game Board

```
158. def makeMove(board, tile, xstart, ystart):
159.     # Place the tile on the board at xstart, ystart, and
     flip any of the opponent's pieces.
160.     # Returns False if this is an invalid move, True if
     it is valid.
161.     tilesToFlip = isValidMove(board, tile, xstart,
     ystart)
```

makeMove() is the function we call when we want to place a tile on the board and flip the other tiles according to the rules of Reversi. This function modifies the board data structure that is passed as a parameter directly. Changes made to the board variable (because it is a list) will be made to the global scope as well. Most of the work is done by isValidMove(), which returns a list of XY coordinates (in a two-item list) of tiles that need to be flipped. (Remember, if the the xstart and ystart arguments point to an invalid move, then isValidMove() will return the Boolean value False.)

```
163.     if tilesToFlip == False:
164.         return False
165.
166.     board[xstart][ystart] = tile
167.     for x, y in tilesToFlip:
168.         board[x][y] = tile
169.     return True
```

On lines 163 and 164, if the return value of isValidMove() was False, then makeMove() will also return False.

Otherwise, isValidMove() would have returned a list of spaces on the board to put down our tiles (the 'X' or 'O' string in tile). Line 166 sets the space that the player has moved on, and the for loop after that sets all the tiles that are in tilesToFlip.

Copying the Board Data Structure

```
172. def getBoardCopy(board):
173.     # Make a duplicate of the board list and return the
     duplicate.
174.     dupeBoard = getNewBoard()
175.
176.     for x in range(8):
177.         for y in range(8):
178.             dupeBoard[x][y] = board[x][y]
179.
180.     return dupeBoard
```

getBoardCopy() is different from getNewBoard(). getNewBoad() will create a new game board data structure which has only empty spaces and the four starting tiles. getBoardCopy() will create a new game board data structure, but then copy all of the pieces in the board parameter. This function is used by our AI to have a game board that it can change around so that it doesn't have to change the real game board. This is like how you may imagine making moves on a copy of the board in your mind, but not actually put pieces down on the real board.

A call to getNewBoard() handles getting a fresh game board data structure. Then the two for loops copy each of the 64 tiles from board to our duplicate board data structure named dupeBoard.

Determining if a Space is on a Corner

```
183. def isOnCorner(x, y):
184.     # Returns True if the position is in one of the four
     corners.
185.     return (x == 0 and y == 0) or (x == 7 and y == 0) or
     (x == 0 and y == 7) or (x == 7 and y == 7)
```

This function is much like isOnBoard(). Because all Reversi boards are 8 x 8 in size, we only need the XY coordinates to be passed to this function, not a game board data structure itself. This function returns True if the coordinates are on either (0,0), (7,0), (0,7) or (7,7). Otherwise isOnCorner() returns False.

Getting the Player's Move

```
188. def getPlayerMove(board, playerTile):
189.     # Let the player type in their move.
190.     # Returns the move as [x, y] (or returns the strings
     'hints' or 'quit')
191.     DIGITS1TO8 = '1 2 3 4 5 6 7 8'.split()
```

The getPlayerMove() function is called to let the player type in the coordinates of their next move (and check if the move is valid). The player can also type in 'hints' to turn hints mode on (if it is off) or off (if it is on). The player can also type in 'quit' to quit the game.

The DIGITS1TO8 constant variable is the list ['1', '2', '3', '4', '5', '6', '7', '8']. We create this constant because it is easier type DIGITS1TO8 than the entire list. (We can't use the isdigit() method because that would allow 0 and 9 to be entered, which are not valid coordinates on our 8x8 board.)

```
192.        while True:
193.            print('Enter your move, or type quit to end the
        game, or hints to turn off/on hints.')
194.            move = input().lower()
195.            if move == 'quit':
196.                return 'quit'
197.            if move == 'hints':
198.                return 'hints'
```

The while loop will keep looping until the player has typed in a valid move. First we check if the player wants to quit or toggle hints mode, and return the string 'quit' or 'hints'. We use the lower() method on the string returned by input() so the player can type 'HINTS' or 'Quit' but still have the command understood by our game.

The code that calls getPlayerMove() will handle what to do if the player wants to quit or toggle hints mode.

```
200.            if len(move) == 2 and move[0] in DIGITS1TO8 and
        move[1] in DIGITS1TO8:
201.                x = int(move[0]) - 1
202.                y = int(move[1]) - 1
203.                if isValidMove(board, playerTile, x, y) ==
        False:
204.                    continue
205.                else:
206.                    break
```

Our game is expecting that the player would have typed in the XY coordinates of their move as two numbers without anything in between them. The if statement first checks that the size of the string the player typed in is 2. After that, the if statement also checks that both move[0] (the first character in the string) and move[1] (the second character in the string) are strings that exist in DIGITS1TO8, which we defined at the beginning of the function.

Remember that our game board data structures have indexes from 0 to 7, not 1 to 8. We show 1 to 8 when we print the board using drawBoard() because people are used to numbers beginning at 1 instead of 0. So when we convert the strings in `move[0]` and `move[1]` to integers, we also subtract 1.

Even if the player typed in a correct move, we still need to check that the move is allowed by the rules of Reversi. We do this by calling `isValidMove()`, passing the game board data structure, the player's tile, and the XY coordinates of the move. If `isValidMove()` returns `False`, then we execute the `continue` statement so that the flow of execution goes back to the beginning of the `while` loop and asks the player for the move again.

If `isValidMove()` does not return `False`, then we know the player typed in a valid move and we should break out of the `while` loop.

```
207.           else:
208.               print('That is not a valid move. Type the x
        digit (1-8), then the y digit (1-8).')
209.               print('For example, 81 will be the top-right
        corner.')
```

If the `if` statement's condition on line 200 was `False`, then the player did not type in a valid move. We should display a message instructing them how to type in moves that our Reversi program can understand. Afterwards, the execution moves back to the `while` statement on line 192 because line 209 is not only the last line in the else-block, but also the last line in the while-block.

```
211.       return [x, y]
```

Finally, `getPlayerMove()` returns a two-item list with the XY coordinates of the player's valid move.

Getting the Computer's Move

```
214. def getComputerMove(board, computerTile):
215.     # Given a board and the computer's tile, determine
        where to
216.     # move and return that move as a [x, y] list.
217.     possibleMoves = getValidMoves(board, computerTile)
```

`getComputerMove()` and is where our AI algorithm is implemented. The `getValidMoves()` function is very helpful for our AI. Normally we use the results from `getValidMoves()` for hints mode. Hints mode will print `'.'` period characters on the board to show the player all the potential moves they can make. But if we call `getValidMoves()` with the computer AI's tile (in `computerTile`), we can get all the possible moves that the computer can make. We will select the best move from this list.

```
219.        # randomize the order of the possible moves
220.        random.shuffle(possibleMoves)
```

First, we are going to use the `random.shuffle()` function to randomize the order of moves in the `possibleMoves` list. Remember that the `random.shuffle()` function will reorder the items in the list that you pass to it. The function also modifies the list directly, much like our `resetBoard()` function does with the game board data structure.

We will explain why we want to shuffle the `possibleMoves` list, but first let's look at our algorithm.

Corner Moves are the Best Moves

```
222.        # always go for a corner if available.
223.        for x, y in possibleMoves:
224.            if isOnCorner(x, y):
225.                return [x, y]
```

First, we loop through every move in `possibleMoves` and if any of them are on the corner, we return that as our move. Corner moves are a good idea because once a tile has been placed on the corner, it can never be flipped over. Since `possibleMoves` is a list of two-item lists, we use the multiple assignment trick in our `for` loop to set `x` and `y`.

Because we immediately return on finding the first corner move in `possibleMoves`, if `possibleMoves` contains multiple corner moves we always go with the first one. But since `possibleMoves` was shuffled on line 220, it is completely random which corner move is first in the list.

Get a List of the Best Scoring Moves

```
227.        # Go through all the possible moves and remember the
        best scoring move
228.        bestScore = -1
229.        for x, y in possibleMoves:
230.            dupeBoard = getBoardCopy(board)
231.            makeMove(dupeBoard, computerTile, x, y)
232.            score = getScoreOfBoard(dupeBoard)[computerTile]
233.            if score > bestScore:
234.                bestMove = [x, y]
235.                bestScore = score
236.        return bestMove
```

If there are no corner moves, we will go through the entire list and find out which move gives us the highest score. The `for` loop will set `x` and `y` to every move in `possibleMoves`. `bestMove` will be set to the highest scoring move we've found so far, and `bestScore` will be set to the best move's score. When the code in the loop finds a move that scores higher than `bestScore`, we will store that move and score as the new values of `bestMove` and `bestScore` (see lines 233, 234, and 235).

Simulate All Possible Moves on Duplicate Board Data Structures

In order to figure out the score of the possible move we are currently iterating on, we first make a duplicate game board data structure by calling `getBoardCopy()` on line 230. We want a copy so we can modify without changing the real game board data structure stored in the `board` variable.

Then we call `makeMove()` on line 231, passing the duplicate board (stored in `dupeBoard`) instead of the real board. `makeMove()` will handle placing the computer's tile and the flipping the player's tiles on the duplicate board.

We call `getScoreOfBoard()` on line 232 with the duplicate board, which returns a dictionary where the keys are `'X'` and `'O'`, and the values are the scores. `getScoreOfBoard()` does not know if the computer is `'X'` or `'O'`, which is why it returns a dictionary with both scores.

By making a duplicate board, we can simulate a future move and test the results of that move without changing the actual game board data structure. This is very helpful in deciding which move is the best possible move to make.

Pretend that `getScoreOfBoard()` returns the dictionary `{'X':22, 'O':8}` and `computerTile` is `'X'`. Then `getScoreOfBoard(dupeBoard)[computerTile]` would evaluate to `{'X':22, 'O':8}['X']`, which would then evaluate to 22. If 22 is larger than `bestScore`, `bestScore` is set to 22 and `bestMove` is set to the current x and y values we are looking at. By the time this `for` loop is finished, we can be sure that `bestScore` is the highest possible score a move can make, and that move is stored in `bestMove`.

You may have noticed that on line 228 we first set `bestScore` to `-1`. This is so that the first move we look at in our `for` loop over `possibleMoves` will be set to the first `bestMove`. This will guarantee that `bestMove` is set to one of the moves when we return it.

Say that the highest scoring move in `possibleMoves` would give the computer a score of 42. What if there was more than one move in `possibleMoves` that would give this score? The `for` loop we use would always go with the first move that scored 42 points, because `bestMove` and `bestScore` only change if the move is greater than the highest score. A tie will not change `bestMove` and `bestScore`.

We do not always want to go with the first move in the `possibleMoves` list if it had not been shuffled on line 220, because that would make our AI predictable by the player. Even though our code always chooses the first of these tied moves, is random which of the moves will be first in the list because the order is random. This ensures that the AI will not be predictable when there is more than one best move.

Printing the Scores to the Screen

```
239. def showPoints(playerTile, computerTile):
240.     # Prints out the current score.
241.     scores = getScoreOfBoard(mainBoard)
242.     print('You have %s points. The computer has %s
     points.' % (scores[playerTile], scores[computerTile]))
```

showPoints() simply calls the getScoreOfBoard() function and then prints out the player's score and the computer's score. Remember that getScoreOfBoard() returns a dictionary with the keys 'X' and 'O' and values of the scores for the X and O players.

That's all the functions we define for our Reversi game. The code starting on line 246 will implement the actual game and make calls to these functions when they are needed.

The Start of the Game

```
246. print('Welcome to Reversi!')
247.
248. while True:
249.     # Reset the board and game.
250.     mainBoard = getNewBoard()
251.     resetBoard(mainBoard)
252.     playerTile, computerTile = enterPlayerTile()
253.     showHints = False
254.     turn = whoGoesFirst()
255.     print('The ' + turn + ' will go first.')
```

The while loop on line 248 is the main game loop. The program will loop back to line 248 each time we want to start a new game. First we get a new game board data structure by calling getNewBoard() and set the starting tiles by calling resetBoard(). mainBoard is the main game board data structure we will use for this program. The call to enterPlayerTile() will let the player type in whether they want to be 'X' or 'O', which is then stored in playerTile and computerTile.

showHints is a Boolean value that determines if hints mode is on or off. We originally set it to off by setting showHints to False.

The turn variable is a string will either have the string value 'player' or 'computer', and will keep track of whose turn it is. We set turn to the return value of whoGoesFirst(), which randomly chooses who will go first. We then print out who goes first to the player on line 255.

Running the Player's Turn

```
257.        while True:
258.            if turn == 'player':
259.                # Player's turn.
260.                if showHints:
261.                    validMovesBoard = getBoardWithValidMoves
        (mainBoard, playerTile)
262.                    drawBoard(validMovesBoard)
263.                else:
264.                    drawBoard(mainBoard)
265.                showPoints(playerTile, computerTile)
```

The `while` loop that starts on line 257 will keep looping each time the player or computer takes a turn. We will break out of this loop when the current game is over.

Line 258 has an `if` statement whose body has the code that runs if it is the player's turn. (The else-block that starts on line 282 has the code for the computer's turn.) The first thing we want to do is display the board to the player. If hints mode is on (which it is if `showHints` is `True`), then we want to get a board data structure that has `'.'` period characters on every space the player could go.

Our `getBoardWithValidMoves()` function does that, all we have to do is pass the game board data structure and it will return a copy that also contains `'.'` period characters. We then pass this board to the `drawBoard()` function on line 262.

If hints mode is off, then we just pass `mainBoard` to `drawBoard()` on line 264.

After printing out the game board to the player, we also want to print out the current score by calling `showPoints()` on line 265.

```
266.                move = getPlayerMove(mainBoard, playerTile)
```

Next we let the player type in their move. `getPlayerMove()` handles this, and its return value is a two-item list of the XY coordinate of the player's move. `getPlayerMove()` makes sure that the move the player typed in is a valid move, so we don't have to worry about it here.

Handling the Quit or Hints Commands

```
267.                    if move == 'quit':
268.                        print('Thanks for playing!')
269.                        sys.exit() # terminate the program
270.                    elif move == 'hints':
271.                        showHints = not showHints
272.                        continue
273.                    else:
274.                        makeMove(mainBoard, playerTile, move[0],
        move[1])
```

If the player typed in the string `'quit'` for their move, then `getPlayerMove()` would have returned the string `'quit'`. In that case, we should call the `sys.exit()` to terminate the program.

If the player typed in the string `'hints'` for their move, then `getPlayerMove()` would have returned the string `'hints'`. In that case, we want to turn hints mode on (if it was off) or off (if it was on). The `showHints = not showHints` assignment statement handles both of these cases, because `not False` evaluates to `True` and `not True` evaluates to `False`. Then we run the `continue` statement to loop back (`turn` has not changed, so it will still be the player's turn when we continue).

Make the Player's Move

Otherwise, if the player did not quit or toggle hints mode, then we will call `makeMove()` to make the player's move on the board.

```
276.                    if getValidMoves(mainBoard, computerTile) ==
        []:
277.                        break
278.                    else:
279.                        turn = 'computer'
```

After making the player's move, we call `False` to see if the computer could possibly make any moves. If `False` returns a blank list, then there are no more moves left that the computer could make (most likely because the board is full). In that case, we break out of the `while` loop and end the current game.

Otherwise, we set `turn` to `'computer'`. The flow of execution skips the else-block and reaches the end of the while-block, so execution jumps back to the `while` statement on line 257. This time, however, it will be the computer's turn.

Running the Computer's Turn

```
281.          else:
282.              # Computer's turn.
283.              drawBoard(mainBoard)
284.              showPoints(playerTile, computerTile)
285.              input('Press Enter to see the computer\'s
     move.')
286.              x, y = getComputerMove(mainBoard,
     computerTile)
287.              makeMove(mainBoard, computerTile, x, y)
```

The first thing we do when it is the computer's turn is call drawBoard() to print out the board to the player. Why do we do this now? Because either the computer was selected to make the first move of the game, in which case we should display the original starting picture of the board to the player before the computer makes its move. Or the player has gone first, and we want to show what the board looks like after the player has moved but before the computer has gone.

After printing out the board with drawBoard(), we also want to print out the current score with a call to showPoints() on line 284.

Next we have a call to input() on line 285 to pause the script while the player can look at the board. This is much like how we use input() to pause the program in our Jokes chapter. Instead of using a print() call to print a string before a call to input(), you can pass the string as a parameter to input(). input() has an optional string parameter. The string we pass in this call is 'Press Enter to see the computer\'s move.'.

After the player has looked at the board and pressed Enter (any text the player typed is ignored since we do not assign the return value of input() to anything), we call getComputerMove() to get the XY coordinates of the computer's next move. We store these coordinates in variables x and y, respectively.

Finally, we pass x and y, along with the game board data structure and the computer's tile to the makeMove() function to change the game board to reflect the computer's move. Our call to getComputerMove() on line 286 got the computer's move (and stored it in variables x and y), and the call to makeMove() on line 287 makes the move on the board.

```
289.              if getValidMoves(mainBoard, playerTile) ==
     []:
290.                  break
291.          else:
292.              turn = 'player'
```

Lines 289 to 292 are very similar to lines 276 to 279. After the computer has made its move, we check if there exist any possible moves the human player can make. If getValidMoves() returns an empty list, then there are no possible moves. That means the game is over, and we should break out of the while loop that we are in.

Otherwise, there is at least one possible move the player should make, so we should set turn to 'player'. There is no more code in the while-block after line 292, so execution loops back to the while statement on line 257.

Drawing Everything on the Screen

```
294.        # Display the final score.
295.        drawBoard(mainBoard)
296.        scores = getScoreOfBoard(mainBoard)
297.        print('X scored %s points. O scored %s points.' %
            (scores['X'], scores['O']))
298.        if scores[playerTile] > scores[computerTile]:
299.            print('You beat the computer by %s points!
            Congratulations!' % (scores[playerTile] - scores
            [computerTile]))
300.        elif scores[playerTile] < scores[computerTile]:
301.            print('You lost. The computer beat you by %s
            points.' % (scores[computerTile] - scores[playerTile]))
302.        else:
303.            print('The game was a tie!')
```

Line 294 is the first line beyond the while-block that started on line 257. This code is executed when we have broken out of that while loop, either on line 290 or 277. (The while statement's condition on line 257 is simply the value True, so we can only exit the loop through break statements.)

At this point, the game is over. We should print out the board and scores, and determine who won the game. getScoreOfBoard() will return a dictionary with keys 'X' and 'O' and values of both players' scores. By checking if the player's score is greater than, less than, or equal to the computer's score, we can know if the player won, if the player lost, or if the player and computer tied.

Subtracting one score from the other is an easy way to see by how much one player won over the other. Our print() calls on lines 299 and 301 use string interpolation to put the integer result of this subtraction into the string that is printed.

Ask the Player to Play Again

```
305.    if not playAgain():
306.        break
```

The game is now over and the winner has been declared. We should call our `playAgain()` function, which returns `True` if the player typed in that they want to play another game. If `playAgain()` returns `False` (which makes the `if` statement's condition `True`), we break out of the `while` loop (the one that started on line 248), and since there are no more lines of code after this while-block, the program terminates.

Otherwise, `playAgain()` has returned `True` (which makes the `if` statement's condition `False`), and so execution loops back to the `while` statement on line 248 and a new game board is created.

Changing The `drawBoard()` Function

The board we draw for our Reversi game is fairly large. But we could change the `drawBoard()` function's code to draw out a much smaller board, while keeping the rest of the game code the same. The new, smaller board would look something like this:

```
   12345678
  +--------+
1|    O   |
2|   XOX  |
3|    O   |
4| XXXXX  |
5|  .OX   |
6|  OOO   |
7| ..O..  |
8|    O   |
  +--------+
You have 8 points. The computer has 9 points.
Enter your move, or type quit to end the game, or
hints to turn off/on hints.
```

Here is the code for this new `drawBoard()` function, starting at line 6. You can also download this code from *http://inventwithpython.com/reversi_mini.py*

```
 6. def drawBoard(board):
 7.     # This function prints out the board that it was
    passed. Returns None.
 8.     HLINE = '  +--------+'
 9.     print('  12345678')
10.     print(HLINE)
11.     for y in range(8):
12.         print('%s|' % (y+1), end='')
13.         for x in range(8):
14.             print(board[x][y], end='')
15.         print('|')
```

```
16.        print(HLINE)
```

Summary: Reviewing the Reversi Game

The AI may seem almost unbeatable, but this isn't because the computer is very smart. The strategy it follows is very simple: move on the corner if you can, otherwise make the move that will flip over the most tiles. We could do that, but it would take us a long time to figure out how many tiles would be flipped for every possible valid move we could make. But calculating this for the computer is very simple. The computer isn't smarter than us, it's just much faster!

This game is very similar to Sonar because it makes use of a grid for a board. It is also like the Tic Tac Toe game because there is an AI that plans out the best move for it to take. This chapter only introduced one new concept: using the `bool()` function and the fact that empty lists, blank strings, and the integer `0` all evaluate to `False` in the context of a condition.

Other than that, this game used programming concepts that you already knew! You don't have to know very much about programming in order to create interesting games. However, this game is stretching how far you can get with ASCII art. The board took up almost the entire screen to draw, and the game didn't have any color.

Later in this book, we will learn how to create games with graphics and animation, not just text. We will do this using a module called Pygame, which adds new functions and features to Python so that we can break away from using just text and keyboard input.

Chapter 16

AI Simulation

Topics Covered In This Chapter:

- Simulations
- Percentages
- Pie Charts
- Integer Division
- The round() Function

"Computer vs. Computer" Games

The Reversi AI algorithm was very simple, but it beats me almost every time I play it. This is because the computer can process instructions very fast, so checking each possible position on the board and selecting the highest scoring move is easy for the computer. If I took the time to look at every space on the board and write down the score of each possible move, it would take a long time for me to find the best move.

Did you notice that our Reversi program in Chapter 14 had two functions, getPlayerMove() and getComputerMove(), which both returned the move selected as a two-item list like [x, y]? The both also had the same parameters, the game board data structure and which tile they were. getPlayerMove() decided which [x, y] move to return by letting the player type in the coordinates. getComputerMove() decided which [x, y] move to return by running the Reversi AI algorithm.

What happens when we replace the call to getPlayerMove() with a call to getComputerMove()? Then the player never types in a move, it is decided for them! The computer is playing against itself!

We are going to make three new programs, each based on the Reversi program in the last chapter. We will make changes to reversi.py to create *AISim1.py*. Next we will make changes to *AISim1.py* to create *AISim2.py*. And finally, we will make changes to *AISim2.py* to make *AISim3.py*. You can either type these changes in yourself, or download them from the book's website at the URL *http://inventwithpython.com/chapter16*.

Making the Computer Play Against Itself

Save the old *reversi.py* file as *AISim1.py* by clicking on **File** and then **Save As**, and then entering *AISim1.py* for the file name and clicking **Ok**. This will create a copy of our Reversi source code as a new file that we can make changes to, while leaving the original Reversi game the same (we may want to play it again). Change the following code in *AISim1.py*:

```
266. move = getPlayerMove(mainBoard, playerTile)
```

To this (the change is in bold):

```
266. move = getComputerMove(mainBoard, playerTile)
```

And run the program. Notice that the game still asks you if you want to be X or O, but it will not ask you to enter in any moves. When we replaced `getPlayerMove()`, we no longer call any code that takes this input from the player. We still press Enter after the original computer's moves (because of the `input('Press Enter to see the computer\'s move.')` on line 285), but the game plays itself!

Let's make some other changes to *AISim1.py*. All of the functions we defined for Reversi can stay the same. But replace the entire main section of the program (line 246 and on) to look like the following code. Some of the code has remained, but most of it has been altered. But all of the lines before line 246 are the same as in Reversi in the last chapter. You can also avoid typing in the code by downloading the source from the URL *http://inventwithpython.com/chapter16*.

AISim1.py

This code can be downloaded from *http://inventwithpython.com/AISim1.py*
If you get errors after typing this code in, compare it to the book's code with the online diff tool at *http://inventwithpython.com/diff* or email the author at al@inventwithpython.com

```
246. print('Welcome to Reversi!')
247.
248. while True:
249.     # Reset the board and game.
250.     mainBoard = getNewBoard()
251.     resetBoard(mainBoard)
252.     if whoGoesFirst() == 'player':
253.         turn = 'X'
```

```
254.        else:
255.            turn = 'O'
256.        print('The ' + turn + ' will go first.')
257.
258.        while True:
259.            drawBoard(mainBoard)
260.            scores = getScoreOfBoard(mainBoard)
261.            print('X has %s points. O has %s points' %
        (scores['X'], scores['O']))
262.            input('Press Enter to continue.')
263.
264.            if turn == 'X':
265.                # X's turn.
266.                otherTile = 'O'
267.                x, y = getComputerMove(mainBoard, 'X')
268.                makeMove(mainBoard, 'X', x, y)
269.            else:
270.                # O's turn.
271.                otherTile = 'X'
272.                x, y = getComputerMove(mainBoard, 'O')
273.                makeMove(mainBoard, 'O', x, y)
274.
275.            if getValidMoves(mainBoard, otherTile) == []:
276.                break
277.            else:
278.                turn = otherTile
279.
280.        # Display the final score.
281.        drawBoard(mainBoard)
282.        scores = getScoreOfBoard(mainBoard)
283.        print('X scored %s points. O scored %s points.' %
        (scores['X'], scores['O']))
284.
285.        if not playAgain():
286.            sys.exit()
```

How the AISim1.py Code Works

The *AISim1.py* program is the same as the original Reversi program, except that the call to getPlayerMove() has been replaced with a call to getComputerMove(). There have been some other changes to the text that is printed to the screen to make the game easier to follow.

When you run the *AISim1.py* program, all you can do is press Enter for each turn until the game ends. Run through a few games and watch the computer play itself. Since both the X and O players are using the same algorithm, it really is just a matter of luck to see who wins. The X player will win half the time, and the O player will win half the time.

Making the Computer Play Itself Several Times

But what if we created a new algorithm? Then we could set this new AI against the one implemented in `getComputerMove()`, and see which one is better. Let's make some changes to our program. Click on **File** and then **Save As**, and save this file as *AISim2.py* so that we can make changes without affecting *AISim1.py*. At this point, *AISim1.py* and *AISim2.py* have the same code. We will make changes to *AISim2.py* and save that file so that *AISim2.py* has the new changes and *AISim1.py* has the original code.

Add the following code. The additions are in bold, and some lines have been removed. When you are done changing the file, save it as *AISim2.py*.

If this is confusing, you can always download the *AISim2.py* source code from the book's website at *http://inventwithpython.com/chapter16*.

AISim2.py

This code can be downloaded from *http://inventwithpython.com/AISim2.py*
If you get errors after typing this code in, compare it to the book's code with the online diff tool at *http://inventwithpython.com/diff* or email the author at al@inventwithpython.com

```
246. print('Welcome to Reversi!')
247.
248. xwins = 0
249. owins = 0
250. ties = 0
251. numGames = int(input('Enter number of games to run: '))
252.
253. for game in range(numGames):
254.     print('Game #%s:' % (game), end=' ')
255.     # Reset the board and game.
256.     mainBoard = getNewBoard()
257.     resetBoard(mainBoard)
258.     if whoGoesFirst() == 'player':
259.         turn = 'X'
260.     else:
261.         turn = 'O'
262.
263.     while True:
264.         if turn == 'X':
265.             # X's turn.
266.             otherTile = 'O'
267.             x, y = getComputerMove(mainBoard, 'X')
268.             makeMove(mainBoard, 'X', x, y)
269.         else:
270.             # O's turn.
271.             otherTile = 'X'
272.             x, y = getComputerMove(mainBoard, 'O')
273.             makeMove(mainBoard, 'O', x, y)
274.
275.         if getValidMoves(mainBoard, otherTile) == []:
```

```
276.                break
277.            else:
278.                turn = otherTile
279.
280.        # Display the final score.
281.        scores = getScoreOfBoard(mainBoard)
282.        print('X scored %s points. O scored %s points.' %
       (scores['X'], scores['O']))
283.
284.        if scores['X'] > scores['O']:
285.            xwins += 1
286.        elif scores['X'] < scores['O']:
287.            owins += 1
288.        else:
289.            ties += 1
290.
291. numGames = float(numGames)
292. xpercent = round(((xwins / numGames) * 100), 2)
293. opercent = round(((owins / numGames) * 100), 2)
294. tiepercent = round(((ties / numGames) * 100), 2)
295. print('X wins %s games (%s%%), O wins %s games (%s%%),
       ties for %s games (%s%%) of %s games total.' % (xwins,
       xpercent, owins, opercent, ties, tiepercent, numGames))
```

How the AISim2.py Code Works

We have added the variables `xwins`, `owins`, and `ties` to keep track of how many times X wins, O wins, and when they tie. Lines 284 to 289 increment these variables at the end of each game, before it loops back to start a brand new game.

We have removed most of the `print()` function calls from the program, and the calls to `drawBoard()`. When you run *AISim2.py*, it asks you how many games you wish to run. Now that we've taken out the call to `drawBoard()` and replace the `while True:` loop with a `for game in range(numGames):` loop, we can run a number of games without stopping for the user to type anything. Here is a sample run where we run ten games of computer vs. computer Reversi:

```
Welcome to Reversi!
Enter number of games to run: 10
Game #0: X scored 40 points. O scored 23 points.
Game #1: X scored 24 points. O scored 39 points.
Game #2: X scored 31 points. O scored 30 points.
Game #3: X scored 41 points. O scored 23 points.
Game #4: X scored 30 points. O scored 34 points.
Game #5: X scored 37 points. O scored 27 points.
Game #6: X scored 29 points. O scored 33 points.
Game #7: X scored 31 points. O scored 33 points.
Game #8: X scored 32 points. O scored 32 points.
```

```
Game #9: X scored 41 points. O scored 22 points.
X wins 5 games (50.0%), O wins 4 games (40.0%),
ties for 1 games (10.0%) of 10.0 games total.
```

Because the algorithm does have a random part, your run might not have the exact same numbers as above.

Printing things out to the screen slows the computer down, but now that we have removed that code, the computer can run an entire game of Reversi in about a second or two. Think about it. Each time our program printed out one of those lines, it ran through an entire game (which is about fifty or sixty moves, each move carefully checked to be the one that gets the most points).

Percentages

Percentages are a portion of a total amount, and range from 0% to 100%. If you had 100% of a pie, you would have the entire pie. If you had 0% of a pie, you wouldn't have any pie at all. 50% of the pie would be half of the pie. A pie is a common image to use for percentages. In fact, there is a kind of chart called a **pie chart** which shows how much of the full total a certain portion is. Here is a pie chart with 10%, 15%, 25%, and 50% portions below. Notice that 10% + 15% + 25% + 50% adds up to 100%.

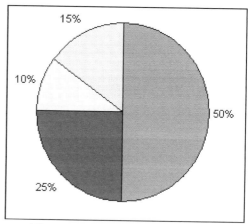

Figure 16-1: A pie chart with 10%, 15%, 25%, and 50% portions.

We can calculate the percentage with division. To get a percentage, divide the part you have by the total, and then multiply by one hundred. For example, if X won 50 out of 100 games, you would calculate the expression 50 / 100, which would evaluate to 0.5. We multiply this by 100 to get a percentage (in this case, 50%). Notice that if X won 100 out of 200 games, we could calculate the percentage with 100 / 200, which would also evaluate to 0.5. When we multiply 0.5 by 100 to get the percentage, we get 50%. Winning 100 out of 200 games is the same percentage (that is, the same portion) as winning 50 out of 100 games.

Division Evaluates to Floating Point

It is important to note that when you use the / division operator, the expression will always evaluate to a floating point number. For example, the expression 10 / 2 will evaluate to the floating point value 5.0, not to the integer value 5.

This is important to remember, because adding an integer to a floating point value with the + addition operator will also always evaluate to a floating point value. For example, 3 + 4.0 will evaluate to the floating point value 7.0 and not to the integer 7.

Try entering the following code into the interactive shell:

```
>>> spam = 100 / 4
>>> spam
25.0
>>> spam = spam + 20
>>> spam
45.0
>>>
```

Notice that in the above example, the data type of the value stored in spam is always a floating point value. You can pass the floating point value to the int() function, which will return an integer form of the floating point value. But this will always round the floating point value down. For example, the expressions int(4.0), int(4.2), and int(4.9) will all evaluate to 4, and never 5.

The round() Function

The round() function will round a float number to the nearest whole float number. Try entering the following into the interactive shell:

```
>>> round(10.0)
10.0
>>> round(10.2)
10.0
>>> round(8.7)
9.0
>>> round(4.5)
5.0
>>> round(3.5)
4.0
>>> round(3.4999)
3.0
>>> round(2.5422, 2)
2.54
>>>
```

As you can see, whenever the fraction part of a number is .5 or greater, the number is rounded up. Otherwise, the number is rounded down. The round() function also has an optional parameter, where you can specify to what place you wish to round the number to. For example, the expression round(2.5422, 2) evaluates to 2.54 and round (2.5422, 3) evaluates to 2.542.

Displaying the Statistics

```
291. numGames = float(numGames)
292. xpercent = round(((xwins / numGames) * 100), 2)
293. opercent = round(((owins / numGames) * 100), 2)
294. tiepercent = round(((ties / numGames) * 100), 2)
295. print('X wins %s games (%s%%), O wins %s games (%s%%),
     ties for %s games (%s%%) of %s games total.' % (xwins,
     xpercent, owins, opercent, ties, tiepercent, numGames))
```

The code at the bottom of our program will show the user how many wins X and O had, how many ties there were, and how what percentages these make up. Statistically, the more games you run, the more accurate your percentages will be. If you only ran ten games, and X won three of them, then it would seem that X's algorithm only wins 30% of the time. However, if you run a hundred, or even a thousand games, then you may find that X's algorithm wins closer to 50% (that is, half) of the games.

To find the percentages, we divide the number of wins or ties by the total number of games. We convert numGames to a float to ensure we do not use integer division in our calculation. Then we multiply the result by 100. However, we may end up with a number like 66.66666666666667. So we pass this number to the round() function with the second parameter of 2 to limit the precision to two decimal places, so it will return a float like 66.67 instead (which is much more readable).

Let's try another experiment. Run AISim2.py again, but this time have it run a hundred games:

Sample Run of AISim2.py

```
Welcome to Reversi!
Enter number of games to run: 100
Game #0: X scored 42 points. O scored 18 points.
Game #1: X scored 26 points. O scored 37 points.
Game #2: X scored 34 points. O scored 29 points.
Game #3: X scored 40 points. O scored 24 points.

...skipped for brevity...

Game #96: X scored 22 points. O scored 39 points.
Game #97: X scored 38 points. O scored 26 points.
Game #98: X scored 35 points. O scored 28 points.
```

```
Game #99: X scored 24 points. O scored 40 points.
X wins 46 games (46.0%), O wins 52 games (52.0%),
ties for 2 games (2.0%) of 100.0 games total.
```

Depending on how fast your computer is, this run might have taken a about a couple minutes. We can see that the results of all one hundred games still evens out to about fifty-fifty, because both X and O are using the same algorithm to win.

Comparing Different AI Algorithms

Let's add some new functions with new algorithms. But first click on **File**, then **Save As**, and save this file as *AISim3.py*. Before the print('Welcome to Reversi!') line, add these functions:

AISim3.py

This code can be downloaded from *http://inventwithpython.com/AISim3.py*
If you get errors after typing this code in, compare it to the book's code with the online diff tool at *http://inventwithpython.com/diff* or email the author at al@inventwithpython.com

```
245. def getRandomMove(board, tile):
246.     # Return a random move.
247.     return random.choice( getValidMoves(board, tile) )
248.
249.
250. def isOnSide(x, y):
251.     return x == 0 or x == 7 or y == 0 or y ==7
252.
253.
254. def getCornerSideBestMove(board, tile):
255.     # Return a corner move, or a side move, or the best
     move.
256.     possibleMoves = getValidMoves(board, tile)
257.
258.     # randomize the order of the possible moves
259.     random.shuffle(possibleMoves)
260.
261.     # always go for a corner if available.
262.     for x, y in possibleMoves:
263.         if isOnCorner(x, y):
264.             return [x, y]
265.
266.     # if there is no corner, return a side move.
267.     for x, y in possibleMoves:
268.         if isOnSide(x, y):
269.             return [x, y]
270.
271.     return getComputerMove(board, tile)
272.
273.
```

```
274. def getSideBestMove(board, tile):
275.     # Return a corner move, or a side move, or the best
     move.
276.     possibleMoves = getValidMoves(board, tile)
277.
278.     # randomize the order of the possible moves
279.     random.shuffle(possibleMoves)
280.
281.     # return a side move, if available
282.     for x, y in possibleMoves:
283.         if isOnSide(x, y):
284.             return [x, y]
285.
286.     return getComputerMove(board, tile)
287.
288.
289. def getWorstMove(board, tile):
290.     # Return the move that flips the least number of
     tiles.
291.     possibleMoves = getValidMoves(board, tile)
292.
293.     # randomize the order of the possible moves
294.     random.shuffle(possibleMoves)
295.
296.     # Go through all the possible moves and remember the
     best scoring move
297.     worstScore = 64
298.     for x, y in possibleMoves:
299.         dupeBoard = getBoardCopy(board)
300.         makeMove(dupeBoard, tile, x, y)
301.         score = getScoreOfBoard(dupeBoard)[tile]
302.         if score < worstScore:
303.             worstMove = [x, y]
304.             worstScore = score
305.
306.     return worstMove
307.
308.
309. def getCornerWorstMove(board, tile):
310.     # Return a corner, a space, or the move that flips
     the least number of tiles.
311.     possibleMoves = getValidMoves(board, tile)
312.
313.     # randomize the order of the possible moves
314.     random.shuffle(possibleMoves)
315.
316.     # always go for a corner if available.
317.     for x, y in possibleMoves:
318.         if isOnCorner(x, y):
319.             return [x, y]
320.
321.     return getWorstMove(board, tile)
322.
323.
```

```
324.
325. print('Welcome to Reversi!')
```

How the AISim3.py Code Works

A lot of these functions are very similar to one another, and some of them use the new `isOnSide()` function. Here's a review of the new algorithms we've made:

Table 17-1: Functions used for our Reversi AI.

Function	Description
getRandomMove()	Randomly choose a valid move to make.
getCornerSideBestMove()	Take a corner move if available. If there is no corner, take a space on the side. If no sides are available, use the regular `getComputerMove()` algorithm.
getSideBestMove()	Take a side space if there is one available. If not, then use the regular `getComputerMove()` algorithm (side spaces are chosen before corner spaces).
getWorstMove()	Take the space that will result in the fewest tiles being flipped.
getCornerWorstMove()	Take a corner space, if available. If not, use the `getWorstMove()` algorithm.

Comparing the Random Algorithm Against the Regular Algorithm

Now the only thing to do is replace one of the `getComputerMove()` calls in the main part of the program with one of the new functions. Then we can run several games and see how often one algorithm wins over the other. First, let's replace O's algorithm with the one in `getComputerMove()` with `getRandomMove()` on line 351:

```
351.            x, y = getRandomMove(mainBoard, 'O')
```

When we run the program with a hundred games now, it may look something like this:

```
Welcome to Reversi!
Enter number of games to run: 100
Game #0: X scored 25 points. O scored 38 points.
Game #1: X scored 32 points. O scored 32 points.
Game #2: X scored 15 points. O scored 0 points.
Game #3: X scored 50 points. O scored 14 points.

...skipped for brevity...
```

```
Game #96: X scored 31 points. O scored 33 points.
Game #97: X scored 41 points. O scored 23 points.
Game #98: X scored 33 points. O scored 31 points.
Game #99: X scored 45 points. O scored 19 points.
X wins 84 games (84.0%), O wins 15 games (15.0%),
ties for 1 games (1.0%) of 100.0 games total.
```

Wow! X win far more often than O did. That means that the algorithm in getComputerMove() (take any available corners, otherwise take the space that flips the most tiles) wins more games than the algorithm in getRandomMove() (which just makes moves randomly). This makes sense, because making intelligent choices is usually going to be better than just choosing things at random.

Comparing the Random Algorithm Against Itself

What if we changed O's algorithm to also use the algorithm in getRandomMove()? Let's find out by changing O's function call on line 351 from getComputerMove() to getRandomMove() and running the program again.

```
Welcome to Reversi!
Enter number of games to run: 100
Game #0: X scored 37 points. O scored 24 points.
Game #1: X scored 19 points. O scored 45 points.

...skipped for brevity...

Game #98: X scored 27 points. O scored 37 points.
Game #99: X scored 38 points. O scored 22 points.
X wins 42 games (42.0%), O wins 54 games (54.0%),
ties for 4 games (4.0%) of 100.0 games total.
```

As you can see, when both players are making random moves, they each win about 50% of the time. (In the above case, O just happen to get lucky and won a little bit more than half of the time.)

Just like moving on the corner spaces is a good idea because they cannot be flipped, moving on the side pieces may also be a good idea. On the side, the tile has the edge of the board and is not as out in the open as the other pieces. The corners are still preferable to the side spaces, but moving on the sides (even when there is a move that can flip more pieces) may be a good strategy.

Comparing the Regular Algorithm Against the CornersSideBest Algorithm

Change X's algorithm on line 346 to use `getComputerMove()` (our original algorithm) and O's algorithm on line 351 to use `getCornerSideBestMove()` (which first tries to move on a corner, then tries to move on a side position, and then takes the best remaining move), and let's run a hundred games to see which is better. Try changing the function calls and running the program again.

```
Welcome to Reversi!
Enter number of games to run: 100
Game #0: X scored 52 points. O scored 12 points.
Game #1: X scored 10 points. O scored 54 points.

...skipped for brevity...

Game #98: X scored 41 points. O scored 23 points.
Game #99: X scored 46 points. O scored 13 points.
X wins 65 games (65.0%), O wins 31 games (31.0%),
ties for 4 games (4.0%) of 100.0 games total.
```

Wow! That's unexpected. It seems that choosing the side spaces over a space that flips more tiles is a bad strategy to use. The benefit of the side space is not greater than the cost of choosing a space that flips fewer of the opponent's tiles. Can we be sure of these results? Let's run the program again, but this time let's have the program play one thousand games. This may take a few minutes for your computer to run (but it would take days for you to do this by hand!) Try changing the function calls and running the program again.

```
Welcome to Reversi!
Enter number of games to run: 1000
Game #0: X scored 20 points. O scored 44 points.
Game #1: X scored 54 points. O scored 9 points.

...skipped for brevity...

Game #998: X scored 38 points. O scored 23 points.
Game #999: X scored 38 points. O scored 26 points.
X wins 611 games (61.1%), O wins 363 games
(36.3%), ties for 26 games (2.6%) of 1000.0 games
total.
```

The more accurate statistics from the thousand-games run are about the same as the statistics from the hundred-games run. It seems that choosing the move that flips the most tiles is a better idea than choosing a side move.

Comparing the Regular Algorithm Against the Worst Algorithm

Now set the X player's algorithm on line 346 to use `getComputerMove()` and the O player's algorithm on line 351 to `getWorstMove()` (which makes the move that flips over the least number of tiles), and run a hundred games. Try changing the function calls and running the program again.

```
Welcome to Reversi!
Enter number of games to run: 100
Game #0: X scored 50 points. O scored 14 points.
Game #1: X scored 38 points. O scored 8 points.

...skipped for brevity...

Game #98: X scored 36 points. O scored 16 points.
Game #99: X scored 19 points. O scored 0 points.
X wins 98 games (98.0%), O wins 2 games (2.0%),
ties for 0 games (0.0%) of 100.0 games total.
```

Whoa! The algorithm in `getWorstMove()`, which always choose the move that flips the fewest tiles, will almost always lose to our regular algorithm. This isn't really surprising at all.

Comparing the Regular Algorithm Against the WorstCorner Algorithm

How about when we replace `getWorstMove()` on line 351 with `getCornerWorstMove()`, which is the same algorithm except it takes any available corner pieces before taking the worst move. Try changing the function calls and running the program again.

```
Welcome to Reversi!
Enter number of games to run: 100
Game #0: X scored 36 points. O scored 7 points.
Game #1: X scored 44 points. O scored 19 points.

...skipped for brevity...

Game #98: X scored 47 points. O scored 17 points.
Game #99: X scored 36 points. O scored 18 points.
X wins 94 games (94.0%), O wins 6 games (6.0%),
ties for 0 games (0.0%) of 100.0 games total.
```

The `getCornerWorstMove()` still loses most of the games, but it seems to win a few more games than `getWorstMove()` (6% compared to 2%). Does taking the corner spaces when they are available really make a difference?

Comparing the Worst Algorithm Against the WorstCorner Algorithm

We can check by setting X's algorithm to `getWorstMove()` and O's algorithm to `getCornerWorstMove()`, and then running the program. Try changing the function calls and running the program again.

```
Welcome to Reversi!
Enter number of games to run: 100
Game #0: X scored 25 points. O scored 39 points.
Game #1: X scored 26 points. O scored 33 points.

...skipped for brevity...

Game #98: X scored 36 points. O scored 25 points.
Game #99: X scored 29 points. O scored 35 points.
X wins 32 games (32.0%), O wins 67 games (67.0%),
ties for 1 games (1.0%) of 100.0 games total.
```

Yes, it does seem like taking the algorithm that takes the corners when it can does translate into more wins. While we have found out that going for the sides makes you lose more often, going for the corners is always a good idea.

Summary: Learning New Things by Running Simulation Experiments

This chapter didn't really cover a game, but it modeled various strategies for Reversi. If we thought that taking side moves in Reversi was a good idea, we would have to spend days, even weeks, carefully playing games of Reversi by hand and writing down the results. But if we know how to program a computer to play Reversi, then we can have the computer play Reversi using these strategies for us. If you think about it, you will realize that the computer is executing millions of lines of our Python program in seconds! Your experiments with the simulation of Reversi can help you learn more about playing Reversi in real life.

In fact, this chapter would make a good science fair project. Your problem can be which set of moves leads to the most wins against other sets of moves, and make a hypothesis about which is the best strategy. After running several simulations, you can determine which strategy works best. You can make a science fair project out of a simulation of any board game! And it is all because you know exactly how to instruct the computer to do it, step by step, line by line. You can speak the computer's language, and get it to do large amounts of data processing and number crunching for you.

That's all for the text-based games in this book. Games that only use text can be fun, even though there simple. But most modern games use graphics, sound, and animation to make much more exciting looking games. For the rest of the chapters in this book, we will learn how to create games with graphics by using a Python module called Pygame.

Chapter 17
Graphics and Animation

Topics Covered In This Chapter:

- Software Libraries
- Installing Pygame
- Graphical user interfaces (GUI)
- Drawing primitives
- Creating a GUI window with Pygame
- Color in Pygame
- Fonts in Pygame
- Aliased and Anti-Aliased Graphics
- Attributes
- The `pygame.font.Font` Data Type
- The `pygame.Surface` Data Type
- The `pygame.Rect` Data Type
- The `pygame.PixelArray` Data Type
- Constructor Functions
- The `type()` Function
- Pygame's Drawing Functions
- The `blit()` Method for `Surface` Objects
- Events
- The Game Loop
- Animation

So far, all of our games have only used text. Text is displayed on the screen as output, and the player types in text from the keyboard as input. This is simple, and an easy way to learn programming. But in this chapter, we will make some more exciting games with advanced graphics and sound using the Pygame library. Chapters 17, 18, and 19 will teach you how to use the Pygame library to make games with graphics, animation, mouse input, and sound. In these chapters we'll write source code for simple programs that are not games but demonstrate the Pygame concepts we've learned. Chapter 20 will present the source code for a complete Pygame game using all the concepts you've learned.

A **software library** is code that is not meant to be run by itself, but included in other programs to add new features. By using a library a programmer doesn't have to write the entire program, but can make use of the work that another programmer has done before them. Pygame is a software library that has modules for graphics, sound, and other features that games commonly use.

Installing Pygame

Pygame does not come with Python. Like Python, Pygame is available for free. You will have to download and install Pygame, which is as easy as downloading and installing the Python interpreter. In a web browser, go to the URL *http://pygame.org* and click on the "Downloads" link on the left side of the web site. This book assumes you have the Windows operating system, but Pygame works the same for every operating system. You need to download the Pygame installer for your operating system and the version of Python you have installed (3.1).

You do not want to download the "source" for Pygame, but rather the Pygame "binary" for your operating system. For Windows, download the *pygame-1.9.1.win32-py3.1.msi* file. (This is Pygame for Python 3.1 on Windows. If you installed a different version of Python (such as 2.5 or 2.4) download the .msi file for your version of Python.) The current version of Pygame at the time this book was written is 1.9.1. If you see a newer version on the website, download and install the newer Pygame. For Mac OS X and Linux, follow the directions on the download page for installation instructions.

Figure 17-1: The pygame.org website.

On Windows, double click on the downloaded file to install Pygame. To check that Pygame is install correctly, type the following into the interactive shell:

```
>>> import pygame
```

If nothing appears after you hit the Enter key, then you know Pygame has successfully been installed. If the error `ImportError: No module named pygame` appears, then try to install Pygame again (and make sure you typed `import pygame` correctly).

This chapter has five small programs that demonstrate how to use the different features that Pygame provides. In the last chapter, you will use these features for a complete game written in Python with Pygame.

A video tutorial of how to install Pygame is available from this book's website at *http://inventwithpython.com/videos/*.

Hello World in Pygame

We are going to create a new "Hello World!" program, just like you created at the beginning of the book. This time, we will use Pygame to make "Hello world!" appear in a **graphical user interface** (GUI, which is pronounced "gooey") window. A graphical user interface gives you a window that color, shapes, and images can be drawn on by your program, as well as accepting mouse input (and not just keyboard input). The basic shapes that we draw on the screen are called **drawing primitives**. GUI windows are used instead of the text window (also called a **console window** or a **terminal window**) that we used for all our previous games.

Pygame does not work well with the interactive shell because it relies on a game loop (we will describe game loops later). Because of this, you can only write Pygame programs and cannot send instructions to Pygame one at a time through the interactive shell.

Pygame programs also do not use the `input()` function. There is no text input and output. Instead, the program displays output in a window by drawing graphics and text to the window. Pygame program's input comes from the keyboard and the mouse through things called events, which we will go over in the next chapter. However, if our program has bugs that cause Python to display an error message, the error message will show up in the console window.

You can also look up information about how to use the Pygame library by visiting the web site *http://pygame.org/docs/ref/*.

Hello World's Source Code

Type in the following code into the file editor, and save it as *pygameHelloWorld.py*. Or you can download this source code by going to this book's website at *http://inventwithpython.com/chapter17*

pygameHelloWorld.py

This code can be downloaded from *http://inventwithpython.com/pygameHelloWorld.py*
If you get errors after typing this code in, compare it to the book's code with the online
diff tool at *http://inventwithpython.com/diff* or email the author at
al@inventwithpython.com

```
 1. import pygame, sys
 2. from pygame.locals import *
 3.
 4. # set up pygame
 5. pygame.init()
 6.
 7. # set up the window
 8. windowSurface = pygame.display.set_mode((500, 400), 0,
    32)
 9. pygame.display.set_caption('Hello world!')
10.
11. # set up the colors
12. BLACK = (0, 0, 0)
13. WHITE = (255, 255, 255)
14. RED = (255, 0, 0)
15. GREEN = (0, 255, 0)
16. BLUE = (0, 0, 255)
17.
18. # set up fonts
19. basicFont = pygame.font.SysFont(None, 48)
20.
21. # set up the text
22. text = basicFont.render('Hello world!', True, WHITE,
    BLUE)
23. textRect = text.get_rect()
24. textRect.centerx = windowSurface.get_rect().centerx
25. textRect.centery = windowSurface.get_rect().centery
26.
27. # draw the white background onto the surface
28. windowSurface.fill(WHITE)
29.
30. # draw a green polygon onto the surface
31. pygame.draw.polygon(windowSurface, GREEN, ((146, 0),
    (291, 106), (236, 277), (56, 277), (0, 106)))
32.
33. # draw some blue lines onto the surface
34. pygame.draw.line(windowSurface, BLUE, (60, 60), (120,
    60), 4)
35. pygame.draw.line(windowSurface, BLUE, (120, 60), (60,
    120))
36. pygame.draw.line(windowSurface, BLUE, (60, 120), (120,
    120), 4)
37.
38. # draw a blue circle onto the surface
39. pygame.draw.circle(windowSurface, BLUE, (300, 50), 20, 0)
40.
41. # draw a red ellipse onto the surface
```

```
42. pygame.draw.ellipse(windowSurface, RED, (300, 250, 40,
    80), 1)
43.
44. # draw the text's background rectangle onto the surface
45. pygame.draw.rect(windowSurface, RED, (textRect.left - 20,
    textRect.top - 20, textRect.width + 40, textRect.height +
    40))
46.
47. # get a pixel array of the surface
48. pixArray = pygame.PixelArray(windowSurface)
49. pixArray[480][380] = BLACK
50. del pixArray
51.
52. # draw the text onto the surface
53. windowSurface.blit(text, textRect)
54.
55. # draw the window onto the screen
56. pygame.display.update()
57.
58. # run the game loop
59. while True:
60.     for event in pygame.event.get():
61.         if event.type == QUIT:
62.             pygame.quit()
63.             sys.exit()
```

Running the Hello World Program

When you run this program, you should see a new GUI window appear which looks like Figure 17-2.

What is nice about using a GUI instead of a console is that the text can appear anywhere in the window, not just after the previous text we have printed. The text can be any color or size.

One thing you may notice is that Pygame uses a lot of tuples instead of lists. **Tuples** are just like lists (they can contain multiple values) except they are typed with parentheses (and), instead of square brackets [and]. The main difference is that once you create a tuple, you cannot change, add, or remove any values in the tuple. For technical reasons, knowing that the contents of the tuple never change allows Python to handle this data more efficiently, which is why Pygame uses tuples instead of lists.

Figure 17-2: The "Hello World" program.

Importing the Pygame Module

Let's go over each of these lines of code and find out what they do.

```
1. import pygame, sys
2. from pygame.locals import *
```

First we need to import the pygame module so we can call the functions in the Pygame software library. You can import several modules on the same line by delimiting the module names with commas. Line 1 imports both the pygame and sys modules.

The second line imports the pygame.locals module. This module contains many constant variables that we will use with Pygame such as QUIT or K_ESCAPE (which we will explain later). However, using the form from moduleName import * we can import the pygame.locals module but not have to type pygame.locals in front of each time we use the module's functions and variables in our program. The * symbol means we should import everything inside the module.

The pygame.locals module contains some constant variables we will use in this program.

If you have `from sys import *` instead of `import sys` in your program, you could call `exit()` instead of `sys.exit()` in your code. (But most of the time it is better to use the full function name so that you know which module the `exit()` is in.)

The `pygame.init()` Function

```
4. # set up pygame
5. pygame.init()
```

The Pygame software library has some initial code that needs to be run before we can use it. All Pygame programs must run this code by calling the `pygame.init()` after importing the `pygame` module but before calling any other Pygame functions.

The `pygame.display.set_mode()` and `pygame.display.set_caption()` Functions

```
7. # set up the window
8. windowSurface = pygame.display.set_mode((500, 400), 0,
   32)
9. pygame.display.set_caption('Hello world!')
```

Line 8 creates a GUI window for our program by calling the `set_mode()` method in the `pygame.display` module. (The `display` module is a module inside the `pygame` module. Pygame is so advanced that even the pygame module has its own modules!)

Just to avoid confusion, you should know the difference between the window that is created is different and the Windows operating system. The graphical user interface is printed as "window" (lower case and singular) and the Microsoft operating system is "Windows" (upper case and plural).

There are three parameters to the `set_mode()` method. The first parameter is a tuple of two integers for the width and height of the window, in pixels. A **pixel** is the tiniest dot on your computer screen. A single pixel on your screen can turn into any color. All the pixels on your screen work together to display all the pictures you see. To see how tiny a pixel is, look at the bottom right corner of the "Hello World!" window. This program sets just one pixel as white.

We want the window to be 500 pixels wide and 400 pixels high, so we use the tuple `(500, 400)` for the first parameter. To get the total number of pixels in our window, multiply the width and the height. Our window is made up of 20,000 pixels, and it doesn't even take up the entire computer screen!

The second parameter is for advanced GUI window options. You won't really need this for your games, so you can always just pass 0 for this parameter. The third parameter is another advanced option called the color depth. You also don't need to know what this means, and can just always pass the value 32.

The `set_caption()` call returns a `pygame.Surface` object (which we will call `Surface` objects for short). Objects are values of a data type that have methods as well as data. For example, strings are objects in Python because they have data (the string itself) and methods (such as `lower()` and `split()`). You can store references to objects in variables just like list reference values. The `Surface` object represents the window and we will include the `windowSurface` variable in all of our calls to drawing functions.

To refresh your memory about the differences between values and reference values, go back to chapter 10.

Colors in Pygame

```
11. # set up the colors
12. BLACK = (0, 0, 0)
13. WHITE = (255, 255, 255)
14. RED = (255, 0, 0)
15. GREEN = (0, 255, 0)
16. BLUE = (0, 0, 255)
```

There are three primary colors of light: red, green and blue. By combining different amounts of these three colors you can form any other color. In Python, we represent colors with tuples of three integers. The first value in the tuple is how much red is in the color. A value of 0 means there is no red in this color, and a value of 255 means there is a maximum amount of red in the color. The second value is for green and the third value is for blue.

For example, we will create the tuple (0, 0, 0) and store it in a variable named BLACK. With no amount of red, green, or blue, the resulting color is completely black. The color black is the absence of any color.

On line 13, we use the tuple (255, 255, 255) for a maximum amount of red, green, and blue to result in white. The color white is the full combination of red, green, and blue. We store this tuple in the WHITE variable. The tuple (255, 0, 0) represents the maximum amount of red but no

Table 17-1: Colors and their RGB values.

Color	RGB Values
Aqua	(0, 255, 255)
Black	(0, 0, 0)
Blue	(0, 0, 255)
Cornflower Blue	(100, 149, 237)
Fuchsia	(255, 0, 255)
Gray	(128, 128, 128)
Green	(0, 128, 0)
Lime	(0, 255, 0)
Maroon	(128, 0, 0)
Navy Blue	(0, 0, 128)
Olive	(128, 128, 0)
Purple	(128, 0, 128)
Red	(255, 0, 0)
Silver	(192, 192, 192)
Teal	(0, 128, 128)
White	(255, 255, 255)
Yellow	(255, 255, 0)

amount of green and blue, so the resulting color is red. Similarly, (0, 255, 0) is green and (0, 0, 255) is blue.

318

These variable names are in all capitals because they are constant variables. It's just easier to type BLACK in our code than (0, 0, 0) every time we want to specify the color black, so we set up these color variables at the start of our program.

If you want to make a color lighter, try adding an equal amount from all three values. For example, the RGB value for gray is (128, 128, 128). You can get the RGB value for a lighter gray by adding 20 to each value to get (148, 148, 148). You can get the RGB value for a darker gray by subtracting 20 from each value to get (108, 108, 108). And you can get the RGB value for a slightly redder gray by adding 20 to only the red value to get (148, 128, 128). Table 17-1 has some common colors and their RGB values.

Fonts, and the pygame.font.SysFont() Function

```
18. # set up fonts
19. basicFont = pygame.font.SysFont(None, 48)
```

A **font** is a complete set of letters, numbers, symbols, and characters drawn in a single style. Figure 17-3 is an example of the same sentence printed in different fonts.

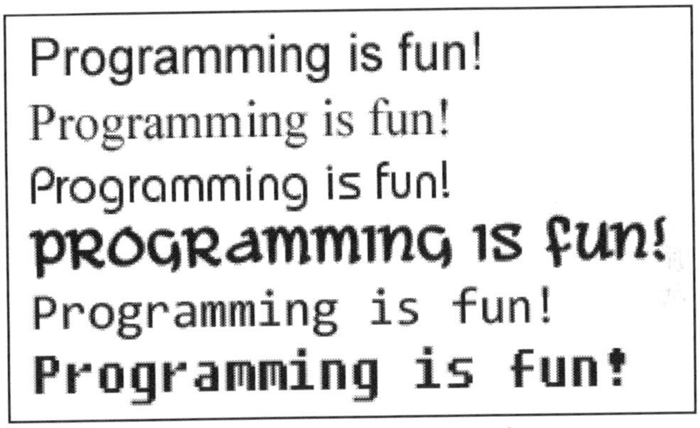

In our earlier games, we only told Python to print out text. The color, size, and font that was used to display this text was completely determined by whatever font your operating system uses for console windows. Our programs could not change the font at all. However, since we will be drawing out letters to a GUI window we need to tell Pygame exactly what font to use when drawing the text.

Figure 17-3: Examples of different fonts.

On line 19 we create a pygame.font.Font object (which we will just call Font objects for short) by calling the pygame.font.SysFont() function. The first parameter is the name of the font, but we will pass the None value to use the default system font. The second parameter will be the size of the font (which is measured in units called **points**). In our call on line 19, we want the font size to be 48 points.

The `render()` Method for `Font` Objects

```
21. # set up the text
22. text = basicFont.render('Hello world!', True, WHITE,
    BLUE)
23. textRect = text.get_rect()
```

The `Font` object that we have stored in the `basicFont` variable has a method called `render()`. This method will create a `Surface` object with the text drawn on it. The first parameter to `render()` is the string of the text to draw. The second parameter is a Boolean for whether or not we want anti-aliasing. Anti-aliasing is a technique for making a drawing look less blocky. On line 22, we pass `True` to say we want to use anti-aliasing. Figure 17-4 is an example of what a line (when we enlarge the individual pixels) looks like with and without anti-aliasing.

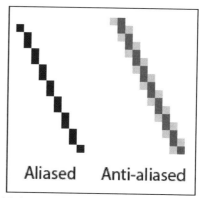

Figure 17-4: An aliased line and an anti-aliased line.

Anti-aliasing can make your text and lines look blurry but smoother. It takes a little more computation time to do anti-aliasing, so although the graphics may look better, your program may run slower (but only just a little).

Attributes

```
24. textRect.centerx = windowSurface.get_rect().centerx
25. textRect.centery = windowSurface.get_rect().centery
```

The `pygame.Rect` data type (which we will just call `Rect` for short) makes working with rectangle-shaped things easy. To create a new `Rect` object call the function `pygame.Rect()`. The parameters are integers for the XY coordinates of the top left corner, followed by the width and height. These integers describe the size in number of pixels.

The function name with the parameters looks like this: `pygame.Rect(left, top, width, height)`

Just like methods are functions that are associated with an object, **attributes** are variables that are associated with an object. The `Rect` data type (that is, the data type of all `Rect` objects) has many attributes that describe the rectangle they represent. Here is a list of attributes of a `Rect` object named `myRect`:

pygame.Rect Attribute	Description
`myRect.left`	The int value of the X-coordinate of the left side of the rectangle.
`myRect.right`	The int value of the X-coordinate of the right side of the rectangle.
`myRect.top`	The int value of the Y-coordinate of the top side of the rectangle.
`myRect.bottom`	The int value of the Y-coordinate of the bottom side of the rectangle.
`myRect.centerx`	The int value of the X-coordinate of the center of the rectangle.
`myRect.centery`	The int value of the Y-coordinate of the center of the rectangle.
`myRect.width`	The int value of the width of the rectangle.
`myRect.height`	The int value of the height of the rectangle.
`myRect.size`	A tuple of two ints: (width, height)
`myRect.topleft`	A tuple of two ints: (left, top)
`myRect.topright`	A tuple of two ints: (right, top)
`myRect.bottomleft`	A tuple of two ints: (left, bottom)
`myRect.bottomright`	A tuple of two ints: (right, bottom)
`myRect.midleft`	A tuple of two ints: (left, centery)
`myRect.midright`	A tuple of two ints: (right, centery)
`myRect.midtop`	A tuple of two ints: (centerx, top)
`myRect.midbottom`	A tuple of two ints: (centerx, bottom)

The great thing about `Rect` objects is that if you modify any of these variables, all the other variables will automatically modify themselves as well. For example, if you create a `Rect` object that is 20 pixels wide and 20 pixels high, and has the top left corner at the coordinates (30, 40), then the X-coordinate of the right side will automatically be set to 50 (because 20 + 30 = 50). However, if you change the `left` attribute with the line `myRect.left = 100`, then Pygame will automatically change the `right` attribute to 120 (because 20 + 100 = 120). Every other attribute for that `Rect` object will also be updated as well.

The `get_rect()` Methods for `pygame.font.Font` and `pygame.Surface` Objects

Notice that both the `Font` object (stored in the `text` variable) and the `Surface` object (stored in `windowSurface` variable) both have a method called `get_rect()`. Technically, these are two different methods. But the programmers of Pygame gave them the same name because they both do the same thing and return Rect objects that represent the size and position of the Font or Surface object.

Also, remember that pygame is a module that we import, and inside the pygame module are the font and surface modules. Inside *those* modules are the Font and Surface data types. The Pygame programmers made the modules begin with a lowercase letter, and the data types begin with an uppercase letter. This makes it easier to distinguish the data types and the modules that the data types can be found in.

Constructor Functions and the type() function.

We create a pygame.Rect object by calling a function named pygame.Rect(). The pygame.Rect() function has the same name as the pygame.Rect data type. Functions that have the same name as their data type and create objects or values of this data type are called **constructor functions**.

You can always find out what the proper name of a value's data type with the type() function. For example, try typing the following into the interactive shell:

```
>>> type('This is a string')
<type 'str'>
>>> type(5)
<type 'int'>
>>> spam = 'Another string'
>>> type(spam)
<type 'str'>
>>> import pygame
>>> pygame.init()
>>> myRect = pygame.Rect(10, 10, 40, 50)
>>> type(myRect)
<type 'pygame.Rect'>
>>> pygame.quit()
```

(You need to call the pygame.quit() function when you are done with typing Pygame functions into the interactive shell. Otherwise you may cause Python to crash.) Notice that the return value from the type() function is not a string, but a value of a data type called "type"! Try typing this into the interactive shell:

```
>>> type(type('This is a string'))
<type 'type'>
```

For the most part, you don't need to know about data types and the `type()` function when programming games. But it can be very useful if you need to find out the data type of the value stored in a variable in your program.

The `fill()` Method for `Surface` Objects

```
27. # draw the white background onto the surface
28. windowSurface.fill(WHITE)
```

This is the first drawing function call in our program. We want to fill the entire surface stored in `windowSurface` with the color white. The `fill()` function will completely cover the entire surface with the color we pass as the parameter. (In this case, we pass `BLACK` to make the background black.)

An important thing to know about Pygame is that the window on the screen will not change when we call the `fill()` method or any of the other drawing functions. These will draw on the `Surface` object, but the `Surface` object will not be drawn on the user's screen until the `pygame.display.update()` function is called. This is because drawing on the `Surface` object (which is stored in the computer's memory) is much faster than drawing to the computer screen. It is much more efficient to draw onto the screen once and only after all of our drawing functions to draw to the surface.

The `pygame.draw.polygon()` Function

```
30. # draw a green polygon onto the surface
31. pygame.draw.polygon(windowSurface, GREEN, ((146, 0),
    (291, 106), (236, 277), (56, 277), (0, 106)))
```

A polygon is any multisided shape with sides that are only straight lines. The `pygame.draw.polygon()` function can draw any shape that you give it and fill the inside space of the polygon. The tuple of tuples you pass it represents the XY coordinates of the points to draw in order. The last tuple will automatically connect to the first tuple to complete the shape.

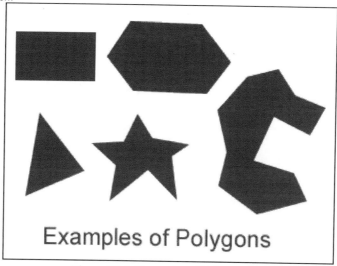

Figure 17-5: Examples of Polygons.

Polygons only have straight lines for sides (circles and ellipses are not polygons). Figure 17-5 has some examples of polygons.

The `pygame.draw.line()` Function

```
33. # draw some blue lines onto the surface
34. pygame.draw.line(windowSurface, BLUE, (60, 60), (120,
    60), 4)
35. pygame.draw.line(windowSurface, BLUE, (120, 60), (60,
    120))
36. pygame.draw.line(windowSurface, BLUE, (60, 120), (120,
    120), 4)
```

The `pygame.draw.line()` function will draw a line on the `Surface` object that you provide. Notice that the last parameter, the width of the line, is optional. If you pass 4 for the width, the line will be four pixels thick. If you do not specify the `width` parameter, it will take on the default value of 1.

The `pygame.draw.circle()` Function

```
38. # draw a blue circle onto the surface
39. pygame.draw.circle(windowSurface, BLUE, (300, 50), 20, 0)
```

The `pygame.draw.circle()` function will draw a circle on the `Surface` object you provide. The third parameter is for the X and Y coordinates of the center of the circle as a tuple of two ints. The fourth parameter is an `int` for the radius (that is, size) of the circle in pixels. A `width` of 0 means that the circle will be filled in.

The `pygame.draw.ellipse()` Function

```
41. # draw a red ellipse onto the surface
42. pygame.draw.ellipse(windowSurface, RED, (300, 250, 40,
    80), 1)
```

The `pygame.draw.ellipse()` function will draw an ellipse. It is similar to the `pygame.draw.circle()` function, except that instead of specifying the center of the circle, a tuple of four ints is passed for the left, top, width, and height of the ellipse.

The `pygame.draw.rect()` Function

```
44. # draw the text's background rectangle onto the surface
45. pygame.draw.rect(windowSurface, RED, (textRect.left - 20,
    textRect.top - 20, textRect.width + 40, textRect.height +
    40))
```

The `pygame.draw.rect()` function will draw a rectangle. The third parameter is a tuple of four ints for the left, top, width, and height of the rectangle. Instead of a tuple of four ints for the third parameter, you can also pass a `Rect` object. In line 45, we want the rectangle we draw to be 20 pixels around all the sides of the text. This is why we want the drawn rectangle's left and top to be the left and top of `textRect` minus `20`. (Remember, we subtract because coordinates decrease as you go left and up.) And the width and height will be equal to the width and height of the `textRect` plus `40` (because the left and top were moved back 20 pixels, so we need to make up for that space).

The pygame.PixelArray Data Type

```
47. # get a pixel array of the surface
48. pixArray = pygame.PixelArray(windowSurface)
49. pixArray[480][380] = BLACK
```

On line 48 we create a `pygame.PixelArray` object (which we will just call a `PixelArray` object for short). The `PixelArray` object is a list of lists of color tuples that represents the `Surface` object you passed it. We passed `windowSurface` object when we called the `PixelArray()` constructor function on line 48, so assigning `BLACK` to `pixArray[480][380]` will change the pixel at the coordinates (480, 380) to be a black pixel. Pygame will automatically modify the `windowSurface` object with this change.

The first index in the `PixelArray` object is for the X-coordinate. The second index is for the Y-coordinate. `PixelArray` objects make it easy to set individual pixels on a `PixelArray` object to a specific color.

```
50. del pixArray
```

Creating a PixelArray object from a Surface object will lock that Surface object. Locked means that no blit() function calls (described next) can be made on that Surface object. To unlock the Surface object, you must delete the PixelArray object with the del operator. If you forget to delete the Surface object, you will get an error message that says pygame.error: Surfaces must not be locked during blit.

The blit() Method for Surface Objects

```
52. # draw the text onto the surface
53. windowSurface.blit(text, textRect)
```

The blit() method will draw the contents of one Surface object onto another Surface object. Line 54 will draw the "Hello world!" text (which was drawn on the Surface object stored in the text variable) and draws it to the Surface object stored in the windowSurface variable.

Remember that the text object had the "Hello world!" text drawn on it on line 22 by the render() method. Surface objects are just stored in the computer's memory (like any other variable) and not drawn on the screen. The Surface object in windowSurface is drawn on the screen when we call the pygame.display.update() function on line 56 because this was the Surface object created by the pygame.display.set_mode() function. Other Surface objects are not drawn on the screen.

The second parameter to blit() specifies where on the windowSurface surface the text surface should be drawn. We will just pass the Rect object we got from calling text.get_rect() (which was stored in textRect on line 23).

The pygame.display.update() Function

```
55. # draw the window onto the screen
56. pygame.display.update()
```

In Pygame, nothing is drawn to the screen until the pygame.display.update() function is called. This is done because drawing to the screen is a slow operation for the computer compared to drawing on the Surface objects while they are in memory. You do not want to draw to the screen after each drawing function is called, but only draw the screen once after all the drawing functions have been called.

You will need to call `pygame.display.update()` each time you want to update the screen to display the contents of the `Surface` object returned by `pygame.display.set_mode()`. (In this program, that object is the one stored in `windowSurface`.) This will become more important in our next program which covers animation.

Events and the Game Loop

In our previous games, all of the programs print out everything immediately until they reach a `input()` function call. At that point, the program stops and waits for the user to type something in and press Enter. Pygame programs do not work this way. Instead, Pygame programs are constantly running through a loop called the game loop. (In this program, we execute all the lines of code in the game loop about one hundred times a second.)

The **game loop** is a loop that constantly checks for new events, updates the state of the window, and draws the window on the screen. **Events** are objects of the `pygame.event.Event` data type that are generated by Pygame whenever the user presses a key, clicks or moves the mouse, or makes some other event occur. Calling `pygame.event.get()` retrieves any new `pygame.event.Event` objects that have been generated since the last call to `pygame.event.get()`.

```
58. # run the game loop
59. while True:
```

This is the start of our game loop. The condition for the `while` statement is set to `True` so that we loop forever. The only time we exit the loop is if an event causes the program to terminate.

The pygame.event.get() Function

```
60.     for event in pygame.event.get():
61.         if event.type == QUIT:
```

The `pygame.event.get()` function returns a list of `pygame.event.Event` objects. This list has every single event that has occurred since the last time `pygame.event.get()` was called. All `pygame.event.Event` objects have an attribute called `type` which tell us what type of event it is. (A list of event types is given in the next chapter. In this chapter we only deal with the `QUIT` event.)

Pygame comes supplied with its own constant variables in the `pygame.locals` module. Remember that we have imported the `pygame.locals` module with the line from `pygame.locals import *`, which means we do not have to type `pygame.locals` in front of the variables and functions in that module.

On line 60 we set up a `for` loop to check each `pygame.event.Event` object in the list returned by `pygame.event.get()`. If the `type` attribute of the event is equal to the value of the constant variable QUIT (which is provided by the `pygame.locals` module), then we know the user has closed the window and wants to terminate the program.

Pygame generates the QUIT event when the user clicks on the X button at the top right of the program's window. It is also generated if the computer is shutting down and tries to terminate all the programs running. For whatever reason the QUIT event was generated, we know that we should run any code that we want to happen to stop the program. You could choose to ignore the QUIT event entirely, but that may cause the program to be confusing to the user.

The pygame.quit() Function

```
62.             pygame.quit()
63.             sys.exit()
```

If the QUIT event has been generated, then we can know that the user has tried to close the window. In that case, we should call the exit functions for both Pygame (`pygame.quit()`) and Python (`sys.exit()`).

This has been the simple "Hello world!" program from Pygame. We've covered many new topics that we didn't have to deal with in our previous games. Even though they are more complicated, the Pygame programs can also be much more fun and engaging than our previous text games. Let's learn how to create games with animated graphics that move.

Animation

In this program we have several different blocks bouncing off of the edges of the window. The blocks are different colors and sizes and move only in diagonal directions. In order to animate the blocks (that is, make them look like they are moving) we will move the blocks a few pixels over on each iteration through the game loop. By drawing new blocks that are located a little bit differently then the blocks before, we can make it look like the blocks are moving around the screen.

The Animation Program's Source Code

Type the following program into the file editor and save it as *animation.py*. You can also download this source code from *http://inventwithpython.com/chapter17*.

animation.py

This code can be downloaded from *http://inventwithpython.com/animation.py*

If you get errors after typing this code in, compare it to the book's code with the online

```
 1. import pygame, sys, time
 2. from pygame.locals import *
 3.
 4. # set up pygame
 5. pygame.init()
 6.
 7. # set up the window
 8. WINDOWWIDTH = 400
 9. WINDOWHEIGHT = 400
10. windowSurface = pygame.display.set_mode((WINDOWWIDTH,
    WINDOWHEIGHT), 0, 32)
11. pygame.display.set_caption('Animation')
12.
13. # set up direction variables
14. DOWNLEFT = 1
15. DOWNRIGHT = 3
16. UPLEFT = 7
17. UPRIGHT = 9
18.
19. MOVESPEED = 4
20.
21. # set up the colors
22. BLACK = (0, 0, 0)
23. RED = (255, 0, 0)
24. GREEN = (0, 255, 0)
25. BLUE = (0, 0, 255)
26.
27. # set up the block data structure
28. b1 = {'rect':pygame.Rect(300, 80, 50, 100), 'color':RED,
    'dir':UPRIGHT}
29. b2 = {'rect':pygame.Rect(200, 200, 20, 20),
    'color':GREEN, 'dir':UPLEFT}
30. b3 = {'rect':pygame.Rect(100, 150, 60, 60), 'color':BLUE,
    'dir':DOWNLEFT}
31. blocks = [b1, b2, b3]
32.
33. # run the game loop
34. while True:
35.     # check for the QUIT event
36.     for event in pygame.event.get():
37.         if event.type == QUIT:
38.             pygame.quit()
39.             sys.exit()
40.
41.     # draw the black background onto the surface
42.     windowSurface.fill(BLACK)
43.
44.     for b in blocks:
45.         # move the block data structure
46.         if b['dir'] == DOWNLEFT:
47.             b['rect'].left -= MOVESPEED
```

```
48.            b['rect'].top += MOVESPEED
49.         if b['dir'] == DOWNRIGHT:
50.            b['rect'].left += MOVESPEED
51.            b['rect'].top += MOVESPEED
52.         if b['dir'] == UPLEFT:
53.            b['rect'].left -= MOVESPEED
54.            b['rect'].top -= MOVESPEED
55.         if b['dir'] == UPRIGHT:
56.            b['rect'].left += MOVESPEED
57.            b['rect'].top -= MOVESPEED
58.
59.         # check if the block has move out of the window
60.         if b['rect'].top < 0:
61.            # block has moved past the top
62.            if b['dir'] == UPLEFT:
63.                b['dir'] = DOWNLEFT
64.            if b['dir'] == UPRIGHT:
65.                b['dir'] = DOWNRIGHT
66.         if b['rect'].bottom > WINDOWHEIGHT:
67.            # block has moved past the bottom
68.            if b['dir'] == DOWNLEFT:
69.                b['dir'] = UPLEFT
70.            if b['dir'] == DOWNRIGHT:
71.                b['dir'] = UPRIGHT
72.         if b['rect'].left < 0:
73.            # block has moved past the left side
74.            if b['dir'] == DOWNLEFT:
75.                b['dir'] = DOWNRIGHT
76.            if b['dir'] == UPLEFT:
77.                b['dir'] = UPRIGHT
78.         if b['rect'].right > WINDOWWIDTH:
79.            # block has moved past the right side
80.            if b['dir'] == DOWNRIGHT:
81.                b['dir'] = DOWNLEFT
82.            if b['dir'] == UPRIGHT:
83.                b['dir'] = UPLEFT
84.
85.         # draw the block onto the surface
86.         pygame.draw.rect(windowSurface, b['color'], b
   ['rect'])
87.
88.    # draw the window onto the screen
89.    pygame.display.update()
90.    time.sleep(0.02)
```

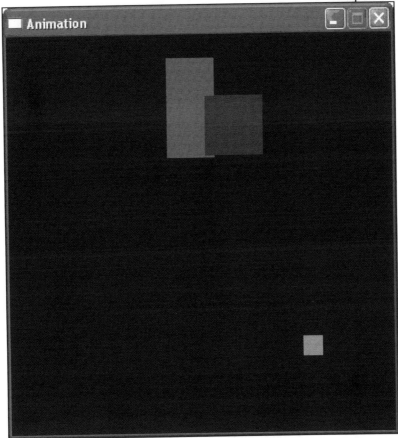

Figure 17-6: The Animation program.

How the Animation Program Works

In this program, we will have three different colored blocks moving around and bouncing off the walls. In order to do this, we need to first consider exactly how we want the blocks to move.

Moving and Bouncing the Blocks

Each block will move in one of four diagonal directions: down and left, down and right, up and left, or up and right. When the block hits the side of the window, we want it to "bounce" off the wall and move in a new diagonal direction. The blocks will bounce as shown in this picture:

The new direction that a block moves after it bounces depends on two things: which direction it was moving before the bounce and which wall it bounced off of. There are a total of eight possible ways a block can bounce: two different ways for each of the four walls. For example, if a block is moving down and right, and then bounces off of the bottom edge of the window, we want the block's new direction to be up and right.

We can represent the blocks with a Rect object to represent the position and size of the block, a tuple of three ints to represent the color of the block, and an integer to represent which of the four diagonal directions the block is currently moving. On each iteration in the game loop, we will adjust the X and Y position of the block in the Rect object. Also in each iteration we will draw all the blocks on the screen at their current position. As the program execution loops through the game loop, the blocks will gradually move across the screen so that it looks like they are smoothly moving and bouncing around on their own.

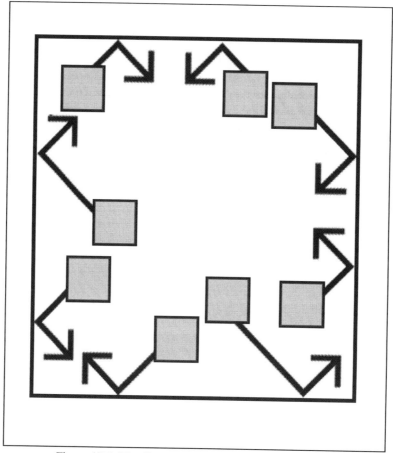

Figure 17-7: The diagram of how blocks will bounce.

Creating and Setting Up Pygame and the Main Window

```
1. import pygame, sys, time
```

In this program, we also want to import the time module.

```
7. # set up the window
8. WINDOWWIDTH = 400
9. WINDOWHEIGHT = 400
10. windowSurface = pygame.display.set_mode((WINDOWWIDTH,
    WINDOWHEIGHT), 0, 32)
```

In this program the size of the window's width and height is used for more than just the call to `set_mode()`. We will use a constant variables to make the program more readable. Remember, readability is for the benefit of the programmer, not the computer. If we ever want to change the size of the window, we only have to change lines 8 and 9.

If we did not use the constant variable, we would have to change ever occurance of the int value `400`. If any unrelated values in the program just happen to also be `400`, we might think it was for the width or height and also accidentally change it too. This would put a bug in our program. Since the window width and height never change during the program's execution, a constant variable is a good idea.

```
11. pygame.display.set_caption('Animation')
```

For this program, we will set the caption at the top of the window to `'Animation'` with a call to `pygame.display.set_caption()`.

```
13. Setting Up Constant Variables for Direction
14. # set up direction variables
15. DOWNLEFT = 1
16. DOWNRIGHT = 3
17. UPLEFT = 7
18. UPRIGHT = 9
```

We will use the keys on the number pad of the keyboard to remind us which belongs to which direction. This will be similar to our Tic Tac Toe game. 1 is down and left, 3 is down and right, 7 is up and left, and 9 is up and right. However, it may be hard to remember this, so instead we will use constant variables instead of these integer values.

We could use any values we wanted to for these directions instead of using a constant variable, as long as we had different values for each direction. For example, we could use the string `'downleft'` to represent the down and left diagonal direction. However, if we ever mistype the `'downleft'` string (for example, as `'fownleft'`), the computer would not recognize that we meant to type `'downleft'` instead of `'downleft'`. This bug would cause our program to behave strangely.

But if we use constant variables, and accidentally type the variable name `FOWNLEFT` instead of the name `DOWNLEFT`, Python would notice that there is no such variable named `FOWNLEFT` and crash the program with an error. This would still be a pretty bad bug, but at least we would know immediately about it and could fix it. Otherwise it may be hard to notice that there is a bug at all.

```
19. MOVESPEED = 4
```

We will use a constant variable to determine how fast the blocks should move. A value of 4 here means that each block will move 4 pixels on each iteration through the game loop.

Setting Up Constant Variables for Color

```
21. # set up the colors
22. BLACK = (0, 0, 0)
23. RED = (255, 0, 0)
24. GREEN = (0, 255, 0)
25. BLUE = (0, 0, 255)
```

We set up constant variables for the colors we will use. Remember, Pygame uses a tuple of three int values for the amounts of red, green, and blue called an RGB value. The integers are from 0 to 255. Unlike our "Hello World" program, this program doesn't use the white color, so we left it out.

Again, the use of constant variables is for readability. The computer doesn't care if we use a variable named GREEN for the color green. But if we later look at this program, it is easier to know that GREEN stands for the color green rather than a bunch of int values in a tuple.

Setting Up The Block Data Structures

```
27. # set up the block data structure
28. b1 = {'rect':pygame.Rect(300, 80, 50, 100), 'color':RED,
      'dir':UPRIGHT}
```

We will set up a dictionary to be the data structure that represents each block. (Dictionaries were introduced at the end of the Hangman chapter.) The dictionary will have the keys of 'rect' (with a Rect object for a value), 'color' (with a tuple of three ints for a value), and 'dir' (with one of our direction constant variables for a value).

We will store one of these data structures in a variable named b1. This block will have its top left corner located at an X-coordinate of 300 and Y-coordinate of 80. It will have a width of 50 pixels and a height of 100 pixels. Its color will be red (so we'll use our RED constant variable, which has the tuple (255, 0, 0) stored in it). And its direction will be set to UPRIGHT.

```
29. b2 = {'rect':pygame.Rect(200, 200, 20, 20),
      'color':GREEN, 'dir':UPLEFT}
30. b3 = {'rect':pygame.Rect(100, 150, 60, 60), 'color':BLUE,
      'dir':DOWNLEFT}
```

Here we create two more similar data structures for blocks that will be different sizes, positions, colors, and directions.

```
31. blocks = [b1, b2, b3]
```

On line 31 we put all of these data structures in a list, and store the list in a variable named `blocks`.

`blocks` is a list. `blocks[0]` would be the dictionary data structure in b1. `blocks[0]['color']` would be the `'color'` key in b1 (which we stored the value in RED in), so the expression `blocks[0]['color']` would evaluate to `(255, 0, 0)`. In this way we can refer to any of the values in any of the block data structures by starting with `blocks`.

Running the Game Loop

```
33. # run the game loop
34. while True:
```

Inside the game loop, we want to move all of the blocks around the screen in the direction that they are going, then bounce the block if they have hit a wall, then draw all of the blocks to the `windowSurface` surface, and finally call `pygame.display.update()` to draw the surface to the screen. Also, we will call `pygame.event.get()` to check if the QUIT event has been generated by the user closing the window.

The `for` loop to check all of the events in the list returned by `pygame.event.get()` is the same as in our "Hello World!" program, so we will skip its explanation and go on to line 44.

```
41.      # draw the black background onto the surface
42.      windowSurface.fill(BLACK)
```

Before we draw any of the blocks on the `windowSurface` surface, we want to fill the entire surface with black so that anything we previously drew on the surface is covered. Once we have blacked out the entire surface, we can redraw the blocks with the code below.

Moving Each Block

```
44.      for b in blocks:
```

We want to update the position of each block, so we must loop through the `blocks` list and perform the same code on each block's data structure. Inside the loop, we will refer to the current block as simply r so it will be easy to type.

```
45.      # move the block data structure
46.      if b['dir'] == DOWNLEFT:
47.          b['rect'].left -= MOVESPEED
```

```
48.                    b['rect'].top += MOVESPEED
49.                 if b['dir'] == DOWNRIGHT:
50.                    b['rect'].left += MOVESPEED
51.                    b['rect'].top += MOVESPEED
52.                 if b['dir'] == UPLEFT:
53.                    b['rect'].left -= MOVESPEED
54.                    b['rect'].top -= MOVESPEED
55.                 if b['dir'] == UPRIGHT:
56.                    b['rect'].left += MOVESPEED
57.                    b['rect'].top -= MOVESPEED
```

The new value that we want to set the left and top attributes to depends on the direction the block is moving. Remember that the X-coordinates start at 0 on the very left edge of the window, and increase as you go right. The Y-coordinates start at 0 on the very top of the window, and increase as you go down. So if the direction of the block (which, remember, is stored in the 'dir' key) is either DOWNLEFT or DOWNRIGHT, we want to *increase* the top attribute. If the direction is UPLEFT or UPRIGHT, we want to *decrease* the top attribute.

If the direction of the block is DOWNRIGHT or UPRIGHT, we want to *increase* the left attribute. If the direction is DOWNLEFT or UPLEFT, we want to *decrease* the left attribute.

We could have also modified right instead of the left attribute, or the bottom attribute instead of the top attribute, because Pygame will update the Rect object either way. Either way, we want to change the value of these attributes by the integer stored in MOVESPEED, which stores how many pixels over we will move the block.

Checking if the Block has Bounced

```
59.            # check if the block has move out of the window
60.            if b['rect'].top < 0:
61.                # block has moved past the top
62.                if b['dir'] == UPLEFT:
63.                    b['dir'] = DOWNLEFT
64.                if b['dir'] == UPRIGHT:
65.                    b['dir'] = DOWNRIGHT
```

After we have moved the block, we want to check if the block has gone past the edge of the window. If it has, we want to "bounce" the block, which in the code means set a new value for the block's 'dir' key. When the direction is set, the block will move in the new direction on the next iteration of the game loop.

We need to check if the block has moved passed each of the four edges of the window. In the above if statement, we decide the block has moved past the top edge of the window if the block's Rect object's top attribute is less than 0. If it is, then we need to change the direction based on what direction the block was moving.

Changing the Direction of the Bouncing Block

Look at the bouncing diagram earlier in this chapter. In order to move past the top edge of the window, the block had to either be moving in the UPLEFT or UPRIGHT directions. If the block was moving in the UPLEFT direction, the new direction (according to our bounce diagram) will be DOWNLEFT. If the block was moving in the UPRIGHT direction, the new direction will be DOWNRIGHT.

```
66.          if b['rect'].bottom > WINDOWHEIGHT:
67.              # block has moved past the bottom
68.              if b['dir'] == DOWNLEFT:
69.                  b['dir'] = UPLEFT
70.              if b['dir'] == DOWNRIGHT:
71.                  b['dir'] = UPRIGHT
```

Here we see if the block has moved past the bottom edge of the window by checking if the bottom attribute (not the top attribute) is *greater* than the value in WINDOWHEIGHT. Remember that the Y-coordinates start at 0 at the top of the window and increase to WINDOWHEIGHT because we passed WINDOWHEIGHT as the height in our call to pygame.display.set_mode().

The rest of the code changes the direction based on what our bounce diagram says.

```
72.          if b['rect'].left < 0:
73.              # block has moved past the left side
74.              if b['dir'] == DOWNLEFT:
75.                  b['dir'] = DOWNRIGHT
76.              if b['dir'] == UPLEFT:
77.                  b['dir'] = UPRIGHT
```

This is similar to the above code, but checks if the left side of the block has moved to the left of the left edge of the window. Remember, the X-coordinates start at 0 on the left edge of the window and increase to WINDOWWIDTH on the right edge of the window.

```
78.          if b['rect'].right > WINDOWWIDTH:
79.              # block has moved past the right side
80.              if b['dir'] == DOWNRIGHT:
81.                  b['dir'] = DOWNLEFT
82.              if b['dir'] == UPRIGHT:
83.                  b['dir'] = UPLEFT
```

This code is similar to the previous pieces of code, but it checks if the block has moved past the rightmost edge of the window.

Drawing the Blocks on the Window in Their New Positions

```
85.            # draw the block onto the surface
86.            pygame.draw.rect(windowSurface, b['color'], b
      ['rect'])
```

Now that we have moved the block (and set a new direction if the block has bounced off the window's edges), we want to draw it on the windowSurface surface. We can draw this using the pygame.draw.rect() function. We pass windowSurface, because that is the Surface object we want to draw on. We pass the b['color'] value, because this is the color we want to use. Then we pass b['rect'], because that Rect object has the information about the position and size of the rectangle we want to draw.

This is the last line of the for loop. We want to run the moving, bouncing, and drawing code on each of the blocks stored in the blocks list, which is why we loop through each of them. Also, if we wanted to add new blocks or remove blocks from our program, we only have to modify the blocks list and the rest of the code still works.

Drawing the Window on the Screen

```
88.    # draw the window onto the screen
89.    pygame.display.update()
90.    time.sleep(0.02)
```

After we have run this code on each of the blocks in the blocks list, we want to finally call pygame.display.update() so that the windowSurface surface is draw on the screen. After this line, we loop back to the start of the game loop and begin the process all over again. This way, the blocks are constantly moving a little, bouncing off the walls, and being drawn on the screen in their new positions. Meanwhile, we also check if the QUIT event has been generated by the Pygame library (which happens if the player closes the window or shuts down their computer). In that case we terminate the program.

The call to the time.sleep() function is there because the computer can move, bounce, and draw the blocks so fast that if the program ran at full speed, all the blocks would just look like a blur. (Try commenting out the time.sleep(0.02) line and running the program to see this.) This call to time.sleep() will stop the program for 20 milliseconds. There are 1000 milliseconds in a second, so 0.001 seconds equals 1 millisecond and 0.02 equals 20 milliseconds.

Some Small Modifications

Drawing as Fast as Possible

Just for fun, let's make some small modifications to our program so we can see what it does. Try adding a # in front of line 90 (the `time.sleep(0.2)` line) of our animation program. This will cause Python to ignore this line because it is now a comment. Now try running the program.

Without the `time.sleep()` function call to intentionally slow down the program, your computer will run through the game loop as fast as possible. This will make the rectangles bounce around the screen so fast, they'll only look like a blur. Now you can see why it is important for us to slow down the program with this line.

Drawing Trails of Blocks

Remove the # from the front of line 90 so that the line is no longer a comment and becomes part of the program again. This time, comment out line 42 (the `windowSurface.fill(BLACK)` line) by adding a # to the front of the line. Now run the program.

Without the call to `windowSurface.fill(BLACK)`, we do not black out the entire window before drawing the rectangles in their new position. This will cause trails of rectangles to appear on the screen instead of individual rectangles. The trails appear because all the old rectangles that are drawn in previous iterations through the game loop don't disappear.

Remember that the blocks are not really moving. We are just redrawing the entire window over and over again. On each iteration through the game loop, we redraw the entire window with new blocks that are located a few pixels over each time. When the program runs very fast, we make it is just one block each time. In order to see that we are just redrawing the blocks over and over again, change line 90 to `time.sleep(1.0)`. This will make the program (and the drawing) fifty times slower than normal. You will see each drawing being replaced by the next drawing every second.

Summary: Pygame Programming

This chapter has presented a whole new way of creating computer programs. Our programs before would stop and wait for the player to enter text. However, in our animation program, we are constantly updating the data structures of things without waiting for input from the player. Remember in our Hangman and Tic Tac Toe games we had data structures that would represent the state of the board, and these data structures would be passed to a `drawBoard()` function to be displayed on the screen. Our animation program is very similar. The `blocks` variable held a list of data structures representing things to be drawn to the screen, and these are drawn to the screen inside the game loop.

But without calls to `input()`, how do we get input from the player? In our next chapter, we will cover how our program can know when the player presses any key on the keyboard. We will also learn of a concept called collision detection, which is used in many graphical computer games.

Chapter **18**

Collision Detection and Input

Topics Covered In This Chapter:

- Collision Detection
- Don't Modify a List While Iterating Over It
- Keyboard Input in Pygame
- Mouse Input in Pygame

A very common behavior in most graphical games is collision detection. **Collision detection** is figuring when two things on the screen have touched (that is, collided with) each other. This is used very often in computer games. For example, if the player touches an enemy they may lose health or a game life. Or we may want to know when the player has touched a coin so that they automatically pick it up. Collision detection can help determine if the game character is standing on solid ground, or if there is nothing but empty air underneath them. In our games, collision detection is determining if two rectangles are overlapping each other or not. Our next example program will cover this basic technique.

Later in this chapter, we will look at how our Pygame programs can accept input from the user through the keyboard and the mouse. It's a bit more complicated than calling the `input()` function like we did for our text programs. But using the keyboard is much more interactive in GUI programs, and using the mouse isn't even possible in our text games. Knowing these two concepts will make our games more advanced and exciting!

The Collision Detection Program's Source Code

Much of this code is similar to the animation program, so we will skip over explaining how to make the bouncer move and bounce off of the walls. (See the animation program in the previous chapter for an explanation of that code.) We will use a list of pygame.Rect objects to represent the food squares. Each pygame.Rect object in the list represents a single food square. On each iteration through the game loop, our program will read each pygame.Rect object in the list and draw a green square on the window. Every forty iterations through the game loop we will add a new pygame.Rect to the list so that the screen constantly has new food squares in it.

The bouncer is represented by a dictionary. The dictionary has a key named 'rect' (whose value is a pygame.Rect object) and a key named 'dir' (whose value is one of the constant direction variables just like we had in last chapter's Animation program). As the bouncer bounces around the window, we check if it collides with any of the food squares. If it does, we delete that food square so that it will no longer be drawn on the screen.

Type the following into a new file and save it as *collisionDetection.py*. If you don't want to type all of this code, you can download the source from the book's website at *http://inventwithpython.com/chapter18*.

---

collisionDetection.py

This code can be downloaded from *http://inventwithpython.com/collisionDetection.py*
If you get errors after typing this code in, compare it to the book's code with the online diff tool at *http://inventwithpython.com/diff* or email the author at al@inventwithpython.com

```
1. import pygame, sys, random
2. from pygame.locals import *
3.
4. def doRectsOverlap(rect1, rect2):
5.     for a, b in [(rect1, rect2), (rect2, rect1)]:
6.         # Check if a's corners are inside b
7.         if ((isPointInsideRect(a.left, a.top, b)) or
8.             (isPointInsideRect(a.left, a.bottom, b)) or
9.             (isPointInsideRect(a.right, a.top, b)) or
10.            (isPointInsideRect(a.right, a.bottom, b))):
11.             return True
12.
13.     return False
14.
15. def isPointInsideRect(x, y, rect):
16.     if (x > rect.left) and (x < rect.right) and (y >
    rect.top) and (y < rect.bottom):
17.         return True
18.     else:
19.         return False
20.
21.
22. # set up pygame
23. pygame.init()
24. mainClock = pygame.time.Clock()
25.
26. # set up the window
```

```
27. WINDOWWIDTH = 400
28. WINDOWHEIGHT = 400
29. windowSurface = pygame.display.set_mode((WINDOWWIDTH,
    WINDOWHEIGHT), 0, 32)
30. pygame.display.set_caption('Collision Detection')
31.
32. # set up direction variables
33. DOWNLEFT = 1
34. DOWNRIGHT = 3
35. UPLEFT = 7
36. UPRIGHT = 9
37.
38. MOVESPEED = 4
39.
40. # set up the colors
41. BLACK = (0, 0, 0)
42. GREEN = (0, 255, 0)
43. WHITE = (255, 255, 255)
44.
45. # set up the bouncer and food data structures
46. foodCounter = 0
47. NEWFOOD = 40
48. FOODSIZE = 20
49. bouncer = {'rect':pygame.Rect(300, 100, 50, 50),
    'dir':UPLEFT}
50. foods = []
51. for i in range(20):
52.     foods.append(pygame.Rect(random.randint(0,
    WINDOWWIDTH - FOODSIZE), random.randint(0, WINDOWHEIGHT -
    FOODSIZE), FOODSIZE, FOODSIZE))
53.
54. # run the game loop
55. while True:
56.     # check for the QUIT event
57.     for event in pygame.event.get():
58.         if event.type == QUIT:
59.             pygame.quit()
60.             sys.exit()
61.
62.     foodCounter += 1
63.     if foodCounter >= NEWFOOD:
64.         # add new food
65.         foodCounter = 0
66.         foods.append(pygame.Rect(random.randint(0,
    WINDOWWIDTH - FOODSIZE), random.randint(0, WINDOWHEIGHT -
    FOODSIZE), FOODSIZE, FOODSIZE))
67.
68.     # draw the black background onto the surface
69.     windowSurface.fill(BLACK)
70.
71.     # move the bouncer data structure
72.     if bouncer['dir'] == DOWNLEFT:
73.         bouncer['rect'].left -= MOVESPEED
74.         bouncer['rect'].top += MOVESPEED
```

```
 75.        if bouncer['dir'] == DOWNRIGHT:
 76.            bouncer['rect'].left += MOVESPEED
 77.            bouncer['rect'].top += MOVESPEED
 78.        if bouncer['dir'] == UPLEFT:
 79.            bouncer['rect'].left -= MOVESPEED
 80.            bouncer['rect'].top -= MOVESPEED
 81.        if bouncer['dir'] == UPRIGHT:
 82.            bouncer['rect'].left += MOVESPEED
 83.            bouncer['rect'].top -= MOVESPEED
 84.
 85.        # check if the bouncer has move out of the window
 86.        if bouncer['rect'].top < 0:
 87.            # bouncer has moved past the top
 88.            if bouncer['dir'] == UPLEFT:
 89.                bouncer['dir'] = DOWNLEFT
 90.            if bouncer['dir'] == UPRIGHT:
 91.                bouncer['dir'] = DOWNRIGHT
 92.        if bouncer['rect'].bottom > WINDOWHEIGHT:
 93.            # bouncer has moved past the bottom
 94.            if bouncer['dir'] == DOWNLEFT:
 95.                bouncer['dir'] = UPLEFT
 96.            if bouncer['dir'] == DOWNRIGHT:
 97.                bouncer['dir'] = UPRIGHT
 98.        if bouncer['rect'].left < 0:
 99.            # bouncer has moved past the left side
100.            if bouncer['dir'] == DOWNLEFT:
101.                bouncer['dir'] = DOWNRIGHT
102.            if bouncer['dir'] == UPLEFT:
103.                bouncer['dir'] = UPRIGHT
104.        if bouncer['rect'].right > WINDOWWIDTH:
105.            # bouncer has moved past the right side
106.            if bouncer['dir'] == DOWNRIGHT:
107.                bouncer['dir'] = DOWNLEFT
108.            if bouncer['dir'] == UPRIGHT:
109.                bouncer['dir'] = UPLEFT
110.
111.        # draw the bouncer onto the surface
112.        pygame.draw.rect(windowSurface, WHITE, bouncer
     ['rect'])
113.
114.        # check if the bouncer has intersected with any food
     squares.
115.        for food in foods[:]:
116.            if doRectsOverlap(bouncer['rect'], food):
117.                foods.remove(food)
118.
119.        # draw the food
120.        for i in range(len(foods)):
121.            pygame.draw.rect(windowSurface, GREEN, foods[i])
122.
123.        # draw the window onto the screen
124.        pygame.display.update()
125.        mainClock.tick(40)
```

When you run this code, this is what the program looks like. The white square (the bouncer) will bounce around the window, and when it collides with the green squares (the food) will disappear from the screen.

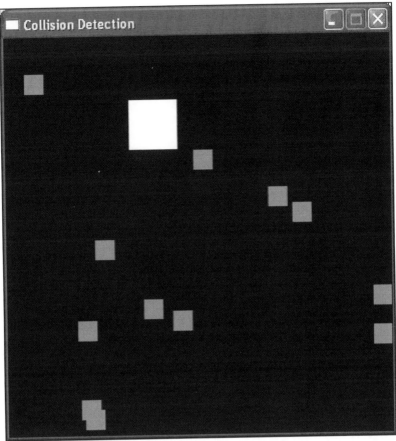

Figure 18-1: The Collision Detection program.

Importing the Modules

```
1. import pygame, sys, random
2. from pygame.locals import *
```

The collision detection program imports the same things as the Animation program in the last chapter, along with the `random` module.

The Collision Detection Function

```
4. def doRectsOverlap(rect1, rect2):
```

In order to do collision detection, we will need a function that can determine if two rectangles intersect each other or not. Here is a picture of intersecting rectangles (on the left) and rectangles that do not intersect (on the right):

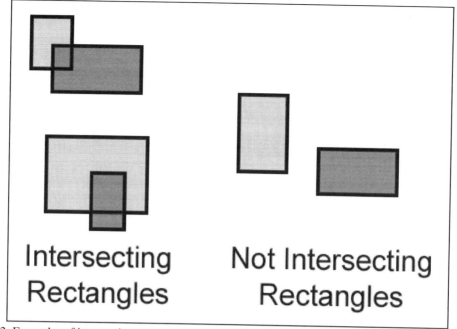

Figure 18-2: Examples of intersecting rectangles (on the left) and rectangles that do not intersect (on the right).

We will make a single function that is passed two pygame.Rect objects. The function, doRectsOverlap(), will return True if they do and False if they don't.

There is a very simple rule we can follow to determine if rectangles intersect (that is, collide). Look at each of the four corners on both rectangles. If at least one of these eight corners is inside the other rectangle, then we know that the two rectangles have collided. We will use this fact to determine if doRectsOverlap() returns True or False.

```
5.      for a, b in [(rect1, rect2), (rect2, rect1)]:
6.          # Check if a's corners are inside b
7.          if ((isPointInsideRect(a.left, a.top, b)) or
8.              (isPointInsideRect(a.left, a.bottom, b)) or
9.              (isPointInsideRect(a.right, a.top, b)) or
10.             (isPointInsideRect(a.right, a.bottom, b))):
11.             return True
```

Above is the code that checks if one rectangle's corners are inside another. Later we will create a function called isPointInsideRect() that returns True if the XY coordinates of the point are inside the rectangle. We call this function for each of the eight corners, and if any of these calls return True, the or operators will make the entire condition True.

The parameters for doRectsOverlap() are rect1 and rect2. We first want to check if rect1's corners are inside rect2 and then check if rect2's corners are in rect1.

We don't want to repeat the code that checks all four corners for both `rect1` and `rect2`, so instead we use a and b on lines 7 to 10. The `for` loop on line 5 uses the multiple assignment trick so that on the first iteration, a is set to `rect1` and b is set to `rect2`. On the second iteration through the loop, it is the opposite. a is set to `rect2` and b is set to `rect1`.

We do this because then we only have to type the code for the `if` statement on line 7 once. This is good, because this is a very long `if` statement. The less code we have to type for our program, the better.

```
13.       return False
```

If we never return `True` from the previous `if` statements, then none of the eight corners we checked are in the other rectangle. In that case, the rectangles did not collide and we return `False`.

Determining if a Point is Inside a Rectangle

```
15. def isPointInsideRect(x, y, rect):
16.     if (x > rect.left) and (x < rect.right) and (y >
    rect.top) and (y < rect.bottom):
17.         return True
```

The `isPointInsideRect()` function is used by the `doRectsOverlap()` function. `isPointInsideRect()` will return `True` if the XY coordinates passed to it as the first and second parameters are located "inside" the `pygame.Rect` object that is passed as the third parameter. Otherwise, this function returns `False`.

Figure 18-3 is an example picture of a rectangle and several dots. The dots and the corners of the rectangle are labeled with coordinates.

The pattern that points inside a rectangle have is an X-coordinate that is greater than the X-coordinate of the left side and less than the X-coordinate of the right side, and a Y-coordinate that is greater than the Y-coordinate of the top side and less than the Y-coordinate of the bottom side. If any of those conditions are false, then the point is outside the rectangle.

We combine all four of these conditions into the `if` statement's condition with `and` operators because all four of the conditions must be `True`.

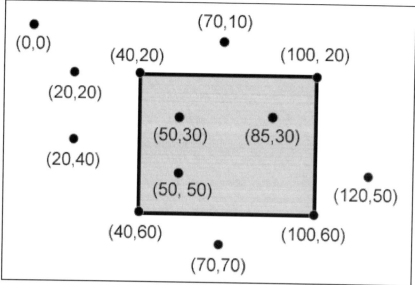

Figure 18-3: Example of coordinates inside and outside
of a rectangle. The (50, 30), (85, 30) and (50, 50) points
are inside the rectangle, and all the others are outside.

```
18.        else:
19.            return False
```

If just one of the four expressions in the condition on line 16 is `False`, then we should
have `isPointInsideRect()` return the value `False`.

This function will be called from the `doRectsOverlap()` function to see if any of the
corners in the two `pygame.Rect` objects are inside each other. These two functions give
us the power to do collision detection between two rectangles.

The `pygame.time.Clock` Object and `tick()` Method

Much of lines 22 to 43 do the same thing that Animation program in the last chapter did:
initialize the Pygame library, set `WINDOWHEIGHT` and `WINDOWWIDTH`, and put together
the color and direction constants. However, line 24 is new:

```
24. mainClock = pygame.time.Clock()
```

In the previous Animation program, we had a call to `time.sleep(0.02)` inside the
game loop in order to slow down the program enough so that we could see the blocks
moving. The problem with this is that the program might run too fast on fast computers and
too slow on slow computers. We want to limit the maximum number of iterations through
the game loop there are per second.

A `pygame.time.Clock` object can do this for us. You can see on line 125 that we call `mainClock.tick(40)` inside the game loop. This call to the `Clock` object's `tick()` method will check if we have iterated through the game loop more than 40 times in the last second. If so, it puts a short sleep into the program for us based on frequently `tick()` is being called. This ensures that the game never runs faster than we expect. Be sure to call `tick()` only once in the game loop.

Setting Up the Window and Data Structures

```
30. pygame.display.set_caption('Collision Detection')
31.
32. # set up the bouncer and food data structures
33. foodCounter = 0
34. NEWFOOD = 40
35. FOODSIZE = 20
```

We are going to set up a few variables for the food blocks that appear on the screen. `foodCounter` will start at the value 0, `NEWFOOD` at 40, and `FOODSIZE` at 20.

```
49. bouncer = {'rect':pygame.Rect(300, 100, 50, 50),
        'dir':UPLEFT}
```

We are going to set up a new data structure called `bouncer`. `bouncer` is a dictionary with two keys. The value stored in the `'rect'` key will be a `pygame.Rect` object that represents the bouncer's size and position. The value stored in the `'dir'` key will be a direction that the bouncer is currently moving. The bouncer will move the same way the blocks did in our previous animation program: moving in diagonal directions and bouncing off of the sides of the window.

```
50. foods = []
51. for i in range(20):
52.     foods.append(pygame.Rect(random.randint(0,
        WINDOWWIDTH - FOODSIZE), random.randint(0, WINDOWHEIGHT -
        FOODSIZE), FOODSIZE, FOODSIZE))
```

Our program will keep track of every food square with a list of `pygame.Rect` objects called `foods`. At the start of the program, we want to create twenty food squares randomly placed around the screen. We can use the `random.randint()` function to come up with random XY coordinates.

On line 52, we will call the `pygame.Rect()` constructor function to return a new `pygame.Rect` object that will represent the position and size of the food square. The first two parameters for `pygame.Rect()` are the XY coordinates of the top left corner. We want the random coordinate to be between 0 and the size of the window minus the size of the food square. If we had the random coordinate between 0 and the size of the window, then the food square might be pushed outside of the window altogether. For example, look at the diagram in Figure 18-4.

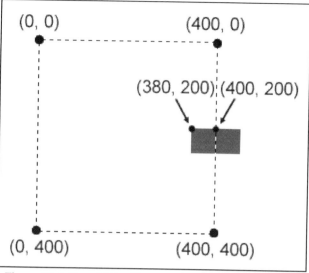

The square on the left has an X-coordinate of its top left corner at 380. Because the food square is 20 pixels wide, the right edge of the food square is at 400. (This is because 380 + 20 = 400.) The square on the right has an X-coordinate of its top left corner at 400. Because the food square is 20 pixels wide, the right edge of the food square is at 420, which puts the entire square outside of the window (and not viewable to the user).

Figure 18-4: For a 20 by 20 rectangle, having the top left corner at (400, 200) in a 400 by 400 window would place the rectangle outside of the window. To be inside, the top left corner should be at (380, 200) instead.

The third parameter for pygame.Rect() is a tuple that contains the width and height of the food square. Both the width and height will be equal to the value in the FOODSIZE constant.

Drawing the Bouncer on the Screen

Lines 71 to 109 cause the bouncer to move around the window and bounce off of the edges of the window. This code is very similar to lines 44 to 83 of our animation program in the last chapter, so we will not go over them again here.

```
111.    # draw the bouncer onto the surface
112.    pygame.draw.rect(windowSurface, WHITE, bouncer
        ['rect'])
```

After moving the bouncer, we now want to draw it on the window in its new position. We call the pygame.draw.rect() function to draw a rectangle. The windowSurface passed for the first parameter tells the computer which pygame.Surface object to draw the rectangle on. The WHITE variable, which has (255, 255, 255) stored in it, will tell the computer to draw a white rectangle. The pygame.Rect object stored in the bouncer dictionary at the 'rect' key tells the position and size of the rectangle to draw. This is all the information needed to draw a white rectangle on windowSurface.

Remember, we are not done drawing things on the windowSurface object yet. We still need to draw a green square for each food square in the foods list. And we are just "drawing" rectangles on the windowSurface object, not on the screen. This `pygame.Surface` object is only inside the computer's memory, which is much faster to modify than the pixels on the screen. The window on the screen will not be updated until we call the `pygame.display.update()` function.

Colliding with the Food Squares

```
114.        # check if the bouncer has intersected with any food
       squares.
115.        for food in foods[:]:
```

Before we draw the food squares, we want to see if the bouncer has overlapped any of the food squares. If it has, we will remove that food square from the `foods` list. This way, the computer won't draw any food squares that the bouncer has "eaten".

On each iteration through the `for` loop, the current food square from the `foods` (plural) list will be stored inside a variable called `food` (singular).

Don't Add to or Delete from a List while Iterating Over It

Notice that there is something slightly different with this `for` loop. If you look carefully at line 116, we are not iterating over `foods` but actually over `foods[:]`. Just as `foods[:2]` would return a copy of the list with the items from the start and up to (but not including) the item at index 2, and just as `foods[3:]` would return a copy of the list with the items from index 3 to the end of the list, `foods[:]` will give you a copy of the list with the items from the start to the end. Basically, `foods[:]` creates a new list with a copy of all the items in `foods`. (This is a shorter way to copy a list than our `getBoardCopy()` function in the Tic Tac Toe game.)

Why would we want to iterate over a copy of the list instead of the list itself? It is because we cannot add or remove items from a list while we are iterating over it. Python can lose track of what the next value of `food` variable should be if the size of the `foods` list is always changing. Think of how difficult it would be for you if you tried to count the number of jelly beans in a jar while someone was adding or removing jelly beans. But if we iterate over a copy of the list (and the copy never changes), then adding or removing items from the original list won't be a problem.

Removing the Food Squares

```
116.            if doRectsOverlap(bouncer['rect'], food):
117.                foods.remove(food)
```

Line 116 is where our `doRectsOverlap()` function that we defined earlier comes in handy. We pass two `pygame.Rect` objects to `doRectsOverlap()`: the bouncer and the current food square. If these two rectangles overlap, then `doRectsOverlap()` will return `True` and we will remove the overlapping food squares from `foods` list.

Drawing the Food Squares on the Screen

```
119.        # draw the food
120.        for i in range(len(foods)):
121.            pygame.draw.rect(windowSurface, GREEN, foods[i])
```

The code on lines 120 and 121 are very similar to how we drew the white square for the player. We will loop through each food square in the `foods` list, and then draw the rectangle onto the `windowSurface` surface. This demonstration of collision detection is fairly easy. This program was very similar to our bouncing program in the previous chapter, except now the bouncing square will "eat" the other squares as it passes over them.

These past few programs are interesting to watch, but the user does not get to actually control anything. In this next program, we will learn how to get input from the keyboard. Keyboard input is handled in Pygame by using events.

The Keyboard Input Program's Source Code

Start a new file and type in the following code, then save it as *pygameInput.py*.

pygameInput.py

This code can be downloaded from *http://inventwithpython.com/pygameInput.py*
If you get errors after typing this code in, compare it to the book's code with the online diff tool at *http://inventwithpython.com/diff* or email the author at al@inventwithpython.com

```
 1. import pygame, sys, random
 2. from pygame.locals import *
 3.
 4. # set up pygame
 5. pygame.init()
 6. mainClock = pygame.time.Clock()
 7.
 8. # set up the window
 9. WINDOWWIDTH = 400
10. WINDOWHEIGHT = 400
11. windowSurface = pygame.display.set_mode((WINDOWWIDTH,
    WINDOWHEIGHT), 0, 32)
12. pygame.display.set_caption('Input')
13.
14. # set up the colors
15. BLACK = (0, 0, 0)
```

```
16. GREEN = (0, 255, 0)
17. WHITE = (255, 255, 255)
18.
19. # set up the player and food data structure
20. foodCounter = 0
21. NEWFOOD = 40
22. FOODSIZE = 20
23. player = pygame.Rect(300, 100, 50, 50)
24. foods = []
25. for i in range(20):
26.     foods.append(pygame.Rect(random.randint(0,
    WINDOWWIDTH - FOODSIZE), random.randint(0, WINDOWHEIGHT -
    FOODSIZE), FOODSIZE, FOODSIZE))
27.
28. # set up movement variables
29. moveLeft = False
30. moveRight = False
31. moveUp = False
32. moveDown = False
33.
34. MOVESPEED = 6
35.
36.
37. # run the game loop
38. while True:
39.     # check for events
40.     for event in pygame.event.get():
41.         if event.type == QUIT:
42.             pygame.quit()
43.             sys.exit()
44.         if event.type == KEYDOWN:
45.             # change the keyboard variables
46.             if event.key == K_LEFT or event.key == ord
    ('a'):
47.                 moveRight = False
48.                 moveLeft = True
49.             if event.key == K_RIGHT or event.key == ord
    ('d'):
50.                 moveLeft = False
51.                 moveRight = True
52.             if event.key == K_UP or event.key == ord
    ('w'):
53.                 moveDown = False
54.                 moveUp = True
55.             if event.key == K_DOWN or event.key == ord
    ('s'):
56.                 moveUp = False
57.                 moveDown = True
58.         if event.type == KEYUP:
59.             if event.key == K_ESCAPE:
60.                 pygame.quit()
61.                 sys.exit()
62.             if event.key == K_LEFT or event.key == ord
    ('a'):
```

```
63.                         moveLeft = False
64.                 if event.key == K_RIGHT or event.key == ord
     ('d'):
65.                         moveRight = False
66.                 if event.key == K_UP or event.key == ord
     ('w'):
67.                         moveUp = False
68.                 if event.key == K_DOWN or event.key == ord
     ('s'):
69.                         moveDown = False
70.                 if event.key == ord('x'):
71.                     player.top = random.randint(0,
         WINDOWHEIGHT - player.height)
72.                     player.left = random.randint(0,
         WINDOWWIDTH - player.width)
73.
74.             if event.type == MOUSEBUTTONUP:
75.                 foods.append(pygame.Rect(event.pos[0],
         event.pos[1], FOODSIZE, FOODSIZE))
76.
77.         foodCounter += 1
78.         if foodCounter >= NEWFOOD:
79.             # add new food
80.             foodCounter = 0
81.             foods.append(pygame.Rect(random.randint(0,
         WINDOWWIDTH - FOODSIZE), random.randint(0, WINDOWHEIGHT -
         FOODSIZE), FOODSIZE, FOODSIZE))
82.
83.         # draw the black background onto the surface
84.         windowSurface.fill(BLACK)
85.
86.         # move the player
87.         if moveDown and player.bottom < WINDOWHEIGHT:
88.             player.top += MOVESPEED
89.         if moveUp and player.top > 0:
90.             player.top -= MOVESPEED
91.         if moveLeft and player.left > 0:
92.             player.left -= MOVESPEED
93.         if moveRight and player.right < WINDOWWIDTH:
94.             player.right += MOVESPEED
95.
96.         # draw the player onto the surface
97.         pygame.draw.rect(windowSurface, WHITE, player)
98.
99.         # check if the player has intersected with any food
     squares.
100.        for food in foods[:]:
101.            if player.colliderect(food):
102.                foods.remove(food)
103.
104.        # draw the food
105.        for i in range(len(foods)):
106.            pygame.draw.rect(windowSurface, GREEN, foods[i])
107.
```

```
108.        # draw the window onto the screen
109.        pygame.display.update()
110.        mainClock.tick(40)
```

This program looks identical to the collision detection program earlier in this chapter. But in this program, the bouncer only moves around when we hold down keys on the keyboard. Holding down the "W" key moves the bouncer up. The "A" key moves the bouncer to the left and the "D" key moves the bouncer to the right. The "S" key moves the bouncer down. You can also move the bouncer by holding down the arrow keys on the keyboard. The user can also use the keyboard's arrow keys.

We can also click anywhere in the GUI window and create new food objects at the coordinates where we clicked. In addition, the ESC key will quit the program and the "X" key will teleport the bouncer to a random place on the screen.

Setting Up the Window and Data Structures

First, we set the caption of the window's title bar to the string to `'Mouse'` on line 12. We set the caption of the window with a call to `pygame.display.set_caption()` the same way as we did in our previous Pygame programs. Next we want to set up some variables that track the movement of the bouncer.

```
28. # set up movement variables
29. moveLeft = False
30. moveRight = False
31. moveUp = False
32. moveDown = False
```

We are going to use four different Boolean variables to keep track of which of the arrow keys are being held down. For example, when the user pushes the left arrow key on her keyboard, we will set the `moveLeft` variable to `True`. When she lets go of the key, we will set the `moveLeft` variable back to `False`. The "W" key affects the `moveUp` variable, the "S" key affects the `moveDown` variable, and the "D" key affects the `moveRight` variable in a similar way.

Lines 34 to 43 are identical to code in the previous Pygame programs. These lines handle the start of the game loop and handling what to do when the user wants to quit the program. We will skip the explanation for this code here since we have already covered it in the last chapter.

Events and Handling the `KEYDOWN` Event

Table 18-1: Events, and what causes them to be generated.

Event	Description
QUIT	Generated when the user closes with window.
KEYDOWN	Generated when the user pressed down a key. Has a `key` attribute that tells which key was pressed. Also has a `mod` attribute that tells if the Shift, Ctrl, Alt, or other keys were held down when this key was pressed.
KEYUP	Generated when the user releases a key. Has a `key` and `mod` attribute that are similar to those for KEYDOWN.
MOUSEMOTION	Generated whenever the mouse moves over the window. Has a `pos` attribute that returns tuple (x, y) for the coordinates of where the mouse is in the window. The `rel` attribute also returns a (x, y) tuple, but it gives coordinates relative since the last MOUSEMOTION event. For example, if the mouse moves left by four pixels from (200, 200) to (196, 200), then `rel` will be `(-4, 0)`. The `buttons` attribute returns a tuple of three integers. The first integer in the tuple is for the left mouse button, the second integer for the middle mouse button (if there is a middle mouse button), and the third integer is for the right mouse button. These integers will be 0 if they are not being pressed down when the mouse moved and 1 if they are pressed down.
MOUSEBUTTONDOWN	Generated when a mouse button is pressed down in the window. This event has a `pos` attribute which is an (x, y) tuple for the coordinates of where the mouse was when the button was pressed. There is also a `button` attribute which is an integer from 1 to 5 that tells which mouse button was pressed: **Value of `button`** / **Mouse Button** 1 — Left button 2 — Middle button 3 — Right button 4 — Scroll wheel moved up 5 — Scroll wheel moved down
MOUSEBUTTONUP	Generated when the mouse button is released. This has the same attributes as MOUSEBUTTONDOWN

The code to handle the key press and key release events is below. But at the start of the program, we will set all of these variables to `False`.

```
44.                if event.type == KEYDOWN:
```

Pygame has another event type called KEYDOWN. On line 41, we check if the event.type attribute is equal to the QUIT value to check if we should exit the program. But there are other events that Pygame can generate. A brief list of the events that could be returned by pygame.event.get() is in Table 18-1.

Setting the Four Keyboard Variables

```
45.                # change the keyboard variables
46.                if event.key == K_LEFT or event.key == ord
     ('a'):
47.                    moveRight = False
48.                    moveLeft = True
49.                if event.key == K_RIGHT or event.key == ord
     ('d'):
50.                    moveLeft = False
51.                    moveRight = True
52.                if event.key == K_UP or event.key == ord
     ('w'):
53.                    moveDown = False
54.                    moveUp = True
55.                if event.key == K_DOWN or event.key == ord
     ('s'):
56.                    moveUp = False
57.                    moveDown = True
```

If the event type is KEYDOWN, then the event object will have a key attribute that will tell us which key was pressed down. On line 46, we can compare this value to K_LEFT, which represents the left arrow key on the keyboard. We will do this for each of the arrow keys: K_LEFT, K_RIGHT, K_UP, K_DOWN.

When one of these keys is pressed down, we will set the corresponding movement variable to True. We will also set the movement variable of the opposite direction to False. For example, the program executes lines 47 and 48 when the left arrow key has been pressed. In this case, we will set moveLeft to True and moveRight to False (even though moveRight might already be False, we set it to False just to be sure).

You may notice that on line 46, in event.key can either be equal to K_LEFT or ord ('a'). The value in event.key is set to the integer ASCII value of the key that was pressed on the keyboard. (There is no ASCII value for the arrow keys, which is why we use the constant variable K_LEFT.) You can use the ord() function to get the ASCII value of any single character to compare it with event.key.

By executing the code on lines 47 and 48 if the keystroke was either K_LEFT or ord('a'), we make the left arrow key and the A key do the same thing. You may notice that the W, A, S, and D keys are all used as alternates for changing the movement variables.

This is because some people may want to use their left hand to press the WASD keys instead of their right hand to press the arrow keys. Our program offers them both!

Handling the KEYUP Event

```
58.                 if event.type == KEYUP:
```

When the user releases the key that they are holding down, a KEYUP event is generated.

```
59.                     if event.key == K_ESCAPE:
60.                         pygame.quit()
61.                         sys.exit()
```

If the key that the user released was the Esc key, then we want to terminate the program. Remember, in Pygame you must call the pygame.quit() function before calling the sys.exit() function. We want to do this when the user releases the Esc key, not when they first Esc key down.

Lines 62 to 69 will set a movement variable to False if that direction's key was let go.

```
62.                     if event.key == K_LEFT or event.key == ord
    ('a'):
63.                         moveLeft = False
64.                     if event.key == K_RIGHT or event.key == ord
    ('d'):
65.                         moveRight = False
66.                     if event.key == K_UP or event.key == ord
    ('w'):
67.                         moveUp = False
68.                     if event.key == K_DOWN or event.key == ord
    ('s'):
69.                         moveDown = False
```

Teleporting the Player

If the user released one of the keys that moves the player, then we want to set the movement variable that corresponds with the key to False. This will tell the later parts of our program to no longer move the player's square on the screen.

```
70.                     if event.key == ord('x'):
71.                         player.top = random.randint(0,
    WINDOWHEIGHT - player.height)
72.                         player.left = random.randint(0,
    WINDOWWIDTH - player.width)
```

We will also add teleportation to our game. If the user presses the "X" key, then we will set the position of the user's square to a random place on the window. This will give the user the ability to teleport around the window by pushing the "X" key (though they can't control where they will teleport: it's completely random).

Handling the MOUSEBUTTONUP Event

```
74.          if event.type == MOUSEBUTTONUP:
75.              foods.append(pygame.Rect(event.pos[0],
     event.pos[1], FOODSIZE, FOODSIZE))
```

Mouse input is handled by events just like keyboard input is. The MOUSEBUTTONUP event occurs when the user clicks a mouse button somewhere in our window, and releases the mouse button. The pos attribute in the Event object is set to a tuple of two integers for the XY coordinates. On line 75, the X-coordinate is stored in event.pos[0] and the Y-coordinate is stored in event.pos[1]. We will create a new Rect object to represent a new food and place it where the MOUSEBUTTONUP event occurred. By adding a new Rect object to the foods list, a new food square will be displayed on the screen.

Moving the Bouncer Around the Screen

```
86.     # move the player
87.     if moveDown and player.bottom < WINDOWHEIGHT:
88.         player.top += MOVESPEED
89.     if moveUp and player.top > 0:
90.         player.top -= MOVESPEED
91.     if moveLeft and player.left > 0:
92.         player.left -= MOVESPEED
93.     if moveRight and player.right < WINDOWWIDTH:
94.         player.right += MOVESPEED
```

We have set the movement variables (moveDown, moveUp, moveLeft, and moveRight) to True or False depending on what keys the user has pressed. Now we will actually move the player's square (which is represented by the pygame.Rect object stored in player) around by adjusting the XY coordinates of player. If moveDown is set to True (and the bottom of the player's square is not below the bottom edge of the window), then we move the player's square down by adding MOVESPEED to the player's current top attribute. We do the same thing for the other three directions as well.

The `colliderect()` Method

```
99.      # check if the player has intersected with any food
      squares.
100.      for food in foods[:]:
101.          if player.colliderect(food):
102.              foods.remove(food)
```

In our previous Collision Detection program, we had our own function to check if one rectangle had collided with another. That function was included in this book so that you could understand how the code behind collision detection works. In this program, we can use the collision detection function that comes with Pygame. The `colliderect()` method for `pygame.Rect` objects is passed another `pygame.Rect` object as an argument and returns `True` if the two rectangles collide and `False` if they do not. This is the exact same behavior as the `doRectsOverlap()` function in our previous Collision Detection program.

```
110.      mainClock.tick(40)
```

The rest of the code is similar to the code in the Input program is similar to the earlier Collision Detection program: draw the food squares and the player squares to the `windowSurface` surface, occasionally add a new food square at a random location to the `foods` list, check if the player square has collided with any of the food squares, and call `mainClock.tick(40)` to make the program run at an appropriate speed.

Summary: Collision Detection and Pygame Input

This chapter introduced the concept of collision detection, which is used in most graphical games. Detecting collisions between two rectangles is easy: we just check if the four corners of either rectangle are within the other rectangle. This is such a common thing to check for that Pygame provides it's own collision detection method named `colliderect()` for `pygame.Rect` objects.

The first several games in this book were text-based. The program output was text printed to the screen and the input was text typed by the user on the keyboard. But GUI programs can accept keyboard and mouse inputs. Furthermore, GUI programs can respond to single keystrokes when the user pushes down or lets up a single key. The user does not have to type in an entire response and press Enter. This allows for immediate feedback when the player presses down any key on the keyboard and much more interactive games.

The Pygame programs we shown so far have drawn rectangles, lines, circles, and even individual pixels to the screen. These are called drawing primitives. But we also want to use pictures and images instead of simple drawing primitives. The next chapter will tell you how to load images and draw them on the screen. We will also learn how to play sounds and music for the player to hear.

Chapter 19
Sound and Images

Topics Covered In This Chapter:

- Image and Sound Files
- Drawing Sprites
- The pygame.image.load() Function
- The pygame.mixer.Sound Data Type
- The pygame.mixer.music Module

In the last two chapters, we've learned how to make GUI programs that have graphics and can accept input from the keyboard and mouse. We've also learned how to draw shapes in different colors on the screen. In this chapter, we will learn how to show pictures and images (called sprites) and play sounds and music in our games.

A **sprite** is a name for a single two-dimensional image that is used as part of the graphics on the screen. Here are some example sprites:

Figure 19-1: Some examples of sprites.

This is an example of sprites being used in a complete scene.

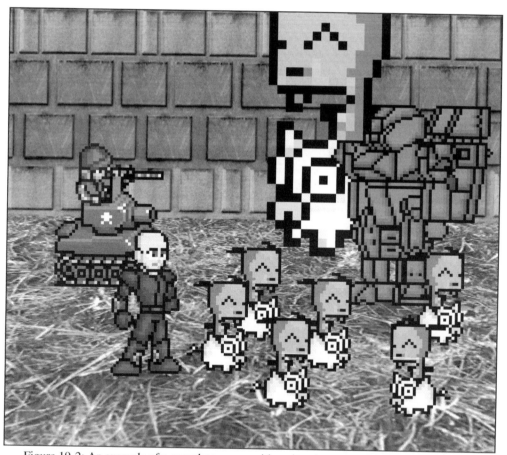

Figure 19-2: An example of a complete scene, with sprites drawn on top of a background.

The sprite images are drawn on top of the background. Notice that we can flip the sprite image horizontally so that the sprites are facing the other way. We can draw the same sprite image multiple times on the same window. We can also resize the sprites to be larger or smaller than the original sprite image. The background image can also be considered one large sprite.

The next program we make will demonstrate how to play sounds and draw sprites using Pygame.

Image and Sound Files

Sprites are stored in image files on your computer. There are several different image formats that Pygame can use. You can tell what format an image file uses by looking at the end of the file name (after the last period). This is called the **file extension**. For example, the file *happy.png* is in the PNG format. The image formats Pygame supports include BMP, PNG, JPG (and JPEG), and GIF.

You can download images from your web browser. On most web browsers, you just have to right-click on the image in the web page and select Save from the menu that appears. Remember where on the hard drive you saved the image file. You can also create your own images with a drawing program like MS Paint or Tux Paint.

The sound file formats that Pygame supports are MID, WAV, and MP3. You can download sound effects from the Internet just like image files, as long as the sound effects are in one of these three formats. If you have a microphone, you can also record sounds with your computer yourself and use them in your games.

Sprites and Sounds Program

This program is the same as the Keyboard and Mouse Input program from the last chapter. However, in this program we will use sprites instead of plain looking squares. We will use a sprite of a little man instead of the white player square, and a sprite of cherries instead of the green food squares. We also play background music and a sound effect when the player sprite eats one of the cherry sprites.

The Sprites and Sounds Program's Source Code

If you know how to use graphics software such as Photoshop or MS Paint, you can draw your own images and use the image files in your games. If you don't know how to use these programs, you can just download graphics from websites and use those image files instead. The same applies for music and sound files. You can also find images on web sites or images from a digital camera. You can download the image and sound files from this book's website at *http://inventwithpython.com/resources/*. You can download the source code in this chapter from the URL *http://inventwithpython.com/chapter19*.

---

spritesAndSounds.py
This code can be downloaded from *http://inventwithpython.com/spritesAndSounds.py*
If you get errors after typing this code in, compare it to the book's code with the online diff tool at *http://inventwithpython.com/diff* or email the author at al@inventwithpython.com

---

```
 1. import pygame, sys, time, random
 2. from pygame.locals import *
 3.
 4. # set up pygame
 5. pygame.init()
 6. mainClock = pygame.time.Clock()
 7.
 8. # set up the window
 9. WINDOWWIDTH = 400
10. WINDOWHEIGHT = 400
11. windowSurface = pygame.display.set_mode((WINDOWWIDTH,
    WINDOWHEIGHT), 0, 32)
12. pygame.display.set_caption('Sprites and Sound')
13.
14. # set up the colors
15. BLACK = (0, 0, 0)
16.
17. # set up the block data structure
18. player = pygame.Rect(300, 100, 40, 40)
19. playerImage = pygame.image.load('player.png')
20. playerStretchedImage = pygame.transform.scale
    (playerImage, (40, 40))
21. foodImage = pygame.image.load('cherry.png')
22. foods = []
23. for i in range(20):
24.     foods.append(pygame.Rect(random.randint(0,
    WINDOWWIDTH - 20), random.randint(0, WINDOWHEIGHT - 20),
    20, 20))
25.
26. foodCounter = 0
27. NEWFOOD = 40
28.
29. # set up keyboard variables
30. moveLeft = False
31. moveRight = False
32. moveUp = False
33. moveDown = False
34.
35. MOVESPEED = 6
36.
37. # set up music
38. pickUpSound = pygame.mixer.Sound('pickup.wav')
39. pygame.mixer.music.load('background.mid')
40. pygame.mixer.music.play(-1, 0.0)
41. musicPlaying = True
42.
43. # run the game loop
44. while True:
45.     # check for the QUIT event
46.     for event in pygame.event.get():
47.         if event.type == QUIT:
48.             pygame.quit()
49.             sys.exit()
50.         if event.type == KEYDOWN:
```

```
51.              # change the keyboard variables
52.              if event.key == K_LEFT or event.key == ord
     ('a'):
53.                  moveRight = False
54.                  moveLeft = True
55.              if event.key == K_RIGHT or event.key == ord
     ('d'):
56.                  moveLeft = False
57.                  moveRight = True
58.              if event.key == K_UP or event.key == ord
     ('w'):
59.                  moveDown = False
60.                  moveUp = True
61.              if event.key == K_DOWN or event.key == ord
     ('s'):
62.                  moveUp = False
63.                  moveDown = True
64.          if event.type == KEYUP:
65.              if event.key == K_ESCAPE:
66.                  pygame.quit()
67.                  sys.exit()
68.              if event.key == K_LEFT or event.key == ord
     ('a'):
69.                  moveLeft = False
70.              if event.key == K_RIGHT or event.key == ord
     ('d'):
71.                  moveRight = False
72.              if event.key == K_UP or event.key == ord
     ('w'):
73.                  moveUp = False
74.              if event.key == K_DOWN or event.key == ord
     ('s'):
75.                  moveDown = False
76.              if event.key == ord('x'):
77.                  player.top = random.randint(0,
     WINDOWHEIGHT - player.height)
78.                  player.left = random.randint(0,
     WINDOWWIDTH - player.width)
79.              if event.key == ord('m'):
80.                  if musicPlaying:
81.                      pygame.mixer.music.stop()
82.                  else:
83.                      pygame.mixer.music.play(-1, 0.0)
84.                  musicPlaying = not musicPlaying
85.
86.          if event.type == MOUSEBUTTONUP:
87.              foods.append(pygame.Rect(event.pos[0] - 10,
     event.pos[1] - 10, 20, 20))
88.
89.      foodCounter += 1
90.      if foodCounter >= NEWFOOD:
91.          # add new food
92.          foodCounter = 0
```

```
93.              foods.append(pygame.Rect(random.randint(0,
       WINDOWWIDTH - 20), random.randint(0, WINDOWHEIGHT - 20),
       20, 20))
94.
95.      # draw the black background onto the surface
96.      windowSurface.fill(BLACK)
97.
98.      # move the player
99.      if moveDown and player.bottom < WINDOWHEIGHT:
100.          player.top += MOVESPEED
101.      if moveUp and player.top > 0:
102.          player.top -= MOVESPEED
103.      if moveLeft and player.left > 0:
104.          player.left -= MOVESPEED
105.      if moveRight and player.right < WINDOWWIDTH:
106.          player.right += MOVESPEED
107.
108.
109.      # draw the block onto the surface
110.      windowSurface.blit(playerStretchedImage, player)
111.
112.      # check if the block has intersected with any food
       squares.
113.      for food in foods[:]:
114.          if player.colliderect(food):
115.              foods.remove(food)
116.              player = pygame.Rect(player.left, player.top,
       player.width + 2, player.height + 2)
117.              playerStretchedImage = pygame.transform.scale
       (playerImage, (player.width, player.height))
118.              if musicPlaying:
119.                  pickUpSound.play()
120.
121.      # draw the food
122.      for food in foods:
123.          windowSurface.blit(foodImage, food)
124.
125.      # draw the window onto the screen
126.      pygame.display.update()
127.      mainClock.tick(40)
```

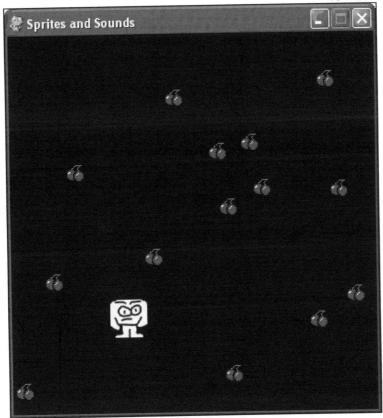

Figure 19-3: The Sprites and Sounds game.

Setting Up the Window and the Data Structure

Most of the code in this program was explained in the previous chapter, so we will only focus on the parts that add sprites and sound.

```
12. pygame.display.set_caption('Sprites and Sound')
```

First, let's set the caption of the title bar to a string that describes this program on line 12. Pass the string 'Sprites and Sound' to the pygame.display.set_caption () function.

```
17. # set up the block data structure
18. player = pygame.Rect(300, 100, 40, 40)
19. playerImage = pygame.image.load('player.png')
20. playerStretchedImage = pygame.transform.scale
      (playerImage, (40, 40))
21. foodImage = pygame.image.load('cherry.png')
```

We are going to use three different variables to represent the player, unlike the previous programs that just used one. The player variable will store a Rect object that keeps track of where and how big the player is. The player variable doesn't contain the player's image, just the player's size and location. At the beginning of the program, the top left corner of the player will be located at (300, 100) and the player will have a height and width of 40 pixels to start.

The second variable that represents the player will be `playerImage`. The `pygame.image.load()` function is passed a string of the filename of the image to load. The return value of `pygame.image.load()` is a `Surface` object that has the image in the image file drawn on its surface. We store this `Surface` object inside of `playerImage`.

The `pygame.transform.scale()` Function

On line 20, we will use a new function in the `pygame.transform` module. The `pygame.transform.scale()` function can shrink or enlarge a sprite. The first argument is a `pygame.Surface` object with the image drawn on it. The second argument is a tuple for the new width and height of the image in the first argument. The `pygame.transform.scale()` function returns a `pygame.Surface` object with the image drawn at a new size. We will store the original image in the `playerImage` variable but the stretched image in the `playerStretchedImage` variable.

On line 21, we call `pygame.image.load()` again to create a `Surface` object with the cherry image drawn on it.

Be sure that you have the *player.png* and *cherry.png* file in the same directory as the *spritesAndSounds.py* file, otherwise Pygame will not be able to find them and will give an error.

The `Surface` objects that are stored in `playerImage` and `foodImage` are the same as the `Surface` object we use for the window. In our game, we will blit these surfaces onto the window's surface to create the window that the user sees. This is exactly the same as the when we got a `Surface` object returned from the `render()` method for `Font` objects in our Hello World program. In order to actually display the text, we had to blit this `Surface` object (which the text was drawn on) to the window's `Surface` object. (And then, of course, call the `update()` method on the window's `Surface` object.)

Setting Up the Music and Sounds

```
37. # set up music
38. pickUpSound = pygame.mixer.Sound('pickup.wav')
39. pygame.mixer.music.load('background.mid')
40. pygame.mixer.music.play(-1, 0.0)
41. musicPlaying = True
```

Next we need to load the sound files. There are two modules for sound in Pygame. The `pygame.mixer` module is responsible for playing short sound effects during the game. The `pygame.mixer.music` module is used for playing the background music.

We will call the `pygame.mixer.Sound()` constructor function to create a `pygame.mixer.Sound` object (which we will simply call a `Sound` object). This object has a `play()` method that when called will play the sound effect.

On line 39 we call `pygame.mixer.music.load()` to load the background music. We will start playing the background music immediately by calling `pygame.mixer.music.play()`. The first parameter tells Pygame how many times to play the background music after the first time we play it. So passing 5 will cause Pygame to play the background music 6 times over. If you pass `-1` for the first parameter, the background music will repeat itself forever.

The second parameter to `pygame.mixer.music.play()` tells at what point in the sound file to start playing. Passing `0.0` will play the background music starting from the very beginning. If you passed `2.5` for the second parameter, this will cause the background music to start playing two and half seconds after the start of the music.

Finally, we have a simple Boolean variable named `musicPlaying` that will tell our program if it should play the background music and sound effects or not. It is nice to give the player the option to run the program without the sound playing.

Toggling the Sound On and Off

```
79.            if event.key == ord('m'):
80.                if musicPlaying:
81.                    pygame.mixer.music.stop()
82.                else:
83.                    pygame.mixer.music.play(-1, 0.0)
84.                musicPlaying = not musicPlaying
```

We will check if the user has pressed the M key. The M key will turn the background music on or off. If `musicPlaying` is set to `True`, then that means the background music is currently playing and we should stop the music by calling `pygame.mixer.music.stop()`. If `musicPlaying` is set to `False`, then that means the background music is not currently playing and should be started by calling `pygame.mixer.music.play()`. The parameters we pass to the `pygame.mixer.music.play()` function are the same as we passed on line 40.

Finally, no matter what, we want to toggle the value in `musicPlaying`. **Toggling** a Boolean value means we set it to the opposite of its current value. The line `musicPlaying = not musicPlaying` will set the variable to `False` if it is currently `True` or set it to `True` if it is currently `False`. Think of toggling as what happens when you flip a light switch on or off.

Toggling the value in `musicPlaying` will ensure that the next time the user presses the M key, it will do the opposite of what it did before.

Drawing the Player on the Window

```
109.        # draw the block onto the surface
110.        windowSurface.blit(playerStretchedImage, player)
```

Remember that the value stored in `playerStretchedImage` is a `Surface` object. "Blitting" is the process of drawing the contents of one `Surface` object to another `Surface` object. In this case, we want to draw the sprite of the player onto the window's `Surface` object (which is stored in `windowSurface`). (Also remember that the surface used to display on the screen is the `Surface` object that is returned by `pygame.display.set_caption()`.)

The second parameter to the `blit()` method is a `Rect` object that specifies where the sprite should be blitted. The `Rect` object stored in `player` is what keeps track of the position of the player in the window.

Checking if the Player Has Collided with Cherries

```
114.            if player.colliderect(food):
115.                foods.remove(food)
116.                player = pygame.Rect(player.left, player.top,
        player.width + 2, player.height + 2)
117.                playerStretchedImage = pygame.transform.scale
        (playerImage, (player.width, player.height))
118.                if musicPlaying:
119.                    pickUpSound.play()
```

This code is similar to the code in the previous programs. But here we are adding a couple of new lines. We want to call the `play()` method on the Sound object stored in the `pickUpSound` variable. But we only want to do this if `musicPlaying` is set to `True` (which tells us that the sound turned on).

When the player eats one of the cherries, we are going to enlarge the size of the player by two pixels in height and width. On line 116, we create a new `Rect` object to store in the player variable which will have the same sizes as the old `Rect` object stored in player. Except the width and height of the new `Rect` object will be 2 pixels larger.

When the `Rect` object that represents the position and size of the player, but the image of the player is stored in a `playerStretchedImage` as a `Surface` object. We want to create a new stretched image by calling `pygame.transform.scale()`. Be sure to pass the original `Surface` object in `playerImage` and not `playerStretchedImage`. Stretching an image often distorts it a little. If we keep restretching a stretched image over and over, the distortions add up quickly. But by stretching the original image to the new size, we only distort the image once. This is why we pass `playerImage` as the first argument for `pygame.transform.scale()`.

Draw the Cherries on the Window

```
121.        # draw the food
122.        for food in foods:
123.            windowSurface.blit(foodImage, food)
```

In our previous programs, we called the `pygame.draw.rect()` function to draw a green square for each `Rect` object stored in the `foods` list. However, in this program we want to draw the cherry sprites instead. We will call the `blit()` method and pass the `Surface` object stored in `foodImage`. (This is the surface that has the image of cherries drawn on it.)

We only use the `food` variable (which contains each of the `Rect` objects in `foods` on each iteration through the `for` loop) to tell the `blit()` method where to draw the `foodImage`.

Summary: Games with Graphics and Sounds

This game has added even more advanced graphics and introduced using sound in our games. The images (called sprites) look much better than the simple drawing primitives used in our previous programs. The game presented in this chapter also has music playing in the background while also playing sound effects.

Sprites can be scaled (that is, stretched) to a larger or smaller size. This way we can display sprites at any size we want. This will come in handy in the game presented in the next chapter.

Now that we know how to create a GUI window, display sprites and drawing primitives, collect keyboard and mouse input, play sounds, and implement collision detection, we are now ready to create a graphical game in Pygame. The next chapter brings all of these elements together for our most advanced game yet.

Chapter **20**

Dodger

Topics Covered In This Chapter:

- The `pygame.FULLSCREEN` flag
- Pygame Constant Variables for Keyboard Keys
- The `move_ip()` Method for `Rect` objects
- The `pygame.mouse.set_pos()` Function
- Implementing Cheat Codes in Your Games
- Modifying the Dodger Game

The last three chapters have gone over the Pygame software library and demonstrated how to use its many features. (You don't need to read those chapters before reading this chapter, though it may make this chapter easier to understand.) In this chapter, we will use that knowledge to create a graphical game with sound that receives input from the keyboard and mouse.

The Dodger game has the player control a small man (which we call the player's character) who must dodge a whole bunch of baddies that fall from the top of the screen. The longer the player can keep dodging the baddies, the higher the score they will get.

Just for fun, we will also add some cheat modes to the game. If the player holds down the "x" key, every baddie's speed will be reduced to a super slow rate. If the player holds down the "z" key, the baddies will reverse their direction and travel up the screen instead of downwards.

Review of the Basic Pygame Data Types

Let's review some of the basic data types used in the Pygame library:

- `pygame.Rect` - `Rect` objects represent a rectangular space's location and size. The location can be determined by the `Rect` object's `topleft` attribute (or the `topright`, `bottomleft`, and `bottomright` attributes). These corner attributes are a tuple of integers for the X- and Y-coordinates. The size can be determined by the width and height attributes, which are integers of how many pixels long or high the rectangle area is. `Rect` objects have a `colliderect()` method to check if they are intersecting with another `Rect` object.

- `pygame.Surface` - `Surface` objects are areas of colored pixels. `Surface` objects represent a rectangular image, while `Rect` objects only represent a rectangular space and location. `Surface` objects have a `blit()` method that is used to draw the image on one `Surface` object onto another `Surface` object. The `Surface` object returned by the `pygame.display.set_mode()` function is special because anything drawn on that Surface object will be displayed on the user's screen.

- Remember that `Surface` have things drawn on them, but we cannot see this because it only exists in the computer's memory. We can only see a `Surface` object when it is "blitted" (that is, drawn) on the screen. This is just the same as it is with any other piece of data. If you think about it, you cannot see the string that is stored in a variable until the variable is printed to the screen.

- `pygame.event.Event` - The `Event` data type in the `pygame.event` module generates `Event` objects whenever the user provides keyboard, mouse, or another kind of input. The `pygame.event.get()` function returns a list of `Event` objects. You can check what type of event the `Event` object is by checking its type attribute. `QUIT`, `KEYDOWN`, and `MOUSEBUTTONUP` are examples of some event types.

- `pygame.font.Font` - The `pygame.font module` has the `Font` data type which represent the typeface used for text in Pygame. You can create a `Font` object by calling the `pygame.font.SysFont()` constructor function. The arguments to pass are a string of the font name and an integer of the font size, however it is common to pass `None` for the font name to get the default system font. For example, the common function call to create a `Font` object is `pygame.font.SysFont (None, 48)`.

- `pygame.time.Clock` - The `Clock` object in the `pygame.time` module are very helpful for keeping our games from running as fast as possible. (This is often too fast for the player to keep up with the computer, and makes the games not fun.) The `Clock` object has a `tick()` method, which we pass how many frames per second (fps) we want the game to run at. The higher the fps, the faster the game runs. Normally we use 40 fps. Notice that the `pygame.time` module is a different module than the time module which contains the `sleep()` function.

Type in the following code and save it to a file named *dodger.py*. This game also requires some other image and sound files which you can download from the URL *http://inventwithpython.com/resources*.

Dodger's Source Code

You can download this code from the URL *http://inventwithpython.com/chapter20*.

dodger.py

This code can be downloaded from *http://inventwithpython.com/dodger.py*
If you get errors after typing this code in, compare it to the book's code with the online diff tool at *http://inventwithpython.com/diff* or email the author at al@inventwithpython.com

```
 1. import pygame, random, sys
 2. from pygame.locals import *
 3.
 4. WINDOWWIDTH = 600
 5. WINDOWHEIGHT = 600
 6. TEXTCOLOR = (255, 255, 255)
 7. BACKGROUNDCOLOR = (0, 0, 0)
 8. FPS = 40
 9. BADDIEMINSIZE = 10
10. BADDIEMAXSIZE = 40
11. BADDIEMINSPEED = 1
12. BADDIEMAXSPEED = 8
13. ADDNEWBADDIERATE = 6
14. PLAYERMOVERATE = 5
15.
16. def terminate():
17.     pygame.quit()
18.     sys.exit()
19.
20. def waitForPlayerToPressKey():
21.     while True:
22.         for event in pygame.event.get():
23.             if event.type == QUIT:
24.                 terminate()
25.             if event.type == KEYDOWN:
26.                 if event.key == K_ESCAPE: # pressing
    escape quits
27.                     terminate()
28.                 return
29.
30. def playerHasHitBaddie(playerRect, baddies):
31.     for b in baddies:
32.         if playerRect.colliderect(b['rect']):
33.             return True
34.     return False
35.
36. def drawText(text, font, surface, x, y):
```

374

```
37.         textobj = font.render(text, 1, TEXTCOLOR)
38.         textrect = textobj.get_rect()
39.         textrect.topleft = (x, y)
40.         surface.blit(textobj, textrect)
41.
42. # set up pygame, the window, and the mouse cursor
43. pygame.init()
44. mainClock = pygame.time.Clock()
45. windowSurface = pygame.display.set_mode((WINDOWWIDTH,
    WINDOWHEIGHT))
46. pygame.display.set_caption('Dodger')
47. pygame.mouse.set_visible(False)
48.
49. # set up fonts
50. font = pygame.font.SysFont(None, 48)
51.
52. # set up sounds
53. gameOverSound = pygame.mixer.Sound('gameover.wav')
54. pygame.mixer.music.load('background.mid')
55.
56. # set up images
57. playerImage = pygame.image.load('player.png')
58. playerRect = playerImage.get_rect()
59. baddieImage = pygame.image.load('baddie.png')
60.
61. # show the "Start" screen
62. drawText('Dodger', font, windowSurface, (WINDOWWIDTH /
    3), (WINDOWHEIGHT / 3))
63. drawText('Press a key to start.', font, windowSurface,
    (WINDOWWIDTH / 3) - 30, (WINDOWHEIGHT / 3) + 50)
64. pygame.display.update()
65. waitForPlayerToPressKey()
66.
67.
68. topScore = 0
69. while True:
70.     # set up the start of the game
71.     baddies = []
72.     score = 0
73.     playerRect.topleft = (WINDOWWIDTH / 2, WINDOWHEIGHT -
    50)
74.     moveLeft = moveRight = moveUp = moveDown = False
75.     reverseCheat = slowCheat = False
76.     baddieAddCounter = 0
77.     pygame.mixer.music.play(-1, 0.0)
78.
79.     while True: # the game loop runs while the game part
    is playing
80.         score += 1 # increase score
81.
82.         for event in pygame.event.get():
83.             if event.type == QUIT:
84.                 terminate()
85.
```

```
 86.            if event.type == KEYDOWN:
 87.                if event.key == ord('z'):
 88.                    reverseCheat = True
 89.                if event.key == ord('x'):
 90.                    slowCheat = True
 91.                if event.key == K_LEFT or event.key ==
    ord('a'):
 92.                    moveRight = False
 93.                    moveLeft = True
 94.                if event.key == K_RIGHT or event.key ==
    ord('d'):
 95.                    moveLeft = False
 96.                    moveRight = True
 97.                if event.key == K_UP or event.key == ord
    ('w'):
 98.                    moveDown = False
 99.                    moveUp = True
100.                if event.key == K_DOWN or event.key ==
    ord('s'):
101.                    moveUp = False
102.                    moveDown = True
103.
104.            if event.type == KEYUP:
105.                if event.key == ord('z'):
106.                    reverseCheat = False
107.                    score = 0
108.                if event.key == ord('x'):
109.                    slowCheat = False
110.                    score = 0
111.                if event.key == K_ESCAPE:
112.                        terminate()
113.
114.                if event.key == K_LEFT or event.key ==
    ord('a'):
115.                    moveLeft = False
116.                if event.key == K_RIGHT or event.key ==
    ord('d'):
117.                    moveRight = False
118.                if event.key == K_UP or event.key == ord
    ('w'):
119.                    moveUp = False
120.                if event.key == K_DOWN or event.key ==
    ord('s'):
121.                    moveDown = False
122.
123.                if event.type == MOUSEMOTION:
124.                    # If the mouse moves, move the player
    where the cursor is.
125.                    playerRect.move_ip(event.pos[0] -
    playerRect.centerx, event.pos[1] - playerRect.centery)
126.
127.        # Add new baddies at the top of the screen, if
    needed.
128.        if not reverseCheat and not slowCheat:
```

```
129.                         baddieAddCounter += 1
130.             if baddieAddCounter == ADDNEWBADDIERATE:
131.                 baddieAddCounter = 0
132.                 baddieSize = random.randint(BADDIEMINSIZE,
      BADDIEMAXSIZE)
133.                 newBaddie = {'rect': pygame.Rect
      (random.randint(0, WINDOWWIDTH-baddieSize), 0 -
      baddieSize, baddieSize, baddieSize),
134.                              'speed': random.randint
      (BADDIEMINSPEED, BADDIEMAXSPEED),
135.                              'surface':pygame.transform.scale
      (baddieImage, (baddieSize, baddieSize)),
136.                             }
137.
138.                 baddies.append(newBaddie)
139.
140.         # Move the player around.
141.         if moveLeft and playerRect.left > 0:
142.             playerRect.move_ip(-1 * PLAYERMOVERATE, 0)
143.         if moveRight and playerRect.right < WINDOWWIDTH:
144.             playerRect.move_ip(PLAYERMOVERATE, 0)
145.         if moveUp and playerRect.top > 0:
146.             playerRect.move_ip(0, -1 * PLAYERMOVERATE)
147.         if moveDown and playerRect.bottom < WINDOWHEIGHT:
148.             playerRect.move_ip(0, PLAYERMOVERATE)
149.
150.         # Move the mouse cursor to match the player.
151.         pygame.mouse.set_pos(playerRect.centerx,
      playerRect.centery)
152.
153.         # Move the baddies down.
154.         for b in baddies:
155.             if not reverseCheat and not slowCheat:
156.                 b['rect'].move_ip(0, b['speed'])
157.             elif reverseCheat:
158.                 b['rect'].move_ip(0, -5)
159.             elif slowCheat:
160.                 b['rect'].move_ip(0, 1)
161.
162.         # Delete baddies that have fallen past the
      bottom.
163.         for b in baddies[:]:
164.             if b['rect'].top > WINDOWHEIGHT:
165.                 baddies.remove(b)
166.
167.         # Draw the game world on the window.
168.         windowSurface.fill(BACKGROUNDCOLOR)
169.
170.         # Draw the score and top score.
171.         drawText('Score: %s' % (score), font,
      windowSurface, 10, 0)
172.         drawText('Top Score: %s' % (topScore), font,
      windowSurface, 10, 40)
173.
```

```
174.            # Draw the player's rectangle
175.            windowSurface.blit(playerImage, playerRect)
176.
177.            # Draw each baddie
178.            for b in baddies:
179.                windowSurface.blit(b['surface'], b['rect'])
180.
181.            pygame.display.update()
182.
183.            # Check if any of the baddies have hit the
        player.
184.            if playerHasHitBaddie(playerRect, baddies):
185.                if score > topScore:
186.                    topScore = score # set new top score
187.                break
188.
189.            mainClock.tick(FPS)
190.
191.        # Stop the game and show the "Game Over" screen.
192.        pygame.mixer.music.stop()
193.        gameOverSound.play()
194.
195.        drawText('GAME OVER', font, windowSurface,
        (WINDOWWIDTH / 3), (WINDOWHEIGHT / 3))
196.        drawText('Press a key to play again.', font,
        windowSurface, (WINDOWWIDTH / 3) - 80, (WINDOWHEIGHT / 3)
        + 50)
197.        pygame.display.update()
198.        waitForPlayerToPressKey()
199.
200.        gameOverSound.stop()
```

When you run this program, the game will look like this:

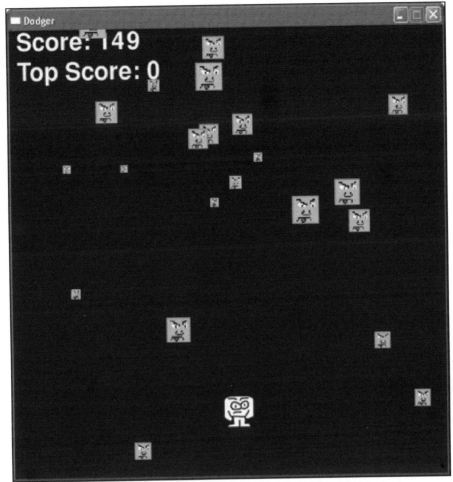

Figure 20-1: A screenshot of the Dodger game in action.

Importing the Modules

```
1. import pygame, random, sys
2. from pygame.locals import *
```

The Dodger game will import the same modules that our previous Pygame games have: `pygame`, `random`, `sys`, and `pygame.locals`. The `pygame.locals` module contains several constant variables that the Pygame library uses such as the event types (`QUIT`, `KEYDOWN`, etc.) and keyboard keys (`K_ESCAPE`, `K_LEFT`, etc.). By using the `from pygame.locals import *` syntax, we can just type `QUIT` instead of `pygame.locals.QUIT`.

Setting Up the Constant Variables

There are several constant variables in this game. We use constant variables because the variable name is much more descriptive than a number. For example, from the line `windowSurface.fill(BACKGROUNDCOLOR)` we know that the argument being sent is a color for the background. However, the line `windowSurface.fill` `(BACKGROUNDCOLOR)` is not as clear what the argument being passed means.

We can also easily change some simple aspects about our game without having the change much of the code by changing the values stored in these constant variables. By changing `WINDOWWIDTH` on line 4, we automatically change the code everywhere `WINDOWWIDTH` is used. If we had used the value `600` instead, then we would have to change each occurrence of `600` in the code. This would be especially confusing because `600` would also be used for the height of the window as well, and we would not want to change those values.

```
4. WINDOWWIDTH = 600
5. WINDOWHEIGHT = 600
6. TEXTCOLOR = (255, 255, 255)
7. BACKGROUNDCOLOR = (0, 0, 0)
```

Here we set the height and width of the main window. Since the rest of our code works off of these constant variables, changing the value here will change it everywhere in our program.

Instead of storing color tuples into a variable named `WHITE` or `BLACK`, we will use constant variables for the color of the text and background. Remember that the three integers in the color tuples range from `0` to `255` and stand for red, green, and blue.

```
8. FPS = 40
```

Just so the computer does not run the game too fast for the user to handle, we will call `mainClock.tick()` on each iteration of the game loop to slow it down. We need to pass an integer to `mainClock.tick()` so that the function knows how long to pause the program. This integer will be the number of frames per second we want the game to run. A "frame" is the drawing of graphics on the screen for a single iteration through the game loop. We will set up a constant variable `FPS` to `40`, and always call `mainClock.tick` `(FPS)`. You can change `FPS` to a higher value to have the game run faster or a lower value to slow the game down.

```
 9. BADDIEMINSIZE = 10
10. BADDIEMAXSIZE = 40
11. BADDIEMINSPEED = 1
12. BADDIEMAXSPEED = 8
13. ADDNEWBADDIERATE = 6
```

Here we set some more constant variables that will describe the falling baddies. The width and height of the baddies will be between `BADDIEMINSIZE` and `BADDIEMAXSIZE`. The rate at which the baddies fall down the screen will be between `BADDIEMINSPEED` and `BADDIEMAXSPEED` pixels per iteration through the game loop.

And a new baddie will be added to the top of the window every `ADDNEWBADDIERATE` iterations through the game loop.

```
14. PLAYERMOVERATE = 5
```

The `PLAYERMOVERATE` will store the number of pixels the player's character moves in the window on each iteration through the game loop (if the character is moving). By increasing this number, you can increase the speed the character moves. If you set `PLAYERMOVERATE` to 0, then the player's character won't be able to move at all (the player would move 0 pixels per iteration). This wouldn't be a very fun game.

Defining Functions

We will create several functions for our game. By putting code into functions, we can avoid having to type the same code several times in our program. And because the code is in one place, if we find a bug the code only needs to be fixed in one place.

```
16. def terminate():
17.     pygame.quit()
18.     sys.exit()
```

There are several places in our game that we want to terminate the program. In our other programs, this just required a single call to `sys.exit()`. But since Pygame requires that we call both `pygame.quit()` and `sys.exit()`, we will put them into a function called `terminate()` and just call the function. This keeps us from repeating the same code over and over again. And remember, the more we type, the more likely we will make a mistake and create a bug in our program.

```
20. def waitForPlayerToPressKey():
21.     while True:
22.         for event in pygame.event.get():
```

There are also a couple places where we want the game to pause and wait for the player to press a key. We will create a new function called `waitForPlayerToPressKey()` to do this. Inside this function, we have an infinite loop that only breaks when a `KEYDOWN` or `QUIT` event is received. At the start of the loop, we call `pygame.event.get()` to return a list of `Event` objects to check out.

```
23.         if event.type == QUIT:
24.             terminate()
```

If the player has closed the window while the program is waiting for the player to press a key, Pygame will generate a `QUIT` event and we should terminate the program. We will call our `terminate()` function here, rather than call `pygame.quit()` and `sys.exit()` themselves.

```
25.              if event.type == KEYDOWN:
26.                  if event.key == K_ESCAPE: # pressing
      escape quits
27.                      terminate()
28.                  return
```

If we receive a KEYDOWN event, then we should first check if it is the Esc key that was pressed. If we are waiting for the player to press a key, and the player presses the Esc key, we want to terminate the program. If that wasn't the case, then execution will skip the if-block on line 27 and go straight to the `return` statement, which exits the `waitForPlayerToPressKey()` function.

If a QUIT or KEYDOWN event is not generated, then this loop will keep looping until it is. This will freeze the game until the player presses a key or closes the window.

```
30. def playerHasHitBaddie(playerRect, baddies):
31.     for b in baddies:
32.         if playerRect.colliderect(b['rect']):
33.             return True
34.     return False
```

We will also define a function named `playerHasHitBaddie()` which will return `True` if the player's character has collided with one of the baddies. The `baddies` parameter is a list of baddie data structures. These data structures are just dictionaries, so it is accurate to say that `baddies` is a list of dictionary objects. Each of these dictionaries has a `'rect'` key, and the value for that key is a `Rect` object that represents the baddie's size and location.

`playerRect` is also a `Rect` object. Remember that `Rect` objects have a method named `colliderect()` that returns `True` if the `Rect` object has collided with the Rect object that is passed to the method. Otherwise, `colliderect()` will return `False`.

We can use this method in our `playerHasHitBaddie()` function. First we iterate through each baddie data structure in the `baddies` list. If any of these baddies collide with the player's character, then `playerHasHitBaddie()` will return `True`. If the code manages to iterate through all the baddies in the `baddies` list without colliding with any of them, we will return `False`.

```
36. def drawText(text, font, surface, x, y):
37.     textobj = font.render(text, 1, TEXTCOLOR)
38.     textrect = textobj.get_rect()
39.     textrect.topleft = (x, y)
40.     surface.blit(textobj, textrect)
```

Drawing text on the window involves many different steps. First, we must create a Surface object that has the string rendered in a specific font on it. The render() method does this. Next, we need to know the size and location of the Surface object we just made. We can get a Rect object with this information with the get_rect() method for Surface objects.

This Rect object has no special connection to the Surface object with the text drawn on it, other than the fact that it has a copy of the width and height information from the Surface object. We can change the location of the Rect object by setting a new tuple value for its topleft attribute.

Finally, we blit the Surface object of the rendered text onto the Surface object that was passed to our drawText() function. Displaying text in Pygame take a few more steps than simply calling the print() function, but if we put this code into a single function (drawText()), then we only need to call the function instead of typing out all the code every time we want to display text on the screen.

Initializing Pygame and Setting Up the Window

Now that the constant variables and functions are finished, we can start calling the Pygame functions that will set up Pygame for use in our code. Many of these function calls are to set up the GUI window and create objects that we will use in the game.

```
42. # set up pygame, the window, and the mouse cursor
43. pygame.init()
44. mainClock = pygame.time.Clock()
45. windowSurface = pygame.display.set_mode((WINDOWWIDTH,
    WINDOWHEIGHT))
46. pygame.display.set_caption('Dodger')
47. pygame.mouse.set_visible(False)
```

Line 43 sets up the Pygame library. Remember, the pygame.init() function must be called before we can use any of Pygame's functions or data types. Line 44 creates a pygame.time.Clock() object and stores it in the mainClock variable. This object will help us keep the program from running too fast.

Line 45 creates a new Surface object which will be used for the window displayed on the screen. We will specify the width and height of this Surface object (and the window) by passing a tuple with the WINDOWWIDTH and WINDOWHEIGHT constant variables. Notice that there is only one argument passed to pygame.display.set_mode(): a tuple. The arguments for pygame.display.set_mode() are not two integers but a tuple of two integers.

On line 46, the caption of the window is set to the string 'Dodger'. This caption will appear in the title bar at the top of the window.

http://inventwithpython.com

In our game, we do not want the mouse cursor (the mouse cursor is the arrow that moves around the screen when we move the mouse) to be visible. This is because we want the mouse to be able to move the player's character around the screen, and the arrow cursor would get in the way of the character's image on the screen. We pass False to tell Pygame to make the cursor invisible. If we wanted to make the cursor visible again at some point in the program, we could call pygame.mouse.set_visible(True).

Fullscreen Mode

The pygame.display.set_mode() function has a second, optional parameter that you can pass to it. The value you can pass for this parameter is pygame.FULLSCREEN, like this modification to line 45 in our Dodger program:

```
45. windowSurface = pygame.display.set_mode((WINDOWWIDTH,
    WINDOWHEIGHT), pygame.FULLSCREEN)
```

Passing pygame.FULLSCREEN will make the program take up the entire space of the screen. It will still be WINDOWWIDTH and WINDOWHEIGHT in size for the windows width and height, but the image will be stretched larger to fit the screen. There may be wasted space along the top and bottom (or the left and right) sides of the screen if you did not set the window size in proportion with the screen's resolution.) To avoid the wasted space, you should set the size of the window to a 4:3 ratio (for every 4 pixels of width, have 3 pixels for height).

If you do not use the fullscreen mode, then you do not need to worry about using a 4:3 ratio for the width and height. Just use whatever width and height works best for your game.

```
49. # set up fonts
50. font = pygame.font.SysFont(None, 48)
```

We need to create a Font object to use when we create a Surface object with the image of text drawn on it. (This process is called "rendering".) We want to create a generic font, so we will use the default Font object that the pygame.font.SysFont() constructor function returns. We pass None so that the default font is used, and we pass 48 so that the font has a size of 48 points.

```
52. # set up sounds
53. gameOverSound = pygame.mixer.Sound('gameover.wav')
54. pygame.mixer.music.load('background.mid')
```

Next we want to create the Sound objects and also set up the background music. The background music will constantly be playing during the game, but Sound objects will only be played when we specifically want them to. In this case, the Sound object will be played when the player loses the game.

You can use any .wav or .mid file for this game. You can download these sound files from this book's website at the URL *http://inventwithpython.com/resources*. Or you can use your own sound files for this game, as long as they have the filenames of *gameover.wav* and *background.mid*. (Or you can change the strings used on lines 53 and 54 to match the filenames.)

The `pygame.mixer.Sound()` constructor function creates a new `Sound` object and stores a reference to this object in the `gameOverSound` variable. In your own games, you can create as many `Sound` objects as you like, each with a different sound file that it will play.

The `pygame.mixer.music.load()` function loads a sound file to play for the background music. This function does not create any objects, and only one sound file can be loaded at a time.

```
56. # set up images
57. playerImage = pygame.image.load('player.png')
58. playerRect = playerImage.get_rect()
59. baddieImage = pygame.image.load('baddie.png')
```

Next we will load the image files that used for the player's character and the baddies on the screen. The image for the character is stored in *player.png* and the image for the baddies is stored in *baddie.png*. All the baddies look the same, so we only need one image file for them. You can download these images from the book's website at the URL *http://inventwithpython.com/resources*.

Display the Start Screen

When the game first starts, we want to display the name of the game on the screen. We also want to instruct the player that they can start the game by pushing any key. This screen appears so that the player has time to get ready to start playing after running the program. Also, before each game starts, we want to reset the value of the top score back to 0.

```
61. # show the "Start" screen
62. drawText('Dodger', font, windowSurface, (WINDOWWIDTH /
      3), (WINDOWHEIGHT / 3))
63. drawText('Press a key to start.', font, windowSurface,
      (WINDOWWIDTH / 3) - 30, (WINDOWHEIGHT / 3) + 50)
64. pygame.display.update()
65. waitForPlayerToPressKey()
```

On lines 62 and 63, we call our `drawText()` function and pass it five arguments: 1) the string of the text we want to appear, 2) the font that we want the string to appear in, 3) the `Surface` object onto which to render the text, and 4) and 5) the X and Y coordinate on the `Surface` object to draw the text at.

This may seem like many arguments to pass for a function call, but keep in mind that this function call replaces five lines of code each time we call it. This shortens our program and makes it easier to find bugs since there is less code to check.

The `waitForPlayerToPressKey()` function will pause the game by entering into a loop that checks for any KEYDOWN events. Once a KEYDOWN event is generated, the execution breaks out of the loop and the program continues to run.

Start of the Main Game Code

```
68. topScore = 0
69. while True:
```

We have finished defining the helper functions and variables that we need for this game. Line 68 is the start of the main game code. The value in the `topScore` variable starts at 0 only when the program first runs. Whenever the player loses and has a score larger than the current top score, the top score is replaced with the player's score.

The infinite loop started on line 69 is technically not the "game loop". (The main game loop handles events and drawing the window while the game is running.) Instead, this `while` loop will iterate each time the player starts a new game. We will set up the code so that when the player loses and we need to reset the game, the program's execution will go back to the start of this loop.

```
70.        # set up the start of the game
71.        baddies = []
72.        score = 0
```

At the very beginning, we want to set the `baddies` list to an empty list. The `baddies` list is a list of dictionary objects with the following keys:

- `'rect'` - The Rect object that describes where and what size the baddie is.
- `'speed'` - How fast the baddie falls down the screen. This integer represents pixels per iteration through the game loop.
- `'surface'` - The Surface object that has the scaled image of the baddie image drawn on it. This is the Surface object that will be blitted to the Surface object returned by `pygame.display.set_mode()` and drawn on the screen.

Next, we want to reset the player's score to 0.

```
73.        playerRect.topleft = (WINDOWWIDTH / 2, WINDOWHEIGHT -
           50)
```

The starting location of the player will be in the center of the screen and 50 pixels up from the bottom. The tuple that we set the `topleft` attribute to will change the location of the `playerRect` object. The first item in the tuple is the X-coordinate of the left edge. The second item in the tuple is the Y-coordinate of the top edge.

```
74.        moveLeft = moveRight = moveUp = moveDown = False
75.        reverseCheat = slowCheat = False
76.        baddieAddCounter = 0
```

Also at the start of the game, we want to have the movement variables `moveLeft`, `moveRight`, `moveUp`, and `moveDown` set to `False`. The `reverseCheat` and `slowCheat` variables will be set to `True` only when the player enables these cheats by holding down the "z" and "x" keys, respectively.

The `baddieAddCounter` variable is used for a counter to tell the program when to add a new baddie at the top of the screen. The value in `baddieAddCounter` will be incremented by one each time the game loop iterates. When the `baddieAddCounter` counter is equal to the value in `ADDNEWBADDIERATE`, then the `baddieAddCounter` counter is reset back to 0 and a new baddie is added to the top of the screen.

```
77.        pygame.mixer.music.play(-1, 0.0)
```

At the start of the game, we want the background music to begin playing. We can do this with a call to `pygame.mixer.music.play()`. The first argument is the number of times the music should repeat itself. `-1` is a special value that tells Pygame we want the music to repeat endlessly. The second argument is a float that says how many seconds into the music we want it to start playing. Passing `0.0` means we want to play the music starting from the beginning of the music file. (Passing `2.0`, for example, would have started the music two seconds into the music file.)

The Game Loop

The game loop contains the code that is executed while the game is being played. The game loop constantly updates the state of the game world by changing the position of the player and baddies, handling events generated by Pygame, and drawing the state of the game world on the screen. All of this happens several dozen times a second, which makes it seem that the game is happening in real time to the player.

```
79.        while True: # the game loop runs while the game part
    is playing
80.            score += 1 # increase score
```

Line 79 is the start of the main game loop. In the main game loop, we will increase the player's score, handle any events that were generated, add any baddies to the top of the screen if needed, move the baddies down a little, and then draw everything on the screen. This code will be executed over and over again as the program execution iterates through the game loop. The loop will only exit when the player either loses the game or quits the program.

First, we will increment the player's score. The longer the player can go without losing, the higher their score will be.

Event Handling

There are four different types of events we will handle in our game: QUIT, KEYDOWN, KEYUP, and MOUSEMOTION. The QUIT event is generated by Pygame if the player closes the program's window or shuts down the computer. In that case, we want the program to close itself. The KEYDOWN and KEYUP events are generated when the player pushes down and releases the keyboard keys, respectively. These events will be how we can tell which direction the player wants to move the character. The player could also have pressed the Esc key to signal that they want to shut down the program. Each time the player moves the mouse, Pygame will generate a MOUSEMOTION event which will tell us the X- and Y-coordinates of the mouse cursor over the window.

```
82.         for event in pygame.event.get():
83.             if event.type == QUIT:
84.                 terminate()
```

Line 82 is the start of the event-handling code. First we call pygame.event.get(), which returns a list of Event objects. Each Event object represents an event that has been created since the last call to pygame.event.get(). We will check the type attribute of the event object to see what type of event it is, and handle the event accordingly.

If the type attribute of the Event object is equal to QUIT, then this tells us that the user has closed the program somehow. The QUIT constant variable was imported from the pygame.locals module, but since we imported that module with the line from pygame.locals import * instead of simply import pygame.locals, we only need to type QUIT and not pygame.locals.QUIT.

```
86.             if event.type == KEYDOWN:
87.                 if event.key == ord('z'):
88.                     reverseCheat = True
89.                 if event.key == ord('x'):
90.                     slowCheat = True
```

If the event's type is KEYDOWN, then we know that the player has pressed down a key. The Event object for keyboard events will also have a key attribute that is set to the numeric ASCII value of the key pressed. The ord() function will return the ASCII value of the letter passed to it.

For example, on line 87, we can check if the event describes the "z" key being pressed down by checking if `event.key == ord('z')`. If this condition is `True`, then we want to set the `reverseCheat` variable to `True` to indicate that the reverse cheat has been activated. We will also check if the "x" key has been pressed to activate the slow cheat in a similar way.

Pygame's keyboard events always use the ASCII values of lowercase letters, not uppercase. What this means for your code is that you should always use `event.key == ord('z')` instead of `event.key == ord('Z')`. Otherwise, your program may act as though the key hasn't been pressed at all.

```
 91.             if event.key == K_LEFT or event.key ==
     ord('a'):
 92.                 moveRight = False
 93.                 moveLeft = True
 94.             if event.key == K_RIGHT or event.key ==
     ord('d'):
 95.                 moveLeft = False
 96.                 moveRight = True
 97.             if event.key == K_UP or event.key == ord
     ('w'):
 98.                 moveDown = False
 99.                 moveUp = True
100.             if event.key == K_DOWN or event.key ==
     ord('s'):
101.                 moveUp = False
102.                 moveDown = True
```

We also want to check if the event was generated by the player pressing one of the arrow keys. There is not an ASCII value for every key on the keyboard, such as the arrow keys or the Esc key. Instead, Pygame provides some constant variables to use instead.

We can check if the player has pressed the left arrow key with the condition: `event.key == K_LEFT`. Again, the reason we can use `K_LEFT` instead of `pygame.locals.K_LEFT` is because we imported `pygame.locals` with the line `from pygame.locals import *` instead of `import pygame.locals`.

Noticed that pressing down on one of the arrow keys not only sets one of the movement variables to `True`, but it also sets the movement variable in the opposite direction to `False`. For example, if the left arrow key is pushed down, then the code on line 93 sets `moveLeft` to `True`, but it also sets `moveRight` to `False`. This prevents the player from confusing the program into thinking that the player's character should move in two opposite directions at the same time.

Here is a list of commonly-used constant variables for the key attribute of keyboard-related `Event` objects:

Table 20-1: Constant Variables for Keyboard Keys

Pygame Constant Variable	Keyboard Key	Pygame Constant Variable	Keyboard Key
K_LEFT	Left arrow	K_HOME	Home
K_RIGHT	Right arrow	K_END	End
K_UP	Up arrow	K_PAGEUP	PgUp
K_DOWN	Down arrow	K_PAGEDOWN	PgDn
K_ESCAPE	Esc	K_F1	F1
K_BACKSPACE	Backspace	K_F2	F2
K_TAB	Tab	K_F3	F3
K_RETURN	Return or Enter	K_F4	F4
K_SPACE	Space bar	K_F5	F5
K_DELETE	Del	K_F6	F6
K_LSHIFT	Left Shift	K_F7	F7
K_RSHIFT	Right Shift	K_F8	F8
K_LCTRL	Left Ctrl	K_F9	F9
K_RCTRL	Right Ctrl	K_F10	F10
K_LALT	Left Alt	K_F11	F11
K_RALT	Right Alt	K_F12	F12

```
104.            if event.type == KEYUP:
105.                if event.key == ord('z'):
106.                    reverseCheat = False
107.                    score = 0
108.                if event.key == ord('x'):
109.                    slowCheat = False
110.                    score = 0
```

The KEYUP event is created whenever the player stops pressing down on a keyboard key and it returns to its normal, up position. KEYUP objects with a type of KEYUP also have a key attribute just like KEYDOWN events.

On line 105, we check if the player has released the "z" key, which will deactivate the reverse cheat. In that case, we set reverseCheat to False and reset the score to 0. The score reset is to discourage the player for using the cheats.

Lines 108 to 110 do the same thing for the "x" key and the slow cheat. When the "x" key is released, slowCheat is set to False and the player's score is reset to 0.

```
111.                    if event.key == K_ESCAPE:
112.                        terminate()
```

At any time during the game, the player can press the Esc key on the keyboard to quit the game. Here we check if the key that was released was the Esc key by checking `event.key == K_ESCAPE`. If so, we call our `terminate()` function which will exit the program.

```
114.                    if event.key == K_LEFT or event.key ==
     ord('a'):
115.                        moveLeft = False
116.                    if event.key == K_RIGHT or event.key ==
     ord('d'):
117.                        moveRight = False
118.                    if event.key == K_UP or event.key == ord
     ('w'):
119.                        moveUp = False
120.                    if event.key == K_DOWN or event.key ==
     ord('s'):
121.                        moveDown = False
```

Lines 114 to 121 check if the player has stopped holding down one of the arrow keys (or the corresponding WASD key). In that event, we will set the corresponding movement variable to `False`. For example, if the player was holding down the left arrow key, then the `moveLeft` would have been set to `True` on line 93. When they release it, the condition on line 114 will evaluate to `True`, and the `moveLeft` variable will be set to `False`.

The `move_ip()` Method for `Rect` objects

```
123.                if event.type == MOUSEMOTION:
124.                    # If the mouse moves, move the player
     where the cursor is.
125.                    playerRect.move_ip(event.pos[0] -
     playerRect.centerx, event.pos[1] - playerRect.centery)
```

Now that we have handled the keyboard events, let's handle any mouse events that may have been generated. In the Dodger game we don't do anything if the player has clicked a mouse button, but the game does respond when the player moves the mouse. This gives the player two ways of controlling the player character in the game: the keyboard and the mouse.

If the event's type is MOUSEMOTION, then we want to move the player's character to the location of the mouse cursor. The MOUSEMOTION event is generated whenever the mouse is moved. Event objects with a type of MOUSEMOTION also have an attribute named pos. The pos attribute stores a tuple of the X- and Y-coordinates of where the mouse cursor moved in the window.

The `move_ip()` method for `Rect` objects will move the location of the `Rect` object horizontally or vertically by a number of pixels. For example, `playerRect.move_ip` `(10, 20)` would move the `Rect` object 10 pixels to the right and 20 pixels down. To move the `Rect` object left or up, pass negative values. For example, `playerRect.move_ip(-5, -15)` will move the `Rect` object left by 5 pixels and up 15 pixels.

The "ip" at the end of `move_ip()` stands for "in place". This is because the method changes the `Rect` object itself, in its own place. There is also a `move()` method which does not change the `Rect` object, but instead creates a new `Rect` object that has the new location. This is useful if you want to keep the original `Rect` object's location the same but also have a `Rect` object with the new location.

Adding New Baddies

```
127.            # Add new baddies at the top of the screen, if
          needed.
128.            if not reverseCheat and not slowCheat:
129.                baddieAddCounter += 1
```

On each iteration of the game loop, we want to increment the `baddieAddCounter` variable by one. However, we only want to do this if the cheats are not enabled. Remember that `reverseCheat` and `slowCheat:` are only set to `True` as long as the "z" and "x" keys are being held down, respectively. And while those keys are being held down, `baddieAddCounter` is not incremented. This means that no new baddies will appear at the top of the screen.

```
130.            if baddieAddCounter == ADDNEWBADDIERATE:
131.                baddieAddCounter = 0
132.                baddieSize = random.randint(BADDIEMINSIZE,
          BADDIEMAXSIZE)
133.                newBaddie = {'rect': pygame.Rect
          (random.randint(0, WINDOWWIDTH-baddieSize), 0 -
          baddieSize, baddieSize, baddieSize),
134.                            'speed': random.randint
          (BADDIEMINSPEED, BADDIEMAXSPEED),
135.                            'surface':pygame.transform.scale
          (baddieImage, (baddieSize, baddieSize)),
136.                            }
```

When the `baddieAddCounter` reaches the value in `ADDNEWBADDIERATE`, then the condition on line 130 is `True` and it is time to add a new baddie to the top of the screen. First, the `baddieAddCounter` counter is reset back to 0 (otherwise, when it keeps incrementing it will always be greater than ADDNEWBADDIERATE and never equal to it. This will cause baddies to stop appearing at the top of the screen.)

Line 132 generates a size for the baddie in pixels. The size will be between BADDIEMINSIZE and BADDIEMAXSIZE, which we have set to 10 and 40 in this program.

Line 133 is where a new baddie data structure is created. Remember, the data structure for baddies is simply a dictionary with keys 'rect', 'speed', and 'surface'. The 'rect' key holds a reference to a Rect object which stores the location and size of the baddie. The call to the pygame.Rect() constructor function has four parameters: the X-coordinate of the top edge of the area, the Y-coordinate of the left edge of the area, the width in pixels, and the height in pixels.

We want the baddie to appear randomly across the top of the window, so we pass random.randint(0, WINDOWWIDTH-baddieSize) for the X-coordinate of the left edge. This will evaluate to a random place across the top of the window. The reason we pass WINDOWWIDTH-baddieSize instead of WINDOWWIDTH is because this value is for the left edge of the baddie. If the left edge of the baddie is too far on the right side of the screen, then part of the baddie will be off the edge of the window and not visible.

We want the bottom edge of the baddie to be just above the top edge of the window. The Y-coordinate of the top edge of the window is 0, so to put the baddie's bottom edge there, we want to set the top edge to 0 - baddieSize.

The baddie's width and height should be the same (the image is a square), so we will pass baddieSize for the third and fourth argument.

The rate of speed that the baddie moves down the screen will be set in the 'speed' key, and is set to a random integer between BADDIEMINSPEED and BADDIEMAXSPEED.

```
138.                    baddies.append(newBaddie)
```

Line 138 will add the newly created baddie data structure to the list of baddie data structures. Our program will use this list to check if the player has collided with any of the baddies and to know where to draw baddies on the window.

Moving the Player's Character

```
140.            # Move the player around.
141.            if moveLeft and playerRect.left > 0:
142.                playerRect.move_ip(-1 * PLAYERMOVERATE, 0)
```

The four movement variables moveLeft, moveRight, moveUp and moveDown are set to True and False when Pygame generates the KEYDOWN and KEYUP events, respectively. (This code is from line 86 to line 121.)

If the player's character is moving left and the left edge of the player's character is greater than 0 (which is the left edge of the window), then we want to move the character's Rect object (stored in playerRect).

We will always move the playerRect object by the number of pixels in PLAYERMOVERATE. To get the negative form of an integer, you can simply multiple it by -1. So on line 142, since 5 is stored in PLAYERMOVERATE, the expression -1 * PLAYERMOVERATE evaluates to -5.

This means that calling playerRect.move_ip(-1 * PLAYERMOVERATE, 0) will change the location of playerRect by 5 pixels to the left of its current location.

```
143.            if moveRight and playerRect.right < WINDOWWIDTH:
144.                playerRect.move_ip(PLAYERMOVERATE, 0)
145.            if moveUp and playerRect.top > 0:
146.                playerRect.move_ip(0, -1 * PLAYERMOVERATE)
147.            if moveDown and playerRect.bottom < WINDOWHEIGHT:
148.                playerRect.move_ip(0, PLAYERMOVERATE)
```

We want to do the same thing for the other three directions: right, up, and down. Each of the three if statements in lines 143 to 148 checks that their movement variable is set to True and that the edge of the Rect object of the player is inside the window before calling the move_ip() method to move the Rect object.

The pygame.mouse.set_pos() Function

```
150.        # Move the mouse cursor to match the player.
151.        pygame.mouse.set_pos(playerRect.centerx,
        playerRect.centery)
```

Line 151 moves the mouse cursor to the same position as the player's character. The pygame.mouse.set_pos() function moves the mouse cursor to the X- and Y-coordinates that you pass it. Specifically, the cursor will be right in the middle of the character's Rect object because we pass the centerx and centery attributes of playerRect for the coordinates. The mouse cursor still exists and can be moved, even though it is invisible because we called pygame.mouse.set_visible(False) on line 47.

The reason we want the mouse cursor to match the location of the player's character is to avoid sudden jumps. Imagine that the mouse cursor and the player's character are at the same location on the left side of the window. When the player holds down the right arrow key, the character moves to the right edge of the window but the mouse cursor would stay at the left edge of the screen. If the player then moves the mouse just a little bit, the player's character would immediately jump to the location of the mouse cursor on the left edge of the screen. By moving the mouse cursor along with the player's character, any mouse movements would not result in a sudden jump across the window.

```
153.                    # Move the baddies down.
154.                    for b in baddies:
```

Now we want to loop through each baddie data structure in the `baddies` list to move them down a little.

```
155.                        if not reverseCheat and not slowCheat:
156.                            b['rect'].move_ip(0, b['speed'])
```

If neither of the cheats have been activated (by the player pushing the "z" or "x" keys which sets `reverseCheat` or `slowCheat` to `True`, respectively), then move the baddie's location down a number of pixels equal to its speed, which is stored in the `'speed'` key.

Implementing the Cheat Codes

```
157.                        elif reverseCheat:
158.                            b['rect'].move_ip(0, -5)
```

If the reverse cheat has been activated, then the baddie should actually be moved up by five pixels. Passing -5 for the second argument to `move_ip()` will move the `Rect` object upwards by five pixels.

```
159.                        elif slowCheat:
160.                            b['rect'].move_ip(0, 1)
```

If the slow cheat has been activated, then the baddie should move downwards, but only by the slow speed of one pixel per iteration through the game loop. The baddie's normal speed (which is stored in the `'speed'` key of the baddie's data structure) will be ignored while the slow cheat is activated.

Removing the Baddies

```
162.               # Delete baddies that have fallen past the
         bottom.
163.               for b in baddies[:]:
```

After moving the baddies down the window, we want to remove any baddies that fell below the bottom edge of the window from the `baddies` list. Remember that we while we are iterating through a list, we should not modify the contents of the list by adding or removing items. So instead of iterating through the `baddies` list with our `baddies` loop, we will iterate through a copy of the `baddies` list.

Remember that a list slice will evaluate a copy of a list's items. For example, `spam` `[2:4]` will return a new list with the items from index 2 up to (but not including) index 4. Leaving the first index blank will indicate that index 0 should be used. For example, `spam` `[:4]` will return a list with items from the start of the list up to (but not including) the item at index 4. Leaving the second index blank will indicate that up to (and including) the last index should be used. For example, `spam[2:]` will return a list with items from index 2 all the way to (and including) the last item in the list.

But leaving both indexes in the slice blank is a way to represent the entire list. The `baddies[:]` expression is a list slice of the whole list, so it evaluates to a copy of the entire list. This is useful because while we are iterating on the copy of the list, we can modify the original list and remove any baddie data structures that have fallen past the bottom edge of the window.

Our `for` loop on line 163 uses a variable b for the current item in the iteration through `baddies[:]`.

```
164.              if b['rect'].top > WINDOWHEIGHT:
165.                  baddies.remove(b)
```

Let's evaluate the expression `b['rect'].top`. b is the current baddie data structure from the `baddies[:]` list. Each baddie data structure in the list is a dictionary with a `'rect'` key, which stores a `Rect` object. So `b['rect']` is the `Rect` object for the baddie. Finally, the top is the Y-coordinate of the top edge of the rectangular area. Remember that in the coordinate system, the Y-coordinates increase going down. So b `['rect'].top > WINDOWHEIGHT` will check if the top edge of the baddie is below the bottom of the window.

If this condition is `True`, then the we will remove the baddie data structure from the baddies list.

Drawing the Window

It isn't enough that our game updates the state of the game world in its memory. Our program will also have to display the game world to the player. We can do this by drawing the graphics of the baddies and player's character on the screen. Because the game loop is executed several times a second, drawing the baddies and player in new positions makes their movement look smooth and natural. But every element on the screen must be drawn one at a time by calling the appropriate Pygame function.

```
167.          # Draw the game world on the window.
168.          windowSurface.fill(BACKGROUNDCOLOR)
```

Now that we have updated all the data structures for the baddies and the player's character, let's draw everything on the screen. First, before we draw anything else on the

Surface object referred to by windowSurface, we want to black out the entire screen to erase anything drawn on it in a previous iteration through the game loop.

Remember that the Surface object in windowSurface is the special Surface object because it was the one returned by pygame.display.set_mode(). This means that anything drawn on that Surface object will appear on the screen, but only after the pygame.display.update() function is called.

Drawing the Player's Score

```
170.            # Draw the score and top score.
171.            drawText('Score: %s' % (score), font,
        windowSurface, 10, 0)
172.            drawText('Top Score: %s' % (topScore), font,
        windowSurface, 10, 40)
```

Next we will render the text for score and top score to the top left corner of the window. The 'Score: %s' % (score) uses string interpolation to insert the value in the score variable into the string. This is the same thing as 'Score: ' + str(score). We pass this string, the Font object stored in the font variable, the Surface object on which to draw the text on, and the X- and Y-coordinates of where the text should be placed. Remember that our drawText() will handle the call to the render() and blit() methods.

For the top score, we do the exact same thing. We pass 40 for the Y-coordinate instead of 0 (like we do for the score) so that the top score text appears beneath the score text.

Drawing the Player's Character

```
174.            # Draw the player's rectangle
175.            windowSurface.blit(playerImage, playerRect)
```

Remember that the information about the player is kept in two different variables. playerImage is a Surface object that contains all the colored pixels that make up the player's character's image. playerRect is a Rect object that stores the information about the size and location of the player's character.

We call the blit() method on windowSurface and pass playerImage and playerRect. This draws the player character's image on windowSurface at the appropriate location.

```
177.            # Draw each baddie
178.            for b in baddies:
179.                windowSurface.blit(b['surface'], b['rect'])
```

We use a `for` loop here to draw every baddie on the `windowSurface` object. Remember that each item in the `baddies` list is a dictionary with `'surface'` and `'rect'` keys containing the `Surface` object with the baddie image and the `Rect` object with the position and size information, respectively.

```
181.            pygame.display.update()
```

Now that we have finished drawing everything to the `windowSurface` object, we should draw this surface to the screen with a call to `pygame.display.update()`.

Collision Detection

```
183.        # Check if any of the baddies have hit the
      player.
184.        if playerHasHitBaddie(playerRect, baddies):
185.            if score > topScore:
186.                topScore = score # set new top score
187.            break
```

Now let's check if the player has collided with any of the baddies. We already wrote a function to check for this: `playerHasHitBaddie()`. This function will return `True` if the player's character has collided with any of the baddies in the `baddies` list. Otherwise, the function will return `False`.

If the player's character has hit a baddie, then we check if the player's current score is greater than the top score. If it is, we set the new top score to be the player's current score. Either way, we break out of the game loop. The program's execution will jump down to line 191.

```
189.        mainClock.tick(FPS)
```

To keep the computer from running through the game loop as fast as possible (which would be much too fast for the player to keep up with), we call `mainClock.tick()` to pause for a brief amount of time. The pause will be long enough to ensure that about 40 (the value we stored inside the `FPS` variable) iterations through the game loop occur each second.

The Game Over Screen

```
191.        # Stop the game and show the "Game Over" screen.
192.        pygame.mixer.music.stop()
193.        gameOverSound.play()
```

When the player loses, we want to stop playing the background music and play the "game over" sound effect. We call the stop() function in the pygame.mixer.music module to stop the background music. Then we call the play() method on the Sound object stored in gameOverSound.

```
195.      drawText('GAME OVER', font, windowSurface,
      (WINDOWWIDTH / 3), (WINDOWHEIGHT / 3))
196.      drawText('Press a key to play again.', font,
      windowSurface, (WINDOWWIDTH / 3) - 80, (WINDOWHEIGHT / 3)
      + 50)
197.      pygame.display.update()
198.      waitForPlayerToPressKey()
```

Now we want to display text on the window to tell the player that the game is over, and they should press a key to start playing a new game. The two calls to our drawText() function will draw this text to the windowSurface object, and the call to pygame.display.update() will draw this Surface object to the screen.

After displaying this text, we want the game to stop until the player presses a key, so we call our waitForPlayerToPressKey() function.

```
200.      gameOverSound.stop()
```

After the player presses a key, the program execution will return from the waitForPlayerToPressKey() call on line 198. Depending on how long the player takes to press a key, the "game over" sound effect may or may not still be playing. We want to stop this sound effect before this loop ends and we start a new game, so we have a call to gameOverSound.stop() here.

Modifying the Dodger Game

That's it for our graphical game. You may find that the game is too easy or too hard. But the game is very easy to modify because we took the time to use constant variables instead of typing in the values directly. Now all we need to do to change the game is modify the value set in the constant variables.

For example, if you want the game to run slower in general, change the FPS variable on line 8 to a smaller value such as 20. This will make both the baddies and the player's character move slower since the game loop will only be executed 20 times a second instead of 40.

If you just want to slow down the baddies and not the player, then change BADDIEMAXSPEED to a smaller value such as 4. This will make all the baddies move between 1 (the value in BADDIEMINSPEED) and 4 pixels per iteration through the game loop instead of 1 and 8.

If you want the game to have fewer but larger baddies instead of many fast baddies, then increase ADDNEWBADDIERATE to 12, BADDIEMINSIZE to 40, and BADDIEMAXSIZE to 80. Now that baddies are being added every 12 iterations through the game loop instead of every 6 iterations, there will be half as many baddies as before. But to keep the game interesting, the baddies are now much larger than before.

While the basic game remains the same, you can modify any of the constant variables to drastically affect the behavior of the game. Keep trying out new values for the constant variables until you find a set of values you like the best.

Summary: Creating Your Own Games

Unlike our previous text-based games, Dodger really looks like the kind of modern computer game we usually play. It has graphics and music and uses the mouse. While Pygame provides functions and data types as building blocks, it is you the programmer who puts them together to create fun, interactive games.

And it is all because you know exactly how to instruct the computer to do it, step by step, line by line. You can speak the computer's language, and get it to do large amounts of number crunching and drawing for you. This is a very useful skill, and I hope you will continue to learn more about Python programming. (And there is still more to learn!)

Here are several websites that can teach you more about programming Python:

- *http://www.python.org/doc/* - More Python tutorials and the documentation of all the Python modules and functions.
- *http://www.pygame.org/docs/* - Complete documentation on the modules and functions for Pygame.
- *http://inventwithpython.com* - This book's website, which includes all the source code for these programs and additional information. This site also has the image and sound files used in the Pygame programs.
- *http://inventwithpython.com/traces* - A web application that helps you trace through the execution of the programs in this book, step by step.
- *http://inventwithpython.com/videos* - Videos that accompany the programs in this book.
- *http://gamedevlessons.com* - A helpful website about how to design and program video games.
- *al@inventwithpython.com* - The author's email address. Feel free to email Al your questions about this book or about Python programming.

Or you can find out more about Python by searching the World Wide Web. Go to the search engine website http://google.com and search for "Python programming" or "Python tutorials" to find web sites that can teach you more about Python programming.

Now get going and invent your own games. And good luck!

Appendix A
Differences Between Python 2 and 3

Most of the programs in this book make use of the newer version 3 of Python. The Pygame games make use of Python 2 because the Pygame library is not yet compatible with Python 3. Python 3 corrects many of the faults with version 2 of the language, however, these changes can also make it impossible to run Python 3 programs with the Python 2 interpreter, and vice versa.

There are only a few changes between the two versions, and this appendix will go through the ones relevant to this book. Learning both Python 2 and 3 is fairly simple. All of the modules imported by the programs in this book (except for the pygame module) are part of the standard library and work with both Python 2 and Python 3.

In short, use Python 3 unless you need to use a library that is not yet compatible with version 3. Learning both Python 2 and 3 is easy because there are only a few changes between them.

The `print()` Function and the `print` statement

In Python 3, `print()` is a function just like `input()` or `len()`. The function version requires parentheses just like any other function call (although you can add parentheses to the `print` statement optionally).

The `print` statement in Python 2 will always print a newline character at the end of the string. To make it print a space instead, put a comma at the end of the print statement:

```
>>> # Python 2
>>> print "Hello",
```

To print something besides a newline at the end of the `print()` function in Python 3, use the keyword argument `end`:

```
>>> # Python 3
>>> print("Hello", end="")
```

The `input()` and `raw_input()` Functions

In Python 2, the function to get input from the keyboard is `raw_input()`. In Python 3, the `input()` function does this. You can simply rename the function wherever it appears in your code.

```
>>> # Python 2
>>> name = raw_input()
```

```
>>> # Python 3
>>> name = input()
```

The `range()` Function's Return Value

In Python 2, the `range()` function returns an actual list with the integers. In Python 3, the `range()` function returns a "range object". Both can be used exactly the same way in `for` loops:

```
>>> for i in range(10):    # Works in Python 2 and 3
...    print(i)
```

However, if you want to create an actual list of integers in Python 3, you must convert the "range object" into a list with the `list()` function:

```
>>> # Python 2
>>> listOfInts = range(10)
```

```
>>> # Python 3
>>> listOfInts = list(range(10))
```

Division with the / Operator

In Python 2, doing division with the / operator results in a floating point number (that is, a number with a decimal point) only if one of the numbers is a float itself:

```
>>> # Python 2
>>> 25.0 / 8
3.125
>>> 25 / 8.0
3.125
```

However, in Python 2, if both of the numbers are integers, then the result of division is the rounded down integer. In Python 3, the result is a floating point number no matter what:

```
>>> # Python 2
>>> 25 / 8
3
```

```
>>> # Python 3
>>> 25 / 8
3.125
```

Formatting Strings with the `format()` Method and %s

In both Python 2 and 3, you can include %s inside a string and follow it with a list of values for each %s such as:

```
>>> # Python 2 and 3
>>> 'My name is %s and I am from %s.' % ('Al',
'Houston')
'My name is Al and I am from Houston.'
```

However, Python 3 adds a new string method called `format()`. This string lets you provide a list of arguments as parameters to format(). Instead of %s, you use {0} and {1} and {2} and so on:

```
>>> # Python 3
>>> 'My name is {0} and I am from {1}.'.format
('Al', 'Houston')
'My name is Al and I am from Houston.'
```

The numbers inside the curly braces are the index of the parameters to `format()`. So switching them around in the string will switch around where the parameters to `format()` are placed:

```
>>> # Python 3
>>> 'My name is {1} and I am from {0}.'.format
('Al', 'Houston')
'My name is Houston and I am from Al.'
```

One nice feature is that you can use the same parameter to `format()` multiple times in the string without making extra parameters to `format()`:

```
>>> # Python 3
>>> 'My name is {0}, {0}, {0}, {0} and I am from
{1}.'.format('Jimmy Four Times', 'Houston')
'My name is Jimmy Four Times, Jimmy Four Times,
Jimmy Four Times, Jimmy Four Times and I am from
Houston.'
```

Along with numeric indexes, you can also put text inside the curly braces. This text can match to keyword arguments passed to `format()`:

```
>>> # Python 3
>>> 'My name is {0} and I like {thing} and I am
from {hometown}.'.format('Al', hometown='Houston',
thing='cats')
'My name is Al and I like cats and I am from
Houston.'
```

Appendix B
Statements, Functions, and Methods Reference

Ack!

This appendix contains a list of all the statements, functions, and methods presented in this book. It doesn't present any new information, but it is a handy list.

As it turns out, there wasn't enough space in this book to include it. But you can find it online for free at *http://inventwithpython.com/appendixb.html*

The rest of the book is also freely available online as well at *http://inventwithpython.com*

Appendix C

Running Python Programs without Python Installed

You may want to share the game programs you make with other people. Having other people play your games is a great way to show off your skills. However, they may not have Python installed on their computer. There is a way to run Python programs without installing the Python interpreter: You will have to compile your .py script into a .exe executable program.

Compiling source code means converting that source code into machine language, which is the programming language your computer understands. Programming in machine language is very long and tedious, and higher-level languages such as Python make programming easier.

This appendix will show you how to compile your .py Python files into .exe programs that can be run on Windows without having Python installed.

Step 1: Download and Install py2exe

First, you will need to download and install a module called py2exe from *http://sourceforge.net/projects/py2exe/files/*. Be sure to download the correct version of py2exe for your version of Python. (For example, download py2exe-0.6.9.win32-py2.6.exe if you have installed Python 2.6 on your computer.)

The py2exe module only works on 2.x versions of Python, and not Python 3. You will have to convert your programs to run on Python 2 if you have written them for Python 3. This is fairly easy. There are not many differences between Python 2 and 3, and they are documented in Appendix A of this book.

After downloading the py2exe installer, double click on it to install it. This installation is much like how you installed Python. Just keep clicking the Next button until you reach the end.

After you have installed py2exe, you can make sure that the installation was successful by running the interactive shell and typing the following:

```
>>> import py2exe
>>>
```

If you do not see anything, then the installation was successful. If you see this error:

```
>>> import py2exe
>>> import py2exe
Traceback (most recent call last):
  File "<stdin>", line 1, in ?
ImportError: No module named py2exe
>>>
```

Step 2: Create Your setup.py Script

After you have installed py2exe and confirmed that it is installed, you will need to create a Python program with the name setup.py. The contents of this program should be as follows:

```
from distutils.core import setup
import py2exe
setup(console=['hello.py'])
```

Replace hello.py in the source code above with the filename of the Python program you want to compile. Be sure to save the setup.py in the same folder as the Python program you want to compile (that is, hello.py, or whatever the filename is).

Step 3: Run Your setup.py Script

Next, you will have to run your setup.py with a command line option. You cannot run setup.py from IDLE by pushing the F5 key or selecting Run Module from the Run menu. You must use the Windows command line.

To start the Windows command line, click on the Start button in the bottom left corner and select "Run". In the windows that opens, type "cmd" and click OK.

A black window with text should appear. Type "cd c:\Python26" (or the folder that you have saved your programs to) to change folders to the folder containing your Python script and setup.py. From that folder, type "c:\Python26\python.exe setup.py py2exe". The first part (c:\Python26\python.exe) runs the Python interpreter from the command line. The first command line option (setup.py) is the script that the interpreter should run. The second command line option (py2exe) tells the script to run with the py2exe option.

There will be a large amount of text from running this program. You can ignore this text.

When the compilation is finished, there will be two new folders, named build and dist. You can delete the build folder because it only contains files that were used during compilation. The dist folder contains all the files you want to give to other people, including the hello.exe binary executable. (Your executable may have a different name. If your setup.py had hello.py, then compilation produces a program named hello.exe.)

Step 4: Distribute Your Program

It's not easy to email all the files in the dist folder to someone. You can use a "zip program" to package these many files into one file (called a zip file because it has the extension .zip). Zip programs can be downloaded from the Internet for free. Some popular, free zip programs are 7-zip from *http://www.7-zip.org/download.html* or WinRAR from *http://www.rarlab.com/download.htm*.

You can rename the dist folder to something else if you wish. The files simply have to be in the same directory.

Summary

The process for turning your .py Python scripts into .exe binary executable programs for Windows is simple:

Step 1: Download and install py2exe from *http://sourceforge.net/projects/py2exe/files/*

Step 2: Create a setup.py file that looks like this:

```
from distutils.core import setup
import py2exe
setup(console=['hello.py'])
```

Step 3: Run "c:\Python26\python.exe setup.py py2exe"

Step 4: Package up the dist folder into a zip file.

Appendix D

Common Error Messages in Python

Error messages in Python can often be confusing. Here is a list of common error messages you may find, along with a plain English explanation. These error messages are the result of runtime errors. They will immediately crash your Here are the error messages explained (your error messages may be slightly different but mean the same thing):

- SyntaxError: invalid syntax
- ImportError: No module named raandom
- SyntaxError: EOL while scanning string literal
- AttributeError: 'str' object has no attribute 'lowerr'
- IndentationError: expected an indented block
- IndentationError: unexpected indent
- IndentationError: unindent does not match any outer indentation level
- TypeError: bad operand type for abs(): 'str'
- TypeError: abs() takes exactly one argument (2 given)
- IndexError: list index out of range
- KeyError: 'spam'

SyntaxError: invalid syntax

This is the most generic error message the Python interpreter will give you. It means that Python was expecting something that isn't there, or there is something there that it didn't expect. Maybe you forgot to include or inserted an extra character. Here are some examples:

```
if guess = 5:
```

In the above case, the programmer used = (the assignment operator) instead of == (the equals comparator operator). Python never expects assignment statements where there should be a condition.

```
def foo(:
```

In the above case, the programmer forgot to match the ending) closing parenthesis.

```
def foo()
```

In the above case, the programmer forgot to put the colon at the end of the def statement. This can also happen with `for`, `while`, `if`, `elif`, and `else` statements.

ImportError: No module named raandom

This error shows up when you try to import a module that does not exist. Most likely, you have a typo in the module name. For example, you may have typed `raandom` instead of `random`.

SyntaxError: EOL while scanning string literal

```
print('Hello world!)
print("Hello world!')
```

This error happens when you do not have two quote marks for a string, or you use different quote marks for the same string. Look at these two examples:

AttributeError: 'str' object has no attribute 'lowerr'

```
'Hello'.lowerr()
'Hello'.append('x')
```

This error appears when you call a method or access an attribute that does not exist. This is most likely because 1) you have a typo in the method or attribute name, or 2) you are calling the method or attribute on a value that is the wrong data type. For example, strings have a method named `lower()`, but not `lowerr()` (that is a typo). And the `append()` method is a list method, so calling it on a string value will cause this error.

IndentationError: expected an indented block

```
def foo():
print('Hello world!')
```

This error happens if you fail to indent your code for a block. In the above example the `print()` call is at the same level of indentation as the `def` statement, when it should have a larger indentation.

IndentationError: unexpected indent

```
def foo():
    print('Hello world!')
     print('Goodbye')
```

An unexpected indent error happens when you add an indentation for no reason. You should only add indentation after a `def`, `if`, `else`, `elif`, `while`, or `for` statment (or any statement that ends with a colon.)

IndentationError: unindent does not match any outer indentation level

```
def foo():
    print('Hello world!')
   print('Goodbye')
```

This indentation error appears when you are decreasing the indentation, but not decreasing it to the same level as the previous indentation. The `print('Goodbye')` call should either be at the same indentation as the other `print()` call (and be inside the `if` block) or at the same indentation as the `if` statement (and be outside of the `if` block).

TypeError: bad operand type for abs(): 'str'

```
abs('Hello')
```

This error occurs when the value of an argument you pass to a function or method is of the wrong data type. In the above example, the abs() function takes an integer or floating point number. Passing a string for the argument results in an error.

TypeError: abs() takes exactly one argument (2 given)

```
abs(42, 50)
```

This error appears when you pass the wrong number of arguments to a function or method, either too many or too few. The abs() function takes exactly one (and only one) argument. In our example we pass two arguments, which results in this error.

IndexError: list index out of range

```
myList = ['spam', 'fizz', 'eggs']
print(myList[3])
```

The IndexError happens when the index you use is larger than or equal to the number of actual items in the list. In our above example, the myList list only has 3 items in it, so the only valid indexes to use are 0, 1, and 2. The index 3 (or any other index larger than 2) is larger than any of these indexes, so the code results in an IndexError.

KeyError: 'spam'

```
myDict = {'fizz':42, 'eggs':100}
myDict['spam']
```

The KeyError happens when you try to access a key in a dictionary object that does not exist. Either the key was never added to the dictionary, was deleted previously with the del operator, or the key you are using has a typo in it.

Glossary

absolute value - The positive form of a negative number. For example, the absolute value of -2 is 2. The absolute value of a positive number is simply the positive number itself.

AI - see, artificial intelligence

algorithm - A series of instructions to compute something.

applications - A program that is run by an operating system. See also, program.

arguments - The values that are passed for parameters in a function call.

artificial intelligence - Code or a program that can intelligent make decisions (for example, decisions when playing a game) in response to user actions.

ASCII art - Using text characters and spaces to draw simple pictures.

assembly language - The simplest programming language. Assembly language instructions are a human-readable form that can directly translate into machine code instructions.

assignment operator - The = sign. Used to assign values to variables.

assignment statement - A line of code that assigns a value to a variable using the assignment operator. This defines, that is, creates the variable when used with a new variable. For example: `spam = 42`

asterisk - The * symbol. The asterisk is used as a multiplication sign.

augmented assignment operator - The `+=`, `-=`, `*=`, and `/=` operators. The assignment `spam += 42` is equivalent to `spam = spam + 42`.

block - A group of lines of code with the same amount of indentation. Blocks can contain other blocks of greater indentation inside them.

boolean - A data type with only two values, `True` and `False`.

boolean operator - Boolean operators include `and`, `or`, and `not`.

break point - A break point can be set on a specific line of code, which will cause the debugger to take over when that line is executed while running the program under a debugger.

break statement - The `break` statement immediately jumps out of the current `while` or `for` loop to the first line after the end of the loop's block.

brute force - In cryptography, to try every possible key in order to decrypt an encrypted message.

bugs - Errors in your program's code. The three types of bugs are syntax errors, runtime errors, and semantic errors.

caesar cipher - A simple substitution cipher in which each symbol is replaced by one and only one other symbol.

cartesian coordinate system - A system of coordinates used to identify exact points in some area of space (such as the monitor, or on a game board). Cartesian coordinates systems commonly have two coordinates, one of the X-axis (that is, the horizontal left-right axis) and one of the Y-axis (that is, the vertical up-down axis).

case-sensitivity - Declaring different capitalizations of a name to mean different things. Python is a case-sensitive language, so `spam`, `Spam`, and `SPAM` are three different variables.

central processing unit - CPU, the main chip that your computer uses to process software instructions.

cipher - In cryptography, an algorithm used to encrypt and decrypt messages with a certain key.

ciphertext - In cryptography, the encrypted form of a message.

comment - Part of the source code that is ignored by the Python interpreter. Comments are there to remind the programmer about something about the code. Comments begin with a # sign and go on for the rest of the line.

commutative property - The property of addition and multiplication that describes how the order of the numbers being added or multiplied does not matter. For example, 2 + 4 = 6, and 4 + 2 = 6. Also, 3 * 5 = 15, and 5 * 3 = 15.

comparison operators - The operators < ("less than"), <= ("less than or equal to"), > ("greater than"), >= ("greater than or equal to"), == ("equal to"), and != ("not equal too").

condition - Another name for an expression, one that exists in an `if` or `while` statement that evaluates to a boolean `True` or `False` value.

constant variables - Variables whose values do not change. Constant variables are often used because it is easier to type the name of the variable then the value that they store. As a convention, constant variable names are typed in all uppercase letters.

convention - A way of doing things that is not required, but is usually done to make a task easier.

conversion specifiers - The text inside a string that makes use of string interpolation. The most common conversion specifier is `%s`, which specifies that the variable it interpolates should be converted to a string.

cpu - see, Central Processing Unit

crash - An event that happens because of a runtime error. After crashing, the program immediately terminates.

cryptanalysis - The science of breaking secret codes and ciphers.

cryptography - The science of making secret codes and ciphers.

data types - A category of values. Some types in Python are: strings, integers, floats, boolean, lists, and NoneType.

debugger - A program that lets you step through your code one line at a time (in the same order that Python executes them), and shows what values are stored in all of the variables.

decrementing - To decrease a numeric value by one.

decrypting - To convert an encrypted message to the readable plaintext version.

def statement - A statement that defines a new function. The def statement begins with the `def` keyword, followed by the function name and a set of parentheses, with any number of parameter names delimited by commas. At the end is a : colon character. For example, `def funcName(param1, param2):`

delimit - To separate with. For example, the string `'cats,dogs,mice'` is delimited with commas.

dictionary - A container data type that can store other values. Values are accessed by a key. For example, `spam['foo'] = 42` assigns the key `'foo'` of the `spam` dictionary the value `42`.

else statement - An `else` statement always follows an `if` statement, and the code inside the else-block is executed if the `if` statement's condition was `False`.

empty list - The list `[]`, which contains no values and has a length of zero. See also, empty string.

empty string - The string `' '`, which contains no characters and has a length of zero. See also, empty list.

encrypting - To convert a message into a form that resembles garbage data, and cannot be understood except by someone who knows the ciphr and key used to encrypt the message.

escape character - Escape characters allow the programmer to specify characters in Python that are difficult or impossible to type into the source code. All escape characters are preceeded by a \ forward backslash character. For example, \n displays a newline character when it is printed.

evaluate - Reducing an expression down to a single value. The expression 2 + 3 + 1 evaluates to the value 6.

execute - The Python interpreter executes lines of code, by evaluating any expressions or performing the task that the code does.

exit - When a program ends. "Terminate" means the same thing.

expression - Values and function calls connected by operators. Expressions can be evaluated down to a single value.

file editor - A program used to type in or change files, including files of Python source code. The IDLE program has a file editor that you use to type in your programs.

floating point numbers - Numbers with fractions or decimal points are not integers. The numbers 3.5 and 42.1 and 5.0 are floating point numbers.

flow chart - A chart that informally shows the flow of execution for a program, and the main events that occur in the program and in what order.

flow control statements - Statements that cause the flow of execution to change, often depending on conditions. For example, a function call sends the execution to the beginning of a function. Also, a loop causes the execution to iterate over a section of code several times.

flow of execution - The order that Python instructions are executed. Usually the Python interpreter will start at the top of a program and go down executing one line at a time. Flow control statements can move the flow of execution to different parts of code in the program.

function - A collection of instructions to be executed when the function is called. Functions also have a return value, which is the value that a function call evaluates to.

function call - A command to pass execution to the code contained inside a function, also passing arguments to the function. Function calls evaluate to the return value of the function.

garbage data - Random data or values that have no meaning.

global scope - The scope of variables outside of all functions. Python code in the global scope cannot see variables inside any function's local scope.

hard-coding - Using a value in a program, instead of using a variable. While a variable could allow the program to change, by hard-coding a value in a program, the value stays permanently fixed unless the source code is changed.

hardware - The parts of a computer that you can touch, such as the keyboard, monitor, case, or mouse. See also, software.

higher-level programming languages - Programming languages that humans can understand, such as Python. An interpreter can translate a higher-level language into machine code, which is the only language computers can understand.

IDLE - Interactive DeveLopment Environment. IDLE is a program that helps you type in your programs and games.

I/O - Input/Output. This is a term used in reference of the data that is sent into a program (input) and that is produced by the program (output).

immutable sequence - A container data type that cannot have values added or deleted from it. In Python, the two immutable sequence data types are strings and tuples.

import statement - A line of code with the `import` keyword followed by the name of a module. This allows you to call any functions that are contained in the module.

incrementing - To increase the value of a numeric variable by one.

indentation - The indentation of a line of code is the number of spaces before the start of the actual code. Indentation in Python is used to mark when blocks begin and end. Indentation is usually done in multiples of four spaces.

index - An integer between square brackets that is placed at the end of an ordered container variable (most often a list) to evaluate to a specific item in that container. The first index starts at 0, not 1. For example, if `spam` refers to the list `['a', 'b', 'c', 'd']`, then `spam[2]` evaluates to `'c'`.

index error - An index error occurs when you attempt to access an index that does not exist. This is much like using a variable that does not exist. For example, if `spam` refers to the list `['a', 'b', 'c', 'd']`, then `spam[10]` would cause an index error.

infinite loop - A loop that has a condition that always evaluates to `True`, which makes the loop keep looping forever. The only way to exit an infinite loop is with a `break` statement.

input - The text or data that the user or player enters into a program, mostly from the keyboard.

integer division - Division that ignores any remainder and rounds the evaluated number down. Integer division occurs when both numbers in the division expression are integers. For example, 20 / 7 evaluates to the integer 6, even though the answer is 6.666 or 6 remainder 2.

integers - Integers are whole numbers like 4 and 99 and 0. The numbers 3.5 and 42.1 and 5.0 are not integers.

interactive shell - A part of IDLE that lets you execute Python code one line at a time. It allows you to immediately see what value the expression you type in evaluates to.

interpreter - A program that translates instructions written in a higher-level programming language (such as Python) to machine code that the computer can understand and execute.

iteration - A single run through of the code in a loop's block. For example, if the code in a while-block is executed ten times before execution leaves the loop, we say that there were ten iterations of the while-block's code.

key-value pairs - In dictionary data types, keys are values that are used to access the values in a dictionary, much like a list's index is used to access the values in a list. Unlike lists, dictionary keys can be of any data type, not just integers.

keys - In dictionaries, keys are the indexes used to

keys - In cryptography, a specific value (usuaully a number) that determines how a cipher encrypts a message. To decrypt the message, you must know both the cipher and the key value that was used.

list - The main container data type, lists can contain several other values, including other lists. Values in lists are accessed by an integer index between square brackets. For example, if spam is assigned the list ['a', 'b', 'c'], then spam[2] would evaluate to 'c'.

list concatenation - Combining the contents of one list to the end of another with the + operator. For example, [1, 2, 3] + ['a', 'b', 'c'] evaluates to [1, 2, 3, 'a', 'b', 'c'].

local scope - The scope of variables inside a single functions. Python code inside a function can read the value of variables in the global scope, but any changes or new variables made will only exist while execution is inside that function call.

loop - A block of code inside a loop (after a for or while statement) will repeatedly execute until some condition is met.

loop unrolling - Replacing code inside a loop with multiple copies of that code. For example, instead of for i in range(10): print 'Hello', you could unroll that loop by having ten lines of print 'Hello'

machine code - The language that the computer's CPU understands. Machine code instructions are series of ones and zeros, and is generally unreadable by humans. Interpreters (such as the Python interpreter) translate a higher-level language into machine code.

methods - Functions that are associated with values of a data type. For example, the string method `upper()` would be invoked on a string like this: `'Hello'.upper()`

module - A separate Python program that can be included in your programs so that you can make use of the functions in the module.

modulus operator - The "remainder" operator that is represented with a % percent sign. For example, while 20 / 7 is 6 with a remainder of 2, `20 % 7` would evaluate to 2.

mutable sequence - A container data type that is ordered and can have values added or removed from it. Lists are a mutable sequence data type in Python.

negative numbers - All numbers less than 0. Negative numbers have a minus sign in front of them to differentiate them from positive numbers, for example, -42 or -10.

nested loops - Loops that exist inside other loops.

None - The only value in the NoneType data type. "None" is often used to represent the lack of a value.

operating system - A large program that runs other software programs (called applications) the same way on different hardware. Windows, Mac OS, and Linux are examples of operating systems.

operators - Operators connect values in expressions. Operators include +, -, *, /, `and`, and `or`

ordinal - In ASCII, the number that represents an ASCII character. For example, the ASCII character "A" has the ordinal 65.

origin - In cartesian coordinate systems, the point at the coordinates 0, 0.

OS - see, operating system

output - The text that a program produces for the user. For example, `print` statements produce output.

overwrite - To replace a value stored in a variable with a new value.

parameter - A variable that is specified to have a value passed in a function call. For example, the statement `def spam(eggs, cheese)` defines a function with two parameters named `eggs` and `cheese`.

pie chart - A circular chart that shows percentage portions as portions of the entire circle.

plaintext - The decrypted, human-readable form of a message.

player - A person who plays the computer game.

positive numbers - All numbers equal to or greater than 0.

pound sign - The # sign. Pound signs are used to begin comments.

print statement - The `print` keyword followed by a value that is to be displayed on the screen.

program - A collection of instructions that can process input and produce output when run by computer.

programmer - A person who writes computer programs.

reference - Rather than containing the values themselves, list variables actually contain references to lists. For example, `spam = [1, 2, 3]` assigns `spam` a reference to the list. `cheese = spam` would copy the reference to the list `spam` refers to. Any changes made to the `cheese` or `spam` variable would be reflected in the other variable.

return statement - The `return` followed by a single value, which is what the call to the function the return statement is in will evaluate to.

return value - The value that a call to the function will evaluate to. You can specify what the return value is with the `return` keyword followed by the value. Functions with no return statement will return the value `None`.

runtime error - An error that occurs when the program is running. A runtime error will cause the program to crash and stop executing.

scope - See, local scope and global scope.

sequence - A sequence data type is an ordered container data type, and have a "first" or "last" item. The sequence data types in Python are lists, tuples, and strings. Dictionaries are not sequences, they are unordered.

semantic error - An error that will not cause the program to crash immediately, but will cause the program to run in an unintended way. A semantic error may cause a runtime error and crash later on in the program.

shell - see, interactive shell

simple substitution ciphers - A cipher where each letter is replaced by one and only one other letter.

slice - A subset of values in a list. These are accessed using the : colon character in between the square brackets. For example, if spam has the value `['a', 'b', 'c', 'd', 'e', 'f']`, then the slice `spam[2:4]` has the value `['c', 'd']`. Similar to a substring.

software - see, program

source code - The text that you type in to write a program.

statement - A command or line of Python code that does not evaluate to a value.

stepping - Executing one line of code at a time in a debugger, which can make it easier to find out when problems in the code occur.

string concatenation - Combining two strings together with the + operator to form a new string. For example, `'Hello ' + 'World!'` evaluates to the string `'Hello World!'`

string formatting - Another term for string interpolation.

string interpolation - Using conversion specifiers in a string as place holders for other values. Using string interpolation is a more convenient alternative to string concatenation. For example, `'Hello, %s. Are you going to %s on %s?' % (name, activity, day)` evaluates to the string `'Hello, Albert. Are you going to program on Thursday?'`, if the variables have those corresponding values.

string - A value made up of text. Strings are typed in with a single quote ' or double " on either side. For example, `'Hello'`

substring - A subset of a string value. For example, if spam is the string `'Hello'`, then the substring `spam[1:4]` is `'ell'`. Similar to a list slice.

symbols - In cryptography, the individual characters that are encrypted.

syntax - The rules for how code is ordered in a programming language, much like grammar is made up of the rules for understandable English sentences.

syntax error - An error that occurs when the Python interpreter does not understand the code because the code is incomplete or in the wrong order. A program with a syntax error will not run.

terminate - When a program ends. "Exit" means the same thing.

tracing - To follow through the lines of code in a program in the order that they would execute.

truth tables - Tables showing every possible combination of

tuple - A container data type similar to a list. Tuples are immutable sequence data types, meaning that they cannot have values added or removed from them. For example, (1, 2, 'cats', 'hello') is a tuple of four values.

type - see, data types

unordered - In container data types, unordered data types do not have a "first" or "last" value contained inside them, they simply contain values. Dictionaries are the only unordered data type in Python. Lists, tuples, and strings are ordered data types. See also, sequence.

user - The person using the program.

value - A specific instance of a data type. 42 is a value of the integer type. 'Hello' is a value of the string type.

variables - A container that can store a value. List variables contain references to lists.

while loop statement - The while keyword, followed by a condition, ending with a : colon character. The while statement marks the beginning of a while loop.

X-axis - In cartesian coordinate systems, the horizontal (left-right) coordinate axis.

Y-axis - In cartesian coordinate systems, the vertical (up-down) coordinate axis.

About the Author

Albert Sweigart (but you can call him Al), is a software developer in San Francisco, California who enjoys bicycling, reading, volunteering, network security, haunting coffee shops, and making useful software.

He is originally from Houston, Texas. He finally put his University of Texas at Austin computer science degree in a frame. He is a friendly introvert, an atheist, a cat person, and fears that he is losing brain cells over time. He laughs out loud when watching park squirrels, which makes people think he's a simpleton.

"Invent with Python" is his first book and will not be his last.

His web site and blog are located at *http://coffeeghost.net*

Made in the USA
Lexington, KY
01 November 2013